OCEANSIDE PUBLIC LIBRARY
330 N COAST HWY
OCEANSIDE, CA 92054

D0950004

Civic Center

EMPTY MANSIONS

EMPTY MANSIONS

The Mysterious Life of
HUGUETTE CLARK
and the Spending of
a Great American Fortune

BILL DEDMAN and
PAUL CLARK NEWELL, JR.

BALLANTINE BOOKS

NEW YORK

Copyright © 2013 by Bill Dedman and Paul Clark Newell, Jr.

All rights reserved.

Published in the United States by Ballantine Books, an imprint of The Random House Publishing Group, a division of Random House LLC, New York, a Penguin Random House Company.

BALLANTINE and the HOUSE colophon are registered trademarks of Random House LLC.

All credits for reproduction of photographs can be found on pages 431–435.

LIBRARY OF CONGRESS CATALOGING-IN-PUBLICATION DATA

Dedman, Bill.
Empty mansions : the mysterious life of Huguette Clark and the spending of a great American fortune / Bill Dedman and Paul Clark Newell, Jr.
p. cm
Includes bibliographical references and index.
ISBN 978-0-345-53452-1
eBook ISBN 978-0-345-54556-5
1. Clark, Huguette, 1906–2011. 2. Heiresses—United States—Biography.
3. Eccentrics—United States—Biography. 4. Recluses—United States—
Biography. 5. Collectors and collecting—United States—Biography.
6. Clark, William Andrews, 1839–1925—Family. 7. Clark, Huguette, 1906–
2011—Family. 8. Clark, Huguette, 1906–2011—Homes and haunts—
United States. 9. Mansions—United States—History.
I. Newell, Paul Clark, Jr. II. Title.
CT275.C6273D33   2013
328.73'092—dc23   2013023933 [B]

Printed in the United States of America on acid-free paper

www.ballantinebooks.com

6 8 9 7 5

Book design by Simon M. Sullivan

31232009738636

FOR HUGUETTE.

P.N. and B.D.

CONTENTS

W. A. Clark Family Tree x

Introduction xiii

An Apparition xxv

Still Life xxvii

CHAPTER ONE
THE CLARK MANSION, Part One
1

CHAPTER TWO
THE LOG CABIN
13

CHAPTER THREE
THE COPPER KING MANSION
35

CHAPTER FOUR
THE U.S. CAPITOL
63

CHAPTER FIVE
THE CLARK MANSION, Part Two
91

CHAPTER SIX
907 FIFTH AVENUE, Part One
123

CHAPTER SEVEN
907 FIFTH AVENUE, Part Two
161

CHAPTER EIGHT
BELLOSGUARDO
191

CHAPTER NINE
LE BEAU CHATEAU
211

CHAPTER TEN
DOCTORS HOSPITAL
225

CHAPTER ELEVEN
BETH ISRAEL MEDICAL CENTER
277

CHAPTER TWELVE
WOODLAWN CEMETERY
301

CHAPTER THIRTEEN
SURROGATE'S COURTHOUSE
323

EPILOGUE
THE CRICKET
351

Authors' Note 361

Acknowledgments 363

Notes 371

Selected Bibliography 419

List of Illustrations 431

Appendix: Siblings of W. A. Clark 437

Appendix: Inflation Adjustment 439

Index 441

THE FAMILY OF W. A. CLARK

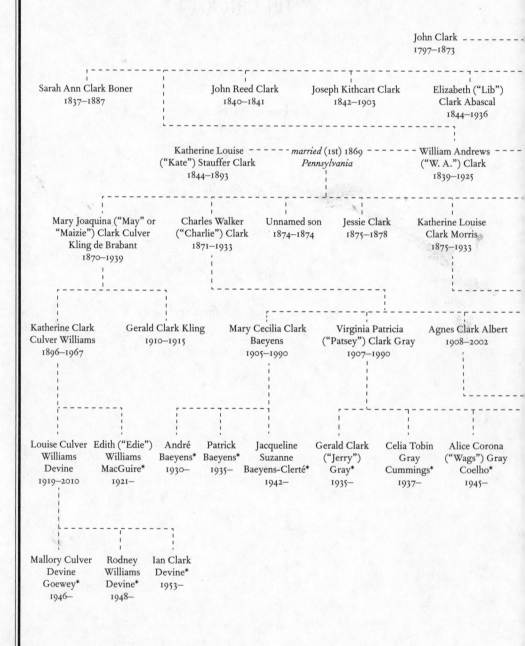

John Clark
1797–1873

Sarah Ann Clark Boner
1837–1887

John Reed Clark
1840–1841

Joseph Kithcart Clark
1842–1903

Elizabeth ("Lib")
Clark Abascal
1844–1936

Katherine Louise
("Kate") Stauffer Clark
1844–1893

married (1st) 1869
Pennsylvania

William Andrews
("W. A.") Clark
1839–1925

Mary Joaquina ("May" or
"Maizie") Clark Culver
Kling de Brabant
1870–1939

Charles Walker
("Charlie") Clark
1871–1933

Unnamed son
1874–1874

Jessie Clark
1875–1878

Katherine Louise
Clark Morris
1875–1933

Katherine Clark
Culver Williams
1896–1967

Gerald Clark Kling
1910–1915

Mary Cecilia Clark
Baeyens
1905–1990

Virginia Patricia
("Patsy") Clark Gray
1907–1990

Agnes Clark Albert
1908–2002

Louise Culver
Williams
Devine
1919–2010

Edith ("Edie")
Williams
MacGuire*
1921–

André
Baeyens*
1930–

Patrick
Baeyens*
1935–

Jacqueline
Suzanne
Baeyens-Clerté*
1942–

Gerald Clark
("Jerry")
Gray*
1935–

Celia Tobin
Gray
Cummings*
1937–

Alice Corona
("Wags") Gray
Coelho*
1945–

Mallory Culver
Devine
Goewey*
1946–

Rodney
Williams
Devine*
1948–

Ian Clark
Devine*
1953–

* *These nineteen relatives challenged the last will and testament of Huguette Clark.*

† *The estate of Timothy Henry Gray joined the challenge to the will after his death.*

‡ *Ella Newell is the grandmother of co-author Paul Newell, Jr.*

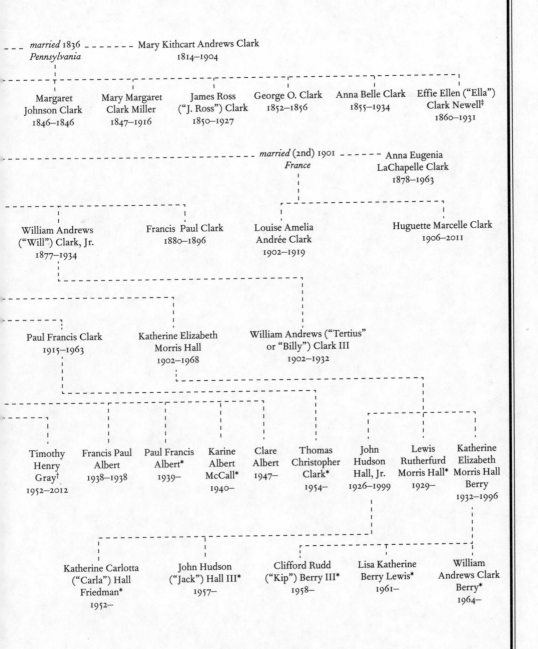

married 1836 — — — — — — Mary Kithcart Andrews Clark
Pennsylvania   1814–1904

Margaret Johnson Clark 1846–1846

Mary Margaret Clark Miller 1847–1916

James Ross ("J. Ross") Clark 1850–1927

George O. Clark 1852–1856

Anna Belle Clark 1855–1934

Effie Ellen ("Ella") Clark Newell‡ 1860–1931

married (2nd) 1901 — — — — — Anna Eugenia
France   LaChapelle Clark
                                                  1878–1963

William Andrews ("Will") Clark, Jr. 1877–1934

Francis Paul Clark 1880–1896

Louise Amelia Andrée Clark 1902–1919

Huguette Marcelle Clark 1906–2011

Paul Francis Clark 1915–1963

Katherine Elizabeth Morris Hall 1902–1968

William Andrews ("Tertius" or "Billy") Clark III 1902–1932

Timothy Henry Gray† 1952–2012

Francis Paul Albert 1938–1938

Paul Francis Albert* 1939–

Karine Albert McCall* 1940–

Clare Albert 1947–

Thomas Christopher Clark* 1954–

John Hudson Hall, Jr. 1926–1999

Lewis Rutherfurd Morris Hall* 1929–

Katherine Elizabeth Morris Hall Berry 1932–1996

Katherine Carlotta ("Carla") Hall Friedman* 1952–

John Hudson ("Jack") Hall III* 1957–

Clifford Rudd ("Kip") Berry III* 1958–

Lisa Katherine Berry Lewis* 1961–

William Andrews Clark Berry* 1964–

NOT SHOWN: *Children of relatives who challenged the will, and children of W. A. Clark's siblings.*

See a detailed family tree at http://ancestry.com/clark.

INTRODUCTION

W E CAME TO THIS STORY by separate paths, one of us by accident and one by birth.

Bill Dedman

I STUMBLED INTO THE MYSTERIOUS WORLD of Huguette Clark because my family was looking for a house, and I got a little out of our price range.

In 2009, my wife's job had been transferred from Boston to New York City, but we wanted to keep in touch with the charms and idiosyncrasies of New England: old stone walls, Colonial houses on country corners, thrifty Yankees who save an *r* sound by keeping their wool socks in a "draw," yet put the *r* to good use when they "draw'r" a picture. While renting we looked at small towns in Connecticut, about an hour northeast of the Empire State Building. Although property values had plunged in the Great Recession, houses came in only two flavors: those we didn't like and those we couldn't afford.

One evening, frustration turned to distraction. I began to scan the online listings for houses we *really* couldn't afford, an exercise in American aspiration. Although some names were familiar—professional talkers Don Imus and Phil Donahue were having trouble selling waterfront mansions on Long Island Sound—other names sent me to Google. One fellow had been able to purchase an $8 million house by selling boxers and briefs on the Internet. ("Buy underwear in your underwear.") I was gobsmacked, however, by the property at the top of the charts.

The most expensive house for sale in Connecticut, in the tony town of New Canaan, was priced at $24 million, marked down from $35 million. Billed as Le Beau Château, "the beautiful castle," this charmer had 14,266 square feet of floor space tucked into fifty-two wooded acres with a river and a waterfall. Its twenty-two rooms included nine bedrooms, nine baths, eleven fireplaces, a wine cellar, elevator, trunk room, walk-in safe, and a room for drying the draperies. The property taxes alone were $161,000 a year, or about four years' income for a typical American family. I didn't recognize the name of the owner, Huguette Clark. Was that a he or a she?

There was an odd note in the records on the town's website: Le Beau Château had been unoccupied since this owner bought it. In 1951. That couldn't be right. Who could afford to own such a house and to not live in it for nearly sixty years? And why would anyone do that?

A beautiful castle wasn't quite in the job description of an investigative reporter, but the next morning, I drove over to New Canaan.

On a winding, narrow lane called Dan's Highway was a tiny hand-made marker for No. 104 and a warning sign, "PRIVATE PROPERTY NO TRESPASSING VIOLATORS WILL BE PROSECUTED." Behind a low red-brick wall with white peeling paint sat two tiny brick cottages. Between them a driveway ran under a rusty gate into the trees and curved out of sight. If there was a beautiful fairy-tale castle, it was deep in the wood. The property showed no sign of humans, only wild turkeys, deer, and birds. It seemed more like a nature preserve than a home. There was no mailbox, no name, no buzzer. Leaning over the wall, I rapped on the window of one of the cottages.

Out shuffled an unshaven man in his white undershirt, a sleepy fellow who introduced himself as the caretaker, Tony Ruggiero. Eighty years old but muscled, he said he used to be a boxer and had sparred once with Rocky Marciano, but now he was watching over "Mrs. Clark's house." He wouldn't open the gate, but he said the house though empty was well cared for. He'd never met the owner in his more than twenty years. All he knew was that his paycheck came from her lawyer in New York City.

Ruggiero thought of something and ducked back inside. He brought out a newspaper clipping from the *New York Post.* An auction house had sold a painting for $23.5 million, Renoir's *In the Roses,* of a woman seated on a bench in a garden, and the newspaper said the portrait came from "the estate of Huguette Clark." Ruggiero kept pointing to those words "the estate of."

"Let me ask you a question," he said. "Do you suppose she's been dead all these years?"

. . .

Finding Huguette Clark's name on an Internet discussion board from Southern California, I discovered that Le Beau Château wasn't her only orphaned house. She had a second, grander home in Santa Barbara, a vacation estate on twenty-three cliff-top acres fronting the Pacific Ocean. But this home was definitely not for sale. A newspaper said she had turned down $100 million some years back. The lush estate was called Bellosguardo, meaning "beautiful lookout." According to the Internet chatter, Huguette had not been seen there in at least fifty years, but the 21,666-square-foot mansion was immaculately kept, with 1930s sedans still in the garage, and the table set just in case the owner should visit.

Though I didn't put much stock in the tale, my curiosity was piqued. Out in Santa Barbara for a business trip a while later, I tried to visit Bellosguardo. The property is hidden on a bluff, separated by a high wall from the Santa Barbara Cemetery, allowing even the dead barely a glimpse of the great house. The back gate to Bellosguardo was open, however, so I walked up the serpentine driveway. At the top of the hill, several gardeners were at work. The main house was out of sight behind a stand of trees. Suddenly, a golf cart barreled toward me, driven by a sturdy man in his fifties giving instructions on a walkie-talkie. He identified himself as the estate manager, C. John Douglas III, and pointed out the half dozen No Trespassing signs. As he sent me back down the driveway, mentioning something about the police, he divulged only two facts: He had worked for "Mrs. Clark" for more than twenty-five years, and he had never met her.

Talking through the locked gate, Douglas was in no mood to help solve a mystery. "I'm just sorry," he said dismissively, "that this is what you have to do to put food on the table for your children."

My family was indeed worrying a bit about curiosity getting the best of me. After all, my wife and I did meet during a prison riot, two journalists breaking *into* the Atlanta Federal Penitentiary to get a better view of the hostages. After I told my brother, a movie buff, about the empty mansions and the search for their mysterious owner, he sent an email with a whispered word: "Rosebud."

Sure, make fun. But where was Huguette Clark? Where did these vast sums of money come from, and why were they being wasted?

. . .

Public records led me to a third residence. Huguette Clark owned not one but three apartments in a classic limestone building in New York City, at 907 Fifth Avenue, overlooking Central Park at Seventy-Second Street. It's a neighborhood of legend and fantasy, near the statue of Alice in Wonderland and the pond where the boy-mouse Stuart Little raced sailboats. Yes, sir, said No. 907's uniformed doorman, in his Russian accent, this is "Madame Clark's building." But no, he hadn't seen Madame or any other Clarks for about twenty years, although he had carried groceries for Martha Stewart, who had a pied-à-terre in the same building. He shrugged, as if to say that doormen see a lot of strange things.

Neighbors and real estate agents filled in a few details. Huguette Clark's apartments took up the entire eighth floor of the building and half the twelfth, or top floor, for a grand total of forty-two rooms and fifteen thousand square feet on Fifth Avenue, the most fashionable street in the most expensive city in America. Her bill from the co-op board for taxes and maintenance was $342,000 a year, or $28,500 a month. Although they'd never seen Huguette Clark, neighbors said they'd heard that her apartments were filled with an amazing collection of dolls and dollhouses. And paintings, too, even a Monet. One neighbor let me into the quiet elevator lobby of Huguette's eighth floor, where rolls of surplus carpet were stored. I rang the buzzer, and no one answered. It didn't seem like a place where anyone would keep a Monet.

So this Huguette Clark owned homes altogether nearly the size of the White House. Where on earth did she reside? And why did she keep paying for this fabulous real estate if she wasn't using it? If I couldn't find out *where* Huguette was, then perhaps I could at least discover *who* she was.

. . .

It turned out that I had wandered through a portal into America's past. Long past. Huguette Clark, then 103 years old, was the heiress to one of

America's greatest fortunes, dug out of the copper mines of Montana and Arizona, the copper that carried electricity to the world. Her father, William Andrews Clark, sounded like the embodiment of the American dream: a Pennsylvania farm boy born in a log cabin, a prospector for gold, a banker, and a U.S. senator from Montana. W. A. Clark was also a railroad baron, connecting the transcontinental lines to a sleepy California port called Los Angeles. And along the way, he auctioned off the lots that became downtown Las Vegas.

The newspapers of the early 1900s couldn't decide who was the wealthiest man in America in that age before the personal income tax. *The New York Times* calculated in 1907 that if you counted only the money already in the banks, oilman John D. Rockefeller was tops. However, if you also included the wealth still to be brought up from underground, the *Times* decided that copper king W. A. Clark might prove to be richer than Rockefeller.

W. A. Clark also had one of the more controversial political careers in American history. He was forced to resign from the U.S. Senate for paying bribes to get the seat in the first place. Undeterred, he was re-elected. While serving in the Senate in 1904, the widower with grown children shocked the political world by revealing a secret marriage to a woman thirty-nine years his junior. At the time of the announcement, the senator and Anna LaChapelle Clark already had a two-year-old daughter, Andrée. The woman I was looking for in 2009, Huguette Clark, was the second child of that marriage, born in 1906 in Paris.

So the name was French: Huguette. The pronunciation took some getting used to, and my Southern accent still has trouble with it. I'm told that the French "u" sound doesn't exist in English. It's not "hue-GET" with an initial "H" sound, nor "you-GET" with a "Y," but somewhere close to "oo-GET." When W. A. Clark died in 1925, he left an estate estimated at $100 million to $250 million, worth up to $3.4 billion today. One-fifth of the estate went to eighteen-year-old Huguette, who was depicted in cartoons as a spoiled poor little rich girl. In the histories and magazine cover stories of his time, the word most often associated with W. A. Clark was "incredible." But after his death, his businesses were sold, and the Clark name faded. He may be the most famous American whom most Americans today have never heard of. Now Huguette, who inherited one-fifth of the copper-mining fortune, also was missing.

The length of history spanned by father and daughter is hard to comprehend. W. A. Clark was born in 1839, during the administration of the eighth president of the United States, Martin Van Buren. W.A. was twenty-two when the Civil War began. When Huguette was born in 1906, Theodore Roosevelt, the twenty-sixth president, was in the White House. Yet 170 years after W.A.'s birth, his youngest child was still alive at age 103 during the time of the forty-fourth president, Barack Obama.

Well, still alive, as far as I knew.

In researching stories about Huguette for the NBC News website, I gradually pieced together that she was indeed alive and had been living for twenty years in self-imposed exile in hospital rooms in Manhattan, although she was said to be in good health. For her own reasons, she had separated herself from the world. She was so reclusive that one of her attorneys, who had handled her business for more than twenty years, had never spoken to her face-to-face, talking to her only on the phone and through closed doors.

And that was, for me, the end of the hunt. I wrote about the mansion mystery, but I wasn't going to barge into a shy old woman's hospital room.

. . .

Then readers started emailing with hints of something nefarious, and the mansion mystery morphed into a criminal investigation. One of Huguette's possessions—one of the rarest violins in the world, a Stradivarius—had been sold for $6 million, and the buyer had been made to promise that he wouldn't tell anyone for a decade where he got it. Meanwhile, a nurse had somehow received millions of dollars in gifts from Huguette's accounts. Huguette's accountant was a felon and a registered sex offender, caught trolling to meet teenage girls over the Internet. And that accountant, along with Huguette's attorney, had already inherited the property of another elderly client.

After my updates about these developments, the Manhattan district attorney had the same questions our readers did: Why would Huguette be selling precious possessions unless she was down to her last copper? Was this eccentric centenarian, who had lived in a hospital for twenty years, competent to manage her affairs? Were her attorney and accountant in line to inherit her fortune, said to be worth more than $300 million?

The reclusive heiress who had withdrawn from the world suddenly had the modern media machine at her doorstep. Huguette Clark was featured on the *Today* show and on page one of the New York tabloids. Although she had been born in the silent film era, she became after her 104th birthday a trending topic of searches on Google and Yahoo, with a biography on Wikipedia, fan pages on Facebook, and a lavish story on the front page of *The New York Times*.

Huguette had been famous in her childhood and was famous again more than a century later, but in between she'd been a phantom. The last known photograph of her, a snapshot of an uncomfortable heiress in furs, jewels, and a cloche hat in the fashionable bell shape, had been taken in 1928. She had managed to escape the world's gaze since then. How? And, more important, why?

Urging further investigation, one of Huguette's own bankers confided to me, "The whole story is utterly mysterious but equally frightening. It has all the markings of a massive fraud. Poor Miss Clark sounds like one in a long list of rich, isolated old ladies taken advantage of by supposedly trustworthy advisers."

If that's what really happened.

· · ·

During my research I was fortunate to meet one of Huguette's relatives. Paul Clark Newell, Jr., is not in line for a claim to her estate, but he was interested in tracing the family history. And he'd gotten a lot closer to Huguette than I had. For one thing, he'd had the good sense to look for her number in the phone book.

Paul Newell

HUGUETTE CLARK WAS MY FATHER'S FIRST COUSIN, although she preferred to identify herself to me as Tante Huguette, using the French word for aunt. My father, Paul Clark Newell, remembered Senator W. A. Clark, who was his uncle and Huguette's father. This famous uncle often visited the Newell family home in Los Angeles. In the last years of his life, my father took up a long-delayed mission, writing a biography of Senator Clark. Unfortunately, his health was failing, so only fragments of that work were completed.

After my father's death, I began to organize our family archives, to visit museums and historical societies, and to develop friendships with relatives who had known W.A. and his second wife, Anna. A few had even met the reclusive Huguette. From the Corcoran Gallery of Art in Washington, D.C., which held the senator's art collection, I learned that Huguette was still alive. She was a generous patron to the Corcoran, sending handwritten checks while insisting that her gifts be attributed to "Anonymous."

Huguette had always been a mysterious presence in family lore. Though they were essentially the same age, my father had never met her, even when he was a guest in Senator Clark's monumental mansion on Fifth Avenue in New York. When I was a youngster, on family trips on the Pacific Coast Highway through Santa Barbara, my father would point out a promontory by the sea and tell me of Bellosguardo, the great Clark vacation estate. I had heard him speak of Huguette's shyness and reclusive tendencies, but I knew little more about her.

Years later, while traveling through Santa Barbara in the 1990s, I checked under Clark in the phone directory, and to my great surprise I found not one but two listings for Huguette M. Clark, giving her phone numbers and street address on the oceanfront Cabrillo Boulevard. Remarkable openness, I thought, for someone whose life was enveloped in secrecy. I dialed one of the numbers and reached her estate manager, John Douglas. He told me a little about his work and said that Madame Clark was a wonderful person to work for, though he said he had never met her. I asked how I might make contact with Huguette, and he provided me with the name of her attorney in New York, Donald Wallace. In November 1994 I wrote to her, through Wallace, introducing myself and saying that I hoped she might cooperate in my family research.

Within ten days I received a voice mail message, chipper and tantalizing. "Hello, Paul, this is your Aunt Huguette. I'm sorry I missed you,

Paul, because I do want to speak with you. I'll call you back soon, Paul, so we can talk. Bye-bye."

Her voice was high-pitched, with a hint of a foreign accent, perhaps reflecting her early years in France or revealing a minor speech impediment. Although she was then eighty-eight years old, her voice was steady. She left subsequent messages, but never a phone number to call her back. *Why not provide me with her phone number?* I pictured her at home in her commodious apartment on Fifth Avenue. Surely she employed a butler or secretary to receive and screen her calls. I telephoned her attorney to inquire about the situation.

"She's not going to provide you a number," he replied curtly.

She missed me again the next month, leaving this message:

> Hello, Paul, this is your Aunt Huguette, and I did call the other number, but I didn't get an answer. So I will call you up soon again, because just now I have the chicken pox—of all things to get at my age. Imagine! So, anyway, I'm getting along fine. The fever went down and everything's okay. And thank you for the photos. Your daughter is beautiful! And your little grandson, Eric—

At that point, the message timed out. Surprisingly, this aged relative, so well known in the family for being reclusive and on guard, seemed comfortable going on informally about personal medical matters and inquiring about my immediate family even though we had never met. But I still didn't have her number.

I continued writing to her through the next year, and in October 1995 I let her know I would be in New York, and gave her the phone number of my hotel. I had accepted an invitation from one of my Clark cousins, André Baeyens, at the French consulate up Fifth Avenue from Huguette's apartment. André, a great-grandson of the senator and a career diplomat, was the French consul general in New York. Huguette had asked André to contact me, and we became friends. Upon my return to my hotel room that night, around eleven, the phone rang.

"Hello, Paul, this is your Aunt Huguette."

At last, nearly a full year after my initial letter, we were in conversation. We remained in conversation for nine years. We talked about six times a year. Sometimes the calls were brief, just a few minutes of light chatter, but on other occasions we talked for a half hour or longer. Selections from our chats are included throughout this book as pieces entitled "In Conversation with Huguette."

She shared with me her favorite books and some of her memories. We discussed current events and family history. And she extended to me the rare treat of visiting her Santa Barbara home, Bellosguardo. I would call her attorney to arrange a time, and Huguette would call as requested, sometimes a few minutes early. What she never shared was her phone number.

Bill Dedman and Paul Newell

IN MAY 2011, just two weeks before her 105th birthday, Huguette Clark died in Beth Israel Medical Center in Manhattan. Court records soon answered one mystery while raising another. Huguette had not signed "a will" to distribute her fortune, but had signed two wills with contrary instructions. Both had been signed in the spring of 2005, when she was nearly ninety-nine.

The first will left $5 million to her nurse and the rest of her fortune to her closest living relatives, who would have inherited anyway if she had signed no will at all. These heirs were not named in the document.

Six weeks later, Huguette had signed a second will, leaving nothing to her relatives. She split her estate among her nurse, a goddaughter, her doctor, the hospital, her attorney, and her accountant, but directed that the largest share go to a new arts foundation at Bellosguardo, her California vacation home.

Thus began a court battle—with more than $300 million at stake—to determine Huguette's true intentions. Nineteen relatives, from her father's first marriage, challenged her last will, saying that Huguette was a victim of fraud, that she was mentally ill, unable to understand what she had signed.

. . .

In *Empty Mansions,* we have joined together to explore the mystery of Huguette Clark and her family. Our aim is to tell their story honestly, wherever it leads. We believe it's a story worth telling, not only for Huguette's sake but because of the light it may throw on American history.

On one level, our tale of the copper king and his family traces the rise and fall of a great fortune. Americans are familiar with the names Rockefeller and Carnegie and Morgan, but why has W. A. Clark nearly vanished from history? At what cost, with what sacrifices, did he achieve wealth and political power? What sort of life did his young wife, Anna, and their daughters, Andrée and Huguette, enjoy amid such incredible wealth and public scrutiny? Why did Huguette withdraw from the public eye? In her old age, was she competent to control her finances or was she, as her relatives assert, controlled by her nurse and her money men? And who would, or should, inherit her fortune?

Yet on another level, above such worldly considerations, the story of the Clarks is like a classic folk tale—except told in reverse, with the bags full of gold arriving at the beginning, the handsome prince fleeing, and the king's daughter locking *herself* away in the tower. The fabulous Clarks may teach us something about the price of privacy, the costs and opportunities of great wealth, the aftermath of achieving the American dream. They can take us inside the mountain camps of the western gold rush, inside the halls of Congress, the salons of Paris, and the drawing rooms of New York's Fifth Avenue amid the last surviving jewels of the Gilded Age.

This book is drawn from interviews, private documents, and public records, as described in the authors' note and line-by-line notes at the back. We have invented no characters, imagined no dialogue, put no thoughts into anyone's head. The sources include more than twenty thousand pages of Huguette's personal papers and the testimony of fifty witnesses in the legal contest for her fortune. Though no work of nonfiction can pretend to map anyone's interior terrain, the Clarks have left enough bread crumbs to lead us back into their fairy-tale world.

AN APPARITION

D R. HENRY SINGMAN, an internist, was making an emergency
house call on a new patient on New York's old-money Upper
East Side. It was a sunny early-spring afternoon, March 26,
1991. Dr. Singman had received a call from a retired colleague, whose
former patient had sent out an SOS.

At the luxury apartment building at 907 Fifth Avenue, the uniformed
doorman greeted the doctor, leading the way up the marble steps and
through the lobby with its elegantly coffered ceiling. The elevator, paneled in mahogany like a plutocrat's library, carried them to the eighth
floor. The doorman then did something he had never dared before. He
unlocked Apartment 8W, admitting the doctor.

Drawn shades blocked the sunlight from Central Park. A single can-
dle lit the entryway—an art gallery nearly forty feet long. The parquet
floor was an obstacle course of French dollhouses and miniature Japanese castles. Mannequins populated a side room, a gaggle of geishas
wearing kimonos. The draperies were green silk damask and red velvet,
the furniture Louis XV gilded oak, the paintings signed by Renoir, Cézanne, Degas, Manet, Monet.

In the half-light, Dr. Singman came face-to-face with "an apparition," a tiny woman, nearly eighty-five years old, with thin white hair
and frightened eyes the color of blue steel. She wore a soiled bathrobe
and had a towel wrapped around her face.

His medical notes give the grim details. The patient was suffering
from several cancers, basal cell carcinomas that had gone untreated for
quite a while. She was missing the left part of her lower lip, unable to
take food or drink without it gushing from her mouth. Her right cheek
had deep cavities. Where her right lower eyelid should have been, there
were large, deep ulcers exposing the orbital bone. She weighed all of
seventy-five pounds, "looked like somebody out of a concentration
camp," and "appeared nearly at death's door."

Dr. Singman urged her to go immediately to a hospital. The patient chose Doctors Hospital, which wasn't Manhattan's finest but was close to a friend's apartment. The patient had no insurance, so her attorney sent over a $10,000 check to the hospital, and the ambulance came that night.

The patient never saw this apartment again, except in photographs. Though she recovered to excellent health, she chose to spend the next twenty years and nearly two months, or exactly 7,364 nights, in the hospital.

As she left her home that spring evening in 1991, Huguette Clark insisted on being carried through the lobby and down the marble steps on a gurney, held high above the shoulders of the ambulance men, like Cleopatra riding on a litter—not for ceremony but for privacy, so the doormen and her neighbors couldn't see her face.

STILL LIFE

BELLOSGUARDO REMAINS TODAY as Bellosguardo was the last time Huguette saw it sixty years ago. The Clark summer estate in Santa Barbara, with its sweeping view of the shimmering Pacific, has been lovingly preserved since the early 1950s at the cost of only $40,000 per month.

Inside the gray French mansion, in the back of the service wing in a room off the kitchen, on the green tile floor lies a white sheet of paper. This typeset sign bears the signature of one of the housemen and has been in place for more than a decade now. It marks the former location of a piece of furniture.

> ON 29 NOVEMBER 2001,
> I MOVED A WHITE,
> WOODEN STEP STOOL FROM
> THIS ROOM TO THE MAIN
> WING ELEVATOR AS AN AID
> TO RESCUE IN CASE THE
> ELEVATOR GETS STUCK.
> *Harris*

Out in the massive garage, formerly a carriage barn and staff dormitory with a ballroom for dances, the automobile shop was once the domain of Walter Armstrong, the Scottish chauffeur for the Clarks. With no Clarks to drive most of the time, Armstrong filled the quiet afternoons at Bellosguardo with the low drone and high melody of his bagpipes.

Armstrong is long gone. After he retired, Huguette paid him his full salary as a pension until he died in the 1970s. Then Huguette paid the pension to his widow, Alma, until she died in the 1990s. But two of the automobiles that Armstrong lovingly cared for are still here, carefully preserved. Huguette turned down repeated offers to buy them.

On the right is a 1933 Chrysler Royal Eight convertible, its top perpetually down, with black paint and cream wheels. The chrome hood mascot of a leaping impala soars over a massive front grille. Huguette recalled Armstrong letting her drive the convertible on the coast road in the Santa Barbara summers of the Great Depression.

On the left is an enormous black 1933 Cadillac V-16 seven-passenger limousine. Its golden goddess hood ornament gleams under the garage's chandelier. Spare tires are affixed at the front of the running boards. Pull-down shades, like those in a drawing room, are ready to provide privacy to occupants of the coach.

On both automobiles, the yellow-and-black California license plates say 1949.

CHAPTER ONE

THE CLARK MANSION

...

PART ONE

THE MOST REMARKABLE DWELLING

HUGUETTE AND ANDRÉE, daughters of the multimillionaire former senator W. A. Clark, arrived in New York Harbor in July 1910, immigrants to their own country. They had sailed from Cherbourg, France, in first-class cabins on the White Star liner *Teutonic*. Wearing broad-brimmed sun hats, the Clark girls posed for newspaper photographers on the pier. Andrée, the adventurous eight-year-old brunette, looked confidently at the cameras, as her tag-along sister, blond four-year-old Huguette, looked down uncertainly.

Huguette's first day in America was filled with conjecture and misinformation. Reporters wrote that the heiresses didn't speak a word of English. Yet their parents were born in Pennsylvania and Michigan, and the girls held American passports, citizens since birth. In fact, they were being well educated by private tutors and governesses, with lessons in three languages: English, Spanish, and French.

Huguette Marcelle Clark was born in Paris on June 9, 1906. Her parents' apartment was on avenue Victor Hugo, at No. 56, a short walk down the wide, tree-lined avenue from the Arc de Triomphe. The baby girl, like the avenue, was named for France's beloved novelist, poet, and dramatist, who had lived just down the block in his last days. The child's name may also have been a nod to her father's French Huguenot ancestry. As a young woman, Huguette sometimes signed her name Hugo, and some of her friends called her Hugs. Andrée was nearly four when Huguette was born. When she had been told that a baby sister was due, Andrée said to her mother, "Let me think it over." Even one hundred years later, Huguette loved to laugh at her sister's cleverness. Huguette's father was old enough to be her great-grandfather. When Huguette was born, W.A. was a vigorous sixty-seven with four grown children from his first marriage, while Huguette's mother, Anna LaChapelle Clark, was only twenty-eight.

Although both parents had accompanied the girls on the ocean crossing, W.A. is the proud parent in the photographs on the pier. Anna stayed off to the side out of the camera's view. In the rare public photos of her, Anna appears standoffish, coolly looking out from under her tilted formal hats. But in the private photos in Huguette's albums, we see another Anna. Wearing her fashionable Continental dresses with a sash around her waist, she smiles warmly, playfully.

When the family arrived in 1910, they had no house in New York to go to. The greatest mansion in the city wasn't quite ready, even after ten years of construction. W.A. sent his wife and daughters west to the Rocky Mountains to Butte, Montana, where he had made his fortune in copper mining. He stayed behind in his New York apartment, sometimes spending the night in the unfinished Clark mansion, changing the plans to make it grander.

. . .

"When this modern palace is completed," the New York *World* reported, "it will rival in beauty and richness the mythical palace of Aladdin." W.A. had selected the site in 1895, paying $220,000 for the northeast corner of Fifth Avenue and Seventy-Seventh Street, prominently situated in the middle of New York's Millionaires' Row, up the avenue from Vanderbilt and Astor, down from Carnegie. By the time it was finished in 1911, observers called it the "biggest, bulliest and brassiest of all American castles," "the most remarkable dwelling in the world," and "without doubt the most costly and, perhaps, the most beautiful private residence in America."

The 121-room mansion was also Huguette's childhood home from age five to eighteen. This was a fairy-tale castle come to life, with secret entrances, mysterious sources of music, and treasures collected from all the world. When Andrée and Huguette would arrive home in their chauffeured automobile, accompanied by a private security guard, they passed through the open carriage gates—bronze gates twenty feet high, fit for a palace.

The bottom half of the six-story Beaux Arts mansion was not so unusual in its day, and might not have stood out if it were W.A.'s bank building. But on the top half, every inch was decorated with Parisian Beaux Arts ostentation, a profusion of lions, cherubs, and goddesses. Oh, but the architects weren't done. Soaring above the mansion was an ornate domed tower reaching nine stories, so pleased with itself that it continued to an open cupola. The overall effect was as if a lavish wedding cake had been designed in the daytime by a distinguished chef, and then overnight a French Dr. Seuss sneaked in to add a few extra layers.

Andrée and Huguette were outdoor girls. In the winter, dressed in matching red coats and red broad-brimmed hats, they went coasting down hills on sleds in Central Park. In the summer, they romped in matching sailor shirts and bloomers gathered above the knee. From any corner of the park, they had a specific home base for navigation: the tower of the Clark mansion. And when they stood in the tower itself, one hundred feet above the sidewalk, Andrée and Huguette could see all of Manhattan spread out below them.

Reporters who toured the home counted twenty-six bedrooms, thirty-one bathrooms, and five art galleries. Below the basement's Turkish baths, swimming pool, and storage room for furs, a railroad spur brought in coal for the furnace, which burned seven tons on a typical day, not only for heat but also to power dynamos for the two elevators, the cold-storage plant, the air-filtration plant, and the 4,200 lightbulbs.

As the girls pulled into the U-shaped driveway, they rode first into an open-air main courtyard and then under an archway into a vestibule decorated with a fountain of Tennessee marble. The fountain displayed a satyr's head projecting from a great clamshell, while two marble mermaids played in the spray. Their carriage then passed into a rotunda, where the young ladies of the house could disembark.

Mass production of the automobile had not yet begun when the plans were drawn up in 1898 by a little-known firm. By 1900, the foundation was being laid, but W.A. kept changing the plans, buying up five neighboring houses to make room for a more extravagant plan by a more famous architect, Henri Deglane, the designer of the Grand Palais in Paris.

W.A. supervised every detail of the house, every furnishing. To hurry along the work, and to keep from being gouged on the prices, in 1905 he bought the Henry-Bonnard bronze foundry, which used copper from his mine in Arizona to make the radiator gratings and door locks. When the price of white granite was raised by a quarry in North Jay, Maine, W.A. bought the quarry next door to undercut the price. He also bought the stone-dressing plant, the marble factory, the woodwork factory, and the decorative-plaster plant.

The plans were modified to include an automobile room after Ransom Olds began selling his Curved Dash Oldsmobile in 1901. After the home was occupied in 1911, photographs show carriages of both types—horse-drawn and horseless—lined up by the gate, with the automobile's driver careful to park in front of the horse.

From the carriage rotunda, Andrée and Huguette could stop on the ground floor to see their father in his private office, situated at the street corner for maximum light. With Santo Domingo mahogany walls, the office was dominated by a Gilbert Stuart portrait above the mantel—the familiar face of George Washington now on the one-dollar bill.

Huguette's girlhood home, the most expensive house in New York, afforded 121 rooms for a family of four. Note both types of carriages awaiting passengers at the Clark mansion on Seventy-Seventh Street at Fifth Avenue.

IN CONVERSATION WITH HUGUETTE

Saints, and religion in general, were more important to the Roman Catholic Anna and her daughters than they were to W.A. He had been a Presbyterian as a youth, then as a prosperous banker he became a more fashionable Episcopalian. Though he helped to build most of the churches in Butte, he admitted, "I am not much of a churchman."

Huguette told me that as a child she asked her father, "Oh, Papa, why can't you be Catholic?"

His reply: "All religions are lovely, my dear."

—PAUL NEWELL

If Andrée and Huguette sneaked through their father's waiting room and down the mirror-lined hallway past his office library, they could peek into the house's male domain, a Gothic-style great hall for smoking and billiards. The room was twenty feet by ninety feet, decorated with a thirteenth-century stained-glass window from a cathedral at Soissons in France.

The billiard room had another oddity: six paintings depicting the heroism, trial, and cruel death of Joan of Arc, France's maiden heroine. Her story was a particular favorite of Andrée's. The French artist of these paintings, Louis-Maurice Boutet de Monvel, had done a children's history of the maiden Joan, and the girls met the artist in France. At first the artist intended these paintings for a chapel near Domrémy, Joan's birthplace. But W.A. had to have them, so instead of being on view for the faithful who made pilgrimages to honor Joan, they were hanging in W.A.'s billiard room.

The cost of building the Clark house, not counting the furnishings, had been predicted to be $3 million, which would have made it as expensive as Rockefeller's and Carnegie's homes combined. As so often happens with home construction projects, the cost climbed—to $5 million, then $7 million, and some newspapers said $10 million, a bill that works out to a bit more than $250 million in today's currency. For perspective, the fifty-seven-story Woolworth Building, a neo-Gothic cathedral of commerce completed in 1913 in Lower Manhattan, cost $13.5 million, and the Woolworth would reign for nearly two decades as the tallest skyscraper in the world. Still, the Clark mansion cost no more than two years' profits flowing from a single Clark copper mine, the United Verde in Arizona. Always watching his pennies, W.A. was able to persuade the courts to lower his property tax bill by valuing the home at only $3.5 million, on the legal theory that it was so expensive to operate that it was of no use to anyone else.

The girls could ride up to the main floor in the elevator, or climb the grand circular staircase. Made of ivory-tinted Maryland marble, the stairs wound their way through a ceiling of oak overlaid with gold leaf. At the top of the stairs, Andrée and Huguette passed two exquisite bronze statues on white marble pedestals, each showing classical Greek heroes in scenes of struggle: on the left a muscular Odysseus bending his bow to show his strength and prove his identity, and on the right a chained Prometheus enduring his endless torture, an eagle eating his liver.

From the top of the stairs, the girls could look down the hallway, of white marble with mottled Breche violette columns, to the marble sculpture hall, with its thirty-six-foot-high octagonal dome made of terra-cotta, in the center of which hung an antique Spanish silver lamp. Here the girls enjoyed playing a game of hide-and-seek. If Andrée, the braver one,

IN CONVERSATION WITH HUGUETTE

On November 3, 2003, Huguette called, her voice strong and clear as usual. I thanked her for the packet of family photos she had sent and asked her about the photo of her father and his guests standing at a long dining table. She said it had been taken in the formal dining room at the Clark mansion on Fifth Avenue in 1913.

Could she tell me who the guests were? She mentioned several, including J. P. Morgan, and . . .

"Oh, what was that character's name? Oh, yes, Carnegie. Andrew Carnegie."

climbed to the third floor and passed through an alcove to the top of the dome, she could look down to see Huguette three floors below.

The main dining room, twenty-five feet by forty-nine feet, was about the same size as a family apartment in New York City. Above its massive fireplace, carved figures of Neptune, god of the sea, and Diana, goddess of the hunt, presided over the stone mantel, attended by cherubs, guarded at their feet by carved lions six feet tall. The ceiling set mouths agape: gilded panels carved from a single English oak supposedly harvested from Sherwood Forest. Over the door was a panel for the new Clark crest. The Clarks had no hereditary coat of arms, so W.A. sketched one out himself with elements fit for a royal house: a lion, an anchor, and a Gothic *C*.

Huguette recalled that her father forbade the girls to run around in the grand salon. W.A. had bought this room, alone the size of a typical house, and had it reassembled here overlooking Fifth Avenue and the woodlands of Central Park. Called the Salon Doré, or "golden room," it gleamed with exquisitely carved and gilded wood panels made in 1770 for a vainglorious French nobleman. W.A. brought the extravagant wall panels intact from Paris, adding reproduction panels to make the square room fit into his larger rectangular space. He decorated the salon with a clock from the boudoir of Marie Antoinette. During the French Revolution, when the former queen was under house arrest at Paris's Tuileries Palace, this gilded clock counted down the hours before her imprisonment and execution. A century later, this room was reserved for formal occasions. The Clark girls were allowed to play in the smaller room next to it, sitting on the Persian carpet of the petit salon.

The girls found more wonders in the tower. Huguette recalled playing hide-and-seek with Andrée there, one hundred feet above the street, discomforting their mother terribly. The tower held its own secret, a suite held in reserve for dark days. This was the quarantine suite, a valued space in these years before antibiotics, with bedrooms and its own kitchen, a refuge in case of a pandemic.

Coming down from the tower, the girls passed the servants' quarters on the fifth and sixth floors. The nursery on the fifth floor was separated into night and day nurseries, each with its own kitchen. A gentleman from *The New York Times* who toured the new house explained, "As the Senator and Mrs. Clark have but two small children, the facilities of

*Brought over from Paris, the golden room, or Salon Doré, was a bit
too formal for Andrée and Huguette to play hide-and-seek in.*

these spacious rooms will not be overtaxed." On the fourth floor was the
Oriental room, with the senator's treasures from the East, and some of
the twenty-five guest rooms. These higher floors were designed at first
to hold apartments to accommodate W.A.'s grown children from his
first marriage, but they already had their own homes, and the apartments were converted to other uses.

There were many nooks for Andrée and Huguette to explore. The
private area of the mansion, the part reserved for the immediate family,
was located on the third floor. Here the most comfortable spot was the
morning room, with a bearskin rug at one end and a tiger rug at the
other. The mirror-paneled walls hid mysterious doors, which opened on
a spring when the right spot was touched, revealing a fire hose, a storage
closet with boxes of cigars, or an entire suite of rooms. Perhaps these
doors were hidden out of whimsy, perhaps with an eye toward security.

The family of four had seventeen servants in residence, including a
houseman, a waitress, two butlers, three cooks, and ten maids. For dish-
ware, W.A. and Anna ordered from Chicago a nine-hundred-piece set
of china, costing $100,000, or about $3 million today. It was a simple
pattern, aside from the gold trim and Clark crest.

The room that Huguette described with the most fondness, years later,

A morning room in the Clark mansion was decorated with a tiger rug at the near end and a bear rug at the far end. The public areas downstairs were cavernous galleries and salons, while the suites upstairs were more warmly decorated for family living, though still featuring European furnishings and the finest Persian rugs.

was the library, warmed by a fireplace from a sixteenth-century castle in Normandy, with armed knights standing guard as andirons. The mantel was carved with a scene of rural revelry, bringing to mind W.A.'s own origins, with a shepherdess, a bagpiper, and dancing men. The ceiling was of carved French mahogany from the 1500s, and the room contained three stained-glass windows freed from a thirteenth-century abbey in Belgium. Its thousands of volumes included Dickens and Conan Doyle, Poe and Thoreau, Ibsen and Twain.

Oh, but from France—their France—the library also held copies of letters of Marie Antoinette, a history of French illustration, and the fables: seventy-five volumes wrapped in red Levant morocco leather and gilt lettering, the works of Jean-Pierre Claris de Florian and his more famous predecessor Jean de La Fontaine. These were French versions of ancient stories still known the world over, such as "The Ant and the Grasshopper" and "The Miser Who Lost His Treasure," along with lesser-known gems, "The Man with Two Mistresses" and "The Cricket."

Huguette recalled nearly a century later how Andrée patiently read to her here, enjoying the fables and fairy tales of the France they had left behind. Of all the rooms in the mansion, the library was the one Huguette missed most of all.

· · ·

Huguette once showed her nurses a photograph of "my father's house" in a book of the great houses of New York. With evident pride she reminisced about how much fun she and her sister had had there. The architectural criticism in that book didn't pierce her memories.

Critics have long been mixed in their opinion of the Clark castle: Some didn't like it, and others thought it awful. It was called an abomination, a monstrosity, and "Clark's Folly." *The Architectural Record* said it would have been a fine home for showman P. T. Barnum. The horizontal grooves in the limestone suggested to some passersby that the building was wearing corduroy pants. Others were offended by the tower, so vulgar and bombastic.

It may be time for a reassessment of the Clark mansion. In his "Streetscapes" column in *The New York Times* in 2011, architectural historian Christopher Gray took the critics to task: "These opinions have been parroted many times but, upon contemplation, this is a pretty neat house. If Carrere & Hastings [architects of the New York Public Library] had designed it for an establishment client, its profligacy would certainly have been forgiven, perhaps lionized."

It's not clear, however, whether the true objection of critics was to the building or to the man it represented. Whatever one thought of the house, it was a perfect embodiment of W. A. Clark's lifelong striving for opulence and recognition, his defiance of criticism, and his self-indulgence.

CHAPTER TWO

THE LOG CABIN

AN AMERICAN CHARACTER

W HEN THE SLIGHTLY BUILT MAN in the black frock coat and silk top hat stepped briskly down New York's Fifth Avenue in the Easter Sunday parade of 1914, the gawkers saw his face and recognized him instantly. His bristly beard and mustache may have turned from auburn to gray, but at seventy-five years of age, he was the picture of sartorial eminence. The proud little man was accompanied by three discreet touches of male vanity: a gold watch chain hanging from his dapper white waistcoat, a polka-dotted silk cravat held tightly to his high collar by a pearl stickpin, and his thirty-six-year-old wife. The publicity-shy Anna walked in the parade by his side, wearing a flowered hat and an uncomfortable expression, perhaps attributable to the tiny steps enforced by her fashionable but thoroughly impractical hobble skirt from Paris.

Uncomfortable in public, Huguette's mother, Anna, does not appear to be enjoying the Easter Parade on New York's Fifth Avenue, which offered a chance for the public to gawk at the tycoons living on Millionaires' Row. On Easter in April 1914, eleven-year-old Andrée walks in the parade, studying her fingernails while her mother gives her hand a tug. Seven-year-old Huguette stayed home.

There strode a man of unusual character, a symbol of two contradictory American archetypes.

W. A. Clark, businessman, was legendary, respected on Wall Street as a modern-day Midas. The epitome of frontier gumption, he was a triumphant mixture of civilizing education, self-reliance, and western pluck, living proof that in America the avenues to corporate wealth were open even to one born in a log cabin.

W. A. Clark, politician, was ridiculed on magazine covers as a payer of bribes, the epitome of backroom graft, and a crass mixture of ostentatious vanity, extravagance, and Washington plutocracy, living proof that in America the avenues to civic power were open only to those with the most greenbacks.

An indefatigable worker, W.A. carried on at a pace that today seems impossible, especially in an era when travel was by steamship and railroad, and communication by letter and telegram. During the first decade of the 1900s, for example, he maintained homes in Paris and Montana; built and furnished the most expensive house in New York City; constructed out of his own pocket a major railroad between Los Angeles harbor and Salt Lake City; subdivided and marketed lots for the city of Las Vegas; oversaw the operation of copper mines in several western states; ran streetcar and electric power companies in the West and a bronze foundry and copper wire factory in the East; grew sugar beets in California; published several newspapers; owned a bank with a good national reputation; was forced to resign from the U.S. Senate, then was reelected and served six more years; fought off a paternity suit filed by a young woman he had met at the Democratic National Convention; traveled through Europe collecting art; maintained good relations with his adult children; married a young wife and sired two daughters. All while in his sixties.

Though often chosen as a leader because of his intelligence, resolve, and deep pockets, he was not blessed with a magnetic disposition. W.A. was introverted and extremely private, a closemouthed man who acted as if he didn't give a damn what people thought of him. If people didn't like what he did, they were wrong. And yet he did give a damn about some things, including family, art, and social prominence. He was a seeker of public attention, not a great orator but a persistent one. He cheerfully took center stage to lead the singing of "The Star-Spangled Banner" at public events and didn't limit himself to the familiar first stanza.

In the pocket of his cutaway coat, W.A. carried two grades of cigars, fine ones for himself and lesser ones to give away.

W. A. CLARK COULD HONESTLY SAY he rose from a log cabin to the most magnificent mansion on Fifth Avenue, a handy trajectory in America's tradition of Horatio Alger's rags-to-riches stories. Yet W.A.'s beginnings were not so impoverished as he let on.

Will Clark, as W.A. was known as a boy, was indeed born in a four-room log cabin on January 8, 1839, but his grandfather owned a 172-acre farm in a remote corner of southwestern Pennsylvania called Dunbar Township. That's southeast of Pittsburgh, about two miles outside the small city of Connellsville, then known for its iron furnaces. This area was becoming connected to a wider world. One of Will's chores was to haul farm produce into town to sell to travelers who were leaving by flatboat on the Youghiogheny River, which led to the Monongahela, then the Ohio, and westward into the expanding nation.

Those were hard times. The nation had fallen into a seven-year economic depression beginning with the panic of 1837. It was not easy to see that the world was on the cusp of the second industrial revolution, when America would begin to take its place as a great power. In 1838, the year before W.A.'s birth, Samuel Morse demonstrated the first long-distance telegraph. A year after his birth, the first customer bought one of Cyrus McCormick's mechanical reapers for harvesting grain. The number of stars on the American flag had doubled from the original thirteen, reaching twenty-six with the addition of Arkansas in 1836 and Michigan in 1837. The people of Dunbar Township were buying their first books written by Americans. Will's father had obtained an account of the westward journey fifty years earlier by Meriwether Lewis and William Clark (no relation).

"The scenes of my joyous childhood," W.A. reminisced some seventy-five years later, were "outlined then by a very limited horizon. Nevertheless, I can recall ambitious speculations engendered in my mind when on winter evenings my father read the thrilling adventures of Lewis and Clark's explorations. . . . This had the effect of strengthening my preconceived but ill-defined idea of adventure. And I recall telling my mother one day at luncheon hour, when I had returned from hoeing corn, and the weeds were really bad, that when old enough I would seek my fortune in the great West."

During his later years, W.A. engaged the British School of Heraldry to trace his ancestry, with results he had the good humor to say were disappointing, for no famous people were found in his lineage. W.A.'s parents were of Scotch-Irish heritage,* a group that arrived in America with little in possessions aside from the Calvinist beliefs of their Presbyterian Church, pride in their work ethic, and the ability to distill a good grade of whiskey. The Clarks had come to Pennsylvania after the American Revolution from county Tyrone in the north of Ireland. W.A.'s father, John, was born in Dunbar in 1797, a few months after George Washington handed the presidency to John Adams, ensuring that America would not return to monarchy. W.A.'s mother, Mary Andrews Clark, was descended from Huguenots, French Protestants who emigrated from France to Scotland to escape religious persecution and then moved on to Ireland and America. W.A.'s red hair was inherited from his mother and shared by all his siblings.

A large family was necessary to work a farm, and John and Mary Andrews Clark had eleven children, eight of whom survived to adulthood. Their first child was a girl, Sarah Ann, born in 1837 and named for Mary's mother. A little over a year later, on January 8, 1839, came William Andrews, or Will.† His sister Elizabeth, also known as Lib, described in a memoir the family's tiring but joyous farm life:

What fun we had in winter too as well as summer! There were always the apples stored in the cellar and nuts we had gathered in the

* Scotch-Irish, not Scots-Irish, has long been the standard name in America for this immigrant group, who were the product not of Scottish and Irish parents, but of Protestant families from Scotland and England who settled in the north of Ireland in the seventeenth century and then moved on to the United States.

† Eight more Clarks were born in Pennsylvania: John Reed, who died in infancy; Joseph Kithcart; Elizabeth; Margaret Johnson, who died in infancy; Mary Margaret; James Ross; George; and Anna Belle.

autumn. . . . I do not remember much about cooking by the fire as Mother had one of the first cooking stoves in the neighborhood. Most of the bread was baked in an outdoor oven. There never was anything in the world better than this bread with butter and homemade maple syrup or homemade apple butter! . . . We lived the outdoor life both winter and summer. . . . We had sleighing and coasting. We were often taken to school in a big sled with all the neighbors' children.

Will's schooling was limited to three months in the winter, because farmwork came first. The Clark children attended the public school, Cross Keys, in Dunbar. As the two oldest, Sarah and W.A. had an advantage over the younger children, going on at age fourteen to Laurel Hill Academy, a selective private school at the Presbyterian church in town. Such academies offered a meager college preparation course: a little algebra, basic Latin, a taste of history and literature, and public speaking.

The Clarks were not in that log cabin for long. With money Will's father made mostly from harvesting trees, they moved into a larger wood-frame farmhouse on the property. When Will was about eleven, he helped his father build a handsome, two-story Federal-style brick residence, which stands today after more than 160 years.

John Clark passed on to his children great energy. He was proud of his fruit trees, prouder still of being a Presbyterian elder for forty years, and he was an advocate of hard work and fair dealing. Mary Andrews Clark gave her children boldness, ambition, and kindness. "Such good common sense," sister Elizabeth said of their mother, "such beauty of body and soul, such refinement, very religious in a tolerant way, progressive with a good sense of fun."

In 1856, at age sixty-two, perhaps a dubious age to start a new venture, John sold the Pennsylvania farm and moved his family west, traveling more than seven hundred miles by rail, steamboat, and stagecoach to the deep, loamy soil of Iowa. Seventeen-year-old Will drove a team of horses by himself the full distance ahead of the family.*

---

* They settled in Van Buren County, near the Missouri border and the Des Moines River village of Bentonsport. The youngest child, Anna Belle, was only six months

Will was "about grown up," Elizabeth recalled, "or at least thought he was." His great shock of wavy hair was dark auburn, matching his florid complexion. He was growing a mustache, which was also red. His eyes were a bluish steel gray, with a piercing stare.

Choosing brains over brawn, Will taught winter school in Iowa in 1857, then enrolled in an academy in Birmingham, Iowa, the following year. In 1859–60, he taught in a one-room school in Missouri. His sister Anna recalled W.A. telling of a man who took one look at the small, twenty-year-old schoolteacher and said, "Young man, you are a failure."

But W.A., as he preferred now to be called, was imbued with his parents' ambition, striving "to better my condition." In 1860, he enrolled in the study of classics and law at Iowa Wesleyan University, a Methodist Episcopal institution in Mount Pleasant. The tuition was twenty-five dollars a year. W.A. was taking classes both as a college freshman and a first-year law student, studying Latin, Greek, and geometry along with his legal contracts. He began a second year of the two-year course. In the spring of 1862, however, he dropped out of school, abandoning any hope of practicing law. Suffering from gold fever, an affliction sweeping the nation, he decided he was not cut out to "sit around in offices and wait for clients."

W.A. was by no means the first of the tens of thousands of men who traveled west in search of El Dorado. Gold had been found in 1848 in California, sparking the 1849 gold rush. The latest strike was in Colorado's Front Range, first at Pikes Peak in 1858 and then more substantially the next year near Central City and Black Hawk, about forty miles west of Denver. Moved, he said, by "a spirit of adventure," W.A. went west to Atchison, Kansas. From there he drove a six-yoke bull team of oxen across the Great Plains to Manitou Springs, near present-day Colorado Springs, a journey of more than eight hundred miles over five months.

Something besides gold may have spurred W.A. and others westward. The first mortars fired on Fort Sumter, South Carolina, in April 1861, when W.A. was twenty-two years old, launched the Civil War.

---

old. In Iowa, three-year-old George died of whooping cough, and the last child, Effie Ellen, was born. Known as Ella, she was the grandmother of co-author Paul Newell.

The Confederacy began drafting soldiers in April 1862, about the time W.A. headed west, and the Union followed suit in March 1863. After W.A. died, a biography written by a bitter former employee claimed that W.A. had fought with the Confederates before deserting, but this idea is contradicted by the available evidence. His home states of Pennsylvania and Iowa both stayed in the Union, and no W. A. Clark of his age and county appears in any service roster, muster roll, or other record for either the Union or Confederate army. If W.A. had any Confederate sympathies, he kept them to himself. Years later, he recalled hearing, near the end of the war, what he referred to as the sad news of President Lincoln's assassination.

W.A. chose three books for his journey west: *Parsons on Contracts,* Hitchcock's *Elements of Geology,* and *Poems of Robert Burns,* "the Ploughman Poet" and favorite son of Scotland. He went on to use all three, becoming in the West a sharp negotiator, a prescient judge of the mineral wealth underground, and a lover of the romantic arts.

I N THE SOUVENIR PHOTOS of tenderfoot gold miners from Colorado in the 1860s, with six-shooters on their hips, there is no reason to think that twenty-four-year-old W. A. Clark stands out from the pack. Though he later listed his height at five feet eight inches to five feet ten on his passport applications, his family and friends described him as five feet five, maybe five feet six in his boots. He weighed 120 to 125 pounds, never as much as 130, with a pipe-cleaner physique, giving the impression of endurance rather than strength.

He also had a lot of nervous energy. He spoke confidently, pointing his long, thin fingers for emphasis. His gait was more a run than a walk. His hands were constantly in motion. W.A. was a dynamo of alert intelligence.

In Colorado in the winter of 1862–63, he started at the first rung of the mining industry, as a hired hand on a small claim at Bobtail Hill, near Central City. "With three others I helped sink a shaft with a windlass, to a depth of 300 feet," he recalled. At most, he made three dollars a day.

News of another gold strike to the northwest spread through the mining camps of Colorado that winter. Gold had been found in what is now Montana, on the banks of a mountain stream called Grasshopper Creek. "The report got into the papers and caused a great deal of excitement," W.A. recalled.

He and two prospector friends left Colorado with two yokes of cattle, a light Schuttler wagon, picks, shovels, gold pans, fresh vegetables, and the certainty that they'd get rich if anyone would. They were headed for a corner of Idaho Territory, for the high, desolate land that would become southwestern Montana. "Our motto then," W.A. recalled, "was Bannack or Bust."

Starting out on May 4, 1863, while the bloody Battle of Chancellorsville was being fought in Virginia, W.A. and his friends traveled into the Wyoming Territory, following the Overland Trail to Fort Bridger, where they

One of these three gold miners in Central City, Colorado, in 1863, would, by the end of the century, own banks, railroads, timber, newspapers, sugar, coffee, oil, gold, silver, and the most profitable copper mines in the world. William Andrews Clark, at right, was about twenty-four here. "There was no lack of opportunities," he said, "for those who were on alert for making money."

were stopped by word of trouble with Shoshone Indians ahead on the Oregon Trail. For safety, they waited to join a long train of twenty-five covered wagons pulled by ox teams. The wagon train consisted of about one hundred people, including a few families with women and children.

The trip from Denver to Bannack, through more than seven hundred miles of wilderness, took sixty-five days. From Fort Bridger they traveled over the Teton Range, up the Snake River, and across the Continental Divide. Only fifteen or so of the party continued all the way on the Montana Trail to Bannack, others being diverted by news of gold in the Boise area. As a reminder of the constant danger on the trail, W.A. "saw the newly made graves of several recently murdered emigrants."

The evening before the Fourth of July 1863, their first night in Idaho Territory, the young men got into a keg of "old rye" whiskey and got to feeling pretty lively, dancing around the campfire. "This we began after supper time," W.A. recalled, "with rattling our tin pans, blowing an old horn, and singing occasionally a few strains of the 'Star-Spangled Banner,' to which we had some very enthusiastic responses from the coyotes in the surrounding hills." The young men called out for any Indians who might be listening to join them: "Come on, you red devils, we are ready for you!" Yet these brave young men were missing the real fight. The Battle of Gettysburg, with some 46,000 men killed, wounded, or missing, was ending in W.A.'s native Pennsylvania that day.

. . .

Despite his ambition, his energy, and his book-learning, W.A. proved to be no genius at prospecting. He described himself as naïve when he arrived in Bannack, where men were streaming out, not in, flocking instead to a new gold strike to the east at Alder Gulch. A group of men hiding from Crow Indians had happened upon gold there, swearing to keep their discovery a secret. That secret hadn't lasted long.

"We found some stampeders already on the way," W.A. later said self-deprecatingly, "some of them afoot, others on horseback, and all we had to do was to follow the crowd." All the claims had been staked out, and W.A.'s group wandered the desolate ridges, hoping to spot quartz veins with gold locked up in the rock, and searching the inside bends of creeks where gold dust might have been deposited. They found nothing promising, but a man named Baugh, for whom they had hauled some whiskey, did them the good turn of staking them in on his claim on a dry gulch, setting aside about two hundred feet for each man to work. An ex-Confederate, Baugh named the area Jeff Davis Gulch. When W.A. went into Bannack to buy grub and lumber for sluice boxes, used for separating gold from the auriferous sands, he was soon down to his last fifty cents. W.A. wrote:

Upon my arrival at Bannack I found five letters from home that anticipated me and had been carried from Salt Lake by a private express which had been established between that place and Bannack. The price of the transportation of a letter at that time was $1.00 each, and I had just $5.00. . . . I had, besides, a fractional greenback currency of the denomination of fifty cents. I gladly dispensed with the $5.00 for the letters, therefore, I was obliged to endeavor to get credit for the lumber and some few other articles which we needed, and this I readily obtained.

His fortunes soon reversed. "During our prospecting trip I had found a very fine pair of elk antlers, which I brought into Bannack, and for which Cy Skinner, who kept a saloon . . . offered to give me ten dollars, and this I readily accepted." W.A. would never again need to ask for credit.

. . .

Sorting out gold on the surface, known as placer (pronounced PLASS-ur) mining, is hard work, and has been since before the Bronze Age, particularly as far from water as these souls were. The idea is to use water to separate the dirt from the gold. To mine their dry Jeff Davis Gulch, W.A. and his pals had to strip off about four feet of the dirt and rock with picks and shovels to reach gold-infused loose sediment near the bedrock. Then they had to haul the sediment half a mile in a cart they had built from the front wheels of their Schuttler wagon. The water of nearby Colorado Creek ran through their handmade sluice boxes, the tiered channels creating eddies that allowed the heavier gold nuggets and gold dust to separate from the dirt and rock, or tailings. The men lived in a cabin they built themselves, with a roof of poles covered with dirt, and worked through the summer and fall until October, as the early snows approached.

They paid off their debts, sold their oxen, and had several thousand dollars each in gold dust to last them the winter in Bannack. "There I found a very lively place," W.A. said. "The gambling houses were open, where they were running a Spanish game with expert Spanish women."

W.A. now had enough money for a warm coat. He wasn't a fop, but he was on his way to being a dandy. Long before he had a valet to tend to his wardrobe, he kept wearing one long coat even after he burned off one of the tails by standing too close to a campfire.

Although W. A. Clark became known as the Midas who got rich in the mines, he actually made his first killing in eggs. As in gold rushes before and since, it wasn't the miners but the merchants who had the best odds. A man might find twenty dollars a day in gold but spend twenty-five dollars on food, axes, and boots, not counting gambling and female company.

The idea of merchandizing did not come to W.A. immediately. He began the winter of 1863–64 working for a hotel owner, cutting fire-wood at two dollars a day plus meals. "The third day I was caught in a fearful blizzard on the mountain, where myself and the horses lost our way, and came very nearly perishing in the storm. I concluded that this was not a good winter job, so I suggested . . . that we each buy a team and wagon and go to Salt Lake and take a look at the Mormons, concerning who we had heard many interesting stories, and to buy something appropriate to the mining camp."

After a ride of nearly four hundred miles into Utah Territory, the men saw the blocks of granite quarried for the Salt Lake Temple and heard preaching by Brigham Young. W.A. later met Young and recorded being "struck with the force of his mentality." W.A. also observed that the Mormon whiskey called "Valley Tan" was "abominable" but that "many of the Mormon girls were very pretty."

In Salt Lake, he loaded up his wagon with flour, butter, tobacco, and eggs. He took a great deal of risk by investing in the eggs, paying a wholesale price of twenty cents a dozen and knowing they would freeze on the return trip north to Bannack. The men shoveled snow for seven days solid on the journey and saw the cattle of other travelers freeze to death in their yokes. When they reached Bannack, W.A. sold the eggs to miners for use in a brandy and eggnog concoction called a Tom and Jerry, each dozen eggs now worth three dollars retail.

. . .

On his way back from Salt Lake City, W.A. met a man who had gotten into a gunfight with robbers, including one robber suspected to be a man named Dutch John. A few days later on the trail, W.A. saw the body of Dutch John, who had been hanged, or, as W.A. put it, "suspended."

This was W.A.'s first contact with the Vigilantes, who carried out a series of executions after brief trials, clearing this part of the Rocky Mountains of a reputed gang of thieves. One of history's best-known incidents of extralegal justice, the Montana Vigilante episode shows the danger of the times in which W.A. made his fortune, and the moral compromises sometimes required. There's no indication that W.A. participated in the hangings—he was away on his moneymaking trip to Salt Lake when the trials and executions began—but he knew several of the actors in this Wild West drama on the American frontier.

Montana was a mostly lawless territory. Although there were miners' courts for settling petty disputes, the nearest courts of law were nearly four hundred miles away in Lewiston, Idaho Territory. Few of those who went west for gold planned to stay long. The aim of many miners was to make a stake and then head back "to the States." Carrying their gold dust home involved a stagecoach ride from Virginia City to Salt Lake, a route that in 1863 was plagued by robbers.

W.A. was acquainted with the suspected leader of the robbers, a gunslinger named Henry Plummer, who also happened to be the newly elected sheriff. Most evenings in Bannack, W.A. would play billiards for an hour, then meet his friend Lloyd Selby at a saloon. Selby preferred to play cards, and his game was Old Sledge, akin to whist, sometimes called All Fours or Seven Up.

"One evening I went to get Selby to go home and found that he was drunk," W.A. recalled. "He had a large amount of gold dust with him in buckskin pouches. I was wearing a blue army overcoat and had my gold in my boots. A pouch of gold dust lay on the table. Henry Plummer, who was present, reached over and picked it up. Thereupon Selby pulled out his revolver and caressing it said, 'There's a friend that has never forsaken me.' Plummer laid down the pouch. Somehow I got Selby home. . . . Ever since that night I have thought it a mystery that we were not robbed on the way home."

After Plummer and his associates were hanged, W.A. came to know many of the Vigilante leaders, who included the leading men of that territory. In early 1864, he became a Mason, joining the ancient fraternal organization's lodge in Virginia City, where the Masonic leader was also the president of the first group of Vigilantes. As the state lodge's long-time secretary, Cornelius Hedges, told it, "We will not say that all the Vigilantes were Masons, but we would not go astray to say that all Masons were Vigilantes." W.A. would rise in 1877 to be the state grand master, or president, his first elected position of leadership.

Although the Vigilante trials swiftly established law and order in the region, their actions are controversial today. The guilt or innocence of Sheriff Plummer is still debated, and many of the later executions, carried out by successors to the original Vigilantes, may have been little more than murder.

But to W.A. and his friends, the morality of the early Vigilante trials was clear. "They had undoubted proof," he told a reunion of the Montana Pioneers in 1917, "of the criminal action of all these men." In a speech the year before in Virginia City, at a Masonic reunion, W.A. joked about the violent period, suggesting that some of his listeners had been far more active participants: "While I had considerable knowledge of the bandits then in the country . . . I did not personally know as much about them as some of you people did." He praised the Masons, among other early members of the Vigilantes, for making the uncivilized Montana Territory safe so honest men like him could earn a living.

"THERE WAS NO LACK," W.A. wrote in his journal, "of opportunities for those who were on the alert for making money."

W.A.'s striving and a good head for figures began to pay off as he bought and sold in dizzying fashion whatever a miner might need. He "traded tobacco at ten dollars a pound for boots at sixteen dollars a pair," earning from the miners such insulting monikers as "Tobacco Billy." When he sold flour, they called him "Yeast Powder Bill."

Here was a man prospering by his wits in the rough high country in winter, trading on his reputation as an honest businessman. He lent money at rates of about 2 percent per month, which would be usurious today but was not out of line in that time and place. His ledgers show him keeping track of every expenditure—at breakfast how much for molasses and butter, in the evening how much for tea. He would open a store, then close it, travel over mountains for new goods, and return to open a new store. When his peaches froze solid on the journey, he sold them as "chilly peaches." He bought tobacco at $1.50 a pound in Boise, Idaho, "with every dollar I had," and sold it in Helena, Montana, at "$5 to $6 a pound." A contemporary marveled at W.A.'s entrepreneurship, saying, "He never touched a dollar except twenty came back in its place."

. . .

In 1867, W.A. found that he could earn a bigger profit by hauling the U.S. mail from the headwaters of the Columbia River, near Missoula in western Montana, through northern Idaho to Walla Walla, then the largest community in Washington Territory, a distance of more than 450 miles. As a subcontractor of the U.S. government, he organized a system of ponies, riders, boats, and way stations that provided mail delivery three times a week.

The dangers of these mountain trails were real and present, but at age twenty-eight, W.A. was courageous—or headstrong. In 1868, he spent days riding his Cayuse pony, a cheap working horse, on his turn on the trail. W.A. followed the Clark Fork* through Indian country, then along the northeast flank of the Bitterroot Mountains into Idaho Territory. At night, he wrote in his journal, marveling at the scenic beauty, grumbling about the difficulty of finding a decent book to read in the wilderness, and calmly recording the dangers.

At one stop, he wrote:

> I was entertained while drinking my tea by this young Welshman, whom I employ to take care of this station on account of the massacre at Ft. Phil Kearney, he having been there at the time, Dec. 21st, 1866, 94 men were massacred within 3 miles of the Post. All were scalped save two and all save one were stripped of their clothing, turned with their faces downward and their backs stuck full of arrow. No bows were found and the arrows were recognized by their peculiar shape to belong to the Sioux, the Arapaho, and the Cheyenne. One was not scalped because of his baldness, but in lieu thereof they took his whiskers and mustache, and another for some reason was not scalped, was left with his face upward, was not stripped of his clothing, and was covered with a buffalo robe. It is supposed they knew him and perhaps had received some act of kindness from his hands, and thus thanked him with respect.

The news of the massacre was fresh in his mind as he traveled through the wilderness, often hearing sounds in the trees. "The weather is very cold and frosty," he wrote in his journal, "and as I rode along solitary through this dense forest of pines I was frequently startled by a loud report near me like the explosion of a blast." It was not gunfire, but was instead "caused by the expansion bursting of the wood or bark of the trees by the frost." Relieved, he stopped at a way station "and took my supper cheerfully by a sparkling fire."

. . .

Indian massacres were not the only dangers W.A. faced. On January 30, 1868, he stepped into a situation that nearly cost him his life.

---

* Named for William Clark (no relation), one of the leaders of the Lewis and Clark Expedition of 1804–1806.

Clear and cold morning, reached crossing of Deer Lodge river at McCarthy's ferry at 10. Found the river frozen over and a beaten track on both sides of the river that led me to believe it a regular crossing. I therefore got off my horse and led him on, feeling carefully and trying to test the ice with my heel.

It gave no indication of breaking and perhaps would have borne me safely over, but no sooner had my horse stepped his whole weight upon it than down we went in five feet of water.

I was fortunate enough to catch on the edge of the ice and prevented myself being swept down by the current and endeavored to raise myself out, but loaded down with overshoes, overcoat and muffler my efforts were futile and in vain did I cry for help.

The ice being very slippery, it was with difficulty I retained my hold until I succeeded in pulling my gloves successively from each hand with my teeth. At this moment my poor horse came up close behind, and placing one foot against his shoulder I made a desperate effort and scrambled out upon the ice next to the shore where it was very thick and firm. My horse again came up to me, nothing being visible except his head and the top of my saddle. I plunged my arm down by the water, uncinched the saddle and threw it off with cantinas on the pommel which contained seven or eight hundred dollars.

Knowing of no means by which I could rescue my horse I began to realize my situation and danger of freezing, being thoroughly drenched in a temperature of 10 degrees below zero. I started to run back one-quarter mile to a house and met two men who had heard my cries and were coming to my relief. They were in time to save my horse, . . . drawing him on the ice with a rope.

I reached the fire just in time as my legs began to get benumbed and my feet were frozen tight in my shoes. Here I remained until evening drying myself and clothes and had a log fire built near which I stood my horse to get warm and dry.

Meticulous as ever, W.A. recorded in his ledger book the cost of his near-death experience:

Paid for getting horse out, $4.00.

. . .

After his narrow—and rather expensive—escape, W.A. was ready for a vacation. His journal reveals his growing interest in the arts, as well as his talent for spotting new sources of revenue.

"Arrived in Helena," he wrote, "when I met numerous friends and acquaintances. Took board at the International Hotel. I was engaged reading among others 'Pickwick Papers' by Dickens." He spent the next few weeks "at Helena amusing myself sleigh riding, attending theaters, reading, writing and billiards."

But Dickens and billiards were not the primary objects of W.A.'s vision. His diary entry for March 6, 1868, reads: "Sent a proposal to convey U.S. Mail from Helena to Missoula for two more years commencing July 1st, '68, for the sum of $22,400 per annum." That's about $400,000 in today's dollars.

W.A. had no intention of hauling the mail through Indian country for the rest of his life, however. In the fall of 1868, he subcontracted out the mail delivery business and took a trip east. He boarded a mackinaw flat-bottomed boat at Fort Benton on the Missouri River. He told friends he was going to bring back a wife.

CHAPTER THREE

THE COPPER KING MANSION

KATE

W.A. HAD SET OFF down the Missouri, intent on seeing a childhood friend back in Pennsylvania. He recalled a girl with dark brown eyes and curly brown hair "who was dear to me when we were children together." In the fall of 1868, the flat-bottom boat W.A. had boarded at Fort Benton docked in Sioux City, Iowa. There W.A. visited with his parents. He then rode by rail back to Pennsylvania to see this childhood friend. At age twenty-nine, he took his mother along for the courting.

The courting began in an Odd Fellows Hall in Connellsville, where W.A. asked Katherine Louise Stauffer to a dance. Brown-eyed "Kate" was no longer a girl, but a beautiful, bright young woman of twenty-four. W.A., a worldly veteran of the western mines, Indian territory, and freewheeling commerce, "wooed and won" her. On the morning of March 17, 1869, they were wed at her parents' large brick house in Connellsville, where her father was a prosperous businessman. A minister of the Church of Christ performed the ceremony. After a morning breakfast

W. A. Clark's first wife, Katherine Louise "Kate" Stauffer Clark, a childhood friend from Pennsylvania.

reception, everyone went uptown to watch the St. Patrick's Day parade. The couple boarded a train heading west, stopping in St. Louis for a working honeymoon, as W.A. bought goods to ship west. They continued by train and stagecoach to their new home, the mining camp of Helena, Montana. When they arrived, they discovered that most of Helena had been destroyed by a fire. The newlyweds set up housekeeping in a friend's spare bedroom.

In addition to a new wife, W.A. had a new business venture. Time and again, he showed great adaptability, switching businesses and cities in search of greater profit. In partnership with a Missouri merchant, he had formed a wholesale mercantile business in 1868. Donnell & Clark shipped groceries and eastern goods to Helena, Montana, by river, rail, and bull or mule teams—a lot of effort for very little profit. After a rough season of drought and poor sales, they consolidated the business in Deer Lodge, a growing town to the west of Helena, in cattle and mining country, and added a third partner, becoming Donnell, Clark & Larabie. In 1870, they adapted to circumstances again, whittling their business down to its most profitable element, banking, which was mostly the business of making the rounds of mining camps, assaying and buying gold dust.

W.A. was shrewd in business, but he was known, like his father, for fair dealing. "When we first knew him he was a ragged, dirty, lousy miner," Montana's *Missoula Gazette* recalled in 1888. "But beneath those rags and gray-backs there was industry, energy, determination and brains, and behind all a resolute, fixed, determined purpose to succeed in the struggle for wealth and honorable distinction."

He had become a family man, too. Kate bore a daughter that January, named Mary Joaquina, usually called May or Maizie. She was followed by Charles Walker, or Charlie, in 1871. In 1874, an unnamed son died at only eight days old. Twin girls, Jessie and Katherine Louise, were born in 1875; the twin Jessie died at age two. William Andrews, Jr., called Will, was born in 1877, and Francis Paul followed in 1880. They were then a family of seven, with W.A., Kate, and the five surviving children.

The Clarks were now prosperous, at least by Deer Lodge standards. The federal census of 1870 shows W.A. as a grocer and banker, with a net worth of $15,000, equal to about $275,000 today. That made him the fourth-wealthiest banker in Deer Lodge, a town of 788 people. The young family lived on a side street in a white frame house with five rooms. Attached to the house was a log lean-to that W.A. used for his assay office. The Clarks traveled the dirt streets in a little horse-drawn buggy.

His wealth began to afford him social status, even a short-term military commission in an Indian war. During the Nez Percé War of 1877, W.A. raised three companies of volunteers and was assigned the rank of major. The fight was then taken over by regular U.S. Army soldiers, who drove Chief Joseph and his band of four hundred warriors off their ancestral lands, in violation of a U.S. treaty with the Indians. The soldiers captured the largest group of Nez Percé refugees near the Canadian border. Although W.A. saw no fighting, his son Charlie recalled watching his father ride off toward the Bitterroot Mountains "to sound the alarm about the Indians," sitting atop a horse called Wild Bill.

In 1872, W.A. gained greater respectability as a banker when he and his partners organized the First National Bank of Deer Lodge, capitalized at $50,000. They soon opened a branch forty miles to the south in Butte, Montana, a failed gold camp with the beginnings of a rebirth as a mining camp for silver and copper. Two of W.A.'s younger brothers, Joseph and Ross, eventually joined him in Butte. After they arrived, W.A. bought out his other partners. It was now solely a Clark operation. Although he may have been something of a loner, his feelings toward family members were deep and affectionate, generously inducting his brothers into his enterprises as soon as they were of age. Joseph worked in the mining operations, and Ross in banking.

There was never any doubt, however, about which Clark was the boss. Their bank, for example, was not called Clark Brothers Bank.

Nor was it W.A. and J. Ross Clark Bank.

The name was W. A. Clark & Brother, Bankers.

ENLIGHTENING THE WORLD

———

THE STREETS OF BUTTE were unpaved and muddy when W.A. brought his banking business there in 1872. The town's gold rush days had passed. Even if underground veins of silver and copper could be found, it would be hard to make them profitable. The town was four hundred miles from the nearest railroad.

In that depressed environment, W.A. saw the right time for an investment. In 1872, the banker bought four old mining claims of uncertain value. They were called the Original, the Colusa, the Gambetta, and the Mountain Chief. To develop his investments, W.A. didn't go at the opportunity the same way most men would. He had two obvious options: He could bear all the risk himself, starting immediately to drill into the Butte hill—he knew something about geology and mining, but he was not by nature a gambler. Or he could wait for others to develop mines nearby, letting them chew up their capital and reap the rewards. But W.A. was not much for waiting.

So he created a third option: Recognizing that his single volume of Hitchcock's *Elements of Geology* was not a sufficient education, he went back to college. Although thirty-three years old and married with two children, the banker took his family east in the winter of 1872–73 to New York, where he studied practical assaying and mineralogy at the School of Mines at Columbia College (now Columbia University). It's hard to imagine that any student ever got a better return on his investment of a single year's tuition.

W.A. learned how to field-test metal-bearing quartz with a blowpipe. He learned how to roast and smelt and refine the ore to remove the precious metals. His ore samples from his four claims in Butte tested out to be promising, particularly in copper. Ore that yielded 5 percent copper would have been rich enough to be worth mining, but the Butte samples were testing closer to 50 percent.

· · ·

Copper was about to become the essential conductor of modern life. In 1858, the warships HMS *Agamemnon* and USS *Niagara* had laid the first transatlantic telegraph cable. In 1876, Bell would patent his telephone. By 1879, Edison would create the first commercially practical incandescent lightbulb. And in 1882, Eduard Rubin of Switzerland would invent the full metal jacket bullet, increasing the distance one could stand from a man while killing him.

All of these advances in communication, everyday life, and warfare would depend on W. A. Clark's copper.

Back in Butte in 1873, W.A. began to explore the Colusa and Gambetta claims, shipping the copper ore by wagon to the nearest point on the Union Pacific at Corinne, Utah Territory. Transportation costs ate up most of the mining profits, so Clark built a smelter to use heat and chemicals to extract the copper locally, increasing his profits considerably. When the Utah & Northern Railway arrived in 1881, connecting Butte to the Union Pacific and valuable markets in the East and West, he was there to meet the first train.

W.A. had an advantage over other entrepreneurs. As a shrewd banker, he had the opportunity to see which mining properties were profitable and which were undercapitalized. And if loans weren't paid, he could foreclose. Although W.A. was not the one who discovered silver in Butte, he found a way into the business. In 1874, a man named Bill Farlin struck silver, and with a loan from Clark's First National Bank of Deer Lodge, he built a stamp mill to process the quartz. When Farlin got overextended in 1880, Clark and his partners became the new owners of both the mine and the mill through foreclosure. Butte would produce 24,000 tons of silver, but its 11 million tons of copper would earn its nickname, "the Richest Hill on Earth."

If not already a millionaire, W.A. was well on his way. The thirty-seven-year-old banker and industrialist had an opportunity to see the future in 1876, representing the Montana Territory as its orator at the world's fair in Philadelphia. Despite another worldwide economic depression, nine million visitors celebrated the centennial of the Declaration of Independence by touring the latest wonders of the world: Bell's telephone and Remington's typewriter, Heinz ketchup and Hires root beer.

Fairgoers could walk up stairs inside a lookout tower to see the entire grounds of the Centennial Exhibition. The tower was part of an unfinished statue brought from Paris. The artist planned the statue as a gift from the French Republic to the United States, and was seeking subscriptions to pay for a pedestal. The work was to be a colossal metallic structure of a woman, fifteen stories tall, but all that was on display was her gigantic right forearm holding a torch and flame. The artist was Frédéric-Auguste Bartholdi, the sculpture was *Liberty Enlightening the World*, and this was America's first glimpse of its Statue of Liberty.

With a fifty-cent ticket, W.A. could climb the stairs to the torch's balcony, looking out on the industrial wonders of the world, touching Lady Liberty's smooth French skin of copper.

A PALACE AND A TEMPLE

BUTTE WAS NO LONGER a muddy, isolated town. As copper was changing the wider world, it transformed Butte. The same railroad that began taking copper out also brought culture in. By the end of the century, Butte's Grand Opera House would be visited by Mark Twain and Sarah Bernhardt. Its Broadway Theatre, one of many in town, claimed to be the largest west of Chicago. W.A. was Butte's dynamo, building its first water supply system, organizing the electric light company and the street railway, and owning *The Butte Miner* newspaper.

He needed the finest house in town, particularly as he began to seek political office. From 1884 to 1888, he supervised every detail of the construction of a thirty-four-room red-brick Victorian mansion with a steeply sloping French mansard roof and dormer windows. Begun in a time of depressed copper prices, the home was W.A.'s testament to confidence in the copper camp. When asked why he was building in Butte, he answered with loyalty, "Because I owe it to Butte. I have made money there."

This first Clark mansion was designed to confer social status, and it was easily the most expensive home in town, costing a quarter of a million dollars, or about $6 million today. The plaster on the walls was painted in swirls of gold in the entryway, bronze in the octagonal reception room, silver in the dining room, and copper in the billiard room. The woodwork was of fine oak, Cuban mahogany, sycamore, bird's-eye maple, and rosewood. W.A.'s silhouette was sculpted above the mantel, and frescoes on the library ceiling represented the arts: literature, architecture, painting, and music. The Clark home didn't have just a staircase; it had the "staircase of nations," with each wood panel representing one nation of the world, leading up to jeweled-glass windows large enough for a church. On the third floor was a ballroom sixty-two feet long.

The house had another special feature, one that was required for an industrialist in that era. On the second floor, hidden in the second bedroom, known as the family bedroom, was a closet that served as a panic room. This closet had a call box that could be used to alert the police, the fire department, or the hospital. This was no extravagance: Wealthy men received threats of all kinds. In 1889, for example, W.A. received a letter threatening his life if he did not pay the writer $400,000. He didn't pay, but he was prepared for trouble if it arrived.

This first Clark mansion, now known as the Copper King Mansion, was located in an area called Uptown, somewhat distant from the worst smoke and fumes from W.A.'s copper smelter, which was called the tallest concrete smokestack in the world. The Butte hill was an industrial moonscape, denuded of trees. Copper was removed from the ore by roasting it in open-air heaps. W. A. Clark's smelter smokestack dispensed sulfurous smoke packed with arsenic, a toxin despite its use by Victorian women to lighten their complexions. Sometimes the smoke was so thick that two people passing on a Butte sidewalk could bump into each other, as in the London fog.

"I must say that the ladies are very fond of this smoky city, as it is sometimes called," W.A. joked at the 1889 state constitutional convention, when he was the presiding officer, "because there is just enough arsenic there to give them a beautiful complexion. . . . I believe there are times when there is smoke settling over the city, but I say it would be a great deal better for other cities in the territory if they had more smoke and less diphtheria and other diseases. It has been believed by all the physicians of Butte that the smoke that sometimes prevails there is a disinfectant, and destroys the microbes that constitute the germs of disease."

. . .

Kate Clark, the lady of Butte's finest home, was known as a charming hostess, but she was not often at home. There's no indication of a lack of affection between Kate and W.A., but she and the children spent most of the years 1884–93 in Europe and New York, seeking better schools and cultural opportunities. W.A., occupied with his business and political career, joined them for vacations, during which he spent much of his time beginning to build his art collection. Well into his forties, W.A.

began to learn French and a smattering of German. The westerner with the bushy red beard nearly always wore refined, well-tailored black suits, dressing elegantly in the tradition of the boulevardiers of Paris. During an extended stay in the German cultural capital, Dresden, W.A. and Kate had their portraits painted. They stand proudly in these paintings, dressed as members of the haute bourgeoisie, W.A. with a silk top hat and knee-length Prince Albert coat, and Kate with an enormous hat and a skirt shaped by a prominent Victorian bustle.

In 1893, while Kate was in Chicago for the World's Columbian Exhibition, she contracted typhoid fever. Amid widespread concern about the poor quality of the city's water supply, officials had assured fairgoers that the water at the fair was filtered or sterilized. (Officials also promised that summers in Chicago were "invariably cool.") Kate died in New York on October 19. She was fifty years old.

W.A. demonstrated his love for Kate by building her a $150,000 mausoleum in the form of a Greek temple. He chose a prominent hillside site, not in Butte but in New York City's Woodlawn Cemetery in the Bronx, north of Manhattan. The stone exterior is of white granite, with intricate mosaics inside. The bronze doors were sculpted by an American living in Paris, Paul Wayland Bartlett, who also designed the pediment for the House wing of the U.S. Capitol. W.A. corresponded endlessly with the artist over every detail. From the massive bronze doors, a portrait of Kate's face looks out mournfully.

W.A. was a fifty-four-year-old widower with five children between the ages of thirteen and twenty-three, all old enough to be away at boarding school or beyond. Soon he was looking for a site for a grand new home in New York City. The only question was, who would be the mistress of the manse?

ANNA

THE WIDOWER W. A. CLARK gained a reputation as one ever ready to help develop young artistic talent, particularly the female sort. Or, as one contemporary said, he was "an ardent admirer, if that's what one wishes to call it, of the fair sex."

His first protégée from the boardinghouses of Butte became an early star of American silent films, but she would not become Mrs. W. A. Clark. Kathlyn Williams was sponsored by W.A. in her early theater career. A blond beauty and the daughter of a boardinghouse operator in Butte, she was born Kathleen Mabel Williams in 1879 but adopted Kathlyn as her stage name. Her father died when she was young, and her mother paid the bills by renting out rooms to miners. As a teenager in the 1890s, Kathlyn starred in Butte theater productions, where she met W.A., the richest man in town.

He agreed to send Kathlyn to New York to study opera, on the condition that she first finish her studies at Montana Wesleyan University, seventy miles away in Helena. The year she graduated, 1901, she turned twenty-two. W.A. was sixty-two.

Kathlyn soon switched from opera to acting, and W.A. paid for her to begin training in New York. By 1903, with W.A. occupied in the U.S. Senate, Kathlyn was married and had moved on to other male sponsors, eventually starring in more than 170 films. In a fan magazine in 1912, Kathlyn thanked Senator Clark, who she said "took a great interest in my welfare." She explained that the senator "has helped so many boys and girls to realize their ambitions." The names of no boys survive.

. . .

At the same time, W.A. was supporting another girl from a Butte boardinghouse, Anna LaChapelle, who had her own plans to become a musician and singer. In 1893 or 1894, soon after Kate's death, W.A.'s eye fell on Anna, who was fifteen or sixteen. After she was well into her twenties, she would become his second wife and the mother of two daughters, Andrée and Huguette.

There are competing stories of how W.A. met Anna. The family version, the official version, has W.A. spotting her on the Fourth of July in a community pageant in which she played a chaste Statue of Liberty. Anna loved to sing and play music, but she was shy and reserved in public. The teenager stood a shapely five feet four with cascading brown hair, a prominent round chin, and an inviting, gap-toothed smile. W.A. recognized her talents immediately.

The unofficial version, printed in anti-Clark newspapers, casts Anna as the forward one. According to this story, Anna called on a banker in Butte, asking him to sponsor her acting career. That man declined but suggested that she contact another banker who might receive her more generously, W. A. Clark.

The family also put forward another story about Anna, one describing her as the daughter of an honored physician who had died before the wealthy W. A. Clark became her guardian and she his ward, as though she were an orphan in need of his legal and financial protection. The facts were quite different, however: Anna's father wasn't quite a doctor, and he was very much alive.

Anna Eugenia LaChapelle was born in the Michigan copper mining town of Red Jacket, now known as Calumet, on March 10, 1878. Her parents were immigrants from Montreal, in French-speaking Quebec, who had arrived in the United States six years earlier as part of a great French Canadian wave of immigration. The family later moved to Butte, settling in one of the rougher neighborhoods on the Butte hill, right below the smoke-belching smelters. Anna was the oldest of three children, two girls and a boy.

The LaChapelles rented out rooms to miners. Anna's mother, Philomene, could speak English, but not read or write it. She worked as a housekeeper. Anna's father, Pierre, had been a tailor and then began selling medical potions such as eye lotions. Later he dispensed eyeglasses. Though his tombstone in Butte's Catholic cemetery identifies him as "Dr. Pierre J. LaChapelle," his obituary says he was studying medicine at the time of his death.

The father was still living when Anna fell under W.A.'s sponsorship. The father's obituary from 1896 places eighteen-year-old Anna already in Paris, studying the concert harp and refining her French. To add some respectability to the arrangement, Anna was described as W.A.'s ward. Court records in Butte show no such guardianship.

At W.A.'s Paris apartment on avenue Victor Hugo, Anna was chaperoned by one of W.A.'s sisters,* who was there with two daughters. These nieces of W.A.'s described Anna as lively and in love with music. She had a puckish sense of humor that kept them entertained. She also liked to joke about her unusual eyes: one blue and one brown. Back in Butte, people noticed that Anna's mother, now a widow, had moved into a fine home one block west of the Clark mansion.

By 1900, as W.A. was serving in the U.S. Senate, Anna visited him in Washington. Newspapers reported that she was "the most interesting lady in Washington," which might have been a polite way of calling her the most gossiped-about woman. *The Denver Post* said she had "a typical French face and the great soulful eyes which are often associated with the artistic temperament." The papers quoted W.A.'s friends as saying that the couple would soon wed and that W.A. planned an opera career for Anna under the stage name Montana. For good measure, the papers added the fiction that Anna's father had been killed in one of W.A.'s mines, stirring the magnanimous industrialist to take pity on the family.

. . .

While Anna was in Paris, W.A. had other romantic entanglements as the new century began.

First, there was Hattie Rose Laube of Huron, South Dakota, a temperance lecturer and political campaigner, who let it be known in 1901 that W.A. had written her a promise of marriage from Europe. All the newspapers covered her announcement, although the Clark family dismissed the claim as false.

Then there was the paternity suit filed by a young newspaperwoman named Mary McNellis. W.A. had met Mary at the 1896 Democratic Na-

---

* The chaperone was Elizabeth Clark Abascal, who accompanied Anna to Paris with Elizabeth's daughters, Anita and Mary.

tional Convention in Chicago, where he was a delegate. In 1901, while W.A. was serving in the Senate, Mary brought a lawsuit against him in New York. She claimed that in October 1900, over a dinner of oysters and champagne at the old Waldorf Hotel, W.A. had promised to marry her. She sought $150,000 for breach of promise, claiming that she had been seduced, debauched, and impregnated.

W.A. admitted in court papers to knowing Mary and to socializing three or four times with this "rather agreeable and very intelligent young woman." But he vigorously denied "that I ever promised to marry Miss McNellis, or ever made love to her or induced her to believe that I was going to marry her." Court records show that a referee found in W.A.'s favor, ordering Mary to pay the senator $1,125 in court costs.

The court records were sealed, keeping the case out of the newspapers for two years, during which time W.A. was courting Anna. Then in 1903, it was revealed that Mary had wanted her attorney to push for a jury trial, but the attorney had persuaded her to accept the referee's decision and give up the case. Mary was surprised to discover that her attorney had owned part of a mining company in British Columbia and that the mine had recently been purchased by W. A. Clark. She filed an appeal, and at that point all the newspapers covered the McNellis case.

Word of the case may have reached Paris, where twenty-five-year-old Anna was still studying the harp. W.A. traveled there at least twice a year by steamship. The girl from the Butte boardinghouse had adopted chic Parisian styles, with hemlines at the ankle and a high waist defined by a luxurious sash. Her brown hair was cut short in bangs hanging nearly to her deep-set eyes. And she began sporting a few expensive gifts: a bracelet with 36 sapphires and 126 small diamonds, a pair of tortoiseshell combs each with 320 diamonds, and a Cartier two-strand pearl necklace with a seven-carat diamond clasp.

W.A. MOVED from rich to superrich after representing Montana at the 1885 World's Industrial and Cotton Centennial Exposition in New Orleans. There he toured the display from Arizona Territory, seeing samples of ore from a particular mine, samples rich in copper, gold, and silver. He made note of it, and promptly forgot about it. But later, in checking the books of a bankrupt ore refinery that he had taken control of, he saw the name of the mine again: the United Verde.

In early 1888, W.A. went to Arizona to visit this mine near the remote town of Jerome. This was high in Yavapai County, at 5,400 feet on the eastern slope of the Black Hills mountains, overlooking the Verde River. It had been operated since 1876, but when miners encountered a leaner ore in 1884, they were no longer able to operate profitably. United Verde's prospects were limited by the lack of access to water or a railroad to transport the copper ore. For a while, the nearest railroad station was three states away, in Kansas. But even after the Santa Fe railroad pushed through Arizona in 1882, worldwide copper prices were depressed, falling to nine cents a pound, and the mine lay idle.

When W.A. visited the mine in 1888, the copper market was ripe, with prices having been driven up to fifteen cents a pound by a French syndicate that was limiting production. He and his mine superintendent went crawling around the mine to take ore samples every twelve inches. Satisfied with what he found, he took an option on the mine and started buying up all the stock, which was scattered across the globe. Eventually, out of 300,000 shares, the Clarks would own 299,000.

Under his ownership, the United Verde would become the richest copper mine in the world. It again showed W. A. Clark's ability to grasp an opportunity. He installed a massive industrial complex for extracting, crushing, and roasting the ore to bring out the vital copper. The mining shafts, lined with concrete, reached two-thirds of a mile deep. W.A. also connected Jerome to the Santa Fe railroad by a narrow-gauge line, cutting his transportation costs dramatically.

For his workers, W.A. built a model town, complete with a library and schools. This planned community, called Clarkdale, was founded in 1912 a mile from the mine. Under the rigid segregation of the day, miners and their families lived in company cottages, with Upper Clarkdale for engineers and bosses. Lower Clarkdale was for working class whites. Mexican immigrants lived in crude buildings in Patio Town closer to the smelter. And out in the desert Native American workers lived in domed huts they built themselves. The company provided a baseball park and four swimming pools, disability insurance, and wages paid on a bonus system, with extra pay given for loading more ore or blacksmithing more pickaxes. Unlike its competitors, the United Verde enjoyed mostly harmonious relations with its unions.

W.A. operated all his businesses under strict secrecy, but he did let out that the United Verde was capable of producing eight million pounds of fine copper per month. Newspapers speculated that its annual profits were $5 million to $10 million, or in today's dollars roughly $140 million to $280 million. With great understatement, W.A. recalled in a speech some years later his impression of the ore samples from United Verde that he had seen in New Orleans: "This was one of the most attractive collections of mineral to be found at the exhibition."

T HE 1880s BROUGHT a flood of pioneers into Southern California. Some came to escape harsh winters elsewhere. Some sought the restoration of their health. And some were prescient entrepreneurs and land speculators. The Clark family contributed immigrants in all three categories, and through W.A.'s enterprise, they built a railroad to open up Los Angeles as the center of business on the Pacific coast, America's gateway for trade with the Orient.

In 1880, Los Angeles was an unimpressive town of 11,000 on the Los Angeles River. In some years, the river flooded in the winter and ran almost dry in the summer. Until 1878, when the Southern Pacific Railroad completed its line from California's biggest city, San Francisco, to its little sister Los Angeles, the only way to make the three-hundred-mile trip was by horse-drawn stagecoach through treacherous mountain passes.

Among the early train passengers was W.A.'s mother, Mary Andrews Clark, age sixty-six, who left Iowa with two of her grown daughters in 1880. W.A.'s father had died five years earlier. They were in the vanguard of a population boom that would push the population of Los Angeles to 50,000 by 1890 and then to 100,000 by the turn of the century.

The Clark business empire was spreading far beyond its roots in Butte. The United Verde mine in Arizona was the biggest moneymaker. W.A. also owned all or part of one of the largest coffee plantations in Mexico; the Colorado Smelter; coal lands in Wyoming; the United States' largest lead mine in Idaho; other mines in Coeur d'Alene, Idaho; thousands of head of cattle; and Shoshone Falls ("the Niagara of the West") on the Snake River in Idaho, where in 1883 he built a ferry and a tourist hotel.

The Clark family was no longer centered in Montana. By 1890, all five of W.A.'s sisters had settled in Los Angeles. His brother Ross soon followed. After W.A. was elected to the U.S. Senate in 1899, then moved to New York, the only remaining Clarks in Montana were his two grown sons, Charlie and Will. Even that connection wouldn't last long, with both sons moving to California by 1907. Although the Clarks still had major mines and other enterprises in Montana, they had become absentee landlords.

W.A. found new investment opportunities wherever he went, and in Los Angeles he went into business again with his brother Ross. Although Joseph died in 1903, Ross was W.A.'s loyal and effective associate for the rest of their lives. W.A. had groomed his brothers in careers that enabled both of them to become very wealthy via their separate enterprises. In the 1890s, they bought land between Los Angeles and its southern neighbor, Long Beach, ten thousand acres they named the Montana Ranch. By 1897, they had planted a thousand acres in sugar beets and had built a state-of-the-art sugar refinery in Rancho Los

W. A. Clark is pictured here in Los Angeles with most of his siblings, as well as other relatives. This was in 1908, a year after he left the U.S. Senate. He had opened the railroad connecting Los Angeles and Salt Lake City in 1905. W.A., age sixty-nine, stands second from the left. His second family, including two-year-old Huguette, is not in the picture. See the appendix on page 437 for a key to people in this photo.

Alamitos. W.A. saw a grander future in Los Angeles than sugar beets. He and Ross entertained the idea of getting into the steamship business.

In 1900, W.A. unveiled an ambitious plan. He acquired several small railroads in the Los Angeles area as the nucleus of a major new rail line connecting San Pedro, which served as the tiny port for Los Angeles, with Salt Lake City, stretching through a thousand miles of desert. W.A. announced that he was putting $25 million into developing the railroad as the last major link in the rail grid that covered the West. At the time, the shortest rail route from Salt Lake City to Los Angeles was by way of San Francisco. Clark's railroad would shorten the trip by four hundred miles. The name of the new line was a mouthful: the San Pedro, Los Angeles & Salt Lake Railroad, often abbreviated as the Salt Lake Route. Informally, it was known as the Clark Road.

This may be the only example in history of an individual financing an entire railroad of significance out of his own pocket. Clark sought to issue bonds through the New York banks, but the response was less than enthusiastic. A railroad to Los Angeles was inevitable, but Los Angeles, still less than one-third the size of San Francisco, was not yet the business center of the West Coast. And there was competition, with the Union Pacific planning its own line to Los Angeles. W.A. replied, "Very well then, gentlemen, I'll build the railroad from my own purse, and I can do it from my income stream alone, without touching my principal."

The Clark Road sparked a bitter railroad war with E. H. Harriman's Union Pacific. The only efficient route was through a narrow gorge in southwest Nevada called Clover Creek Canyon, and there was room for only one set of tracks. While Clark and Harriman were fighting over the issue in the courts, their competing construction crews were battling it out in the dirt. In one skirmish, two hundred Harriman men pushed their way through Clark's forces, "driving their horses back with shovels." In another, Clark's men scattered Harriman's men into retreat with picks. Harriman and Clark tried to buy the loyalty of the opposing workers, raising wages from $1.75 a day all the way up to $2.50.

The two owners soon settled the railroad war by merging their interests, with Harriman in the shadows and Clark out front as president. It took a while for the news to reach their men, however, and even as the two tycoons were shaking hands on the armistice and toasting each other, their men in the mountains were still battling over every inch of ground.

The Clark Road began operation in May 1905, with brass bands and gifts of flowers for the passengers slowing down the first run so much that it arrived in Salt Lake four hours late.

W.A. threw a rolling party, inviting Salt Lake notables, including two apostles of the Mormon Church, for a return trip to Los Angeles. The *Los Angeles Times* headline read, "Saints and Elders Greet Us— Handclasps for Our Salt Lake Friends." The visitors wore red badges with this inscription: "We just arrived on the brand new track. You've a hot old town but we're going back." W.A. was honored at a banquet, with one of the visitors toasting him: "The two cities are wedded, and Senator Clark has provided the ring."

. . .

In the Nevada desert, the Clark Road needed a maintenance point for switching railcars and storing water and fuel. W.A.'s men found a working ranch in the right spot, an abandoned Mormon missionary camp.

W.A. had more land than he needed after the railroad opened, and saw an opportunity for profit. In 1905, he subdivided 110 acres to create a small town of 1,200 lots. People came from Los Angeles on a special Clark train for the auction, held on May 15 in desert heat above 100 degrees. Bidders paid as little as $100 for residential lots and as much as $1,750 for the corner commercial lots on the main street, called Fremont. At the end of the second day, W.A.'s auction company had sold half of his properties, pocketing more than $250,000.

The missionary camp became Los Vegas Rancho (deliberately spelled differently from Las Vegas, New Mexico). Then it was Stewart Ranch. Clark called the new town Clark's Las Vegas Townsite, but everyone else left off the Clark name, calling it Las Vegas, which eventually became the glittering gambling capital of the world. W.A. traveled to Las Vegas in February 1905, riding in the luxury of his new private Pullman car with its two apartments, a dining room for twelve, and an observation room finished in English oak and brass. He told the citizens they

*Owner of the railroad that established the town of Las Vegas in 1905, W. A.
Clark greets the town's citizens from his private railcar that year. His company
auctioned off the lots that became downtown Las Vegas, now in Clark County.*

would soon have a decent town with schools, churches, water, and roads.
In 1909, a new Clark County was carved out with Las Vegas as its seat,
one of the few lasting memorials to the Clark name.

. . .

From the time that his mother and siblings relocated to Los Angeles,
W.A. visited at least once a year, generally staying in his mother's Victorian home on South Olive Street, a few blocks from the current location of the Biltmore hotel and Pershing Square. He continued his visits
after his mother died in 1904 and then threw himself into a philanthropic
project there named for her, a group residence for young working
women called the Mary Andrews Clark Memorial Home.

W.A.'s sister Ella had proposed that they create a memorial to their
mother, in anticipation of the one hundredth anniversary of her birth
coming up in 1914. W.A. said he preferred something practical, rather
than a park or a statue. They agreed on building an affordable place
where young, single women pursuing a career could live in a safe and
wholesome environment. Now into his seventies, W.A. selected the site

on Crown Hill, west of downtown Los Angeles, hiring an architect and taking a hands-on interest in the design and materials, much as he had with his own mansions. The Clarks donated the massive 150-room French château to the Young Women's Christian Association (YWCA), which operated it from 1913 as a dormitory for stenographers, office assistants, saleswomen, dressmakers, nurses, artists. The rules were strict—no men allowed upstairs, no slacks or curlers at dinner.

After dinner at Ella's home when W.A. would visit, the Clark family would tell stories while enjoying their dear departed mother's favorite dessert, *île flottante,* or floating island, a meringue floating on custard.

Ella's son, Paul Clark Newell, Sr., recalled years later those family dinners, and a demonstration of the power held by someone owning a railroad.

Among the more vivid recollections of my boyhood, growing up in Los Angeles in the early part of the century, were the occasional visits to our home of my uncle. During the years that I knew him W.A., as the family called the senator, came out to Los Angeles about once a year, usually in the fall, arriving in his private railcar on his own railroad. He came out from his palatial home on Fifth Avenue in New York, his private railcar linked to other rail lines, by way of Butte, and on to the connection point in Salt Lake City.

I remember his visits to our house most, perhaps, because of his eccentricities. On two occasions upon his departure he headed for the hall closet door, instead of the front door, which was considerably larger. This amused me, and suggests some absent-mindedness, resultant perhaps from his intense concentration of thought.

On occasions when he dined with us, following the saying of grace by my minister father, W.A. would remove from his vest pocket a small flask of whiskey, pour out two tablespoons full, and enjoy a drink. My parents and my aunts were all teetotalists, except for Aunt Elizabeth, who had joined her brothers in Montana in the early days.

On one of these visits, W.A. was relishing warm family reminiscences with his sisters, his brother Ross, and their spouses, when his valet appeared at the living room door, nervously to announce that the train W.A. was boarding for the East that evening had already been held up for an hour for his accommodation. W.A., in only slightly disguised irritation, informed his valet that the train could wait. And wait it did for an hour or longer.

The train happened to be the evening departure of the San Pedro, Los Angeles and Salt Lake Railroad, bound for Salt Lake City, to the rear of which was attached W.A.'s private car, and of which he was builder, president, and principal owner. It seemed obvious that to my uncle, being a railroad president was the ultimate power and glory.

I N JULY 1904, Senator W. A. Clark, one of the richest men in the world, sent a telegram containing an announcement so surprising, so incredible, that his own newspaper got scooped. The editor of *The Butte Miner* delayed publishing the news, fearing that W.A.'s political opponents had planted the preposterous story as a hoax.

W.A.'s telegram explained that he and his ward, Anna LaChapelle, had been secretly married in the Mediterranean port of Marseille. The wedding hadn't happened that week, or even that year, but three years earlier, on May 25, 1901. On that wedding day, W.A. was sixty-two years old, and Anna was twenty-three. That must have been a busy year for W.A., as he was sponsoring the actress Kathlyn Williams and dealing with newspaperwoman Mary McNellis's paternity suit, as well as the publicity over temperance lecturer Hattie Rose Laube's campaign for an engagement.

The wedding wasn't Senator Clark's only secret: The couple had a daughter, Andrée, already nearly two years old. "THEY'RE MARRIED AND HAVE A BABY," thundered a front-page headline in the opposition Montana newspaper, *The Anaconda Standard*.

Louise Amelia Andrée Clark had been born on the southern coast of Spain on August 13, 1902, a date more than a year after the supposed marriage. The announcement was so haphazard that her name was misspelled in the newspapers as Audree.

W.A.'s *Miner* took pains to stress the next day that the situation had been a chaste one, with his ward, Anna, chaperoned in Paris by the senator's sister and nieces as she studied the harp. Over time, however, "he learned that his early affection for this beautiful girl had ripened into love." And Anna was certainly now of legal age, twenty-three at the time of the supposed marriage. Her sixty-two-year-old bridegroom was still vigorous enough that year to defend himself during a street robbery in Paris, slugging one of the thieves in the mouth.

W.A.'s announcement attempted to explain the delay in making the marriage public, pointing to Anna's shy manner:

Mrs. Clark did not care for social distinction, nor the obligations that would entail upon my public life. She was anxious to remain in Europe for a time to continue her studies, and felt she could do this with more freedom. Personally I would have preferred to have her with me at all times, but my extensive interests compelled me to spend a great deal of time travelling through the United States. I did not have the necessary time myself to devote to social obligations and their extensive requirements. . . . Then again, I wanted my child to be educated in America and brought up a resolute and patriotic American.

. . .

The marriage—and the baby—were a surprise to W.A.'s grown children from his first marriage. They suddenly had a new half-sister, not to mention a new stepmother who was younger than they were. His children were, as one headline put it, in for "A Very Rude Shock." Their inheritance was now in peril. Their father was a widower, free to do as he pleased, but this match, to a nobody from Butte, certainly didn't enhance the social standing of the Clark scions.

After sending his announcement from Paris, W.A. visited his daughter Katherine in New York. After talking with her sister, May, she wrote to their brother Will:

A line only, dearest Will, as of course you know by now of father's marriage—and while both May and I are greatly grieved and dreadfully disappointed we must all stand by dear Father, and try and make it as easy for him as possible as already he realizes his mistake—your heart would have ached could you have seen him the night before he left us for St. Louis, and indeed I can't get over the way he looked so badly. Don't let anyone know I have written you—father will tell you himself—and dear, be as good and kind to him as you can be for it is hard for dear father. . . . Poor May is all broken up.

If W.A. indeed realized the wedding was a mistake, there's no indication that he treated Anna rudely. He spent far more time with her than he had with his first wife during their marriage, when he was primarily engaged in the acquisition of wealth and political power. He showered Anna with jewels and presents, and there is no indication that W.A. continued his tomcatting around. Well into his sixties, W.A. finally matured.

The week after the announcement, W.A. wrote to son Will from the 1904 Democratic National Convention in St. Louis, assuring him that his "alliance" with Anna would not dim his affections for his adult children, that Anna did not have designs on his fortune, and that she would receive only a small sum after his death.

In his public statement, W.A. had acknowledged that "it has been stated that my family objected to this union." But he said that any initial apprehension of his children had been overcome and "their approval of these relations were so essential to my happiness."

There was speculation in the family that the birth of Andrée had been followed by a second pregnancy, a boy, Paul, who died within hours of his birth, and that this second event sparked Anna to pressure W.A. to announce a backdated marriage. The birth of a son, if it happened, is undocumented.

Not everyone believed that W.A. and Anna were legally married, certainly not married in May 1901 in Marseille. Clark's political opponents quickly pointed out that his own newspaper in Butte had interviewed him that month about his European travels, which by his account hadn't taken him anywhere near Marseille. The supposed marriage also caused a legal complication. Montana law required a married man to obtain his wife's signature if he signed a deed, and during recent years W.A. had signed several deeds, indicating on each one that he was an unmarried man. Either he was lying on the deeds or he was lying now.

Aside from such political sniping, there was the Clark family Bible, where family marriages and births are listed. W.A.'s 1869 marriage to Kate L. Stauffer is recorded in his handwriting, but no marriage to Anna is mentioned there, though later deaths are listed. Perhaps that's merely a sign of his first family's reluctance to accept the younger second wife. The Bible had been in the home of W.A.'s mother in Los Angeles.

When Anna was required to show proof of their marriage, in a Montana court after W.A.'s death, all she could offer was a postnuptial declaration that the couple signed in 1909 at the American embassy in Paris. In this document, W.A. and Anna swore under oath that "no record of said marriage is known to exist."

With or without a marriage certificate, Anna was now writing letters with her eighteen-carat-gold Cartier fountain pen, opening replies with her fourteen-carat-gold Tiffany letter opener, checking the time on her Cartier gold and diamond watch, applying a bit of dark red with her eighteen-carat-gold and diamond lipstick holder, fixing her hair with her Cartier diamond and rock crystal hairpin, mending clothes with her fourteen-carat-gold safety pins, trimming her nails with her fourteen-carat-gold manicure set, carrying coins in her eighteen-carat-gold-mesh purse with five inset emeralds, and praying with fourteen-carat-gold and jade rosary beads. Her Tiffany toiletry case was engraved AEC, for Anna Eugenia Clark.

CHAPTER FOUR

THE U.S. CAPITOL

SATURDAY AFTERNOONS FROM THREE TO SIX

W HEN SENATOR W. A. CLARK brought his newly revealed young bride to New York from Paris for a visit in 1905, he began a public campaign for acceptance into fashionable society. With an absence of subtlety, W.A. announced in the newspapers his plan to join the Social 400, New York's informal list of old merchant and landowning families, a list guarded by Caroline Astor. The 400 may have been a dying concept by this time, but the Clarks and other nouveau riche newcomers still chafed under Mrs. Astor's impenetrable defenses.

Along with another "westerner" from Pennsylvania, Charles M. Schwab, who gave the world the steel beam and thus the skyscraper, W.A. threatened to set up their own social set if not added to the 400. After all, if the Vanderbilts had been admitted to the list, albeit with some reluctance, why not a couple of newer millionaires?

A spouse with an outgoing personality might have helped W.A.'s social standing. But Anna, uninterested in the celebrity and gossip that their secret marriage had engendered, preferred to stay at home. W.A.'s wealth was enough to gain his admission to the proliferating social clubs of the era: the New York Yacht Club (with J. P. Morgan), the Lotos Club (called "the Ace of Clubs" by member Samuel Clemens), the National Arts Club (with Theodore Roosevelt), and, outside the city, the Sleepy Hollow Country Club (with the Astors and the Vanderbilts). His wife, however, rarely accompanied him, except to the opera and chamber concerts. Now in possession of wealth and power, Anna exhibited no ambition for social glory.

So W.A. brought society to his home. After he settled his young family into the Clark mansion in early 1912, W.A. printed up cards, distributing them whenever he met a friendly face of the right social caste.

This Card Will Admit _____ to the galleries at my residence, 962 Fifth Avenue, on _____, from 3 to 6 o'clock.

Bearing a facsimile of his signature, the cards allowed New Yorkers to visit the Clark home, usually on Saturday afternoons, and to tour his five art galleries. If W.A.'s lineage could not impress the members of the 400, he could demonstrate his good taste through one of the best art collections in America. The art, said his eldest daughter Katherine, was "my father's great joy in life."

Starting in 1878, W.A. was one of the best customers of the art dealers of Europe. At home in Butte, he was derided as "the Paris millionaire," but he was more swayed by the opinion of a French ambassador, who praised Clark's "finest collection of French art in the United States."

The mansion's five art galleries were enormous windowless rooms under large skylights, with dark red woolen baize lining the walls of Istrian limestone. The art filled the walls, in rows stacked two or three high, as was common then in the galleries of Paris and the homes of New York.

W.A.'s collection was an eclectic mix of the best of Europe: Rembrandt's *Man with a Sheet of Music,* *The Judgment of Midas* by Rubens, the ephemeral ballet dancers of Degas, Van Goyen's panoramic Dutch landscapes and seascapes, a sunny field in France by Rousseau, Gainsborough's flattering portraits of the landed gentry, and drawings by Titian, Leonardo, and Raphael.

The main picture gallery, a full ninety-five feet by twenty feet, doubled as a ballroom. Beyond was the small picture gallery, then two more galleries framing the music room, which contained Anna's gilded concert pedal harps and a few of the seven pianos in the house. W.A. fancied more than paintings, with his galleries fringed by easels holding delicate lace from Venice and France. Guests walked on the finest great silk carpets from Persia and India and Turkey, fit for a royal tent or a throne.

After W.A. had all these treasures installed in the house, he added few more, explaining that if he acquired more paintings, he would have to remove something, and he was happy with things as they were.

· · ·

W.A. personally led visitors down the back stairs of the Clark mansion, giving tours of a hidden art gallery close to his heart and his social ambitions. It was a long room alongside the driveway court, a room lined with tapestries and two dozen glass cases. Huguette remembered this room well. A few of the shelves were devoted to antique sculptures from Greece and Egypt. Inside the rest of the cases were, well, dishes.

But such dishes. These earthenware plates and three-dimensional forms—vases, inkwells, figurines—conveyed the refinement, status, and classical education of their owner. Under the names majolica in Italy and Spain, faïence in France and Germany, and delft in the Netherlands, this decorated pottery from the fifteenth and sixteenth centuries passed through the most honored families of Europe.

Though paintings dominate art auctions today, in the Italian Renaissance great value was also placed on tapestries, furniture, fine lace, and these earthenware pots. They were glazed white with tin oxide, then brightly painted with colors from the earth: copper produced green hues; cobalt, blue; manganese, purple; antimony, yellow; and iron, ocher, orange, and red. The artists used brushes made from the whiskers of mice.

Clark's pieces showed a great variety of themes—whimsical, religious, grotesque. Christ as a man of sorrows. The tragic lovers Pyramus and Thisbe. Saint George slaying the dragon. Icarus flying too close to the sun. Saint Catherine of Alexandria appearing as a vision to Joan of Arc. Satyrs and nymphs and drunken Bacchus.

To understand the collection, one needed a grounding in literature, mythology, and music. For a man such as W.A. with a classical, though interrupted, education, leading a tour of his faïence gallery conveyed a clear message. These art pieces had been owned by the Borgias and the Medicis and were now right where they belonged, with the Clarks.

. . .

In the rotunda of the sculpture hall on the main floor, where Huguette and Andrée enjoyed their games, was a small marble statue of Eve that W.A. had bought directly from Rodin, who had created it for his masterwork, *The Gates of Hell*. Rodin's *Eve* is a powerful portrait of shame, her head bent, her eyes open, barely hiding her nakedness.

Dominating the rotunda, however, was a life-size marble sculpture of another female nude, the delicate *Hope Venus*, commissioned by the

English collector Thomas Hope from the eighteenth-century Italian sculptor Antonio Canova, who was renowned for making marble look like human skin. Venus, the Roman goddess of love and beauty, stands as though surprised in her dressing room, inadequately covering herself with her garment, her hand touching her right breast.

The *Hope Venus* found its way into the rotunda because the seller knew enough to raise the price. Most of Clark's contemporaries in the mining world had hardly any education and even less interest in foreign travel and culture. However, those who achieved great wealth felt it incumbent on them to decorate their mansions with expensive art. They bought capriciously, often through order-taking dealers who exploited their naïveté. As a result, many ended up with hodgepodge collections of mediocre, repainted, or counterfeit work. One critic reported that of the eight hundred landscapes executed by the French artist Jean-Baptiste-Camille Corot, American millionaires owned more than eleven hundred.

Clark approached the collection process with considerable advantages. He had, at a minimum, a dilettante's knowledge of fine art. In addition, he found intrinsic value in art for his own enjoyment. He tended to be conservative in his acquisitions, choosing the established work of old masters and the prevailing Barbizon school. And by willingly paying the highest prices, usually buying paintings with a clear provenance, he was less susceptible to buying fakes. He held twenty-three scenes by Corot (most of them legitimate), twenty-two landscapes and scenes of everyday life by Cazin, and a better collection of Monticellis than held by the Musée du Louvre. W.A. did buy those daring but vulgar new Impressionists, but he was a bit late in betting on them. He bought a Pissarro in 1897 and then at the turn of the century two Degas studies of ballet dancers, but he could have snatched up the entire studios of Monet and Van Gogh for pocket change.

W.A. made a splashy entrance into New York society as an art buyer in 1898, paying an extravagant price for a Fortuny painting, *The Choice of a Model*. The subject of this kitschy work is a nude woman posing before an assemblage of male artists. W.A.'s purse strings could be loosened by female pulchritude. He paid $42,000, a record price for a painting, which commanded New York's attention: Who *was* this westerner?

To advise him on his collection, W.A. had been induced to hire Joseph Duveen, a shrewd British purveyor of fine art to American millionaires. To get the commission, Duveen somehow learned details of Clark's house plans and spent $20,000 on a model of the manse—a dollhouse based on the Clark home. This plaster model was accurate down to the carpets, tapestries, and light fixtures—all to be purchased from Duveen.

Duveen's taste was impeccable and his contacts superb, but his ethics questionable. Among the pieces he located was the *Hope Venus,* which was available for $25,000. A Parisian dealer persuaded Duveen that this was not a sufficiently important price to interest Clark, who had spread the word that he wanted the best in the market. Duveen raised the price to $110,000, and Clark bought it.

· · ·

As guests toured the Clark collection on Saturday afternoons, the main attraction was not any particular piece of art, but the music one heard throughout the galleries. The music came from an enormous pipe organ

One of the five art galleries in the Clark mansion was dominated by a wall of pipes belonging to the $120,000 organ, which filled all the galleries with music.

set into the wall above the entrance to a picture gallery. It was the finest organ anyone ever thought of putting in a private home. It was the size of organs at metropolitan churches, with 4,496 pipes encased in a grill-work of oak. Hidden ducts carried the sound to the art galleries, enveloping visitors with music.

The original price of the organ was $50,000, but W.A. demanded the most wonderful chamber organ in the world, driving the cost up to $120,000, or roughly $3 million today. Critics declared its sound "the most perfect ever heard," and on one occasion two hundred members of the Mormon Tabernacle Choir stood in W.A.'s gallery to sing. He and Anna hired their own church organist, and he stayed on staff, well salaried, for the next fourteen years.

W.A.'s QUEST FOR SOCIAL ACCEPTANCE could have overcome the obstacles of a shy wife with no social ambitions, even the lack of a marriage certificate. His campaign was thwarted, however, by the stain from his messy political career.

One political cartoon of the early 1900s showed W. A. Clark firing a cannon in battle—with bags of money used as ammunition at the rate of a thousand dollars a second. Another showed W.A. working in a barn as "the new chore boy," feeding not corn but millions of dollars to a raggedy mule named Democracy. A third depicted W.A. as a stray cat with dollar signs for eyes—a cat that keeps returning to the door of the U.S. Senate.

W.A.'s public profile was summed up, or solidified, by Mark Twain, coiner of the derisive term "the Gilded Age" and the principal American voice of the era. In an essay penned in 1907, Twain excoriated W. A. Clark of Montana. "He is said to have bought legislatures and judges as other men buy food and raiment. By his example he has so excused and so sweetened corruption that in Montana it no longer has an offensive smell."

Twain was just getting started. "His history is known to everybody; he is as rotten a human being as can be found anywhere under the flag; he is a shame to the American nation, and no one has helped to send him to the Senate who did not know that his proper place was the penitentiary, with a chain and ball on his legs."

There was a personal connection between Mark Twain and W. A. Clark, which the author did not disclose.

. . .

W. A. Clark's desire in the last twenty years of the nineteenth century was a title, and his quest made him nearly a permanent political candidate in the first days of the state of Montana, which denied him the honor time after time. He presided over two conventions that wrote constitutions for the new state, supporting the vote for women and immigrants while leading the opposition to taxation of mines. But that wasn't enough for W.A. The title he wanted was senator, and the quest for it left his reputation forever stained.

He had a few handicaps as a candidate. He was not the friendliest campaigner. He was a Protestant in a state with a heavily Irish Catholic workforce that could be motivated by its employers to vote as it was told. And many of those workers were employed by Marcus Daly, W.A.'s main rival in the copper mining business in Montana, who seemed determined to keep W.A. out of office.

Both men were Democrats, and both owned mines, but they had little else in common. Daly, a burly extrovert born in Ireland, never ran for office and lived on a Montana ranch, where in the 1890s he bred some of the fastest racehorses in America. Clark, a reed-thin introvert born in Pennsylvania, spent time in Europe, where he collected works by Rodin and Renoir.

But they did have one other thing in common: They were family. Marcus Daly's wife's sister, Miriam Evans, married W. A. Clark's brother Ross. Huguette said she was fond of her Aunt Miriam. And after both men were dead, their widows lived in the same exclusive apartment building in New York City.

W.A. was nominated to be the Montana Territory's delegate to Congress in 1888 but was defeated when Daly, though a Democrat, told his miners to support the Republican candidate. Clark's campaign was afflicted with what today would be called gaffes: criticizing an Irish newspaperman as a traitor, putting on a huge feast for Daly's mostly Catholic miners on a Friday but serving them steak instead of fish. He lost handily.

"The conspiracy was a gigantic one," W.A. wrote to an ally, "well planned, and well carried out, even though it did involve the violation of some of the most sacred confidences. . . . The day of retribution may come when treason may be considered odious. . . . For the time being, I retire politically."

Two years later, in 1890, he was elected to be the first U.S. senator from Montana—or so it seemed. As the Founding Fathers prescribed, senators were chosen not by the people but by their elected state legislators. Unfortunately for W.A., he was not elected by Montana's only legislature. Democrats and Republicans both claimed the majority that year and caucused in separate halls, electing two different men to fill the open Senate seat. In Washington, the Senate seated the Republican, and W.A. was still without his title.

. . .

The first political battle W.A. won was not for office. Montana had become a U.S. territory on May 26, 1864, and the forty-first state on November 8, 1889. The question was where to put its capital. In 1894, Clark's political forces won a raucous battle over Daly's supporters when Helena, rather than the Daly-backed Anaconda, was selected as the capital. That night, the Clark partisans celebrated by taking on the role of horses, pulling W.A. in his carriage through the streets of Helena. W.A. repaid the honor by buying drinks for the whole town.

In Montana in the 1890s, as in the United States in the 2010s, the laws were loose enough to allow men of means to spend unlimited sums of money, either personally or through their companies, to put candidates into office. Bribery was forbidden, but virtually any "campaign expense" was allowed.

According to W.A., although he may have put $250,000 into the capital fight, his opponent Daly had spent $1 million. And although Daly never held public office, he wielded enormous power in Montana through his Anaconda Copper Mining Company. Clark claimed that he saw men in a voting line getting paid $5 apiece for their votes, and in some Anaconda precincts twice as many people voted as were registered.

The Montana legislature attempted to rein in both men. After the fight over the capital, an anti-bribery law forbade any candidate to spend more than $1,000 on his own campaign or anyone to give more than $1,000 to a political committee in any county. The law was little regarded and poorly enforced.

In public, W.A. spoke often about integrity. He attributed his career in business to it. "The most essential elements of success in life are a purpose, increasing industry, temperate habits, scrupulous regard for one's word . . . courteous manners, a generous regard for the rights of others, and, above all, integrity which admits of no qualification or variation."

Another quotation often ascribed to him is more direct: "I never bought a man who wasn't for sale." Although there seems to be no proof in the record that W.A. ever said anything of the sort, the comment is attributed to him in dozens of books.

Clark was determined to try again for the Senate, with or without the backing of Daly or the state Democratic committee. In the summer of 1898, his twenty-seven-year-old son, Charlie, a Yale graduate, helped organize his campaign committee. W.A. later admitted giving Charlie and others nearly $140,000 (about $4 million today) to run the campaign, without making any report of how it was spent.

W.A. said that the money was used only for "legitimate" expenses, such as paying hotel bills for about three hundred friends and political operatives, paying men to accompany legislators so the Daly faction could not get to them, and compensating newspapers for their endorsements. Indeed, it was not unusual at the time for a candidate to buy a newspaper before an election, use the paper's editorials to endorse himself, and then sell the newspaper back to the previous owner after the election was over.

W.A. cast the 1898 Senate election as having one goal, "overthrowing the power of one man in the state of Montana: Mr. Daly." If there was any evil in buying an election, he seemed to be saying, it was necessary in order to do good. He said that he did not seek the office but was persuaded to do so to end "this state of despotism."

"Nobody could expect to have any recognition whatever," W.A. later said, "unless he bowed the knee and crawled in the dust to these people. It was impossible to break their power in that state unless large sums of money were used, legitimately, to do it."

For his part, Daly was said to have threatened "to run W. A. Clark and his family out of the state of Montana." He denied making the statement, testifying, "I have not the slightest personal feelings against Mr. Clark or any member of his family, and it is a villainous lie."

The stage was set for a three-ring circus of a legislative session, one that would send W. A. Clark to Washington.

. . .

Violence broke out before the legislative session even began. During the election of the state legislators themselves in November 1898, two armed men burst into Butte's Precinct 8, an Irish stronghold known as Dublin Gulch, in an attempt to steal either the ballot box or cash. One election judge was shot and killed. The Daly forces blamed Clark, calling him "the arch-boodler of the century." Clark's forces claimed that the robbery had been staged to discredit W.A.

On January 9, 1899, the day before voting for the new U.S. senator began, a state senator named Fred Whiteside dropped a bombshell. On the floor of the state senate, he presented thirty crisp thousand-dollar bills that he claimed had been directed by Clark's forces to be delivered to legislators. Whiteside, who had been a whistle-blower in a previous corruption case, said he had launched his own sting operation, putting out the word that he could be bribed. "My object was to break up the band of boodlers that have so long infested this state."

Whiteside described how the payoffs worked. One of Clark's attorneys would show a legislator ten one-thousand-dollar bills, seal them inside an envelope, and then have the man write his initials on the outside. The attorney would keep the envelope and deliver it to the legislator only if he voted for Clark throughout the session, whether or not Clark won. It was bribery and blackmail rolled into one act.

Whiteside said that he did not think Clark knew all the details but that W.A. did know in a general way what his men were doing. "There seems to be no end to the supply of money," Whiteside testified. "I think they expected to use nearly $1 million, and, as near as I can judge, have already paid out about $200,000. . . . They ran short of money several times, because large-sized bills were hard to get."

He went on, quoting Clark's campaign manager, John B. Wellcome. "Every man who votes for Clark is to be paid. And the man who votes for him without being well paid is a fool."

Clark's newspaper, *The Butte Miner,* responded that it was all a Daly trick.

A DAMNABLE CONSPIRACY—DALY CROWD SPRING
THEIR PROMISED SENSATION—BUNGLING WORK
AT THE OUTSET

ABORTIVE ATTEMPT TO STAMPEDE MEMBERS OF THE
LEGISLATURE BY THE EXHIBITION OF MONEY AND CHARGES
OF BRIBERY—WHOLE THING BEARS EVIDENCE OF HAVING
BEEN COOKED UP BY THE ARCH-CONSPIRATORS

And that was just part of the headline.

A grand jury began investigating even while the legislators started voting for senator on January 10, 1899. Clark was in fourth place on the first ballot, receiving only seven votes to thirty-six for the leading Republican. No candidate had a majority, so the voting continued. Nearly every day for three weeks, there was a new ballot. W.A. crept into third place, then second. By January 23, he was in the lead. On January 26, the grand jury failed to indict anyone.

In a precursor to the alternative realities displayed a century later by competing cable news outlets, Clark's *Butte Miner* hailed the grand jury's decision:

HIS VINDICATION IS COMPLETE....
CONSPIRATORS FOILED

Daly's *Anaconda Standard* lamented:

THEY SIMPLY FELL DOWN FLAT

The day after the grand jury failed to issue an indictment, Republicans began crossing party lines, tilting toward the Democrat Clark. Not all were persuaded by money; some went over to W.A. because he had declared himself to be a protectionist, favoring tariffs to aid Montana products such as wool, lead, and hides.

On January 28, Clark won on the eighteenth ballot, by a vote of

A QUIET DINNER

To celebrate his election to the U.S. Senate, W.A. gave a banquet for a couple of hundred friends and supporters, held at the Helena Hotel on Tuesday evening, February 7, 1899. A copy of the menu, printed in French, survives. It is presented here with an English translation in parentheses. Alcoholic beverages were listed in capital letters.

Caviar à la Russe (caviar with egg, cream, and vodka)
Huîtres à l'écaille (oysters on the half shell)
Céleri (celery)
HAUT SAUTERNE (French sweet white wine from Bordeaux)
Green Turtle (soup)
XERES AMONTILLADO (Amontillado sherry)
Cheese Straws
Radis (radish)
Pompano Planche (planked fish)
Pommes Parisiennes (Parisian potatoes)
Ris de Veau en Caisse (veal sweetbreads dressed in paper)
PONTET-CANET (French red wine from Bordeaux)
Côtelettes d'Agneau (lamb chops)
Petit Pois Français (French peas)
PUNCH A LA ROMAINE (lemon, orange rind, egg white meringue, wine, and rum punch)
Cailles Farcies aux Truffes (quail stuffed with truffles)
Salade Laitue (salad with lettuce)
DRY MONOPOLE–EXTRA (champagne)
Asperges à la Vinaigrette (asparagus in vinaigrette)
Biscuit Glacé (a dessert with cream or ice cream, fruit)
Fromage–Dessert (cheese–sweets)
Café–LIQUEURS (coffee–liqueurs)

54 to 39. The young state had elected its fifth U.S. senator and its first Democrat. At long last, W.A. would be Senator Clark.

Clark's *Miner* rejoiced:

VOICE OF THE PEOPLE HEARD.

Daly's *Standard* summed up:

THEY TOOK THE ARCH-BOODLER'S GOLD.

Handbills were distributed:

THERE WILL BE A HOT TIME. GRAND
CELEBRATION TO-NIGHT TO ENDORSE THE
ELECTION OF HON. W. A. CLARK TO THE UNITED
STATES SENATE. PROCESSION. FIREWORKS.
MEETING AT THE AUDITORIUM. EVERYBODY
WELCOME.

W.A. again bought drinks for the town. His son Charlie spent half the next day signing checks to the bars.

A S SOON AS W.A. TOOK HIS SEAT in the U.S. Senate in 1899, a delegation of citizens from Montana petitioned to throw the rascal out, to have his election invalidated on account of bribery. After a delay of nearly a year, the Senate Committee on Privileges and Elections held a trial lasting from January to April 1900.

Witnesses were caught in lies. Others were paid to testify. A few were paid by one side, then changed their testimony when paid more by the other. And who put up unlimited sums to pay for the detectives to produce evidence, the attorneys to prosecute the case, and the newspapers to editorialize about it? Marcus Daly, who testified he had no interest in politics.

The evidence that hurt W.A. the most was the changed economic circumstances of the Montana legislators who voted for him.

W. W. Beasley, a Republican who started voting for Clark on the eighteenth ballot, ended the session with $5,000 in his pocket, including at least one thousand-dollar bill, which he claimed to have taken to Helena and kept in his vest pocket the entire session, even as he owed his boardinghouse $400.

H. H. Garr, who began the legislative session with $75 and had to borrow $25 for the trip to Helena, ended it with enough money to buy a ranch for $3,500, in the name of his wife's aunt. He testified that he didn't know what it meant when he wrote his initials on the back of one of those fat envelopes.

John H. Geiger, who had no regular job, carried home $2,600 from the legislative session, including $1,100 he said he found in his room and $1,500 he said he won by gambling at faro, a popular card game (and one often rigged in favor of the house).

H. W. McLaughlin sold his woodlots and sawmills to W.A., who set him up with a job.

D. G. Warner's ranch and building lots were sold to an employee of Charlie Clark for $7,500.

E. C. Day, leader of the Clark forces in the state house, received personally from W.A. $5,000 after the vote "as a testimonial of friendship."

And for S. S. Hobson, the chairman of the Republican caucus, who owed $22,000 to the Fergus County Bank, W.A. bought the whole bank and cleared his debt.

The total paid out was estimated at $431,000, but there was no way to know the exact figure.

. . .

When it came his turn to testify, W.A. said that he had not campaigned for the Senate at all, that he had never sought the office, that he had left any electioneering to his son and others, that he couldn't recall what instructions he might have given in letters because he dictated as many as one hundred letters a day and required the use of two or three stenographers, that he had no knowledge of any money being paid to anyone, and that when the subject of money was raised by anyone fishing for a payout, he would say firmly, "I don't expect to secure any votes for a financial consideration." He said that Charlie had the authority to write checks on his account. "I never asked a question of any of them where they spent a dollar. . . . Of course I did not authorize or expect that they would spend any money unlawfully."

As for the canceled checks themselves, they were drawn on the bank W. A. Clark & Brother and were nowhere to be found. "About every six months," W.A. explained, "I destroy all my checks."

The best case that W.A.'s lawyers could make was that he had not been directly tied to any bribery. "A man does not forfeit his seat because he obtained it under suspicious circumstances." The case against him was based on "hearsay evidence, rumors, the gossip of the street corners and barrooms." No one had been convicted, or even accused, of a crime. The Daly banks were the ones that had run short of thousand-dollar bills. In sum, the attorneys claimed that the case against Clark assumed a scheme of political corruption more degraded than the world had seen, committed in the open, clumsily, in front of witnesses.

Yet, in private, W.A. conceded to a friend that "it cannot be overlooked that money has been used improperly."

Indeed, the Senate committee vote against him was unanimous. Even if W.A. didn't make any payoffs himself, the senators found that "the friends of Senator Clark illegally and improperly used large amounts of money." The Senate committee found on April 23, 1900, that "the election to the Senate of William A. Clark, of Montana, is null and void on account of briberies, attempted briberies, and corrupt practices by his agents." This was not the final verdict. The full Senate would have to ratify the committee's recommendation, but that seemed inevitable.

The gossipy *New-York Tribune* described W.A.'s reaction: "His face was somewhat flushed, but his voice was calm and his manner collected."

A SERIES OF SURPRISES

I N MONTANA, Governor Robert B. Smith, a lawyer by training, didn't suspect a thing. He was offered a side job, an easy $2,000 for a bit of freelance work examining the title to a valuable mining claim. All he had to do was take the train from Helena to San Francisco, a trip that happened to keep him out of Montana for several days. Thus began a most daring political scheme.

In Washington, before the full Senate could ratify the committee's decision to throw him out, W. A. Clark gave a tearful speech to the Senate on May 15, 1900, condemning "the most devilish persecution that any man has ever been subjected to in the history of any civilized country." He said the men who had paid off their debts during the legislative session must have come by it honestly. He likened his situation to the renowned case of Alfred Dreyfus, the French artillery officer who had been presumed guilty of treason, convicted based on false evidence, and imprisoned before finally being exonerated.

He closed with a flourish: "I was never in all my life, except by such characters as are now pursuing me, charged with a dishonorable act, and I propose to leave to my children a legacy, worth more than gold, that of an unblemished name."

And then, after weeks of saying he would never quit, he surprised the Senate by revealing that he had written a resignation letter.

Here's how the entire scheme unfolded.

1. W.A. addressed his resignation letter to "His Excellency, the Governor of Montana." No name, only a title.
2. The governor, Robert B. Smith, was not a friend to Clark.
3. The lieutenant governor, one A. E. Spriggs, was friendlier, a manager of W.A.'s Ruby mine.
4. The newspapers spread the word that Lieutenant Governor Spriggs was out of the state, in South Dakota, at a weeklong convention of his Populist Party.

5. Clark's men arranged the publication in the Montana papers of a firm statement that he would never resign.

6. Trusting too much in all this, Governor Smith was induced by a Clark associate to travel by train to San Francisco to examine the mining claim.

7. Immediately after the governor left the state, W.A. made his resignation speech, and his son Charlie sent a telegram to Lieutenant Governor Spriggs in South Dakota with the agreed-upon signal that it was time to return to Montana: "Weather fine, cattle doing well."

8. Spriggs rushed back to Helena. Charlie filled in the date on his father's resignation letter, then handed it to the lieutenant governor, who filled in the name on an order appointing Clark's successor in the Senate.

9. That successor? W. A. Clark. Forced to resign on a charge of corruption, he was now appointed to fill his own vacancy.

10. The lieutenant governor wired a confirmation to W.A., adding, "I trust you will accept the appointment." He did.

The headlines in the *New York Herald* captured the plot: "Clark Resigns; Then Appointed. Daly Caught Napping. All a Series of Surprises."

After the scheme was found out, W.A.'s supporters said that he had no idea of the shenanigans done on his behalf, that reckless son Charlie must have been responsible. It aided their narrative that Charlie drank and gambled and womanized too much, and failed to repay loans. (Several years later, in 1908, W.A. wrote with optimism to a friend, "Chas is with me and is in fine shape and has not drunk anything spirituous. . . . I am happy over it and I do hope it will last always.") Charlie is usually credited with making the comment during the campaign, "We'll put the old man in the Senate or in the poorhouse."

The idea that Charlie was to blame was bolstered when he was implicated in 1902 in another scandal in which he was accused of offering $250,000 to a judge to fix a case. Before he could be served with a warrant, he left Butte for San Francisco, leaving behind his lovely French château not far from his father's mansion. For many years thereafter, Charlie dared not enter the state of Montana.

W.A.'s correspondence, however, shows that he was intimately involved in this cynical scheme to lure the governor out of the state, as he was intimately involved in all his business. On April 28, 1900, before he resigned, he wrote to a fervent supporter, John S. M. Neill, editor of the friendly *Helena Independent*. Responding to Neill's description of the plans, W.A. objected at that point, not on moral grounds but on practical ones: "I have canvassed the proposition referred to in your letter. The plan of getting a certain party out of the State while action might be taken by another is not feasible."

After the plan was indeed executed and W.A. was appointed to succeed himself, he wrote again to Neill, this time approvingly, with his usual confidence that he was in the right: "The appointment by the Governor improves the situation and has thrown consternation into the ranks of the enemy. So far as we have been able to discover there is no legal reason why the Senate should not immediately order the oath of office administered upon the presentation of the credentials made in accordance with the appointment of Governor Spriggs."

Cleverness was not enough. Governor Smith heard the news in San Francisco, was back in Helena in three days, and sent notice to the Senate to disregard this "contemptible trickery." The seat stayed vacant, leaving the people of Montana missing a voice in the Senate for the next fourteen months.

"This man, Clark, has been convicted by the United States Senate of perjury, bribery, and fraud," Governor Smith told the newspapers, somewhat overstating the case, "and it is an insult to the Senate to send him back to that body. It is a disgrace, a shame and humiliation upon the people of Montana, and the Senate should adopt the resolution and show him that they do not want him there, as it seems he can take the hint in no other way."

. . .

The comical events made Montana a laughing-stock, and had long-lasting effects on W.A. and on the nation.

For the United States, the Montana episode strengthened the voices calling for an end to the Founding Fathers' design for state legislators to choose U.S. senators. The Clark case was an important event in the long march toward the Seventeenth Amendment, ratified by the states in 1913. This amendment gave the people the power to elect senators.

For W. A. Clark, the election scheme left a blot on his reputation. His supporters, then and now, argue that frontier politics were notoriously corrupt. Clark's partisans echoed his claim that he had to put up his own money to get elected, fighting fire with fire, to stop Daly money from controlling the state.

The voice of history, however, was summed up, or influenced, by Mark Twain's evisceration of W. A. Clark as a shame to the American nation. W.A. could have been the greatest Horatio Alger character, the boy who made good by hard work, education, and luck, but his was a legacy squandered in pursuit of political power and baronial extravagance. "Life was good to William A. Clark," wrote Montana historian Michael Malone, "but due to his own excesses, history has been unkind."

It mattered not a bit that Twain himself may have been carrying water for W.A.'s opponents in business, and corrupt opponents at that. Twain cast his 1907 essay as though he'd happened upon an evening with Clark, suffering through the senator's long, self-adoring pronouncements over dinner at the Union League Club in New York. Twain decried "the assfulness and complacency of this coarse and vulgar and incomparably ignorant peasant's glorification of himself." Despite his excesses, W.A. was no ignorant peasant. What Twain also failed to mention was that one of Clark's main opponents in the Montana copper business, the Standard Oil man Henry Huttleston Rogers, had rescued a failed businessman named Samuel Clemens from bankruptcy. Clemens called Rogers "my closest and most valuable friend." The muckraker Ida Tarbell called the ruthless Rogers "as fine a pirate as ever flew his flag in Wall Street." Rogers was CEO of Rockefeller's Standard Oil, the company's main financial strategist and the leader of its attempts to corner the worldwide market in copper.

In one of the great stock swindles of the age, Rogers, Rockefeller, and their Standard Oil cronies moved into Montana copper in 1899, setting up the Amalgamated Copper Company, absorbing Daly's Anaconda Copper. They were hoping to buy Clark's Montana copper interests, too, if the price was low enough, a goal they achieved in 1910. Rogers made his best friend, Samuel Clemens, one of the first people to get in on the stock.

"For a week now, the Vienna papers have been excited over the great Copper combine," Clemens wrote to Rogers on May 10, 1899, urging his patron to invest the money the writer had banked with him. "I feel perfectly sure that you are arranging to put that $52,000 under that hen as soon as the allotment of stock begins, and I am very glad of that." Clemens urged, "Put it in! You don't want all that money stacked up in your daily view; it is only a temptation to you. Am I going to be in the Board?"

The public shareholders of Amalgamated Copper put up most of the money for the company and were fleeced by stock manipulations. The Standard Oil men and their bank, National City Bank of New York, took the profits. The man who hatched the plan, financier Thomas W. Lawson, lamented that Amalgamated was "responsible for more hell than any other trust or financial thing since the world began." The inside shareholders, including Samuel Clemens, profited handsomely. "You know how to make a copper hen lay a golden egg," Clemens wrote to Rogers in delight.

The scathing essay by Clemens's alter ego, the writer Mark Twain, wasn't published until long after both men were gone. Twain may have written it only for his own pleasure. He may have been truthfully appalled by W.A., or jealous of his wealth. It's also possible that he wrote it to impress his benefactor Rogers. The wallet of Samuel Clemens may have been doing the talking for Mark Twain.

The Amalgamated deal was one of the leading examples cited by supporters of a new wave of antitrust efforts in Washington. The twist is that this deal was just the sort of scheme by which the robber barons earned their name, and the sort that W. A. Clark abhorred.

Although Clark was a wealthy industrialist during the Gilded Age, that didn't make him a robber baron. W.A. was a tough competitor in business, but he generally played by the rules of his age. He didn't want any stockholders, who would be entitled to information. None of W. A. Clark's enterprises profited from trusts or monopolies or stock manipulation, as did Rockefeller, Carnegie, Harriman, Rogers—and Mark Twain.

W.A. supported fair wages, even opposing wage reductions when copper prices fell, and as a result he didn't suffer from strikes. He also offered model healthcare for workers, and when Daly opposed a law requiring safety cages in the mines, Clark supported it—even if only for political advantage. He also supported voting rights for women. "I am in favor of giving to women everything that they want," he said, "upon the principle that I have the utmost confidence in their intelligence." Although he was accused of cutting timber on public land and fought to keep taxes paid by mines to nearly zero, he mostly paid his own way.

To the public, however, Twain's motivation for attacking W.A. was beside the point. Clark's too-clever trickery in politics made it irrelevant whether or not he had been abused by an unjust prosecution. He would remain in the American memory, to the extent he was remembered at all, as a copper king tarnished by political shenanigans.

W.A. could have found the explanation for this perception in his own library, in the words of Victor Hugo: "True or false, that which is said of men often occupies as important a place in their lives, and above all in their destinies, as that which they do."

M OST MEN would have slunk off in shame after the Senate scandal, but eight months after his humiliation, W. A. Clark was elected to the U.S. Senate by the Montana legislature, perhaps honestly.

His election in January 1901 was aided by the decline of Marcus Daly, who died in November 1900 in New York City at age fifty-eight. It was also helped by W.A.'s timely support for reducing the workday of miners to eight hours instead of ten. His campaign button said simply, "W. A. Clark, U.S. Senator, 8 Hours."

Senator Clark served quietly from March 1901 to March 1907, having the misfortune of being in the wrong party, a Democrat in a heavily Republican Congress, and in the wrong time, a Progressive Era dominated by Republican presidents. The Republicans soon had an energetic young man in the White House, Theodore Roosevelt, after William McKinley was assassinated in September 1901. W.A. campaigned for a Nicaraguan alternative to Roosevelt's Panama Canal plan in 1904, hoping that route could be achieved more quickly. (Better shipping routes would help W.A.'s business interests in the West.) He supported Roosevelt's Pure Food and Drug Act of 1906 but criticized Roosevelt for his obsession with hunting, or killing animals for sport. His six years in the Senate are best remembered, however, for his opposition to Roosevelt's conservationist campaign for national parks and forests.

Clark left Washington after only a single term, having secured for life his coveted title of "Senator Clark." In a farewell address to the Senate in 1907, he explained his view of the responsibilities of one generation to another in regard to the earth's resources: "In rearing the great structure of empire on the Western Hemisphere we are obliged to avail ourselves of all the resources at our command. The requirements of this great utilitarian age demand it. Those who succeed us can well take care of themselves."

Back in New York full-time after leaving the Senate, W.A. announced that he was abandoning his plans to enter the Social 400. "My house in New York is now open, and we entertain our friends almost daily," he told reporters in 1912. "But we seek our friends among people of artistic inclinations and from them we receive the pleasure which others may find in other forms of society, but which I do not consider worth my while."

W.A. and Anna appeared frequently in the social notes through the 1910s and early 1920s. In the home where Huguette and Andrée grew up, they played host to dinners and parties to raise money for the families of French soldier-artists, for the Institute for Crippled and Disabled Men, the School Art League, the Unique Book and Handcraft Salon. All these events were held at the Clark mansion. As W.A. had threatened, the Clarks had set up their own social set, one mostly confined to their own home and directed at the arts and generosity.

Because he opened his home so often to share its art and music, W.A. told the reporters, "I am not likely to be lonely."

CHAPTER FIVE

THE CLARK MANSION

. . .

PART TWO

THE CLARK GIRLS were frequent transatlantic travelers, accustomed to the luxurious staterooms of the Cunard and White Star luxury liners. In 1911, newspapers across America carried a photo of Andrée, nearly nine years old, arm in arm with her niece of the same age, Katherine Morris, who was holding hands with Huguette, nearly five. They were standing on the deck of the RMS *Adriatic*, crossing the Atlantic to attend the coronation of George V, king of the United Kingdom, grandson of Queen Victoria and grandfather of Queen Elizabeth II.

The next summer, their crossing for a vacation was delayed. In April 1912, before a trip to France, W.A. showed the girls a brochure with the floor plan of their first-class staterooms on a new White Star liner. The Clarks were booked for passage from New York to Ireland to Cherbourg. This crossing would be a treat, the second voyage of the largest ship afloat: the RMS *Titanic*.

Instead, W.A. ended up meeting survivors of the *Titanic* in New York, and the family delayed their trip while they mourned a loss. Huguette's first cousin Walter Miller Clark, the son of W.A.'s brother Ross, had gone down with the *Titanic*. Walter had been playing cards in the smoking room when the great ship scraped an iceberg. His wife, Virginia, was saved, bobbing in lifeboat No. 4 with the pregnant Madeleine Astor, watching the ship sink with their husbands among the 1,502 people lost in the icy North Atlantic.

The *Titanic* launched another scandal for the Clarks, as Walter's widow remarried five months after the sinking. She and Walter had an infant son, who was at home in Los Angeles when the *Titanic* sank. For months, the newspapers were filled with the resulting custody battle between the boy's mother and his paternal grandparents over the "Millionaire Baby." The parties eventually settled on joint custody.

During the family's annual summer vacation to France, W.A. and Anna took Andrée and Huguette to their Paris apartment on avenue Victor Hugo, then out by rail to a luxurious seaside resort called Trou-

IN CONVERSATION WITH HUGUETTE

"We didn't get on the *Titanic*," Huguette explained matter-of-factly. "We were booked to go. But then actually it never got to New York, because it sank before it got in. So we took another boat out. I think it was the *George Washington*."

Huguette remarked on how sad she was at her cousin Walter's death on the *Titanic*. Although she commented on Walter's drinking problem and how his wife remarried so quickly after his death, her memories focused more on the reason for her family's planned trip to France. Andrée was especially interested in attending a commemoration of the five hundredth year since Joan of Arc's birth. "She wanted to be there for the Joan of Arc birthday."

ville, near Deauville in Normandy. W.A.'s first family had summered in Trouville as far back as 1880, and this was a regular summer spot for his second family as well.

The family rented a villa at the end of the beach, at 11B, rue des Roches Noires, facing the giant black rocks captured on canvas by Courbet and Boudin, whose paintings inspired the young Monet. While W.A. went on to business meetings in England and Vienna, Anna and the girls stayed in Trouville. Anna played her harp two or three hours a day, while Andrée and Huguette hunted among the black rocks for small crabs and shrimp, attended by their governess and tutor, Madame Sandré, who taught them how to swim. The tides at Trouville were gentle, making the area safe for swimming, though the water was cold even in August. The family also had the use of a yacht in the harbor.

That summer was a high-water mark for the Clarks, and for France, with the entire family together and the nation enjoying the peace and prosperity of the Belle Epoque. Yet relations between France and Germany, already strained, were pushed into the headlines when the German gunboat *Panther* sailed into the French Moroccan port of Agadir. This provocation led to the expansion of British promises to protect France in case of a German attack. In a letter from Paris to his business manager in Montana, Clark observed that the "Socialists in Germany have become so strong that the Emperor might think that war is the only way to save his throne."

The Clarks had left anxiety behind at home as well. On March 22, 1914, when Huguette was eight, a parade of a thousand anarchists and union activists marched up Fifth Avenue from Madison Square to 107th Street, with orator Emma Goldman at the head of the parade, urging the poor to take what they need from the rich. With a banner vowing "demolitione," the passing parade cursed the Clark mansion, where frightened servants gathered at the windows. The parade ended with the singing of "The Worker's Marseillaise," the revolutionary French national anthem ("The rich, the exploiters . . .").

Huguette often described the summers of 1911–14 in France as the idyllic days of her childhood. The family rented a castle called the château de Petit-Bourg, in the hamlet of that name, sixteen miles south of the center of Paris, known today as Evry-sur-Seine. Those were care-free days. Well-thumbed photos in Huguette's album show her father decked out in casual white pants and a straw hat, standing in a wheat field; Anna, smiling, in a white summer dress on a park bench; Andrée striding in front of the castle with a broad grin; and little Huguette, at about age seven, sitting proudly on a horse with a white diamond-shaped mark on its nose.

The girls rode bicycles and explored the castle's secret tunnels, which led down to the banks of the Seine. They were not alone on their adventures, always chaperoned by Madame Sandré, as the fear of kidnapping and other dangers was ever present. Their mother forced them inside every day for music lessons—the piano for both girls, as well as the harp for Andrée (like her mother) and the violin for Huguette. For good behavior, they received gold coins from their father as an allowance. Eighty years later, Huguette told the following story to her nurses.

In late August 1914, with the German army sweeping through Belgium and approaching Paris from the east, word came from the ambassador that all American citizens must leave France. W.A. prepared to remove his family, but how to pay for the trip? The banks were closed, and he didn't have enough cash to hire a car and driver. The mine owner and banker was worth well over $50 million. Yet at that moment, he was a little light in the wallet, even as the German First Army approached the outskirts of Paris, within fifty miles of Petit-Bourg.

Andrée and Huguette came up with a clever solution: They handed over their gold coins, which W.A. used to hire a car to the coast. From there they found passage to England, departing on September 4. Two days later, the French and British engaged the Germans in the First Battle of the Marne, preventing the occupation of Paris and beginning four years of trench warfare. Safe in England as the great powers went into battle, W.A., Anna, Andrée, and Huguette enjoyed the mineral waters of the posh Royal Leamington Spa. W.A. had no fear of being drafted into service when America entered the Great War three years later, in 1917. His war, the one he was of age to serve in, had been the American Civil War.

. . .

During the war years of 1914–18, the girls escaped New York's summer heat by taking vacations in the West, seeing the geysers at Yellowstone and staying at the family's lakefront hideaway in Montana. Photos show them swimming and enjoying time with their half-brother Will and his retinue. Whatever strains his marriage to Anna may have caused, W.A.'s first and second families were vacationing together. The retreat, called Mowitza Lodge, after an American Indian word meaning "running deer," was situated on Salmon Lake, northwest of Helena, a tranquil spot for swimming, hiking, and bird-watching among ponderosa pine, western larch, and Douglas fir. In the 1910s, the favorite game at the lodge was Ping-Pong, a British import that had taken Montana by storm.

In September 1916, the girls signed Will's guest book, first fourteen-year-old Andrée with a bold signature, listing her address nostalgically as Paris, France. Andrée said later that although her parents had been born in America, she was still a French girl. Ten-year-old Huguette followed, signing below her sister's name in a distinctive, metronomic hand, each letter precisely the same height, and ending with a ditto, indicating her home as Paris, too. Both girls still spoke with a slight French accent.

Photos from one of these trips show the sisters, always together, in bathing caps and knee-length swimming dresses on a pier, in matching hiking dresses, and with matching Kodak Brownie box cameras in the woods, and posing in fancy dresses and high-laced shoes. In two of the photos, Andrée is looking directly at the photographer, while Huguette is examining her own camera or looking shyly at the ground.

A highlight of these annual trips to Montana was a return to Butte. They rode W.A.'s streetcar east to Columbia Gardens, W.A.'s gift to the people of Butte in 1899. The brightest spot in a depressing town, the amusement park featured a dance pavilion, lake, and picnic area. With obvious pride, W.A. showed the girls his flower gardens. Wearing a black bow tie and a bowler hat, he had his picture taken with the girls, who stood in embroidered dresses, white gloves, and matching broad-brimmed hats.

More than eighty years later, Huguette recalled putting on a hard hat and taking a ride down into one of her father's mines in a four-man steel cage. At the height of copper production, around 1917, the Butte-Anaconda area had fourteen thousand men working underground, an amalgamation of Irish, Italians, Chinese, Serbians—the story was that immigrants looking for work were told, "Don't stop in America, go straight to Butte."

In hard-rock mining, the men had the most dangerous occupation in America. Deep in Clark's Belmont mine, workers wore long underwear and bib overalls to protect themselves from the 135-degree heat. Men rigging sticks of powder dynamite were warned to "tap 'er light," but it wasn't unusual for a finger to be found still sporting a wedding ring. Diggers were crushed by falling timbers. Motormen and swampers were suffocated when trapped by underground fires. Rail benders stood in acidic water so strong it would eat anything metal. Because drilling produced black dust, the drills were called widow makers. "We were," as one old miner named Tom Holter put it, "damn close to hell."

In August 1917, the same summer that the Clark girls took a sojourn in Butte, a union organizer named Frank Little was working for the Wobblies, the Industrial Workers of the World, speaking out against U.S. entry into World War I. Relations between the union workers and the mine owners were complicated. In 1892, men at W.A.'s Original mine gave him a walking stick with an engraved silver top as a sign of

IN CONVERSATION WITH HUGUETTE

On June 28, 1998, Huguette and I spoke of my recent tour of Butte and her memories of the town. She said that she had not been to Butte for years, explaining that it was "too sad for me, with memories of my father." She sent me a photo of herself, at about age four, on the porch of her father's mansion there. She is sitting on the railing, wearing an enormous white hat, and is surrounded by a dozen of her dolls.

She told me she understands that Butte is not a healthful place to live.

their affection. Yet the mine yards were surrounded by ten-foot electrified fences in case of union trouble.

Early on the morning of August 1, 1917, Frank Little was found hanged from a railroad trestle in Butte. On his chest was a note with the words "First and last warning" and the numbers 3-7-77, an obscure code used by the Montana Vigilantes. With copper prices and demand at record levels, the war was going to make a lot of money for Butte, its workers, and its mine owners.

. . .

The following year, the girls' vacation in Montana ended in tears. The parting had gone badly, with a quarrel between Anna and sixteen-year-old Andrée, who wrote her mother this letter:

Mowitza Lodge, Aug. 27, 1918

My Dearest Little Mother,
    I know that you will not answer me nor do I think that you will read this letter, but if you do, you will know that you are the best friend that I ever have had, or will ever have. We all had a most beautiful, wonderful time at the Lake, and we regret so much that it is all over!!! And we are all indebted (especially me) to you for this lovely summer we have had. We had a very sunny, windy, incidental trip to Butte and we arrived here

at quarter to seven. We all had dinner at the house and then, separated. This afternoon Daddy is going to take me to the Gardens to see his marvelous begonias. . . .

I am ever so sorry to have made you unhappy yesterday for I was heartbroken to see you cry and send me away without one of your smiles and fond kisses which are worth to me more than a world. I hope you will forgive me. Whether you write to me or not or do not open my letters, I am going to write to you, every week or so and it may prove to you, or it may not, that I love you above anybody else on this earth and that though I am selfish, I'd die first, before anything could happen to you. Good-by, dearest little Mother, and please forgive me.

Your loving daughter,
Andrée

THE CLARK SISTERS SHARED a bedroom in the Clark mansion until Andrée was fourteen and Huguette ten. Decades later, Huguette told her night nurse about the bedtime routine of the young sisters. "Her sister was a wonderful writer and reader," said the nurse, Geraldine Lehane Coffey, "and she would tell her stories at night. And she would not finish them."

So, each night, Huguette would ask, "Will you continue tomorrow night?" And Andrée always would.

At age sixteen, Andrée had grown moody and tempestuous, which is to say she was a teenager. She also had a physical ailment, a bad back, and was taking exercises at home with a gym teacher, Alma Guy, who saw that the older daughter needed more than physical therapy. Andrée needed to have some time out of the smothering atmosphere of the Clark home.

Andrée was "shy and timid and afraid to call her soul her own," Miss Guy recalled. "Her parents were so occupied with other things that they really did not know what was happening to their daughter in the hands of maids and governesses. Andrée was never allowed to do anything for herself."

Miss Guy pressed for Andrée to be allowed to join some activity outside the home, an outlet for self-expression. She suggested the Girl Scouts, a group that had formed in 1912 and was flourishing during World War I. At first Anna wasn't sure this was a proper activity, saying that it sounded "too democratic for the daughter of a senator," but finally she relented.

And so in the winter of 1918–19, after the armistice was signed, Andrée joined Sun Flower Troop, which drew its recruits from the wealthy homes of Manhattan. She exchanged her au courant French fashions for the dark blue middy blouse and skirt, light blue sateen cotton neckerchief, blue felt campaign hat, and black shoes and stockings of the Girl

Scouts. Each Tuesday afternoon, Girl Scout day, she worked toward her Tenderfoot pin, then her Second Class patch, struggling to make an American flag with all forty-eight stars. "I have made everything of the flag except the stars!" she wrote to a friend. "They are hopeless!!!" She learned Red Cross work, such as wrapping bandages and treating wounds, and built an open-air fire in the woods. She also volunteered with the Scouts at the Lighthouse, a recreational program of the New York Association for the Blind, where Miss Guy was the activities director.

"Scouting really made a different girl of Andrée," Miss Guy recalled. "She was quite determined to come down to the Lighthouse and start a troop for the blind girls there, she loved it so."

Andrée had other adventures with her Girl Scout friends, far from the overbearing reach of governesses. At age sixteen, in a letter to a friend, she described riding with a group of girls through a suburban town in a Scout leader's yellow jalopy, nicknamed the Yellow Peril, "a topsy-turvy, yellow flivver and we had our bloomers on, and were packed up in sweaters and coats, like sausages!!!! And the whole family of dogs was with us! Can you imagine us, bumping up and down on the crowded Main Street!!!!"

. . .

The summer before Andrée's seventeenth birthday, in July and August 1919, she and Huguette took an outdoors trip with their mother, traveling north to a fishing club in Quebec, not far from the hometowns of Anna's parents, and then to a resort area in the Maine woods near the Canadian border. Hotels and primitive camps lined Maine's Rangeley Lakes, below Saddleback Mountain, a few years before the area became well known to hikers on the new Appalachian Trail.

On the trip, Andrée fell ill, first with a simple fever, which quickly grew worse and was accompanied by a severe headache. Anna and the girls were two days' travel from home, far from the quarantine suite in the tower at 962 Fifth Avenue. Their father's personal physician, William Gordon Lyle, rushed up from New York to assist the local doctor. For four days, Andrée lay ill at a house on Rangeley Plantation, on the south side of the lake, with Anna and Huguette by her side.

The doctor found that Andrée's ailment was "probably tubercular meningitis," a devastating inflammation of the membranes covering the brain and spinal cord. It would be twenty-five years before penicillin would be reported as effective in treating meningitis. On August 7, 1919, Louise Amelia Andrée Clark, the firstborn child of Anna and W.A. and the older sister of Huguette, died a week before her seventeenth birthday. W.A., who had been in Butte on business, was speeding eastward on the Empire State Express when he received a cable with the news.

The funeral service "was most beautiful," W.A. wrote to a friend. "We had the entire boy choir of the church," W.A. wrote. "We laid the precious body away in the mausoleum in Woodlawn Cemetery."

The Episcopalian rector from St. Thomas Church on Fifth Avenue read W.A.'s favorite poem, "Thanatopsis," a young man's meditation on death, from Andrée's poetry book. The poet, William Cullen Bryant, argues that death should not be feared, for there is great company in it.

> *Yet not to thine eternal resting-place*
> *Shalt thou retire alone, nor couldst thou wish*
> *Couch more magnificent.*
> *Thou shalt lie down*
> *With patriarchs of the infant world, with kings,*
> *The powerful of the earth, the wise, the good,*
> *Fair forms, and hoary seers of ages past,*
> *All in one mighty sepulcher.*

W.A. wrote to his brother Ross, "Mrs. Clark is very sad, but very brave." And to a business associate he wrote, "Mrs. Clark has wonderful fortitude, and little Huguette is also very courageous."

. . .

After the funeral, W.A. and Anna discovered Andrée's diary, which revealed that their older daughter had had an unhappy childhood, more desperately unhappy than they had suspected. She'd had great difficulty making the transition from France to America. Her father told a friend how devastated he was by reading it.

The diary brightened, however, when Andrée wrote about her Tuesday Girl Scout meetings. She told of the camaraderie of hiking with the girls and of the uplifting effect of being allowed to do a task however she decided was best. She included a folded manuscript of a story she had written, "The Four Little Flowers," with characters from Sun Flower Troop.

"Scouting has been a hand in the dark to me," she wrote. "It has changed me from a moody, thoughtless girl, and has shown me what life may be."

Her family sought solace in making a contribution to the Girl Scouts. The Clarks knew an area around Scarsdale, north of the city, where they often spent weekends with W.A.'s daughter Katherine in her twenty-one-room manor house. Looking for a proper memorial, Anna and W.A. helped scour the countryside for just the right spot. In 1919, they donated 135 acres in the village of Briarcliff Manor, where primitive land with a brook and a small lake became the first national Girl Scout camp, called Camp Andrée Clark.

Thirteen-year-old Huguette stood grimly at her father's side as he handed over the deed to the camp at a Scout office in the city. While sixteen uniformed Girl Scouts sat or kneeled on the floor, Huguette stood. Not a Scout herself, she was dressed in city clothes, with her long blond hair flowing down her back toward the fur cuffs of her coat. During the ceremony, she held her emotions in check, resting her hand reassuringly on her eighty-year-old father's shoulder.

For the rest of Huguette's life, members of her family would speculate about the great emotional trauma she must have felt at her sister's death. She had lost her only sibling, her playmate, an older sister with whom she had spent her entire life. In later years, at her bedside on Fifth Avenue, she kept a photograph of her sister in a small, oval Cartier frame. She also kept Andrée's letter to their mother from the year before she died, and a lock of Andrée's hair.

Camp Andrée, as the girls called it, became a progressive camp, democratic in spirit, with the girls directing many of their own activities. Each group of girls had its own rustic quarters; there was no dining hall, no dormitory, though Anna made certain that the camp had a small hospital and a nurse. Still in existence today, the camp has trained thousands of Scout leaders and given generations of girls a summer experience of close community in the wilderness.

For years after Andrée's death, Girl Scouts wrote letters to Anna, thanking her for making it possible for them, too, to see what life may be.

CULTIVATE IMAGINATION

HUGUETTE'S UPBRINGING was already artistically strong, with music lessons, painting lessons, and a family home that was essentially a public art gallery. Her sense of imagination was enhanced by her high school education in the 1920s at Miss Spence's Boarding and Day School for Girls.

Miss Spence's was one of the favorite schools in Manhattan for the daughters of the elite. Admission was a patent of American nobility. The same year that Huguette enrolled as a day student at the school, three of her half-nieces, her peers in age, enrolled as well. These were the daughters of Huguette's half-brother Charlie. Karine McCall, the daughter of one of those nieces, Agnes Clark Albert, said that Agnes had been told by her mother to keep an eye on Huguette, to watch out for her, as though Huguette needed protection. Her protector, Andrée, was gone.

Classes at Miss Spence's met in a converted brownstone residence on West Fifty-Fifth Street, where the chauffeurs of the Carnegies, Fricks, and Clarks lined up at the curb.

The school's lively, artistic tone was set by its founder, Clara Spence, a Scottish actress who loved to read Shakespeare aloud and could be talked into dancing the Highland fling. Miss Spence emphasized standards of scholarship, for this was the highest education most of her young ladies would receive. Of the fifty-six students in Huguette's class of 1925, only fourteen were aiming for college. The rest, including Huguette, were on the marriage track. Within a few years after Huguette's class of 1925, that ratio would reverse, with most Spence girls headed to college. Along with elocution and Latin, Huguette and her classmates studied sewing and practical math, needed to manage a home budget. The sewing class, in which the girls made baby clothes to be pinned into a scrapbook, was a Spence tradition.

The teaching was warm and the curriculum innovative, with options such as fencing lessons. The art classes appealed particularly to Huguette. She recalled that one of her dance teachers was Isadora Duncan, known for her modern choreography, her outspokenness about political and sexual matters, and her flowing silk scarves, including the one that killed her when it became caught in the wheel of an automobile.

Miss Spence's motto for her school was the Latin *"Non scholae sed vitae discimus,"* meaning "Not for school but for life we learn." She urged her ladies to emphasize more than just book knowledge, more than reason:

> I beg you to cultivate imagination, which means to develop your power of sympathy, and I entreat you to decide thoughtfully what makes a human being great in his time and in his station. The faculty of imagination is often lightly spoken of as of no real importance, often decried as mischievous, as in some ways the antithesis of practical sense, and yet it ranks with reason and conscience as one of the supreme characteristics by which man is distinguished from all other animals. . . . Sympathy, the great bond between human beings, is largely dependent on imagination—that is, upon the power of realizing the feelings and the circumstances of others so as to enable us to feel with and for them.

Decorum, morals, and good judgment were expected. The girls wore simple skirts extending at least three inches below the knee. Parents were urged to send their girls to school without extravagances: no jewelry except a simple ring and a simple pin, no perfume, no scented face powder, no lipstick. Church attendance was mandatory. Spence girls curtsied to their elders. One student who received an overly affectionate telegram from her beau was surprised to learn that she had two choices, either leave school or announce her engagement.

Each spring the girls took turns playing host at a round of teas for their classmates. Huguette threw other parties as well. "Miss Huguette Clark, daughter of Mr. and Mrs. William Andrews Clark of 962 Fifth Avenue entertained a party of girlfriends yesterday at Sherry's," the popular restaurant, *The New York Times* reported in May 1922, when Huguette was nearly sixteen.

At commencement, as the entire school filed in to Mozart's "March of

Eighteen-year-old Huguette, middle front, with her 1925 graduating class at Miss Spence's Boarding and Day School for Girls. Even at the most exclusive school in New York, she was far wealthier than nearly all of her classmates.

the Priests" from *The Magic Flute,* the youngest led the procession. Huguette's commencement was held at the old Waldorf-Astoria, where in five years would rise a new structure, the Empire State Building. In a photo, the girls are dressed all in white, holding flowers. Everyone has the newly fashionable short hairstyle. Huguette would become the last surviving member of the Spence class of 1925, but we do have a few memories of her from classmates, secondhand.

Louise Watt, a banker's daughter, recalled having good times with her, including a clandestine visit to a speakeasy—the proper Spence girls exploring the city during Prohibition, when whom should they see at a table but Jimmy Walker, the mayor of New York. Louise described Huguette as her best friend.

A different portrait came from Dorothy Warren, a classmate from an old Yankee family and a year older than Huguette though in the same grade. She described her as always polite and gracious but often not socializing with the other girls. Most of the Spence girls had visited one another's houses, but none had been to the Clark home. Warren said that

Huguette was something of an odd bird, and the girls who knew her only casually were flummoxed by her. Was she too proud of her family, which was so much richer and better traveled than most of the other families? Was she embarrassed about her father's wealth or his failed campaign for social standing? The other girls couldn't quite figure her out.

ONE OF THE PHOTOGRAPHS in Huguette's album, one she particularly liked to share in her later years, shows her in an American Indian costume and feathered headdress, sitting beside her father. She looks about seven years old, which would make him about seventy-four. The family was on a sojourn in Greenwich, Connecticut, known for its art colony. Huguette had taken a fall while playing in the yard and had cried a bit before the photo was taken. Her eyes are puffy, but she's smiling, and her arm is draped across the old man's shoulder. W.A. looks dapper in his black sport coat, white pants, and white nubuck shoes, his gray hair billowing as he hugs her proudly.

Given Huguette's shyness, in contrast to her outgoing father, it's not

Huguette hugs her dapper father on a family weekend in Connecticut about 1912. He showed great affection for his youngest child, whom he called Huguetty. She called him Papa.

IN CONVERSATION WITH HUGUETTE

Huguette in 1999 described her memories of a family trip to Hawaii. Even at age ninety-three, her memory was excellent, as she remembered clearly the name of the beautiful trees in Honolulu, and the name of the handsome Olympic champion who took them out paddling on surfboards. I had begun by asking if she'd traveled to the islands.

Huguette: Oh yes, I was there. . . . I went there several times.

Paul: You traveled with your family there?

Huguette: With my father, in 1915. We went to Honolulu at Waikiki Beach. It was lovely there! I think it was more pleasant in those days, because it wasn't so built-up.

Paul: It's very commercial now.

Huguette: Very commercial.

Paul: Yes. Was the Royal Hawaiian Hotel built at that time?

Huguette: Yes, that's where we were, the Royal Hawaiian Hotel.

Paul: Oh, how nice!

Huguette: Is it still there?

Paul: It's still there, yes, it is. And the other one, I think it's called the Awani, or something like that, is also still there.

Huguette: That's the one where we went in 1915! The Moana Hotel. Is it still there, too?

Paul: Yes, in fact Leslie [my daughter] said she was there just recently. . . .

Huguette: Did you ever see the rainbow shower blossoms? They're beautiful! They're called Rainbow Shower.

Paul: It's a blossom? On a tree, you mean?

Huguette: Yes.

Paul: I don't think so. How did your father enjoy Hawaii? Did he like it over there?

Huguette: He enjoyed it. He used to go in the water. He went swimming there.

Paul: With all his high-finance and business activity, was he able to have some fun, too?

Huguette: Oh yes. We used to surfboard ride with Kahanamoku, you know. The Hawaiians, they used to take us out on the surfboard. Duke Kahanamoku, he was the champion swimmer at the time. . . . Because, you see, they used to have sharks around there. And if you go with them, you'd be more safe. Sometimes the sharks would come through the coral reef.

And then, as she often did, she ended the call abruptly but cheerfully.

Huguette: Well, nice talking with you, Paul. I won't keep you. . . . And I'll talk to you soon again. I'll get you on the phone. Bye-bye.

surprising that there were Clark family stories claiming that W.A. wasn't keen on her, even that he wasn't actually her father, but these tales are belied by his warm mentions of her in his correspondence. In 1921, for example, W.A. wrote to a friend while he, Anna, and Huguette were on a Hawaiian vacation, describing with enthusiasm how mother and daughter sunned and rode surfboards at Waikiki Beach: "They take great delight in swimming and the beach at the Moana Hotel is very good. The board riding is particularly interesting to them." Later he wrote, "They enjoy the swimming very much and go in generally twice a day." In this letter, he refers to his daughter affectionately as Huguetty.

W.A.'s wife and children showed him great affection as well. A relative recalled Anna snuggling up to the old man and tugging on his whiskers playfully, with frolicsome affection.

As W.A. passed his eightieth birthday, his weight began to fall, from his usual 125 to about 108. He continued to walk up to five miles a day, and he continued smoking his cigars. He remained devoted to his business correspondence on "the Clark interests," approving expenditures on political committees, deflecting requests to give to colleges and convents. But he was growing weaker, and in 1922 he signed his last will and testament.

That year, W.A. traveled to France with Anna and Huguette. They had been forced to wait four years after the end of the Great War until the mines were cleared from the French coast. Forever a friend of France, W.A. laid roses at the new Tomb of the Unknown Soldier at the Arc de Triomphe. In the photograph from that day, he looks noticeably weaker. This would be his last trip to France.

By 1925, W.A. was no longer going to his office at 20 Exchange Street, off Wall Street, instead having his mail brought to him at home. "Becoming vaguer all the time," he seemed "not to grasp matters regularly," his son Will wrote in January of that year. W.A., who shunned automobiles after a couple of bad accidents, also had hurt his leg severely in a fall while running to catch a bus.

Then a cold turned worse, and he was dead within a few days. He died on March 2, 1925, at age eighty-six, attended by Dr. William Gordon Lyle, the same doctor who had tried to save Andrée. Anna, Huguette, and most of the children from his first marriage were by his side.

"Ex-Senator Clark, Pioneer in Copper, Dies of Pneumonia," read the front-page headline in *The New York Times*. The headline continued, "His Career Picturesque. Went to Montana with Ox Team and Acquired One of Biggest Fortunes in America."

W.A.'s last will and testament called for a "decent and Christian burial in accordance with my condition in life, without undue pomp or ceremony." More than three hundred people gathered for a service at the Clark mansion, in the main art gallery on the second floor, under his beloved Corot landscapes. "Thanatopsis" was read aloud, as it had been at Andrée's funeral, and the thirty boy choristers from St. Thomas Church again sang as the organist played an old Scottish hymn: "Swift to its close, ebbs out life's little day. / Earth's joys grow dim, its glories pass away. / Change and decay in all around I see. / Oh, Thou who changest not, abide with me!"

Among the more than four hundred floral tributes were orchids and lilies of the valley sent by President Calvin Coolidge, a Republican.

Anna and Huguette joined the cortège, which also included W.A.'s children and grandchildren from his first marriage, accompanying his coffin north to the mausoleum he'd had built on the hilltop at a prominent intersection of Woodlawn Cemetery. His new neighbors were Pulitzer, Macy, Gould, and Woolworth.

Andrew Carnegie's theory was that life should be divided into three stages: education, making money, and giving all the money away. Little towns all across America still have Carnegie libraries. In a similar vein, Rockefeller Center in New York City and the Rockefeller Foundation carry on that name. Clark did donate to churches and universities, and he frequently opened his home for charity galas. He built Columbia Gardens for the people of Butte. However, he rejected a friend's advice to endow a great university in Montana. Though he lived to age eighty-six, he never fully entered Carnegie's third stage.

Out of his estate, estimated to be worth between $100 million and $250 million, W.A.'s will left only about $600,000 in cash to charity, mostly to social welfare causes emblazoned with the Clark name: $350,000 to the Paul Clark Home for children in Butte, named for a son who died as a teenager; $100,000 to the Katherine Stauffer Clark Kindergarten School in New York, named for his first wife, including money to continue his custom of giving Christmas presents to the children and to allow the children to spend a fortnight each year in the country; $100,000 to benefit his company mining town of Clarkdale, Arizona; and $25,000 to the Mary Andrews Clark Memorial Home for Women, honoring his mother, in Los Angeles.

W.A. also remembered friends from long ago in Montana. He left $25,000 for aged, indigent, and disabled Masons; $2,500 to the Masons in Deer Lodge to be used for charity; $25,000 to each of his sisters; $10,000 each to two nieces and nephews; $10,000 to his business managers in Butte; $5,000 to his managers in Missoula; $2,500 to the editor of his newspaper and political adviser in Butte; $2,500 to his butler; his gold watch and chain to his elder son, Charlie; and his gold match safe to his younger son, Will.

To Anna he left a limited sum, as he had promised his children from his first marriage. She received $2.5 million in cash, the furnishings from the Paris apartment, and an unknown amount already paid to her as a result of an antenuptial agreement referred to in the will. Although it was not specified in the will, Anna also received Bellosguardo, their summer home ninety miles up the coast from Los Angeles, in Santa Barbara.

The rest of the estate, including all of Clark's mining companies and his business empire, was divided among his five surviving children, Huguette and her four older half-siblings.

It's impossible to know the exact amount of W.A.'s estate. For tax purposes in Montana, it was reported to be only $48 million. If one uses $250 million, a commonly cited value, he easily ranks among the fifty richest Americans ever, relative to the economy of his time. The only ones more affluent at Clark's death during the Roaring Twenties were the oilman John D. Rockefeller, the automobile maker Henry Ford, the banking Mellon brothers, and Cyrus H. K. Curtis, publisher of *The Ladies' Home Journal* and *The Saturday Evening Post*. To put it another way, W.A. died with personal wealth equivalent to one day's share of the entire gross national product in 1925. On that scale, he would rank third today on the Forbes 400, far ahead of Google's founders or Rupert Murdoch, behind only Bill Gates and Warren Buffett, and just ahead of the industrialist Koch brothers, who have brought a new spotlight to the influence of money in politics.

As an indication of his great love for his youngest child, who was still a minor when he signed his will, W.A. took special care to provide for her. In addition to her housing and education, he specified that Huguette should receive an allowance, up to $90,000 a year, or in today's dollars about $1.1 million, until she reached age twenty-one. He explained that he wanted her to experience "the actual handling and care of money during her minority."

Others also wanted that opportunity, as Huguette had to face false claims to the copper fortune. In 1926, three sisters from Missouri presented themselves to the probate court in Butte, saying they were the daughters of W. A. Clark. Their case was a farce. The man whom Alma, Effie, and Addie Clark described as their father, William Anderson Clark, had, like W.A., taught school in Missouri and was a Mason, but for most of his life he'd been a druggist in Stewartsville, Missouri, a dealer in books and notions, while William Andrews Clark had graced the halls of Congress and the galleries of Paris. As Charlie Clark testified, his father "would not have been content to operate a farm, to conduct a small business, a picayune business, when he was engaged in the big development that he was concerned with here in the West, banking, mining, the development of the country."

W. A. Clark's family apparently wanted to make a show of defeating the claim of the three sisters so thoroughly as to scare off any others. Who knew what offspring W.A. might have in Iowa or Montana or New York. Witnesses to support Huguette and her half-siblings as the true heirs were found by Pinkerton detectives and brought out to Butte from Missouri and Pennsylvania on the train. They testified that the two men looked nothing alike, with the druggist standing about five feet eleven, weighing about 160 pounds, having brown hair, and usually being clean-shaven. The jury quickly rejected the three sisters' claim, securing Huguette's inheritance.

W.A.'s WILL DIRECTED that his art go to America's most prominent museum, the Metropolitan Museum of Art, just up Fifth Avenue from the Clark mansion. The Clark collection would be a permanent monument to his name—if the Met would accept certain terms. Here, even after death, W.A. overplayed his hand.

The Met could have most of his art—more than 800 objects, including 225 paintings and drawings—if it agreed to three conditions: The entire collection must be kept together, in a separate gallery solely for its display, forever.

The first problem, the Met's leaders said, was that keeping the Clark collection together would prevent the pieces from being integrated into the Met by time period and style. Second, the collection was huge, and unless the Met bought Clark's home, it had no suitable space for it.

Left unsaid by the Met, but pointed out by the press in 1925, was the fact that Clark's collection was also uneven—spectacular in some areas but no better in others than the pieces the Met already had, not to mention a few frauds or "misattributed" pieces, as was common in most private collections. His version of *The Judgment of Midas* was apparently not by Rubens but by another artist in Rubens's studio. His *Man with a Sheet of Music*, attributed to Rembrandt, had the same uncertainty.

Even Clark's *Hope Venus*, it turned out, was a fake, or at least a copy. Lord Duveen had assured Clark that Canova made more than one version of the statue. But Clark's *Venus* had been offered first to newspaper publisher William Randolph Hearst, who had seen the original in Florence and knew better than to buy this copy. After Clark's death, his *Venus* was judged to have been made by an English artist after Canova's death.

People wrote to the Met, some urging that it accept the Clark collection, despite its flaws, even if it meant the Met had to buy the Clark mansion to hold it all. Others urged the Met not to indulge a millionaire's vanity. After long debate, the Met said no.

The collection was offered next to W.A.'s backup choice, the Corcoran Gallery of Art in Washington, D.C., a second-tier museum in a city with a culture more political than artistic. Clark was no stranger to the Corcoran, having donated $100,000 to endow prizes for American painters and serving as a trustee from 1914 until his death. He lent the museum eighty-six works in his collection to be shown while his New York house was under construction, taking President Theodore Roosevelt on a private tour there in 1904. Despite T.R.'s environmental regulations and his criticism of the "malefactors of great wealth," he and W.A. shared a love of art.

The Corcoran quickly said yes, eager to bring to Washington's cultural swamps a major collection of European paintings. Although W.A. had insisted on a private space for his collection, he hadn't left the museum any funds to pay for it. His heirs put up $700,000 for the Corcoran to add a neoclassical Clark Wing to its Beaux Arts building, located just southwest of the White House. Anna made a contribution, as did Huguette and her half-sisters, Mary Joaquina and Katherine. The Corcoran built a space exactly designed to fit W.A.'s golden room, Salon Doré. President Coolidge opened the W. A. Clark Collection in 1928. The heirs relaxed their father's restrictions, agreeing that not all the collection had to be on view at once and pieces that turned out to be misattributed could be kept off the walls.

In New York, the Clark house-museum was now without its art.

ONE GOOD CIGAR

————

T HE DEATH OF HER FATHER meant that Huguette would soon be evicted from her childhood home. This, she may not have anticipated.

W.A. had promised his grown children that his second wife, Anna, would not inherit the mansion. His will gave Anna and Huguette until June 1928 to move out. At his death in March 1925, only three more years were left. Anna didn't need three years. The house was W.A.'s hobby, not hers, built for social standing, in which she had no interest. In less than a year, she and Huguette had moved into an apartment down Fifth Avenue.

"The most remarkable dwelling in the world," which had taken thirteen years to move from architect's drawings to becoming the Clark family home, had been occupied for only fourteen years.

These showgirls on the console of the pipe organ at the Clark mansion were hired by the home's buyer to lead public tours before the demolition.

Huguette and her half-siblings had trouble, however, finding a buyer for the mansion. Exactly as W.A. had told the property assessor, the Clark mansion was fit for only one owner. It was too expensive to operate, almost too expensive to tear down. Built for $7 million to $10 million, it sold for less than $3 million. The money from the sale was divided among the children.

In the summer of 1927, the tower of the Clark mansion came down, making way for the next wave in architecture, an apartment building with elegant interiors. Other mansions on Fifth Avenue were disappearing as well. The palace of Vincent Astor, the château of Mrs. Cornelius Vanderbilt—many mansions yielded to modernity. The Gilded Age was past.

At auction, the Clark heirs sold a silver candelabra, hundreds of yards of red velvet wall hangings, porcelain soup plates with gold trim and the Clark crest—nearly half a million dollars in furnishings, or in today's values more than $6 million. A collector took the bronze carriage gates

The Clark mansion's marble staircase, made of creamy, ivory-tinted Maryland marble, lasted only sixteen years.

to his farm. W.A.'s daughter May moved the walls of two entire rooms to her mansion on Long Island. The mirror-paneled walls and doors went to the city's children's hospital. When no buyer was found for the grand marble staircase, it was loaded onto a scow and dumped at sea.

Before the pinch bars and hammers began the demolition, the new owner of the Clark mansion allowed curiosity seekers inside to gawk at its bones, stripped of its art collection and furnishings. Among more than sixteen thousand tourists paying fifty cents for a peek was Charlie Chaplin. To promote the tours, showgirls posed for photographs: eight showgirls standing in front of the dining room fireplace, then the same eight clowning on the pipe organ.

Ah, the pipe organ. No one thought to auction off Anna and W.A.'s $120,000 marvel. The real estate developer asked the man handling the demolition if he could take it home, thinking the organ might look good in his home or his church. He was prepared to pay a few thousand dollars, but the wrecker told him, "You can have the organ, if you'll give me a cigar." The developer soon realized his folly. The pipe organ was too inextricably built into the walls of the house to be removed intact. It was dumped to fill a swamp in Queens. He had wasted a perfectly good cigar.

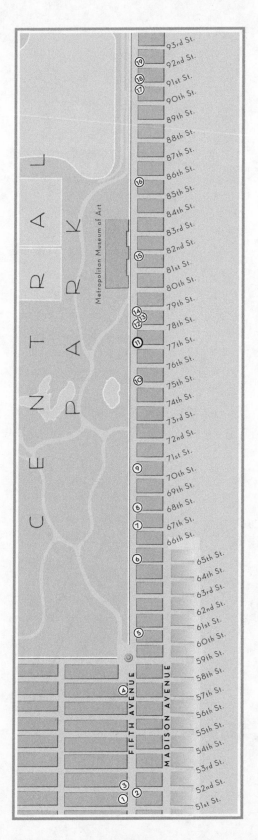

NEW YORK'S DISAPPEARING MILLIONAIRES' ROW

Prominent residences on Fifth Avenue in 1914, shown as a walking tour from south to north. Dates indicate the life span of each building.

1. **William H. Vanderbilt.** 1881–1942. *Replaced by commercial buildings.*
2. **Morton Plant.** 1905–. *Cartier since 1917.*
3. **William Kissam Vanderbilt.** 1882–1926. *Replaced by a commercial building.*
4. **Cornelius Vanderbilt II.** 1882–1927. *Replaced by Bergdorf Goodman.*
5. **Elbridge Gerry.** 1897–1929. *Replaced by the Pierre hotel.*
6. **Caroline Astor, son John Jacob Astor IV.** 1896–1926. *Replaced by Temple Emanu-El.*
7. **George J. Gould.** 1908–1961. *Replaced by apartments.*
8. **William C. Whitney.** 1884–1942. *Replaced by apartments.*
9. **Henry Clay Frick.** 1914–. *The Frick Collection since 1935.*
10. **Edward S. Harkness.** 1908–. *The Commonwealth Fund since 1952.*
11. **W. A. Clark.** 1911–1927. *Replaced by an apartment building.*
12. **James B. Duke.** 1912–. *New York University Institute of Fine Arts since 1957.*
13. **Harry Payne Whitney.** 1906–. *Cultural Services of the French Embassy since 1952.*
14. **Isaac D. Fletcher.** 1899–. *Ukrainian Institute of America since 1955.*
15. **Benjamin N. Duke.** 1901–. *Owned by Mexican billionaire Carlos Slim since 2010.*
16. **William Starr Miller.** 1914–. *Neue Galerie New York since 2001.*
17. **Andrew Carnegie.** 1902–. *Cooper-Hewitt, National Design Museum since 1976.*
18. **Otto Kahn.** 1918–. *Convent of the Sacred Heart school since 1934.*
19. **Felix Warburg.** 1908–. *The Jewish Museum since 1947.*

SOURCES: *Great Houses of New York, 1880–1930,* Michael C. Kathrens; *Gilded Mansions,* Wayne Craven. Dates of completion are approximate.

CHAPTER SIX

907 FIFTH AVENUE

...

PART ONE

DOWNSIZING

FOR THEIR NEW HOME, Anna and Huguette found an apartment five blocks south at 907 Fifth Avenue, at the corner of Seventy-Second Street. This was a super-luxury building, in the style of an Italian Renaissance palazzo, but not showy, turning a refined limestone face to the street.

Anna's tastes were not altogether different from her husband's, but she added a touch of the religious, with a dark, mysterious air. When the massive wooden door to Apartment 12W was opened, the visitor passed into a paneled Jacobean gallery, thirty-seven feet long with herringbone floors. From the eleven-foot ceilings hung an ornate brass lantern with a maiden encircled by branches and leaves of gold. On the long wall to the right was an old red tapestry, about twelve feet square, depicting Crusaders bargaining with a caliph for prisoners. On the left hung stained-glass windows, facing the building's open courtyard. These colorful panels of red and blue, apparently dating from seventeenth-century Zurich, depicted angels, knights, and coats of arms.

Though they were downsizing, the Clarks still had a marvelous view. On their twelfth floor—the top floor—a string of nine oversize windows ran the entire length of the building alongside the avenue, allowing them a view of the rapidly changing city skyline. The best view, however, was left to the servants, who had quarters on the roof, as was common in the day.

Looking down into the park in the foreground, Anna and Huguette could see Japanese cherry trees, the oval sailboat pond called Conservatory Water, and children sledding on Pilgrim Hill, with its statue commemorating the *Mayflower*'s landing at Plymouth Rock. Huguette painted this view straight across the park, a lovely scene showing the French gables of the Dakota apartment building on Central Park West. Her painting is missing the iconic twin towers of the San Remo, which wouldn't rise until after 1929.

To the right, far beyond the north end of Central Park, they could see the Hudson River Bridge to New Jersey beginning to be built in 1927, before it was named for George Washington. To the left, looking south down Fifth Avenue, they were able to watch the Empire State Building begin its ascent in 1930.

Anna wanted nothing but the best, and this apartment had a respectable heritage as the most expensive in the city. Their neighbors included W. C. Durant, a founder of General Motors. The previous tenant of their twelfth-floor apartment, Herbert Lee Pratt, was a name familiar to the Clarks, as Pratt and his father had been partners in Standard Oil with John D. Rockefeller. Pratt had paid $30,000 a year to rent the entire twelfth floor, with its twenty-eight rooms, advertised when the building opened in 1916 as "the finest apartment in the world." The Clarks took only half that space, five thousand square feet. Their rent was $12,000 a year, or about $150,000 in today's dollars.

Most people, when downsizing from 121 rooms to only 17, would have to figure out which furnishings to sell off. Anna, however, didn't own the contents of the Clark mansion. Those belonged to the estate, which was to be divided among the five children. So she went shopping. Her tastes looked back to old Europe, nothing modern. She chose a French bed with a sumptuous green silk damask bedspread, a Queen Anne walnut wing chair covered in needlepoint, a small Jacobean inlaid and carved oak cabinet, a French library table of the Henri II period, a Chippendale mahogany bookcase; the bill of sale from Charles of London runs on for eight pages. In the last two months of 1925, Anna spent $92,210 at Charles, quite a bit more than the $75,000 President Coolidge earned in salary for the year. In today's dollars, her new furnishings cost about $1.2 million.

Where W.A. had thrown open the Clark mansion to photographers and sketch artists from the world's newspapers and magazines, no photos of their apartments were published while Anna or Huguette were alive. They would have guests over for musical afternoons and small dinners, but access was carefully controlled.

Anna did add one touch from the Clark mansion: A door was concealed in the paneling of the gallery. A burglar could have spent a good while in Apartment 12W, wandering the parquet floors, meandering through the dining room with its wallpaper of pheasants and flowers, through the living room with Anna's French harps, and through the study and the breakfast room—without finding any bedrooms. All were hidden behind this door, which led to its own hallway, four bedrooms, four walk-in closets, and two sitting rooms.

In Anna's bedroom, the furniture was all in an ornate Louis XV style, oak with gold trim: a rolltop desk, a dressing table with three oval mirrors. The bedside table had photos of a young Huguette in a red dress resting her head on her father's shoulder and several photos of Andrée looking a bit forlorn. In the bathroom was one bit of modern technology: a scale built into the floor tile, with a dial on the wall showing the person's weight.

All of this luxury served only two Clarks, who soon expanded into a second apartment in the building. Anna moved down to an equally sumptuous apartment on the eighth floor.

The plan was for Anna to live alone and for Huguette to find a husband.

TADE

NEARLY EVERY WEEKDAY AFTERNOON in her late teens and twenties when the Clarks were in New York, Huguette walked thirteen blocks down Fifth Avenue to Central Park South, then a block over to the apartments at No. 36, to visit the man she called Cher Maître, or "Dear Master." It was time for her painting lesson.

Tadeusz Styka, called Tadé, was the favorite artist of the Clarks. From a well-known Czech-Polish family of painters, Tadé was a boy genius whose precocious talent at drawing was studied in Paris by the French psychologist Alfred Binet, inventor of the IQ test. After immigrating to the United States in 1921, he was popular among the New York social set of the 1920s and 1930s as a fast-painting portraitist, not only of people but also of family pets. He painted a lot of young women, though burlesque artist Gypsy Rose Lee threw him out of her dressing room when he expected the teenage stripper to pose nude. He also painted presidents: His *Rough Rider* portrait of Theodore Roosevelt hangs in the West Wing of the White House, and Harry Truman sat for him, too. Tadé painted at least a dozen portraits of the Clarks and was well paid for it. But his first job for the family was as a painting instructor for young Huguette.

Although becoming a painter was not a typical goal for one of Miss Spence's young ladies, Huguette was raised in an artistic household with music lessons and a family home that doubled as a public art gallery. Her father was not the only voracious collector in the family. On a single day when Huguette was twenty-three, she and her mother bought Renoir's *Chrysanthemums,* Pissarro's *Landscape,* and a small, stunning Degas, *Dancer Making Points,* showing a ballerina pointing her toe, a gentle figure in bold yellow and orange. That day was November 11, 1929, just two weeks after the Wall Street crash, which began the Great Depression. For most people.

Women at the time usually painted with pastels. They weren't thought capable of handling oil paints, which require more skillful preparation of the canvas, mixing of the colors, and layering of the paint. Oils, used by male artists, were associated with fine art. Huguette, meticulous in all things, always painted with oils.

One of her self-portraits shows her at the easel, turning to look over her shoulder as though surprised by a visitor. Her blond, shoulder-length hair is wavy, but not in a fancy do. She is wearing a simple peach-colored painter's smock, not a debutante's dress. For once, there is no strand of pearls at her neck. She holds an Impressionist's palette of intense colors arranged from crimson to yellow to emerald green. The unglamorous smock, the uncertain look, and the large palette all combine as if to say, *This is who I am. I am an artist.*

. . .

Huguette had an early love of Japan, a love she shared with her mother. Much of France had fallen under the spell of Japanese art in the late 1800s—a craze known as Japonisme. Huguette developed that love into a quiet career as an artist. Her paintings, often life-size portraits of Japanese geishas, focus more on the costumes and hairstyles than on the revealed emotional lives of the women: A woman with a dragonfly pin in her hair smokes a cigarette, another holds a fan looking at a castle, and a third delicately cuts flowers. Huguette's geishas are women trained to keep their emotions hidden.

One of her smallest paintings, only six by nine inches, shows Huguette's dedication to detail. A young geisha stands barefoot, her eyes averted pensively. She is wearing a floor-length robe with a large golden bow. Her black hair is decorated with a dozen combs, ornaments, and tassels of gold. The subtle lighting brings to life the exquisite textures of silk and gold.

Huguette's shelves were stacked with illustrated and scholarly books on Japan, in several languages: *The Changing Social Position of Women in Japan, Palaces of Kyoto, Japanese Court Poetry, Japanese Art of the Heian Period.* These books resided alongside her wider collection of Homer, Virgil, Plato, Descartes, Lao-tzu, and Oscar Wilde.

The paintings in her home studio in Apartment 12W show how she immersed herself in Japanese culture, an archaeologist studying the markers of Japanese nobility: traditional calligraphy, the Osuberakashi hairstyle tied in the back with a ribbon, elaborate hair accessories, richly brocaded silk fabrics in red and gold. She didn't only study these objects in books; she collected them, filling shelves with delicate wooden boxes of kimonos and hairpieces. These details are lifelike in her paintings.

Huguette was also influenced by the work of illustrators and artists of her native France, from Parisian magazine illustrations to the Monets and Renoirs hanging on her walls. While the Impressionists applied a Japanese aesthetic to European subjects, Huguette's artwork shows an Impressionist style applied to Japanese subjects.

Though her art shows years of training, it doesn't quite match the technical skill of her instructor, Tadé Styka. While some Impressionist art conveys a hurried approach, trying to render the light as they experienced it, Huguette's landscapes of Japanese castles and bridges look as if they were painted entirely in her apartment from detailed photos, without exposure to real life. And when she painted people, it's possible that Huguette, as her social contacts declined, used herself as the body model for her paintings of Japanese women.

Nevertheless, her works show a dedication to excellence and an ability to adapt to newer styles. Her painting of an ornate bowl of pink and yellow tulips, with two still-fresh petals lying on the table, is a bit disjointed, shown from more than one perspective at once, just as Cézanne did in the still life of an earthenware jug hanging on Huguette's wall. Huguette finished many paintings of this scene, always with two petals fallen.

She signed many of these paintings in an Asian style with an artist's chop, or personal stamp. She arranged the letters of her first and last names in two vertical columns inside a rectangle.

For many of the women she painted, Huguette also chose a name, which she painted in Japanese characters into the corner of the canvas. On into the 1940s and 1950s, she corresponded with Japanese advisers, discussing appropriate names for a modern princess—a "young lady of a good family." She wanted to know the proper names indicating gentleness, goodness, and grace. Among her favorites were Ume-ko Hime (Princess Plum Blossom) and Fuji-ko Hime (Princess Wisteria). After she learned that the American government in postwar Japan had abolished the peerage and its titles, she went with names such as Yoshi-ko (meaning "graceful and noble").

Another of her life-size paintings shows a sober maiko, or apprentice geisha, in a brilliant red, pink, and white kimono, holding a long, silver tobacco pipe that is smoldering. In a round seal next to Huguette's signature is the name she associated with this woman, Ku-Raku, meaning "sorrow and joy."

. . .

Perhaps as a personal favor to its twenty-two-year-old benefactor, the Corcoran museum in Washington showed seven of her paintings in 1929. "From the day of her birth," said the catalog for the two-week showing, "Huguette Clark has lived in an artistic atmosphere. She has been surrounded with the many treasures of various Schools and Periods, contained in the notable art collection bequeathed to this Gallery by her father, the late William Andrews Clark. She has had the benefit of extensive European travel; and, added to these advantages, she is endowed with unusual natural talent."

The Associated Press later carried a glowing report of the exhibition: "Her paintings received high praise from critics at an exhibition at the Corcoran galleries in Washington last year and now she is planning an exhibition in Paris. She is an accomplished musician."

Her paintings displayed at the Corcoran were titled *Scene from My Window—Night; Scene from My Window—After the Snow Storm; Typical French Doll; Typical Japanese Doll; La Rentrée d'une Soirée* (Returning from the Party); *Study of Hydrangeas;* and *Portrait of Myself.*

Huguette apparently never exhibited her paintings again, but she had a few printed as holiday cards. Her friends and relatives could see, if they looked closely, her signature on the artwork. We don't know how late in life Huguette continued her painting. She may have given away some of her work to staff or friends: The delicate barefoot geisha sold on eBay in 2010 for $104.

. . .

Huguette's most affecting painting, of those we have seen, is a snowy view from her apartment window: The Manhattan skyline, streetlights, and automobile taillights are diffused by the moist air of a blue-gray night. The scene is reminiscent of the urban paintings of Edward Hopper or Georgia O'Keeffe, but with more warmth. The dominant feature is the brown grid of Huguette's window looking south on Fifth Avenue toward the Empire State Building and the RCA Building. In the foreground, reflected in the window, glows a lamp with a golden base, its white shade supported by a delicate Japanese porcelain figure of a woman in a kimono standing on a golden pedestal. The artist reveals only this part of her private space illuminated by the lamp, nothing more. The woman in the kimono is smiling, her face partly hidden behind a lady's fan.

Outside the window, it is cold, dark, noisy, uncertain, offering the energy and engagement of city life. Inside, it is warm, bright, refined, cultured, offering the slow pulse and detachment of solitude.

This view disappeared in the 1950s. The builder of 907 Fifth Avenue had outfitted these apartments with south-facing windows, looking down Fifth Avenue, but had failed to acquire the air rights above the townhouses to the south. This failure became manifest when the townhouses were torn down and the glazed, white-brick 900 Fifth Avenue was built in 1959—shouldering right up against the windows of the Clark apartments. The effect was that Anna and Huguette's south-facing windows in the dining and living rooms were bricked up, part of their views snuffed out.

. . .

In early days at least, Huguette painted from live models. One of Tadé Styka's portraits shows her, at perhaps age eighteen to twenty, working intently on a large canvas. She is seated on an upholstered bench in his studio, her legs stretched out to her full five feet six inches. She is dressed in a knee-length pencil skirt and an artist's collared shirt with a necktie, affecting the "garçon look," with her hair in an undulating marcel wave reminiscent of Jean Harlow. At the right of the canvas, almost out of sight, stands a well-toned nude male model, his back to the viewer. Perhaps to save her modesty, the artist shows Huguette's eyes fixed firmly on her canvas. In her apartments, among her hundreds of paintings, Huguette had other nudes of men and women.

Another of Tadé's powerful images of Huguette, as a young woman of about eighteen, shows off her rose-colored cheeks, which match her high-necked blouse, offset by a short strand of pearls. Her blond-auburn hair is parted and falls to her shoulders. Her face looks warm and generous—not a model's face, but with a Mona Lisa smile and cheerful blue eyes.

Through the years, there was Clark family speculation that Huguette was in love with her handsome Cher Maître, or that he was in lust with her. Tadé Styka was mentioned occasionally in newspapers as a possible suitor of celebrities and the wealthy. In early 1923, when Huguette was just sixteen and Tadé was thirty-four, he was named as a rival to Charlie Chaplin for the affections of the sultry Polish actress Pola Negri, whom he had painted many times. But she moved on to the film heartthrob Rudolph Valentino, and Tadé wouldn't marry until the 1940s.

BILL

T WENTY-YEAR-OLD HUGUETTE was the most prominent debutante introduced to New York society in December 1926. Her father's estate had been settled. She was free now to find a husband.

A newspaper cartoon imagined the life of Huguette, the "spoiled little rich girl." Breakfast in bed served by a French waitress. Stepping into her limousine, bound for a shopping tour to spend $333 a day. Donning gorgeous evening clothes and setting out for the opera. Attending a deb-

Huguette poses for a photograph in her debutante days, a time when young ladies were presented to society so they could attract a husband. She graduated from high school at a time when most of the girls at Miss Spence's planned to get married, but in a few years most in the graduating classes were looking forward to college.

utante dance, where, because of her wealth and beauty, she is the center of attention.

In truth, Huguette focused more attention on her fellow Spence alumnae, playing hostess for luncheon parties for her debutante friends at Pierre's French restaurant. A newspaper society photograph inadvertently captured her. The photo concentrates on a beautiful young woman in a sleeveless gown, seated at the center of a party, smiling as two tuxedoed young men ask her to dance. The woman is not Huguette, although she is in the photo, sitting off to the side, out of the limelight. And in the background of the party, another man sits by himself. His name is Bill Gower.

In December 1927, Mrs. W. A. Clark announced the engagement of her daughter, Huguette Marcelle, to William MacDonald Gower. Bill was a year older than Huguette, a tall, not unattractive man. They had known each other since they were children. There are signs that it may have been an arranged marriage, an attempt by Anna to find someone close to the family to wed her quiet daughter. Or it may have been an attempt to separate Huguette from any possible entanglement with Tadé Styka, her painting instructor. It could have just been time for marriage, and this was the young man she liked.

This was not the usual Clark marriage. W.A.'s children from his first marriage had aimed higher, shooting for European royalty or its American equivalent. When Katherine married a descendant of a signer of the Declaration of Independence, W.A. gave her a present of $4 million in

Huguette's husband, Bill Gower, was a Princeton graduate and law student working as a clerk on Wall Street. They wed at Bellosguardo in 1928, when Huguette was twenty-two and Bill twenty-three.

real estate and issued six thousand invitations to her wedding, held just two weeks after he was forced to resign from the Senate.

The Gowers were certainly not poor. They lived in suburban New Rochelle, had a Park Avenue apartment, and spent summers playing pinochle and tennis in Lake Placid, New York. Bill had been on the track team and active in theatricals at the elite Trinity School in Manhattan and then received his Princeton degree in history at age twenty, one of the youngest members of the class of 1925. While studying law at Columbia, he was employed at thirty dollars a week at the firm of J. & W. Seligman, an investment bank that had financed Jay Gould's railroads and the Panama Canal. While the bride-to-be was a Roman Catholic and the daughter of a Democratic senator, her fiancé was a Presbyterian and a Republican.

Bill was also the son of W. A. Clark's accountant, William Bleckly Gower, the longtime comptroller of the United Verde and twenty other mining companies. As part of his service to the Clarks, the elder Gower had presented a paper at the American Mining Congress in Denver in 1920 strategizing how to fight the onerous burden of taxes placed on

IN CONVERSATION WITH HUGUETTE

Huguette recalled the 1925 earthquake in Santa Barbara in a conversation in August 1999, as she had been watching TV news of the devastating earthquake in Turkey. She was nineteen when the quake struck California.

"I was in Santa Barbara during the 1925 earthquake. . . . Thirteen people were killed. . . . The movie theater we used to go to—that all came down. Imagine! Many people would have been killed. . . . It was six in the morning, so many people were saved."

You were at Bellosguardo in Santa Barbara at the time? I asked.

"Yes. That's why Mother built another house, because it wasn't very solid. . . . It was something, you know, all that shaking. Terrible, yes. But it was nothing in comparison to Turkey."

W.A. and other mine owners by World War I, the same war that was making them rich. Because Huguette was now a co-owner of the Clark empire she had inherited from her father, her employee would now be her father-in-law.

Huguette in her wedding gown, 1928.

· · ·

Huguette had the experience of an elaborate society wedding in New York, but not as a bride. When she was seventeen, in January 1924, she was a bridesmaid for her half-niece, Katherine Morris Hall. And in 1928, Huguette was again a bridesmaid for a friend, Emily Hall Tremaine, who became a prominent art collector and patron of Jasper Johns and Andy Warhol. Emily credited Huguette with introducing her to great art and the value of artistic expression. At Emily's wedding, Huguette was dressed in a pink taffeta frock and a Juliet cap; she carried spring flowers.

Her own wedding was a private one, held in Santa Barbara at the Clark summer home, Bellosguardo. W.A. and Anna had vacationed on the California coast with Huguette in 1923 and then decided to buy a home there. A few months after W.A.'s death in 1925, the home was shaken in the June earthquake, which burst a dam and started a fire, destroying much of Santa Barbara's downtown. After the earthquake, Anna began making plans to renovate and expand the home, but it remained livable enough for Huguette's wedding.

Mr. and Mrs. William Gower were married by a Catholic priest on August 18, 1928. The bride wore a formal white gown of lace with a nearly endless cathedral train. The Santa Barbara newspaper, *The Morning Press,* struggled for any scraps of news: "Miss Clark and her mother have been at their Santa Barbara home, Bellosguardo, since their return from Europe early this summer and have taken an active part in the summer social life. . . . The wedding will be extremely quiet."

Her maid of honor, one of the few guests other than family, was the wife of Dr. Lyle, the Clark family physician. The groom was twenty-three, the bride twenty-two. A special car was ready for the honeymoon. Anna had bought a gray-green 1927 Rolls-Royce with silver door handles and a black leather top. It cost $25,750, or about $300,000 in today's dollars. This was the Phantom I, a town car in which the driver sat out in the open air while the passengers enjoyed the comfort and quiet in the salon, as the rear passenger seat was called. The Clark chauffeur, Walter Armstrong, described driving Huguette and Bill around the West before the couple left from San Francisco on a honeymoon cruise to Hawaii, accompanied by the bride's governess, Madame Sandré.

Huguette and Bill were accosted by a newspaper photographer. They posed awkwardly. And then Huguette was trapped for a photo alone. She stands swathed in fur, clutching her handbag tightly, her usual strand of pearls around her neck, her wrists decorated by Cartier Art Deco bracelets of diamonds and emeralds. She looks most uncomfortable.

This was not the last photograph taken of Huguette, but it was the last the public would see while she lived for the next eight decades.

. . .

At home again in New York, the newlyweds moved into her mother's building, 907 Fifth Avenue, with their wedding gifts, including a fifteen-inch sterling silver serving platter with Huguette's new monogram, "H.C.G.," and their wedding date, "8-18-1928." They took a subscription to Box 9 for matinees at the Metropolitan Opera, and Tadé Styka painted Bill Gower's portrait.

"No married couple," the *New York Herald* opined, "ever started married life under more brilliant auspices."

Within nine months, the newspapers had caught on to a split. Bill was back with his parents on Park Avenue. A typical newspaper headline of the time read: "Why America's $50,000,000 Heiress Cast Off Her $30-a-Week Prince Charming."

Some papers blamed the groom. "Those who should know whereof they speak tell me the cause for the failure of the union of nine months can be laid directly at young Gower's door," wrote a gossip columnist. Others said Huguette was simply interested in art, while he was interested in finance. The story among Huguette's half-siblings was that she didn't want what marriage implied, physically. The same bell was rung in a bitter tell-all biography of W. A. Clark and his family in 1939: "Huguette refused to consummate the marriage." The author, William D. Mangam, must have gotten his information from his former employer and law school buddy, Huguette's half-brother Will, who lived all the way across the country in Los Angeles.

Yet Mangam may have been right. Seventy years later, Huguette would be asked about her brief marriage by her nurse, Hadassah Peri. An immigrant, the nurse summarized Huguette's answer in broken English: "It didn't stay long. On my honeymoon, I have to go home."

To FORMALLY END HER MARRIAGE, Huguette left New York by private railcar, headed for Reno, Nevada. Anna went with her. It was May 1930, nearly two years after her wedding, though the couple had already been separated for more than a year. Before leaving on the trip, Huguette completed the purchase of a painting, one of Monet's Water Lilies, from a dealer in Paris.

Divorces were difficult to obtain everywhere in the United States in the early 1900s, especially in heavily Roman Catholic states such as New York, where the only legal ground for dissolving a marriage was

Newspapers speculated about the reasons for Huguette and Bill's Reno divorce in 1930. This article says the heiress was more interested in art, and the young financial clerk more interested in making a fortune. The floor plan shows the Reno hotel floor Huguette and her mother occupied.

adultery. These restrictions presented a business opportunity for states willing to grant divorces easily with short residency requirements. Before Nevada had gambling, it had divorce. In 1927, it had reduced its residency rule to three months, solidifying the state's status as "the Great Divide." Before the decade ended, more than thirty thousand couples had "Reno-vated" their marriages.

Though the Clarks kept to themselves for their three months in Reno, their desire for privacy attracted attention. The town usually yawned at wealthy divorce vacationers—Cornelius Vanderbilt, Jr., had made do in Reno with a single room—but Huguette and Anna rented an entire floor of the fashionable Riverside Hotel, arriving with a retinue of six servants. One headline summarized crisply, "Reno Agog."

The deed was done on August 11, 1930, with a quick visit to court. Bill did not appear to contest the divorce, which in the court papers was ascribed to his alleged desertion.

Her divorce secured, Huguette sailed again from San Francisco to Honolulu, this time with her mother, on a reverse Hawaiian honeymoon.

DISSOLUTION

T HE W. A. CLARK BUSINESS EMPIRE was not built for longevity, collapsing soon after its founder handed it to his children.

While his Gilded Age contemporaries typically operated through hierarchies of executives and managers, creating vast corporate entities, W.A. ran his companies as essentially sole proprietorships, which he ruled autocratically. Having attended to every detail of his companies personally W.A. failed in succession planning.

In August 1928, three years after W.A. died, his heirs cashed out of the Clark interests in Montana, selling out to his longtime opponent, the Anaconda Company, which had taken over the Daly interests. Now the Clarks had no real connection to Montana except Will's lakefront lodge. They still held the family's largest asset, the United Verde copper mine in Arizona.

Sons were expected to take over a business, but W.A.'s two sons were dissolute in their personal habits and enthusiasms. And they were not blessed with their father's longevity.

Charlie Clark, the older son and chairman of the United Verde Copper Company, lived like a European prince. His drinking, gambling, and womanizing were well chronicled. He had his own private racetrack at his San Mateo estate, El Palomar, and the longest private railcar ever built, which he sold to Howard Hughes. Charlie married three times and gave hardly anything to charity. He died of pneumonia in April 1933 in New York, at age sixty-one, having never achieved the sobriety his father hoped for him.

His younger brother had pursuits of a more intellectual sort. W.A. Jr., known as Will, had a law degree from the University of Virginia, ran minor industries with his father's financing in Montana, and was vice president of the United Verde. After settling in Los Angeles in 1907, Will built an elaborate jewel-box Italian Renaissance library with rare books on shelves made of copper. He specialized in seventeenth- and eighteenth-century English literature, and also built perhaps the finest collection pertaining to Oscar Wilde. A music lover and skilled violin-ist, Will founded the Los Angeles Philharmonic Orchestra in 1919 and subsidized it for its first eight years of operation. He was also a major donor in the construction of the Hollywood Bowl, an outdoor amphi-theater.

Will died in June 1934 at age fifty-seven of a heart attack at his Mo-witza Lodge in Montana. At his funeral in Los Angeles, his father's favorite poem, "Thanatopsis," was read by a Shakespearean actor. He was laid to rest in the most exquisite private mausoleum in Los Angeles, on an island in the center of a scenic pond at Hollywood Memorial Park Cemetery.

Will's reputation was marred after his death by the tell-all biography published by a college friend and former employee, William Mangam. Will was labeled as a binge drinker and a profligate and reckless homo-sexual and chaser of much younger men. Such claims were more shock-ing in the Los Angeles of the 1930s than today, and their truth has not been established. Mangam made other conjectures that turned out to be wrong. We have only his word, because Will's papers were burned after his death.

His generosity is better documented. He willed his home compound and his library to the public institution that became the University of California, Los Angeles. He gave a building to the University of Nevada, Reno, to honor his first wife, and another to the University of Virginia to honor his second. A statue of Beethoven marks Will's founding of the Philharmonic—in unusual fashion for a Clark, he said he didn't want a statue of himself. The statue now stands forlornly in a remote corner of Pershing Square, a gathering area for the city's homeless.

Will Clark left little to his relatives, and a large share of his estate went to the seventeen-year-old son of his housekeeper. George Palé, child of a Basque immigrant whose husband had abandoned her, was eight or nine when he met Will, who paid for his schooling. They spent most weekends together, and George spent weeks during the summer at the lodge in Montana. After Will's own son died in 1932, Will began to talk of adopting George, with George's mother's permission. He began signing his letters "Your father" and "Daddy Clark." He also referred to

George fondly as "Sonny" and "General Pershing," reflecting the family's fondness for the general who saved France. Will's letters to young George show a touching paternal love. George explained, "Mr. Clark told me that I filled a void in his heart after the death of his son." After receiving his inheritance, George married a trombonist's daughter from the Los Angeles Philharmonic and named his first son Clark.

The family's best hope for an executive had been Will's only child, the manager of the United Verde. W. A. Clark III was known as Billy, or within the family as Tertius, the Latin word for third. In May 1932, at age twenty-nine, W. A. Clark III died while taking flying lessons with Jack Lynch, a former barnstorming buddy of Charles Lindbergh. It's not clear who was at the controls, but Clark and Lynch were practicing flying blind, with the windshield covered, just as Lindbergh had flown from New York to Paris in 1927 with a gas tank blocking his forward view. They crashed near Clemenceau, Arizona, not far from the United Verde mine. Tertius's young wife saw the plane go down.

This run of male self-destruction left the empire in the hands of W.A.'s daughters, who showed little interest in business. Katherine died in 1933, May had no husband or son with business experience, and Huguette was in her twenties.

Although copper was at a historic low price during the Depression days of 1935, May and Huguette sold off the United Verde mine in Arizona. The last mine of W. A. Clark, who had built a model company town with good healthcare and fair wages for his workers, was sold to the Phelps Dodge Corporation, notorious for its anti-union activity.

W. A. Clark's empire had been dissolved, and his name drifted toward obscurity. The abandoned home of his grandson W.A. III outside the model mining town of Clarkdale remained vacant for eighty years. It was eventually used as a set for a low-budget film about a haunted brothel and in 2010 was destroyed by fire.

· · ·

In Montana, the legacy of W. A. Clark is still debated.

First, mining is a proud part of the state's history. Fourteen steel structures from the mines still rise over Butte today. These headframes were used to support the ten-ton cables that hoisted men, mules, and equipment in and out of the mines. The men called them gallows frames, employing the dark humor of workers toiling in a deadly environment. But they are the symbols of Butte as surely as the Eiffel Tower is Paris.

Butte is still paying for its copper past. The Clark Fork is today America's largest Superfund environmental disaster site. The Clark Fork ends its 479-mile journey at the Pend Oreille River, where W.A. hauled the mail, exclaiming at the beauty, "The firmament sheweth His handiwork." It begins that journey as Silver Bow Creek, near the Butte mines. Water and wind spread the copper arsenic, cadmium, nickel, and lead, from the mines and smelters of Butte and Anaconda more than a hundred miles downstream, killing fish and fouling drinking water. Remediation of the watershed has been under way for thirty years, at a cost of nearly a billion dollars. One can still find blue-green sediment alongside the river.

Some locals lay more of the blame on Marcus Daly and his Anaconda Copper Mining Company, which remained in business longer and left more reminders. There's "the Stack," a massive brick smokestack built in 1919 and still standing in Anaconda, northwest of Butte, a relic nearly sixty stories tall and easily large enough to fit the Washington Monument inside it. Today the Stack is the centerpiece of Anaconda Smoke Stack State Park, a monument too toxic to allow any visitors close by.

The successor to Daly's Anaconda Company turned several Butte neighborhoods into an open strip mine, the Berkeley Pit, in 1955. After W.A.'s Columbia Gardens burned in a suspicious fire in 1973, the pit expanded, gobbling up the gardens so dear to W.A. and the community. The new owners, the Atlantic Richfield Company (ARCO), shut down the mine in 1982 in the face of foreign competition, but the Berkeley Pit remained, slowly filling with water contaminated with sulfuric acid, arsenic, and lead. Now it's a massive lake, a Superfund disaster site with a viewing stand for tourists. Hundreds of migrating snow geese died after landing in the pit, so recorded gunfire is played at intervals to keep birds away.

W.A. had his own smelter smokestack, the tallest in the world, spreading its arsenical debris far from his "smoky city." Worse for his reputation, he moved to New York, selling most of his Montana mining interests to the Standard Oil men in 1910.

"The cumulative sentiment here," said Keith Edgerton, a professor of history at Montana State University who is researching a Clark biography, "is that he made a fortune off of the state's resources in the free-wheeling laissez-faire times of the late nineteenth century, prostituted the political system with his wealth and power, exploited the working class for his own gain, left an environmental wreck behind, and took his millions to other places to benefit a handful of others. And in some ways, the state has never really recovered from it all."

Clark never acknowledged any awareness of such resentments. He described himself as one of "those men, those brave pioneers who have come out here and made the wilderness bloom as the rose, and opened up these great mountains and brought their hidden wealth to light."

THE GODDAUGHTERS, LEONTINE AND ANN

WITH ONE DAUGHTER DECEASED and the other occupied with her painting, Anna befriended other children, two goddaughters, who came to her apartment for weekend lunches and chamber music concerts.

The first goddaughter, Leontine Lyle, was also known as Tina. She was born in 1926, twenty years after Huguette, and was the daughter of the family physician, Dr. Lyle, who had attended to Andrée and W.A. at their deaths.

The second, Ann Ellis, born in 1928, was the daughter of the family attorney, George Ellis, of Clark, Carr & Ellis, a law firm that had represented the Clarks for many years.

Anna invited Leontine and Ann, usually one at a time, over for Sunday lunches or private chamber music concerts. The girls would put on their party dresses and shiny black patent leather shoes for an afternoon among the Renoirs. Both goddaughters called Anna "Lani" (LAH-nee), which she fancifully told them meant "godmother" in Hawaiian.

They ate in the formal dining room, with place cards in silver holders to mark their spots. Water was poured into crystal glasses from a Tiffany pitcher. Bread was served in a double-ended sterling silver barge engraved "W.A.C." and stamped on the bottom with the Clark crest (the lion, anchor, and Gothic *C*).

They loved Anna, both goddaughters recall. She gently corrected their manners, watching the placement of every silver butter knife, being very firm that they were not to drink if they had food in their mouths, and to sip, not gulp.

The lunches were not about etiquette alone. As the years passed, Anna wanted to soak up every detail of their lives: school, boys, their débuts, dating, marriage. Anna gave Leontine a Cartier gold watch for her debutante season and sent her personal assistant, Adele Marie, known as "Missie," to Bergdorf Goodman to buy clothes for Leontine's wedding. "She was to me a completely caring person, beyond belief generous," Leontine said. "You never felt the generosity had a string attached."

She recalled, "One day I can remember clearly, I was almost in tears. I wanted Mummy to let me have a dog, and I was telling Lani all this, at age thirteen or fourteen, very dramatic. And the next thing I knew, three days later, a miniature black poodle arrived at the house, with instructions that it was not to be returned. We called it Parie, like Paris."

Both goddaughters remember Anna as stunning, mannered, very French, immaculately dressed, trim, tactful, and not at all nouveau riche. There was no talk of Butte or Jerome, no talk of Butte copper or political scandals. There was no talk of where Anna came from either, no mention of Calumet or Quebec. Her French-accented English sounded Parisian to their ears. "It never occurred to me," Leontine said, "that she was anything but French."

The goddaughters remember Huguette shyly stopping by their little parties with Anna, but only once did she stay for lunch. Ann remembers Huguette sending her gifts, but not to her taste: "horrible, formal dolls." These weren't Huguette's friends, but the very young friends of her mother. They knew nothing of her paintings or art projects. "She was a waif that passed through the room," Ann said. "A fairy light that came and went."

· · ·

Once you were Anna's friend, you stayed friends. This was a trait Huguette inherited. Anna talked regularly on the phone with Leontine's mother, the widow of the family doctor, and sent her checks for years. After Anna died, Huguette kept on sending the checks, increasing the amounts.

Both goddaughters, born in the decade after the Nineteenth Amendment gave all American women the right to vote, seized on new opportunities. Ann Ellis Raynolds raised four children, then went back to school for a doctorate and became an instructor in psychiatry on the Harvard Medical School faculty and a professor at Boston University. Leontine Lyle Harrower worked on the staff of Senator Prescott Bush of Connecticut, father of a president and grandfather of another. She served on the Republican National Committee and worked in the gu-

Anna hosted many musical afternoons at 907 Fifth Avenue, the luxury apartment building at Seventy-Second Street and Central Park. Eventually Huguette had fifteen thousand square feet.

bernatorial campaign of Nelson Rockefeller of New York, the grandson of W.A.'s contemporary John D. Rockefeller.

The only foray into politics by Anna and Huguette seemed to be in 1940, when they supported the Republican presidential candidate Wendell Willkie, who was urging greater American intervention to stop Germany in Europe. This policy would have appealed to the Francophile Clarks, who each gave $5,000 to Democrats for Willkie—the largest contributions in New York. Anna and Huguette, the wife and daughter of a U.S. senator, never registered to vote.

Only now, the goddaughters say, have they begun to realize that Anna's relationship with them was a bit odd. "It seems strange," Leontine said, "that so much attention was paid to a little girl. In a funny way, I filled a need, like a surrogate daughter. There was a sadness there."

These girls were the daughters of the family doctor and lawyer, prominent but not in the same social class as the Clarks. As Ann's father explained to her, in his legal work for rich families he was merely a servant. But that sort of distinction didn't seem to matter to Anna. Nevertheless, Leontine said, it was odd that Anna restricted her social circle so tightly to people paid by the family: the family doctor, the family lawyer. Anna made some friends through music and art but seemed not to be comfortable developing relationships unless she was the boss. Perhaps these friendships showed an admirable sort of class neutrality on Anna's part, but also a kind of self-limiting only to circumstances she could control.

And then Leontine stopped speculating and said, "It's too complicated. You can't know someone's mind."

THE STAFF

In 1940, there were ten servants in residence at 907 Fifth Avenue to take care of a family of two. Well, actually, a family of three, because an aunt of Anna's, Pauline De Lobel, had moved in. A few of the servants lived in the two apartments with Anna and Huguette, but most were in the small rooms on the roof. Here are those thirteen residents, as enumerated by the census taker, with their birthplace and education. Notice the countries where the staff hail from, and which country is missing from the list.

The family:

Anna E. Clark, 62, widow, Michigan, one year of high school.
Huguette Clark, 33, divorced, France, four years of high school.
Pauline De Lobel, 65, widow, Belgium, grade eight.

And the staff:

Helen Ives, personal maid, 52, single, England, salary $1,500/
year, grade eight.

Hilda Carlson, personal maid, 48, single, Sweden, $1,080, grade eight.

Shyra Golden, cook, 40, widow, Sweden, $1,080, two years of high school.

James Smith, butler, 38, widower, New York, $1,010, grade eight.

Anna Flatley, waitress, 36, single, Ireland/Galway, $1,008, one year of high school.

Joseph Jones, chauffeur, 42, single, New York, $980, grade eight.

Margaret Duffy, parlor maid, 39, single, Northern Ireland, $960, grade eight.

Paula Hauger, cook, 57, single, Norway, $900, grade eight.

Gurbild Berker, assistant cook, 34, widow, Sweden, $840, one year of high school.

Anna Erickson, chamber maid, 27, single, Finland, $840, grade eight.

Which country is missing from the list of the staff? France. The Clarks could keep confidences by speaking and writing in French.

The Clarks paid wages slightly better than was typical in the building. An annual salary of $1,000 in 1940 would be equal to about $16,400 today, not counting room and board. Their downstairs friend and neighbor, Margaret Price Daly, widow of W.A.'s old antagonist Marcus Daly, made do with a staff of only five.

O NE MIGHT HAVE GUESSED that Anna, as the much younger second wife, would have had little connection with W.A.'s children from his first marriage. Indeed, the terms "gold dig- ger" and "adventuress" were thrown around a bit in some quarters of the family, but quite a few Clarks speak of Anna fondly, remembering her as vivacious, a warm hostess, a lot of fun at a cocktail party, and a bit salty in her humor. Even the closest Clarks, however, never developed a connection with Anna's daughter Huguette.

In the years between the world wars, Anna often invited the children of her stepson Charlie Clark over for musical afternoons in Apartment 8W at 907 Fifth Avenue. She enjoyed playing the harp and gossiping about music and musicians with Charlie's three daughters, Mary, Agnes, and Patsey. They were close to Huguette in age, her half-nieces, though that sort of "half-niece" phrase was not one the family ever used. Raised in California, all three had spent some time in New York with Huguette at Miss Spence's, and attended debutante parties at Pierre's. Huguette said later that she was very fond of Agnes and her sisters and that her mother had continued to invite the nieces for short summer visits to Santa Barbara so the girls could stay in touch.

The next generation, however, never made much of a connection with their great-aunt Huguette. Patsey's son, Jerry Gray, recalled a time in the early 1940s when a group of them were sitting on the sand or in low chairs near the beach house at Bellosguardo. He was about nine and Huguette was in her thirties. Anna was animated and participated in the conversation, but Huguette, staring silently at him, never said a word. Afterward, Jerry's father said, "She has never been able to grow up." And his mother said, "It's so sad that all she can do is play with dolls."

Huguette's attachment to her dolls was indeed unusual. A photograph survives of a Clark dinner party in a restaurant, with a group including Anna and Huguette, who looks to be about sixteen, so this would be about 1922. Anna is recognizable in her bangs, resting her chin on her white-gloved hand. One of Huguette's half-nieces, wearing a corsage, is also at the table. The three gentlemen in the photo are dressed in black tie. Seated at the right, next to one of the men, is Huguette, wearing a party dress and a strand of pearls, her eyes fixed on something in the distance. In her lap, she holds a doll with well-coiffed coal-black hair, wearing its own party dress.

Family members began to say Huguette was "slow" or "emotionally immature." Her father was too old when she was conceived, they'd say, or she must have been damaged by her sister's death or her brief marriage. The children in the family heard these stories and accepted them as fact, having little other information to go on. They knew nothing of her life, of her painting. Some in the next generation didn't even know that Huguette ever had a sister.

Huguette was well aware of her relatives. She knew the names of the children and grandchildren. When she saw photos, she expressed concern when a relative seemed to appear in failing health.

After the death, in 2002, of her half-niece Agnes Clark Albert, who had gone to Miss Spence's with her, Huguette sent a handwritten card to Agnes's son.

Dear Paul. Your kind letter regarding your dear mother deeply touched me. Your mother was a very remarkable person and had such great talent as a musician. I admired her greatly and was very fond of her. You had reason to be very proud of her. With my very deepest sympathy, Dear Paul, and much love. Tante Huguette.

Small acts of generosity were observed but didn't change the family narrative. Another of Charlie's grandchildren, Jacqueline Baeyens-Clerté, was about ten when she met Huguette at an afternoon tea at Bellosguardo in 1952. Huguette and Anna were excited to be spending time with these relatives living in France. "Aunt Huguette was very shy," Jacqueline recalled, "and her mother did all the talking." Without prompting, however, Huguette gave Jacqueline and her cousin tiny cameras as welcoming gifts.

For the most part, however, Huguette kept her distance through the decades. She sent flowers to a list of friends every New Year—azaleas or triple amaryllises—but there were no relatives on the list. She called a few relatives at Christmas and Easter. And when relatives called occasionally to invite her out, she would beg off with an excuse that became a running joke in the family. Each time she would say in French, *"Je suis enrhumée"*—"I have a little cold."

. . .

The most detailed family memory of a visit to 907 Fifth Avenue was told by Huguette's niece Agnes, and is relayed by her daughter Karine. It's a story of a valuable painting and of rare musical instruments, and it reveals something of the family dynamic between Huguette and her mother. In one afternoon shopping trip, Anna made it easier for her daughter to spend more time with her, and she founded one of the noted chamber music groups of the twentieth century.

Anna was mad about chamber music, quite an unusual avocation for someone with only an eighth-grade education. She sang choral music with her low contralto voice as a member of the Oratorio Society of New York. She was a dedicated student of the harp, taking afternoon lessons at her Fifth Avenue apartment, precisely at four o'clock, from Marcel Grandjany, a Frenchman who taught at the Juilliard School in New York. Grandjany was an influential composer and teacher on a difficult and little understood instrument and may be the third-best-known harpist of all time, after King David and Harpo Marx. He dedicated many works to his patron, Anna, and later to her daughter Huguette, including a suite based on "La Belle au Bois Dormant," or "Sleeping Beauty."

For years, nothing prevented Anna from going out to hear chamber music—not for the society, not to be seen, but for Haydn and Brahms and Debussy. On one occasion, a musician recalled, she attended a three P.M. matinee at the Town Hall in New York, stayed in her seat awaiting the five-thirty twilight concert, and was back for the evening recital at eight-thirty.

But as Anna moved into her sixties, her hearing grew dismal. She used the latest newfangled hearing aid, an electronic box that she held out to pick up sound, with a wire attached to her ear. Anna began to take her music only at home, inviting musicians to play at 907 Fifth Avenue.

Huguette sometimes came downstairs to her mother's apartment for the music, but rarely for the conversation.

One of the musicians who encountered Huguette on these musical afternoons was violinist Henri Temianka, who offered a memory of meeting her. He said Huguette "was strangely withdrawn and had the curious habit of maneuvering backward while engaged in conversation." As they spoke in one of the large rooms in Anna's apartment, Huguette stepped back, and the violinist stepped forward, continuing the conversation, "executing a series of mincing steps that ultimately landed her and her partner in conversation at the opposite end of the room."

One afternoon in December 1945, just after the end of the Second World War, Anna had a few guests over to 907 Fifth Avenue for one of her home concerts. But the events of that afternoon were most unusual, as Anna found a clever way to solve two problems with a single excursion.

The first problem was Madame Cézanne.

"You see Cézanne's portrait of Madame Cézanne?" Anna told her guests. "My daughter Huguette won't come in here because she hates the painting so much."

Anna had bought *Madame Cézanne in a Red Dress*, one of Paul Cézanne's portraits of his longtime mistress and eventual wife, many years earlier from a Paris dealer. Apparently, Cézanne didn't have much understanding of women, and his wife didn't much care for his paintings of her. One can see why. In this depiction, she is an awkward subject with disfigured hands and a confused or worried look in her eyes. Still, there is something tender or vulnerable in her affect, which is not nearly as angry as in the well-known *Woman in a Green Hat* or as grotesque as in *Madame Cézanne with Unbound Hair*. Yet, as Karine tells the story, something in Madame Cézanne's look bothered Huguette, who came downstairs to visit her mother less often than Anna would have liked.

The second problem was how to outfit a new string quartet with proper instruments.

Anna and Huguette had long sponsored musicians, including the well-regarded Loewenguth String Quartet in Paris, for whom Huguette wrote a check to buy four instruments made by the renowned Amati

*Because this portrait of a stern Madame
Cézanne was off-putting to Huguette,
Anna found a clever use for it.*

family. Word of the Clark patronage got around, and it was not unusual
for musicians to play at Anna's apartment.

Anna had been introduced to a cellist in need of a quartet, a cellist
who she had thought was dead. Robert Maas was well known for his Pro
Arte Quartet of Brussels, which Anna had followed closely. Maas had
been reported as killed soon after the Germans invaded Belgium in
1940, but he was only wounded. Stranded in his native country, he was
ordered by the Nazis to form a quartet with German musicians. He refused and spent the war playing for meal money in a café in Brussels,
while his Pro Arte colleagues escaped to Wisconsin.

Maas was a forceful cellist, his immense bald head leaning forward as
he drove his bow "deep into the strings to produce a tone of unique vi-
brancy and breadth," as one fellow player described him. "Yet, for all his
dramatic power and fervor, his playing was characterized by classic reserve and impeccable taste."

On that afternoon in 1945, with the Germans and Japanese defeated,

Maas was in New York, in Anna's living room, playing Bach sonatas. He was a frequent guest, as Anna had grown quite fond of him. Maas was accompanied on the 1940 Steinway grand piano by Agnes, Huguette's niece.

"Robert," Anna said to Maas, "you must form another string quartet." If he did, she promised to fund it. But what instruments would the new quartet play, instruments befitting the quality of the players and the reputation of their patron?

Maas told Anna that he had seen four remarkable instruments at the New York studio of Emil Herrmann, a dealer in rare instruments. All were made by Antonio Stradivari in Cremona, Italy, between 1680 and 1736, and all had been owned by the Italian violinist and composer Niccolò Paganini in the 1800s. The four had been split up, sold off by Paganini's heir and illegitimate son. Herrmann had reassembled the group and would sell them only if they stayed together. But who could afford to buy four Stradivarius instruments at once?

Anna immediately took Madame Cézanne down from the wall and called for the chauffeur. A couple of hours later, she returned home to find Robert Maas and Agnes Albert still playing sonatas. She told them she had gone to Fifty-Seventh Street and Madison Avenue, to Knoedler & Co., one of the favored galleries of the Clarks and their peers. There she had sold Madame Cézanne. We're not sure what she got for the portrait, but it was enough to continue on to her second errand, on West Fifty-Seventh Street near Carnegie Hall, where she spent $200,000 at Emil Herrmann's penthouse studio.

Anna and the chauffeur were carrying four instruments in their cases—each three hundred years old, with finely carved maple backs and thick orange varnish: two violins, an exceptionally rare Stradivarius viola, and, for Maas, a cello, inscribed inside in Latin in the hand of Antonio Stradivari himself: "Made in my ninety-third year." These were among the finest musical instruments in the world, and Anna had bought them on a whim with the money from the Cézanne.

"Now, Robert," she said, "you have a wonderful quartet of Strads to use. Go and form a string quartet."

At that moment was born the Paganini Quartet, which recorded for RCA Victor, performed the full Beethoven quartet cycle in six concerts at the Library of Congress, and presented public concerts in halls around the world.

In addition to founding a world-class quartet, Anna had removed an impediment to her daughter coming downstairs to visit.

Besides, the Clarks had another Cézanne.

Sometimes even Huguette's closest niece couldn't get in to see her. One day in the mid-1950s, Agnes brought her children by to visit, but Huguette said she had a little cold. Not one to take no for an answer, Agnes sent word through the doorman that she would go out by the street and wave to Huguette. So there they stood on the sidewalk along Fifth Avenue, waving up at the twelfth-floor windows, unable to see whether Huguette was waving back.

SIXTEEN FIRST DATES

FTER HER DIVORCE, Huguette reclaimed her maiden name, but she kept the "Mrs.," perhaps indicating that she was no longer in the market for a husband. For the rest of her life, her staff called her Mrs. Clark or Madame Clark, in the French style of extending that title of marriage to older, unmarried women.

There were newspaper accounts in 1931, apparently false, that Huguette was ready to wed an Irish nobleman named Edward FitzGerald, the Seventh Duke of Leinster. The duke, a compulsive gambler and ne'er-do-well, later admitted in court that he was bankrupt when he came to America "with the idea of marrying someone rich." He died by suicide, penniless.

Not that a marriage for Huguette was out of the question. Anna made further attempts to find her daughter a husband, even into Huguette's forties, but only within a carefully circumscribed group of friends, even relatives. She was scheduled to go on dates with one young man in particular, appointments that became a comical series of sixteen attempted first dates.

Anna's dear sister, Amelia, was married to T. Darrington Semple, the treasurer of suburban Westchester County, New York. It was Amelia's third marriage and his second. He had a son, T. Darrington, Jr., known as Darry, who served in the Army Air Corps during World War II, graduated from Harvard, and studied law in Alabama. Darry was family, but not a blood relative, and he was twenty years younger than Huguette.

Speaking sixty years later from a nursing home in Montgomery, Alabama, Darry described how Anna and Amelia conspired to set him up on dates with Huguette. He said the Clarks were kind and generous, observing that "they gave money away like it was water." As for Huguette, he said, "from all the family stories, she was just shy, introverted, didn't like crowds. But very smart." Huguette was not unattractive, with her Japanese-print, floor-length summer dresses. He was willing to go out with her, but there were complications.

"I had sixteen dates to meet her, a proper social date," Darry said. "Every time, her hair wasn't right, or she had to do something else, or there was some other excuse. Every time, she couldn't go. Sixteen times it got called off at the last minute."

He soon found another woman to marry, and they had children and grandchildren. In 2010, when Huguette Clark was in the hospital at age 104 and Darry Semple was suffering from Parkinson's disease, both of them in the last year of their lives, he still had his sense of humor. "If I saw her now," he said, "I'd say, 'Let me know if you got your hair done.'"

He never knew that Huguette already had a boyfriend.

CHAPTER SEVEN

———

907 FIFTH AVENUE

· · ·

PART TWO

LOVE OF HALF A LIFE

T HE CLOSEST ROMANTIC CONNECTION of Huguette's life began on the beaches of Normandy. On their summer jaunts to Trouville before World War I, the Clarks made friends with a family by the name of Villermont. The grandfather was a painter, as were the mother and father, and they must have had much to discuss with the art-collecting Americans. The Villermonts were a proud old Roman Catholic family, with roots in the French nobility but not much money to show for it since the Revolution. One of their sons was just two years older than Huguette.

Etienne Allard de Villermont was called Etienne (pronounced AY-tyin), the French name for Stephen. Although Etienne and Huguette played together as school-age children, they didn't cement their friendship until he came to America in the 1930s.

Marquis Etienne de Villermont in 1936.

The Marquis de Villermont was a well-known name in the society columns of New York and Los Angeles from 1935 to 1944. He attended parties with Hollywood royals Errol Flynn and Pola Negri, and also with actual royalty: Russian princes, British countesses, and Indian maharajahs. And he was a frequent guest of Anna and Huguette Clark at society dinners, musical afternoons at 907 Fifth Avenue, and during their summer vacations at Bellosguardo in Santa Barbara.

Etienne was tall, with brown hair, a kind face, and a debonair manner. He looked dapper in his black bow tie, with a sharp jaw and high forehead. A French book about high-society parties in Trouville in the late 1930s described the marquis as a handsome man with a flair for playing the piano at parties.

In 1936, an announcement was made of the engagement of the French nobleman to an American heiress, not from a copper fortune but from coffee. Before there was Starbucks, there was Arbuckles', the first national coffee brand, known as "the cowboy's favorite." Etienne snagged an Arbuckles' heiress. Newspaper front pages across the country showed Etienne with tall redhead Claire Smith, who was known for wearing $1.5 million in jewels just for an average evening.

It was not unusual for Europeans of noble birth to come to America shopping for heiresses to refill their coffers, as the Irish duke had done in 1931 when his name was linked to Huguette's. The newspapers in 1936 said the coffee heiress had chosen the marquis over his best friend, a Russian prince. But a month later, Walter Winchell, the nation's best-known gossip columnist, said mysteriously that it had been called off.

In May 1939, Etienne was back in Winchell's "On Broadway" column in more than two thousand newspapers, with a new heiress: "The Marquis de Villermont and Huguett [*sic*] Clark probably will wed this summer." It had been three years since Etienne's engagement broke up, and nine years since Huguette was divorced. Both were now approaching their middle thirties.

Etienne's source of income was a bit vague. While Winchell said the marquis was "due for a post with the French Diplomatic Service," one newspaper said he was an importer of French perfumes. Another said he was representing France at the New York World's Fair in 1939–40, as the French fell under the thumb of the Nazis.

In fact, the family's greatest source of support was Anna Clark. W.A. and Anna had sent money to the Villermonts for decades. In 1942, during World War II, the Clarks apparently helped Etienne find a position with the new Vermont Copper Company, formed to take advantage of the wartime demand for the metal. Etienne became a naturalized U.S. citizen in 1943. The president of the copper company was a Clark attorney, the father of Anna's goddaughter Ann Ellis—who also visited the family in France in 1949, a visit arranged by Anna. She recalled Etienne as "a quite handsome Frenchman," and the family farm quite simple. Etienne's extended family kept mentioning how grateful they were to him for helping support them, Ann Ellis recalled, though she said it seemed clear that in fact the money was coming from Anna Clark.

Though Huguette never became the Marquise de Villermont, she remained deeply interested in royalty the rest of her life, a theme infusing her artwork and her reading. For one of her Japanese projects in the 1950s, she was ordering a silk costume for a marquise, the wife of a marquis, when her intermediary sent the bad news that noble titles had been abolished in Japan. Still, into old age, she was an avid reader of the magazines that follow the goings-on of the nobility.

Curiously, Etienne continued to be a frequent social guest of the Clarks. In 1941, he took a long train ride to the West Coast to visit Bellosguardo, and was their guest at a party for Santa Barbara's big fiesta, the Old Spanish Days. Gloria Vanderbilt was there, along with the dukes and duchesses of the Montecito summer colony.

It's hard to imagine that Anna broke up the marriage—tying her family to French nobility must have appealed to her, especially when she knew the Villermont family so well; and if she opposed the marriage, why would she still play host to Etienne at Bellosguardo? It's hard to imagine that Etienne ended it—why would he pass up a chance at a wealthy American bride? So it must have been Huguette who opposed the marriage—perhaps any marriage. After all, she never did marry again. There is one secondhand account that Huguette and Anna had a spat on that 1941 stay at Bellosguardo, and that Huguette's reclusivity became more pronounced when they returned to New York. "It was roughly right around there that she started, well, stopped coming out of the house." That's the story Huguette's personal assistant, Chris Sattler, said he heard decades later. But we can't be sure. Sattler knew no details, referring to the Marquis de Villermont as "the duke of something from France."

One could suppose that this connection between Etienne and Huguette was simply another nobleman's play for a fortune, if not for the fact that these two remained friends and pen pals for life. If Huguette Clark ever had a soul mate, he was the Marquis Etienne Allard de Villermont.

. . .

From the 1940s to the early 1980s, Huguette and Etienne exchanged hundreds of postcards, letters, and telegrams. Dozens of his notes to her survive, and a few of hers to him as well—mostly telegrams, nearly always in French. And their relationship was not only long-distance. Etienne crossed the Atlantic to New York a couple of times a year, staying in an apartment that it seems Huguette paid for.

They stayed in touch even after Etienne married in 1953 at age forty-nine. His wife, Elisabeth, got on with Huguette, and they corresponded as well. Elisabeth was sickly, and she and Etienne had separate bedrooms. Even though Etienne described himself to Huguette as "split emotionally," there is no hint in their correspondence that his relationship with her was a threat to his marriage.

On March 21, 1965, Etienne wrote to Huguette:

> *I join you through my thoughts, and neither distance nor time alters the bond of love of half a life, which will never disappear. . . . My encouragement comes from knowing that we will see each other again this year in New York.*

In February 1968, he sent Huguette a postcard with a picture of two young lovers about to kiss, protected from a shower of hearts by the

From Etienne de Villermont, writing in French to Huguette in 1965 from France: "I join you through my thoughts, and neither distance nor time alters the bond of love of half a life, which will never disappear. . . ."

broad white brim of the young woman's hat. The woman hides a gift behind her back in a white-gloved hand, and he offers a bouquet of roses. Etienne wrote, in French:

> *It's Valentine's Day and I am thinking of you with great affection.*
> *I send you this bouquet but the mimosas are under the snow. We will take the boat in the middle of March, the United States. It will be a joy to see you, I can't wait. I hope you are well, will try to call you.*

He added in English, "Much love, always, Etienne."

Like her mother, Huguette sent money to the Villermont family, $10,000 and $20,000 at a time, and even helped Etienne and Elisabeth adopt an orphaned girl born in 1962, Marie-Christine. Huguette began to shower the child with gifts: a bicycle, a stuffed toy donkey. Etienne sent back photos of himself with Marie-Christine. In one snapshot taken on a street corner in France, handsome Etienne is standing beside his little girl, buttoned up in her gray coat, and the toy donkey, both about the same size. They had named the donkey Cadichon after the mischievous character in a children's book.

TELEPHONE CONFIRMATION FILED JUL 17 338EST   JUL 17 1959

LT ETIENNE DE VILLERMONT BONNNEVILLE SUR TOUQUES PAR TOUQUES CALVADOS NORMANDIE

CHER ETIENNE J ESPERE QUE VOUS N AVEZ PAS TROP SOUFFERT DE LA GRANDE CHALEUR ET QUE TOUT VA BIEN ET QUE MA LETTRE VOUS EST BIEN ARRIVEE SERAIT CONTENTE D'AVOIR DE VOS NOUVELLES PENSE SERIEUSEMENT FAIRE UN PETIT SEJOUR EN FRANCE QU EN PENSEZ VOUS AFFECTUEUSEMENT

HUGUETTE

"Dear Etienne, I hope you have not suffered too much from the great heat and that all is well and that my letter has reached you. I would be happy to hear from you. I am thinking seriously of taking a short stay in France. What do you think of that? Affectionately, Huguette."

It doesn't appear that Huguette visited Etienne in France, or ever returned to her native country after a trip there with her mother in 1928, although she did consider making the journey. On July 17, 1959, she sent Etienne a telegram saying that she was planning a visit, one she apparently couldn't quite accomplish.

THE LAST PHOTOGRAPH taken of Huguette was not the uncomfortable one from the time of her marriage in 1928. She continued to have photos taken, but kept them inside the family. In her late thirties, she presented to Anna a portrait of herself standing elegantly in a Japanese-print floor-length gown, with the note, "To my darling Mother, With all my love, Huguette."

A devoted amateur photographer, Huguette bought for herself and friends the latest cameras—from the highest-end models of the 1930s to the newfangled instant Land Cameras introduced by Polaroid in 1948. She kept many snapshots of the gardens and rooms at the Clark summer home, Bellosguardo, and of the view across Central Park from No. 907. She studied the light, painstakingly recording on the backs of her prints the light and camera settings: "September 30, 1956, one floodlight, opening 4, counted four seconds."

On Easter and Christmas through her forties and fifties, she sat for photographs at home, perhaps self-portraits that she composed. Time after time, she placed a chair in a corner under a Cézanne still life, or sat by the 1940 Steinway piano topped with Easter flowers or a simple white Christmas tree. From year to year, the photos are nearly identical, although the costumes change and she ages. In one she is wearing high-heeled shoes and a smart, slimming dress with polka dots, in another a similar dress with sheer sleeves. Always her hair is in a wave, always a strand of pearls at her neck. Often a Japanese doll is standing on the bureau behind her.

Only one year did her mother participate in this photo session, late in Anna's life, perhaps in the early 1960s. In the photo, Anna stands alone in front of the still life. In place of the Japanese doll is a vase of flowers. Next to Anna is one of her magnificent golden French harps, much taller than she, even in her high heels and black Mamie Eisenhower dress with its sheer back. Her back is all we see, for Anna is facing away from the camera.

. . .

Anna Eugenia LaChapelle Clark died at New York's Mount Sinai Hospital on October 11, 1963, at age eighty-five, after several years of decline. The Catholic funeral Mass was private. In the newspapers, brief obituaries of Mrs. William Andrews Clark listed her only survivors: her sister, Amelia, and daughter, Huguette. Anna's last will and testament, carefully drawn up in 1960 and sealed with a purple ribbon and red wax, named four executors: Huguette along with Anna's brother-in-law, attorney, and banker. The will shows a devotion to her family, to her employees, and to charity. Most of the bequests were simple to carry out. Anna left sums of $12,000 to $20,000 each to her sister, her sister-in-law, and her nieces, all on the LaChapelle side. She provided for several friends and relatives by establishing trusts. She directed $50,000 to be set aside for each of her goddaughters, Leontine and Ann. Her former aide Adele Marie ("Missie") received $100,000, and other employees were remembered with smaller sums.

Among the charities, Anna left $125,000 to the Girl Scouts to support the memorial to her older daughter, Camp Andrée Clark; $100,000 to the Corcoran Gallery to support her husband's art collection; and $100,000 each to the United Hospital Fund of New York, the Red Cross, and the Juilliard School of Music. Smaller bequests included $10,000 to the Franciscan Friars of the Atonement to serve the needy and $5,000 for the orphans at the Paul Clark Home in Butte.

Anna was interred in the mausoleum at Woodlawn Cemetery, the one with the image of W.A.'s first wife, Kate, on the brass door. She was laid to rest in a crypt next to W.A. and below Andrée.

At that moment, Huguette herself had no place to be buried. Every spot in the mausoleum was occupied. But Huguette was only fifty-seven years old. She would wait more than forty years to address this issue.

. . .

Writing to Etienne's family in France about Anna's death, Huguette was protective of their feelings, while masking her own grief. She cautioned that there was no need to upset any of their older relatives with such news: "It would be useless to give this great sorrow."

Etienne comforted Huguette, making plans to visit her in New York. He wrote to her on October 14, 1963:

My dear friend Huguette: Your news of your mother passing filled me with sadness, but she left us only temporarily, and she is in a better place now with the angels, Andrée, her parents and God. She is probably happier since her last years were difficult. She will be with you forever, though there is emptiness for you now. Wish I could be with you and I want to come back as soon as possible. Her memory will always live among us, with her great kindness and courage. She will be a star in our lives. Heaven will have one more great soul, which will shine forever to bring light and guidance to your life. And on earth you will always have the ones who love you. I am so anxious to see you again, dear, dear Huguette. I am not forgetting your dear mother in my prayers, and also you, dear Huguette. I kiss you with all my heart, with much love. Your devoted, Etienne.

Huguette replied to this letter with a short telegram on October 30:

Thank you for your letter, dear Etienne, and for your words of sympathy which touched me very much. I am fine. . . . I wish Elisabeth a prompt recovery. Affectionate kisses. Huguette.

Her words seem more formal than his, less intimate. This may always have been the case, yet it's worth noting that we have copies of only Huguette's papers, not Etienne's. We see only the confirmation copies of her telegrams, and do not have her letters. Of course, he also was married.

In a letter dated November 2, 1963, Etienne tells Huguette of his plan to have his wife, Elisabeth, and daughter, Marie-Christine, come to New York in the spring:

Thinking of you and your mother, I have a cold again, Elisabeth is staying here for the treatments which seem to help. She is helped by a nice country woman, so I will be able to leave in peace, and the cute little orphan we were entrusted with will keep her company. Once her

treatments are finished and she is completely recovered, she and the lit-
tle Marie-Christine will join me in New York. In the meantime I am
going alone again and I can't wait to be in New York. You know how I
am split emotionally and how hard it is for me to be away so long, so I
will come as soon as possible. . . . Here is a photo of Marie-Christine
and my vegetable garden. Alas, my hair is so gray! Thinking of you
and your dear mother who left such emptiness! See you soon . . .

He signed the letter, in English, "With much love always. Etienne."

. . .

Huguette had projects to throw her grief into. First, she arranged to
move into her mother's apartment, spending much of the next year re-
decorating and updating Apartment 8W, while holding on to 12W. A.d
before Etienne's next visit she went on a clothes shopping binge. She was
looking furiously for the right style, not by visiting one of the boutiques
on Madison Avenue, one block from her home, but by sending telegrams
to Paris. She contacted La Maison Jean Patou, the fashion designer, in
an effort to find two-piece silk dresses, for summer and winter. She was
especially eager, at age fifty-seven, to find styles that would be slimming. The house of Jean Patou was about to get a dose of the Huguette
Clark experience.

Cable of March 19, 1965, to Mme. Peggy, Jean Patou, Paris:

The two-piece pleated silk dress is less slimming than the shantung
dresses, which are perfect measurement-wise. Please make the black
pleated silk dress that I ordered with 3 inches extra above and below
the chest, and the belt looser. The skirt is fine. Try to make this dress
in a style that would be as slimming as possible. With all my thanks.

. . .

Etienne did visit several times after Anna's death, including at least one
visit with his wife and daughter. On his way home from one of his trips,
as he crossed the Atlantic, he described how difficult the parting was.
On May 29, 1966, he wrote:

Very dear Huguette: It was wonderful to see you, even though it was too short. . . . It was hard to leave you. You are always in my thoughts and heart. Kisses . . . [In English] *With much love, always, Etienne.*

Marie-Christine, now in her fifties, said she remembers visiting Huguette at 907 Fifth Avenue when she was a child, with her father and mother. She said she can bring up only three details.

Tante Huguette was germophobic, afraid of catching an illness.

The long gallery in her apartment was completely lined with armchairs, each providing a seat for a doll.

After dinner, Marie-Christine had a delicious tarte aux pommes, the best apple tart she ever tasted.

. . .

Huguette also continued her financial support of Etienne and his extended family, spreading her generosity widely. From 1960 into the 2000s, she sent monthly bank drafts to half a dozen of Etienne's relatives. She helped Etienne's sad-sack younger brother, Henri, always starting a new agricultural venture while struggling as a bureaucrat. Huguette made sure that her physician saw all of Etienne's family for checkups on his annual trips to Paris. She sent her handyman all the way to France to deliver vitamins and to help Etienne with the chores. After hearing that a drought had affected the cows in Normandy, she sent the family powdered milk.

Huguette established an account with Monsieur Cognin, the grocer at 42, rue Gambetta in Deauville, sending him orders for essentials and treats to be delivered to Etienne and his extended family. From 907 Fifth Avenue in New York, transatlantic telegraph cables, made of seven twisted strands of pure copper strung across the ocean floor, carried Huguette's messages to the corner grocer 3,517 miles away. She even made sure to ask for the trading stamps, so the family could save on other purchases.

On July 2, 1962, she cabled to Monsieur Cognin:

Received your nice letter. I just sent you a little more than the price of the order because I would like to order four cartons of fat-free milk, a few bars of Cemoi chocolate, and also a can of instant chocolate Nesquik. With my thanks, Huguette Clark.

She also sent the family gifts, including the high-priced Rolleiflex cameras from Germany, the newest film projectors. She sent small televisions to her French friends so they could watch America's Apollo space flights. From the fabled Parisian toy store Au Nain Bleu in Paris, she ordered thoughtful gifts for the children, suited to their ages: for the girls, a musical blue goblin, Barbie dolls, a bedroom mirror and dresser with little perfume bottles, porcelain boxes filled with jewels, and lots of bows and ribbons; for the boys, not only a train set but an entire wooden village.

The Villermont family was already grateful to America for defending their country in the great wars. "Without your country," Etienne wrote in 1968, "there would be no more France." But they were also grateful to their Tante Huguette. An older relative prayed for her on pilgrimages to Lourdes. Henri, Etienne's brother, wrote in 1954, "I will never forget that you saved us from utter misery and that you eased our dear mother's last years with your tireless kindness. . . . You distribute happiness every chance you get for the well-being and joy of others. It is an admirable form of ideal, from which everyone must draw the most beautiful Christian virtue—forget the self in favor of the others. You practice this virtue incessantly."

In 2001, when Huguette was ninety-five, Marie-Christine's cousins made an illustrated French children's book for her called *Une Princesse Merveilleuse* (A Marvelous Princess). They wrote:

Once upon a time there was a princess who loved children very much. Every Christmas, she gave them lots of wonderful presents, and every time, the children were very happy. This princess loved the children's toys a lot, and she would have liked to get presents, too. And this year in 2001, she received some mail. In this letter there was a gift. This gift was made by children. These children had made a book, the drawings and story were created by them. The princess was very, very, very happy. It was the first time that she had received a gift from the children who had made the book. And this princess, guess what her name was? Tante Huguette.

When Huguette got too hard of hearing to talk with Etienne's family on the phone, she had a friend make the calls to swap news, which from the French side usually involved complaints about transit workers on strike—except when the postal workers were on strike.

Marie-Christine continued to correspond with Huguette for many years, and Huguette counseled her through a difficult divorce, praising her for her bravery in striking out on her own. She says she doesn't know what her father's relationship with Huguette was, except that they were friends. She has now seen her father's correspondence with Huguette. In a letter dated September 5, 1966, apparently after a gap in communication, Etienne describes returning to the beach at Trouville, where he and Huguette were children together:

> *Very dear Huguette: It was wonderful to receive your cable. Although your note "as well as possible" is worrisome, this note from you was a flower in my life as it is very hard not to hear from you, since in spite of our separate lives, my heart always beats with you. The years will always live. . . .*
>
> *On the Trouville-Deauville beach, I thought a lot about you and your mother while looking at the same place where your vacation home was. The houses have been remodeled so it's not possible to identify which house from among the others. Very nice restorations. In spite of the rain, there were lots of families and children. . . . I kiss you with all my heart. With much love, always, Etienne.*

· · ·

Andrew Etienne Allard de Villermont died on April 8, 1982, in one of the nicer neighborhoods of Cannes on the French Riviera. He was seventy-seven. A funeral Mass was said in a church in the wealthiest district of Paris. Etienne was entombed in the ancient monumental cemetery in Rouen, the historic capital city of Normandy, an hour from the beach at Trouville where Huguette met the young marquis.

As it turns out, Etienne was not a marquis, despite being called so by the newspapers for years. His family held no noble title, though it had come close. Known for centuries as the Allards, the family had been on the way to nobility—Etienne's great-great-great-grandfather bought an office as adviser to the king, but didn't hold the post long enough—when the French Revolution interrupted their ascent. Etienne's obituary, placed by Elisabeth and Marie-Christine, makes no mention of nobility. In Paris, the association of French noble families does not list his family. In the early 1900s Etienne's father added a gloss, changing the family name to Villermont, which to French ears would have suggested nobility.

Though Etienne's tomb is near those of the novelist Flaubert, the artist Duchamp, and many people with noble-sounding names, his position even after death is insecure. His spot in the cemetery is not guaranteed forever, but lasts only as long as someone pays to maintain his monument.

Huguette would outlive Etienne by twenty-nine years. She continued for nearly all that time to wire money to his widow, Elisabeth. The two women carried on a fond correspondence, sending love and kisses with all their hearts.

THE LITTLE PEOPLE

═══

THE HOUSE OF CHRISTIAN DIOR held fashion shows at the palatial French consulate in New York, just up Fifth Avenue from Huguette's apartment, with models showing the latest Parisian fashions. On the afternoon of one of these shows in the late 1950s, a familiar name showed up on the guest list.

"Mrs. Huguette Clark!" exclaimed the consul general, Baron Jacques Baeyens, who had married Huguette's niece. "Look, she's not going to come. She's my aunt, and she never goes out."

The representative from Christian Dior replied, "Oh, yes, she will. She wants to see the dresses to dress her dolls."

And she did. Huguette, then just past fifty, walked the three blocks up Fifth Avenue to the consulate to view the latest fashions from Paris.

. . .

Huguette Clark, who grew up in the biggest house in New York, was, like her father, a meticulous designer of extravagant houses, only on a smaller scale. These were dollhouses, but more than dollhouses. These one-of-a-kind tabletop models were story houses, theaters with scenes and characters painted on the walls. And like her father with his art collection, Huguette spared no expense. She commissioned religious houses with Joan of Arc, forts with toy soldiers, cottages with scenes from old French fables, and house after house telling her favorite fairy tales: Rapunzel, the long-haired maiden trapped in the tower. Sleeping Beauty, the princess stuck in sleep until a handsome prince awakens her with a kiss. Rumpelstiltskin, with the girl forced to spin straw into gold.

Focused on every detail, Huguette tried to get the artisans, some of them up to four thousand miles away, to be more careful with their measurements when they made her dollhouses. The houses had to be in proportion to the dolls that went with them. The following cable is typical, sent when Huguette was fifty-eight years old to an artist who made small, posable dolls based on fairy-tale characters and sold them door-to-door in a Bavarian town.

Cable of October 6, 1964, to Mrs. Edith von Arps, Burgkunstadt, West Germany:

> *Rumpelstiltskin house just arrived. It is beautifully painted but unfortu-nately is not same size of last porridge house received. Instead of front of house being 19¾ of an inch wide it is only 15½ inch wide. Please make sure religious house has front of house 19¾ of an inch wide. Would also like shutters on all the windows. Would like another Rumpelstiltskin house with same scenes with scene where hay is turned to gold added as well as scene before hay is turned but with wider front and also wooden shutters on every window. With many thanks for all your troubles and kindest regards. Huguette Clark, 907 Fifth Ave NYC.*

. . .

Rudolph Jaklitsch, born in Austria-Hungary in 1910, immigrated to New York from Yugoslavia before World War II and fought in the U.S. Army during the war. Trained as a cabinetmaker and restorer of antiques, Rudolph was hired by Huguette after the war to work on her dollhouses. When the houses arrived from their makers, Huguette would send them to Rudolph's apartment in Sunnyside, Queens, for modifications. His wife, Anna, made the little curtains.

Their daughter Linda Kasakyan recalls the frequent phone calls at home in the evening. It would be Madame Clark with an idea for a change to one of her houses. Then five minutes later, another instruction. The phone might ring six times in a night. Rudolph would say, it would be so much easier to know what she wanted if he could sit down with her. But she would talk with him only on the phone or through her apartment door. Rudolph worked for Huguette for thirty years and saw her only twice.

His daughter said it bothered Huguette terribly if the measurements weren't right. She liked to place dolls in the houses and move them through various activities—drinking tea, walking in the garden, having conversations. Sometimes, however, the ceilings in the houses were too low for the dolls. One time Huguette called Rudolph with an urgent problem:

"The little people are banging their heads!"

. . .

In her dollhouse building, as in her many other art projects, Huguette blended an artistic sensibility and imagination with a meticulous drive for precision, a commanding self-assurance, and an overwhelming generosity.

Even as an adult, she was not happy with the fables and fairy tales as they were written, often excising the unpleasant parts. On August 16, 1962, she cabled instructions to Manon Iessel, a renowned French illustrator, who was helping her with illustrations for a story house:

> *Thank you for your kind letter. I would like that the Sleeping Beauty house tale not continue after the kiss as I do not like the rest of the story. I also would like an interior staircase going from the first to the second floor, and a detachable garden with rose bushes (with thorns) placed in the garden and on the surrounding fence. Also, the house should be able to be opened on one side, but not the garden side. The figurines should be sketched according to the models you received, in color, with some fairies wearing pointy headdresses.*

In the rest of the story, Sleeping Beauty and the prince marry and have children. An ogress demands that the children and princess be cooked and served to her, though they are saved. Disney's animated films also left out that part, agreeing with Huguette's editing.

Huguette also ordered dollhouses from Au Nain Bleu in Paris. When she didn't get what she wanted, she'd send it back, politely but firmly. For example, in a cable to Au Nain Bleu dated June 14, 1963, she wrote:

> *Received the wall and garden. Unfortunately, they are useless. The door for the wall being in front of the elevator, it is impossible to open it. This door should open into the kitchen. The second-floor windows are not necessary as there is so little space to place the furniture. The window to the left of the door is the only one that is well-placed. The*

measurements of the garden are not the same as in the model I sent
you, and the sides are too short. I am sending it back to you. With all
my thanks. Huguette Clark.

She desired not only the dolls and dollhouses but also the accessories
that gave the appearance of daily life. For a breakfast scene, she cabled
Au Nain Bleu asking for tiny French breads: croissants, brioches, madeleines, mille-feuilles, and turnovers. But she wasn't done. In a May 7,
1956, cable to the store, she wrote:

For the lovely pastry shop please send the following: waffles, babas,
tartelettes, crepes, tartines, palmiers, galettes, cups of milk, tea and
coffee with milk, small butter jars, fake jam and honey, small boxes of
chocolate, candies and candied fruits, and small forks. Thank you.

The dolls needed costumes. From Paris, Huguette ordered satin for
her antique dolls with musical recordings inside them. She was having
trouble finding the right satin for the Jumeau dolls, famous for their
great beauty and big, soulful eyes.

On August 9, 1962, in a cable to "Mme. Gervais, La Maison Christian Dior, Paris," she wrote:

Received your nice letter with the samples. If Sample B2 could be
slightly darker and in satin it would be fine, as the color is the closest
to the original. Sample A2 for the singer doll is perfect when it comes
to softness and lightness, but is too dark. The color of Sample A3 is
perfect, but the fabric is too heavy. I think it would be better to wait
until you find the perfect fabrics for those little costumes. Please send
me your new sketches. With all my thanks.

· · ·

Rudolph, her dollhouse cabinetmaker, found Huguette charmingly
frustrating. But she paid so extravagantly that he could never say no. In
addition to paying for his time, she sent gifts to his children and grandchildren, including an early computer, a puppet theater with one hun-

dred fairy-tale characters, and a second puppet theater so large that the family gave it to a school. She sent monetary gifts to the family as well.

At Christmastime, Huguette would take three weeks to send out her dozens of Christmas cards, carefully redrafting each one until it suited her. ("I don't like holidays," she said with mock suffering, "because there is so much to do. Too much!") Rudolph's family was one of many to receive her "small gift," a check for $20,000. Later, the little gifts grew to $30,000, then $40,000.

When Rudolph died in 2000, Huguette kept sending the checks to his widow. When his widow died, the checks kept arriving in the names of their children. All the grandchildren of Rudolph and Anna Jaklitsch went to good colleges, paid for by Huguette and her "little people."

I N JAPAN, a rare type of cedar was reserved by the so-called sumptuary laws for use only in imperial buildings and castles, where a roof
made of its bark could last for seventy years. But a wealthy woman in
the United States sought permission to buy and export a small quantity
of this cedar. After months of discussion, the normally formidable bu-
reaucracy of the prefecture finally knew it was beaten.

The cedar was purchased, and an aging Japanese artist cut the valuable wood into tiny slivers. He was making tiles for the roof of a
dollhouse-size castle. This authentic model took two or three years to
construct and cost $80,000.

One of Huguette's great enthusiasms, for half a century, was authenticity, in the form of designing tabletop models of real-life Japanese
buildings—castles, teahouses, cake shops—which she commissioned
from Japan. These were pieces of art in wood and fabric, miniatures
with exquisite detail and authentic materials. She insisted that they
have detachable roofs so she could see the interior surfaces and furnishings.

Through a go-between in California and several translators, Huguette corresponded with the Japanese artist who cut the cedar for her
roof, an old man she knew simply as "the artist." The man, Saburo
Kawakami, took long trips for her in Japan, once changing trains four
times in a single day to reach Hirosaki Castle, so he could take photographs and measurements of each wall and tower.

The measurements in her detailed designs had to be converted from
English inches to metric centimeters to traditional Japanese *shaku,* and
then the artist's replies had to be converted back again. The costs were
considerable. In 1991, she accepted an additional charge of $38,600 just
to add doors to a wood house. In 1992, she sent $67,000 for a castle, and
on they went to the next project.

"She knew what she wanted to have done," said her go-between, Caterina Marsh. "If she was not pleased, not that many times, she was gra-

cious, but you understood you were going to have to redo it. If we believe in something, we're not going to take a poor substitute for it."

Mrs. Caterina, as Huguette called her, had married into the family of an old-line dealer in Asian art and artifacts, G. T. Marsh and Company. Though she and Huguette enjoyed hundreds of letters and phone calls through the years, she never had Huguette's phone number.

"She had a very happy voice," Caterina said. "It was cute. One of her favorite words was 'peculiar.' 'Isn't that peculiar, Mrs. Caterina,' she'd say.

"I still have that voice in my ear. She was always polite, always asked about my husband and my son. She was just a delightful person. I think she had fun—don't you think?—doing these projects that were not easy."

"The artist," Saburo Kawakami, was a bit overwhelmed by the relentless requests from his "Clark-san." At one point, Caterina cautioned Huguette, "It seems the artist is becoming more and more nervous every time he receives our letters."

The castle projects continued nearly to the end of Huguette's life. For example, in February 2004, when she was nearly ninety-nine, she had the artist working simultaneously on a small palace, a garden with a red bridge, and new screens for a theater. Eventually she wore out her Japanese artist, who was becoming too ill to continue. A new artist was brought on, but Huguette wasn't happy with his work, finding his style too modern.

. . .

Huguette was an avid collector of rare, historic Japanese dolls, particularly the tiny ones representing the emperor, the empress, and their ladies-in-waiting and court musicians. These figures are known as *hina-ningyo,* or hina dolls.

These are not merely playthings, as they might be in the West— young Japanese children usually aren't allowed to handle them—but rather objects of religious celebration and national pride. On March 3 of each year, the third day of the third month, Japan celebrates the festival known as Hina-matsuri, or Girl's Day, an ancient day of purification for the nation. The hina serve as protective talismans, absorbing malevolent spirits.

IN CONVERSATION WITH HUGUETTE

In a conversation in 1999, Huguette started by telling me about her Japanese dolls. She seemed uninhibited in expressing her interest in topics normally thought of as juvenile. I was unfamiliar with these dolls, so she patiently explained.

Paul: So, well, now, now, what are you doing for fun these days?
Huguette: Well, nothing special, you know. I'm getting my hina dolls together. I'm making a collection of hina dolls. I don't know if you know what they are?
Paul: No, I don't know. How do you spell that?
Huguette: H-I-N-A.
Paul: H-I-N-A.
Huguette: It's a festival that takes place in Japan. . . . They have a festival in March and they have all these dolls.
Paul: Are these a big part of your doll collection—Japanese dolls?
Huguette: Yes, the hina collection. They are hard to get. They go way down to the Meiji period.
Paul: Where will these be shown? Where will they be exhibited?
Huguette: They're not exhibited. I mean to say, people collect them. But they're hard to get, very hard to find. You've never heard of them?
Paul: No, I haven't. I'll have to read about it. . . . Are you contributing to a show for this purpose?
Huguette: No, no, they have it in their home, you see? For three days they exhibit these dolls. They invite all their friends.
Paul: And will you be having a celebration in your home for this?
Huguette: No, no, no. . . . But, I mean, they're very lovely dolls, you know. . . . I think you'll enjoy them for your little granddaughter. Does she still dance the ballet?

I asked Huguette how many times she had visited Japan. Had she gone to the doll temple in Kyoto? Seen Hirosaki Castle?

Oh no, she answered cheerfully, I've never been to Japan.

Huguette prized her hina dolls, especially the tiny ones—called *mame-bina,* about five inches high, with heads the size of a bean—and the three-inch *keshi-bina,* with heads the size of a seed. She said one of her favorite movies was Akira Kurosawa's *Dreams,* which has a sequence about hina dolls that come to life to punish a boy's family for cutting down some sacred peach trees.

Huguette said her favorite novel was *The Hidden Flower,* a love story written by Pearl S. Buck. Huguette corresponded with Buck in the 1940s and gave money to her humanitarian efforts for children in Asian countries.

The Hidden Flower, published in 1952, describes a forbidden love between an American serviceman and a young Japanese American woman living in postwar Japan. The woman, Josui, was born in the United States but returned to her ancestral home rather than submit to a life behind barbed wire in the Japanese American internment camps established during World War II. Now, however, Josui finds herself feeling as out of place in Japan as she did in America. Hers is a story of beauty and pain, of a woman's quiet, dignified courage as she attempts to move from one culture to another—not unlike Huguette's own story.

. . .

Caterina Marsh said that neither Huguette nor her hobbies seemed the least bit odd—once you talked with her.

"We are all taken by customs and culture," she said. "I have a brother who became fascinated by trains. There's nothing strange about having a fascination like collecting stamps.

"She developed an incredible knowledge about the art and culture of Japan. It was astonishing what she knew, all the legends and folklore. To me, she was the last of an era.

"We are all a little peculiar, as she would say."

THE GOOD FAIRY

HUGUETTE'S FAVORITE MAGAZINE in her youth was a popular French weekly for young girls, *La Semaine de Suzette*, which holds an important place in the collective memory of France. *Suzette* included games, crafts, recipes, and dress patterns for the doll Bleuette. Available only through the magazine from 1905 to 1960, Bleuette was about eleven inches high, about half the size of today's American Girl dolls. Most important, the magazine included stories with lavish color illustrations.

Huguette did more than fondly remember or collect these souvenirs of her youth. In her middle age, she applied her own brand of generosity, reaching out to the magazine's illustrators, becoming their patron, their friend, and their savior. An entire generation of the greatest illustrators in France found themselves blessed by an unseen benefactor from America.

She remembered one illustrator in particular from *Suzette*, and also from her books of fairy tales and fables, filled with "Le Maître Chat" (the mischievous Puss in Boots), "Le Petit Poucet" (the tiny Tom Thumb), and "Cendrillon" (the underdog Cinderella). His name was Félix Lorioux. American audiences may not know that name, but they're certainly familiar with this one: Walt Disney.

Lorioux was an early inspiration to Disney, who worked in France after the Great War in 1919. Lorioux was hired by Disney to illustrate early Mickey Mouse books, including the French version of *Mickey and Minnie*. In 1916, Lorioux had created the character of a comic goose in a sailor suit, a goose that looks a lot like Donald Duck. A humble man, Lorioux was often credited by others for creating Donald Duck, but Disney published his illustrations for decades without crediting him. As a silent protest or wink, Lorioux would hide the names of his family in his drawings for Disney.

In France, Lorioux is as well known as, say, Beatrix Potter is in England. Lorioux illustrated more than one hundred books and has been called one of the most influential artists of the twentieth century. Whom did he influence? Well, to name one, Picasso, who riffed on Lorioux's tragicomic Don Quixote.

In her forties, Huguette went looking for Félix Lorioux. In 1950, Artine Courbalk, a French bookbinder in New York who had known Huguette since childhood, sought out Lorioux on her instructions. Courbalk was the intermediary, a courier for instructions from Huguette to the arts. In his many letters to Lorioux, Courbalk offered a detailed portrait of Huguette's personality. He described her, in French, as a "rare bird," very kind, compassionate, and generous, who "always keeps her smile, the smile of a child." She doesn't drink, doesn't smoke, never seems to age, and doesn't wear makeup—"she is ravishing and does not need it." Courbalk explained that Huguette lived in a separate apartment from her mother, though they were "very close and insepa-rable." He said Huguette suffered from epistolophobia—the fear of writing letters—which is why she mostly used the telephone and sent telegrams. He tipped off Lorioux that Huguette was "rich, very rich," and capricious, confiding that her whims "are really a command, and will be well paid for." He said she wants light colors, pastels, and fairy scenes and doesn't like to hear bad news or to express any criticism. In short, Courbalk described Huguette as "a comet."

Through Courbalk, Huguette commissioned works from Lorioux—starting with illustrated legends of France, then a series of fairy tales—"except the unpleasant scene where Snow White is laying down poisoned," and without the witch, she cautioned—and sought his help in finding all the back issues of *La Semaine de Suzette,* particularly those for the years 1912 and 1913, when she was six and seven. The artist's daughter-in-law sent Huguette her personal collection. Lorioux and Huguette exchanged lively letters for decades, and he opened the door for her to support an entire generation of illustrators in France.

Like Huguette, Lorioux was a bit uncomfortable among people, feel-ing more at home with his fantasy figures and insects. He painted vivid watercolors for Huguette's eyes only, portraying her as a princess among the fawning inhabitants of a miniature world of lovable insects in fancy clothes.

One hand-painted birthday card, sent to her in 1952, shows a royal grasshopper, sitting high on pillows in the blossom of a giant purple flower, studying herself in a mirror, while a colorful host of ladybugs scramble up a rickety ladder carrying, and spilling, gifts for her: jewels, jelly beans, a picnic, a bouquet of flowers. In 1954, Félix sent Huguette a drawing of an aging butterfly suitor giving flowers and jewels to a bashful butterfly princess.

Huguette supported Lorioux and his wife, Lily, with her generous "little gifts" for many years, and in 1989 she gave an arts group $100,000 for an exhibition in New York of his scholarly crows, pompous bureaucrats, and robins wearing spats. Lily called Huguette "our benevolent fairy."

When Félix died in Paris in 1964, at age ninety-one, Huguette cabled Lily:

Dear Madame, very sad to learn of the sad news of your great loss and immense sorrow. What a loss also for the whole world to lose dear Mr. Lorioux, such a great artist and a great soul. Allow me to kiss you tenderly with all my affectionate sympathy.

. . .

Félix Lorioux was not the only French artist to benefit from Huguette's patronage. She sought out others. At least four illustrators—Jean Mercier, Manon Iessel, J. P. Pinchon, and the pen-named Chéri Hérouard— were all supported by Huguette until they died. She commissioned illustrations of children's songs, drawings of all the female saints of France, and maps of the history of each region of the country. "You know how loyal I have remained," she wrote to Pinchon, "to the French traditions and folkloric past of France."

Huguette became closest to Hérouard, known for his lighthearted and fantastic covers and illustrations for the society magazine *La Vie Parisienne*. He was a specialist in fairy godmothers, witches, ogres, and dragons. He also, under the pen name Herric, illustrated erotic books with scenes of sadomasochism: sex with the maid, sex between the maids. He sent Huguette a crate of his original drawings, including a few of his "daring" ones.

Huguette put Hérouard to work painting watercolors of Sleeping Beauty, instructing him to make the costume changes historically accurate when the princess wakes up after a hundred years. She also sent him to Petit-Bourg to draw the ruins of her family's summer castle, which the retreating Nazis had burned during World War II. And she had the old man tracking down more old copies of *Suzette*. At age seventy-five, the artist was placing classified ads for the magazines in French newspapers, supplementing his effort with prayers to Saint Anthony of Padua, the patron saint of seekers of lost items. After finding the last issue of 1912, Hérouard was philosophical, thinking of that innocent time before France was plunged into conflict:

> In spite of their fragile state, these Suzettes from such a distant era went through the two most important wars in history. And as I was looking at these slightly yellowed pages, I was thinking that many little girls, who would open them with delight and carelessness, were to cry two years later at the sight of their father going away toward a most dangerous fate.

He did have just one request, from the Frenchwoman who was giving up her *Suzette* collection to the heiress in America: "The person who provided them is a widow. She has been keeping them since her youth, and in her response to my purchase offer, she asked if she could keep them for another two weeks to give her a chance to look at them one last time."

After Hérouard's death in 1961, his widow sent along his last drawing, which he had intended for Huguette's birthday.

Another of the artists, J. P. Pinchon, summed up his relationship with the American heiress. He wrote to Huguette in 1953, accepting in his eighties a new commission, even as he recognized he was near death. "The fairy tale continues, and you make my life beautiful. At the beginning of our acquaintance, I compared you to a good fairy who made the dream of any artist at the end of his career come true. Your magic wand never stopped, and I work with joy."

These artists never knew what their good fairy looked like. The Lorioux family sent photos to Huguette but never received any in return.

They knew only her telegrams and her high voice, as Huguette would call to inquire about the illustrator's grandchildren. The Lorioux family had invited Huguette to France many times, but she always begged off. No, she said, she wouldn't be able to return there. They asked why. She explained: the French Revolution.

Huguette said she was afraid she might be kidnapped or killed if there were another revolution, sounding as if a guillotine were always ready for the highborn. After all, to the long-lived Huguette, the French Revolution was only a little more than one lifetime before her birth.

CHAPTER EIGHT

BELLOSGUARDO

ANDREE'S COTTAGE

E NCHANTED FOR MOST of the twentieth century by the mystery of the Clark summer estate hidden on a hill, the residents of Santa Barbara created their own legends of Bellosguardo. One day in 1986, Huguette's California attorney sent to her New York attorney a detailed report of misinformation spread as a new trolley bus for tourists made its daily run past East Beach toward Montecito. The tour guide explained over the loudspeaker that the Clarks were the owners of the Anaconda Copper Company. (False.) The Clarks didn't think they were going to be able to have children. (False.) So they adopted a French orphan. (False.) She never married. (False.) And the daughter maintains a home in Paris. (False.)

Huguette's New York attorney discussed with her what action to take to correct these falsehoods. None, she said. Wanting to maintain her privacy at all costs, she agreed that they wouldn't make a fuss. Still, from time to time, the California attorney sent his secretary to ride the Montecito trolley, just to monitor the tour guides.

Though the details were all wrong, the legend of Bellosguardo was, in essence, true. The mansion had been frozen in Huguette's memory, unchanged since the Truman administration. It was the most important place to Huguette, her mother's place.

The name Bellosguardo ("beautiful lookout," pronounced BELL-os-GWAR-doe) was attached to the coastal estate on this oceanfront mesa by the Oklahoma oilman William Miller Graham and his wife, Lee Eleanor Graham, who built a 25,000-square-foot Italian villa there in 1903. One party thrown by the theatrical Mrs. Graham included a psychic, a juggler, and a trained monkey. The estate was used several times as a film set during the silent film era, serving as a Roman emperor's palace for the 1913 one-reeler *In the Days of Trajan*.

After a divorce and bankruptcy put Lee Eleanor Graham into a house-poor situation, she leased Bellosguardo to Frederick W. Vanderbilt, grandson of the Commodore. The next summertime tenants were

Anna, W.A., and their seventeen-year-old daughter, Huguette. The copper king's family liked the house so much that in December 1923, W.A. offered Mrs. Graham $300,000 cash for it, adding, "Take it or leave it." W.A. had only a year and a few months to enjoy this acquisition before his death. Bellosguardo would be Anna's mansion, not his.

In 1933, eight years after the Santa Barbara earthquake and five years after Huguette's wedding there, Anna began to have the old Graham home razed. It had been too severely damaged by the earthquake, and Anna wanted something more quakeproof—a home built of reinforced concrete and sheathed in granite, with walls sixteen inches thick.

She also wanted something more French. The architectural style is late-eighteenth-century French with Georgian influences, a formal style somewhat unusual for an oceanfront setting in California. It was designed by the renowned architect Reginald Johnson, who had designed the Santa Barbara Biltmore. After Anna allowed extensive archaeological explorations of the site, the house was completed in 1936, with twenty-seven rooms and 23,000 square feet, or about twice the size of Jefferson's Monticello. The building permit estimated the cost at $300,000, but it ended up at $1 million, in Depression prices, or about $17 million today.

The Clarks were proud of a side benefit of Anna's project—creating jobs in a desperate time—and Huguette often repeated the story that Anna ordered her overseer to hire as many workers as possible. "My dear Mother put so much of herself into its charm," Huguette wrote to Santa Barbara's mayor, Sheila Lodge, in 1988, "and had the satisfaction of knowing that during the great depression she was a bit helpful in giving much needed employment."

. . .

Anna and Huguette visited Bellosguardo regularly from the mid-1920s until the early 1950s. The Clarks' Pullman car would park on a siding at the Santa Barbara train station, and chauffeur Walter Armstrong would pick them up in the black 1933 Cadillac limousine or the gray-green 1927 Rolls-Royce, while the baggage followed in the wood-paneled Plymouth station wagon.

Although the Clarks' Bellosguardo had none of the social whirl of the

Graham era, guests were welcome on occasion. Anna opened the grounds to garden clubs and held small concerts for friends. The Paganini Quartet played on an elevated platform set nine feet up in an oak tree near the tennis court, the world-famous musicians bowing Anna's priceless Stradivarius instruments as their music rested on stands made of bamboo.

Anna and Huguette made social connections, too. Huguette was a founding member, in 1928, of the Valley Club, a prestigious golf course and social club, though it's not known if she ever golfed. She also joined the Santa Barbara Museum of Art in 1949, subscribing to its newsletters on contemporary and Asian art.

. . .

Bellosguardo is located just inside the eastern boundary of the city, adjoining the affluent community of Montecito, home to many movie stars. The Clark estate has twenty-three and a half acres, with nearly one thousand feet of ocean frontage, incongruously sharing the bluff with the Santa Barbara Cemetery. The cliff-top site, sixty feet above the public beach, affords great privacy. Visitors entered the grounds through a gate, usually locked, on Cabrillo Boulevard, from which the house can barely be seen.

The main driveway ascends cliffside next to tall eucalyptus, pine, and Monterey cypress trees. A short way up the driveway, one can stop at a pergola, an open structure of white columns, to sit in the mottled sunlight under the latticed arbor, surrounded in summer and fall by the flowering San Diego Red bougainvillea. The vast Pacific Ocean fills the view.

An enormous floating wooden deck was stored near the rustic beach house, ready to be towed out at the beginning of the summer, so that Huguette and her guests could go swimming, protected by a "lifeline" with wooden floats leading to the shore.

By the driveway, an enormous sign, nine feet wide, blares a warning: "PRIVATE KEEP OUT." The vast expanse of lawn sweeps out to a tree-lined pathway that skirts the sharp drop where the cliff falls off to the beach. On a clear day, one can see to the south as far as the Channel Islands, twenty-four miles offshore. On a foggy day, one can barely make out the volleyball players on Santa Barbara's East Beach below.

At the top of the cliff, with a hairpin turn to the left, one gets the first glimpse of the house, or one wing of it at least. The massive light gray structure gives a stately, institutional impression, with exquisite granite masonry in an interlocking pattern of grays and tans. This house is the creation of the quiet Anna, not her flamboyant husband. It is framed by a wall covered with green Boston ivy, which turns brilliant shades of orange and red in the fall. A queen palm soars over the thirteen chimneys.

The gardens close to the house are examples of symmetry, restraint, and severity. A field of orange California poppies leads up to the front of the house, with its entrance court. The court is itself a work of art, a floral design of beach stones in grays, whites, and blacks hand-selected from nearby Carpinteria Beach. No parking was allowed on the court, which is still trimmed in the pink, sweet-smelling flowers known as naked ladies.

Up two short flights of stairs, through the front door, and into the main entry hall, one is greeted by a portrait of a proud older gentleman in a military uniform. The most prominent place in the house is given not to W. A. Clark but to General John J. "Black Jack" Pershing, the man who saved the Clarks' beloved France in the Great War of 1914–18. Pershing, with salt-and-pepper hair and a gray mustache, stands weary but resolute, his thumb tucked confidently in the belt of his high-collared uniform, which is adorned with three rows of ribbons. This portrait, like so many others in the house, was painted by Tadé Styka.

The house is mostly a U-shaped structure, with east and west wings extending away from the sea in the front and toward the Santa Ynez Mountains in the back. Between the wings, visible as one enters the home, is a courtyard with a long, dark reflecting pond with blue-black stone tiles. One enters via a great central corridor, or galleria, that runs nearly the full length of the main section of the house. Portraits show an older W. A. Clark, with his intense blue eyes and white beard, and Anna, with her dark bangs and pearls.

The largest space in the home is the music room, measuring forty-six feet by twenty-three feet. This is where Anna played her forty-three-string pedal harp, a marvel made for her in a Louis XVI style adorned with gilt sculptures and paintings, and Huguette played her second-best

Huguette Clark was shy but not sad. Her friends and the few relatives who knew her described her as cheerful, gracious, stubborn, devoted to her art, and generous to friends and strangers.

The flamboyant W. A. Clark and his first wife, Kate, built this home in the mining town of Butte, Montana, in 1884–88. Designed to confer social status, it was easily the most expensive home in town, costing about $6 million in today's currency.

Huguette, at about age four, sits with her doll collection on the porch of her father's Butte mansion. W.A.'s two daughters from his second family—Andrée, born in 1902, and Huguette, born in 1906—stayed here in 1910–11 while their grand new home in New York was being finished.

On a family vacation in Connecticut in about 1912, near the time when the family held tickets on the Titanic's *return trip to Europe, Huguette sits with their father, W.A., while Andrée is beside their mother, Anna Eugenia LaChapelle Clark. The girls were about six and ten.*

Though appearing reserved and even cold in public, Anna
was warm and easygoing in private and had a salty sense of
humor. The child of French Canadian immigrants who lived
in a smoky mining section of Butte, she became the second
wife of the copper millionaire W. A. Clark, who was thirty-
nine years her senior.

W. A. Clark's new mansion in New York, finished in 1911, was known as the most expensive in America. Its 121 rooms included five galleries for works of art, including this painting by Degas. W.A. purchased the golden room called the Salon Doré in Paris and had it shipped to New York. Huguette recalled that their father would not let the girls play in the eighteenth-century room, which is now in the Corcoran Gallery of Art in Washington, D.C.

On a summer visit to Montana in about 1917, W.A. posed with daughters Andrée, left, and Huguette at Columbia Gardens, the family park he built for the people of Butte. The girls were about fifteen and eleven. W.A. loved to show off his flowers at Columbia Gardens.

The Clark mansion at Fifth Avenue and Seventy-Seventh Street by Central
Park, "the most remarkable dwelling in the world" and Huguette's childhood
home, was occupied for only fourteen years. It cost about $180 million in today's
dollars, but after her father died in 1925, it was deemed too expensive for anyone
to maintain and was torn down. In this view in 1927, a demolition debris chute
extends from the window of the Salon Doré toward Fifth Avenue. A sign on the
building advertises modern apartments to come.

violin by Stradivari, which she kept wrapped in four Japanese scarves. Two Steinway pianos sat back-to-back for duets. Bellosguardo was alive with music when the Clarks were in residence.

In the wood-paneled library, above the fireplace, is a large Styka portrait of Andrée, who died fifteen years before the house was built. Matching portraits of the girls show them sitting on benches, Andrée with a book, the younger Huguette cradling a doll. The house is full of portraits of Andrée, paintings sometimes two to a room. Her deep-set eyes are everywhere. In one large painting by Styka, the older sister sits on a giant cut log in a rushing mountain stream, dressed in a middy blouse with neckerchief, surrounded by the nature she loved. Her sad blue eyes are filled with portent.

. . .

The lost sister is also remembered in two memorials outdoors at Bellosguardo. The first is a small brown-and-white cottage tucked behind the tennis court and framed by green tamarix junipers. This cottage wouldn't have been out of place in England or Normandy in the fifteenth century. It's a half-timbered structure in the mock Tudor style, with a thatched roof, a stone chimney, and oddly undulating windowpanes. Built of clear heart redwood, the two rooms are rustic, with a black cast-iron stove from the early 1900s and simple country furniture.

The Clarks didn't build this cottage but inherited it from the Grahams, who built it as a playhouse for their daughter, Geraldine. The Clarks took down the sign in Old English script reading "Geraldine Graham's Cottage" and replaced it with a nearly identical one saying "Andrée's Cottage." The cottage was lovingly maintained. When the roof needed repairs, for example, thatchers came from England to do the work. Although Barbara Hoelscher Doran, the estate manager's daughter, remembers using it as a playhouse, to the Clarks it was more of a memorial, and they spoke with solemn voices in its vicinity.

That's how Anna's goddaughters recall the cottage. In addition to their regular visits to 907 Fifth Avenue, Anna allowed each goddaughter one trip west to the summer home at Bellosguardo. Leontine went with her family for Huguette's wedding in 1928. Her mother was the maid of honor, and Leontine was two and a half.

Music filled the rooms at Bellosguardo. In this photo from about 1940, one of Anna's harps and a piano sit at one end of the music room, with portraits of Huguette, right, and her late sister, Andrée, prominently displayed.

Ann's trip came when she was eight, nearly nine. In May 1937, her godmother pulled her out of school for a surprise cross-country train trip. Ann's mother and a governess also made the trip. Huguette, at age thirty-one, did not.

The leg from Chicago to Los Angeles was the first regular run of the Super Chief, a new high-speed train also known as "the Train of the Stars." The passenger list included ventriloquist Edgar Bergen and his sidekick Charlie McCarthy. Anna, having been married to railroad royalty, had lifetime courtesy passes on all the nation's railroads, a perk recorded on a list registered with Congress. On this train, she had her own china in her stateroom to use for tea parties with her goddaughter. "She was," Ann recalled, "a sweet person to children."

Ann remembers that while they were at Bellosguardo, the Paganini Quartet played a concert just for them. "It was idyllic."

Both goddaughters said that the subject of Anna's elder daughter never came up. The girls knew that something bad had happened, so bad that it was never spoken of. Ann recalled the thatched-roof Andrée's cottage as "a shrine—we had to be very quiet around that."

. . .

The second memorial to Andrée was provided by Huguette. In August 1928, before her wedding here, Huguette honored her sister by giving $50,000 to the City of Santa Barbara to create the Andrée Clark Bird Refuge on city land just behind Bellosguardo. Her donation eventually turned the marshy inlet from a foul-smelling eyesore into a lake with three man-made islands. The city had drawn up plans for the refuge at Anna's request, and Huguette came up with the donation from her own money. This donation benefited the Clarks, too, removing a blight from the neighborhood, but the thirty-one-acre refuge was primarily Huguette's memorial to her sister, just as Camp Andrée was her parents'.

For more than eighty years, the Andrée Clark Bird Refuge has been a serene lagoon and garden for wild ducks, snow geese, and other waterfowl heading south for the winter, as well as a year-round home for herons, cormorants, and other water birds. It is also a sanctuary for people, but on Huguette's terms. Her donation included strict limits on its use: no camping, no boating, no swimming, no concessions, and no parking alongside the boulevard. And it must forever be named for Andrée.

After the lake filled up with algae, in 1989 Huguette donated an additional $30,000 for its cleanup and for educational programs. Still in some years a foul odor comes off the water from decomposing algae, and in 2012 the cost of needed rehabilitation was estimated at $1 million. The lake, like a life well lived, needs constant replenishment with fresh oxygen.

PRIVATE SPACES

THE DAUGHTER of the estate manager, Barbara Hoelscher Doran, recalls playing dolls with Huguette in the early 1950s at Bellosguardo.
Little Barbee, as she was called, said she didn't think for a moment
about the difference in ages. Barbee Hoelscher was born in 1944 and was
still a child in the early 1950s, while Huguette was in her forties. "Huguette would phone our house and invite me over for afternoon tea. I
would walk over with the dogs and sit with Huguette and Anna on the
terrace under the big umbrellas, overlooking the great lawns and ocean.
I remember having lemonade, tea, and lovely cakes and cookies made by
the French chef who came with the ladies from New York."

Usually the Clark estate had no Clarks, only servants. There was
work to be done, of course. Anna's English butler, the tall and quite
proper Thomas Morton, was responsible for the dining room, with its
hundreds of dark wood panels. This is one of three rooms in the house
salvaged from the old Clark mansion on Fifth Avenue. (Anna, who of
course didn't inherit the house, did not save these rooms, but had to buy
them back from an antiques dealer.) The ceiling is a wonder, made of
canvas, trimmed in gold, and painted with comical human figures and
colorful cherubs. There were maids to supervise, but no work of urgency. Morton found time to become expert at cultivating bonsai.

Into the 1960s, Bellosguardo operated on the forty-eight-hour rule.
The staff was expected to have the house ready for the family within two
days' notice of a Clark visit. Sometimes, Barbara recalls, Anna and Huguette "would arrive on such short notice that Mother offered to help
whip off the dust sheets covering the furniture and brighten the rooms
with flower arrangements."

Then the house would spring to life. Anna would show off to visitors
her harps and her collection of ladies' fans from the courts of France.
Huguette had her own enthusiasms: photography and painting. Her
photo albums show that she roamed the grounds freely with her camera,
capturing the symmetrical steps by the reflecting pool and a still life of

fruit leaves in a bowl. She documented every room repeatedly. Years later, she would astonish the staff by calling to request a certain book on Japanese culture, telling them which shelf it was on, and that it was the seventh book over from the right.

Her artist's studio was tucked into the back for maximum privacy. There she kept not only paintings but the Japanese dolls that she loved to paint. The studio has its own kitchenette, and a private stairway up to the bedrooms, allowing Huguette to live and work without having to pass through the main hallway of the house.

Huguette was not content to work on her own paintings, but also offered a bit of editing. Outside the music room hangs a depiction of an older W.A. with a wild shock of white hair and brilliant blue eyes. Nattily dressed in a vest, her father is wearing a pearl stickpin and also a pinkie ring. The surprising part is the signature. At the lower right is "Tadé Styka 1925." Below that is another signature, "Hugo C." Huguette made amendments to this work, touching up her painting instructor's view of her father, and co-signed it with her nickname.

On the upper level of the east wing are suites for Anna and Huguette—W.A. needed no room here, as it was built after he died. Each suite includes a sitting room with a fireplace and a wardrobe closet paneled in book-matched bird's-eye maple. In Anna's suite, a portrait of W.A. sits on the desk by the window, near photos of both girls playing as children. One of her enormous golden French harps stands at the foot of the bed. Her bathroom features an astonishing oversize bathtub, carved from a solid block of yellow-and-pink marble with gold trim. She had a French kneeling desk, or prie-dieu, for prayer, and a felt-lined box from Cartier held a crucifix.

Through the windows, they could see Anna's rose garden, once the grandest in Santa Barbara. Its concentric circles were separated by low hedges of dwarf myrtle and walkways of red sandstone. At the center of the garden stands a fountain, a three-tiered Italian stone sculpture, topped by a bathing nude woman fixing her long hair.

The estate manager's daughter, living at Bellosguardo year-round, had far more time to explore these wonders than Huguette did. Amid all this luxury, she remembers the Clarks most of all for their generosity. "Huguette wanted my mother to have the very best piano for our home on the property, and spent days trying out pianos until she found one that had the quality she wanted," Barbara Hoelscher Doran recalled. "She loved the latest technology and innovations, and would buy the newest camera or sixteen-millimeter projectors, one for her and one for our family.

"They were very quiet, lovely, giving ladies."

A FRIEND ATTACKS

O N DECEMBER 3, 1941, Huguette wrote a jaunty note in French to Tadé Styka from Santa Barbara. She was still in touch with her former painting instructor, who had sent her chocolates and a corsage for her journey west. She wrote that she was tanning in the beautiful sun, "turning the color of chocolate."

Four days later, the Japanese attack on Pearl Harbor drew the United States into World War II. Huguette, who had studied Japanese culture and art, told her friends she was crushed by the sneak attack.

Bellosguardo changed during the war, as fear of invasion dominated the Pacific coast. An infantry regiment brought up to Santa Barbara had a post in the Clark beach house. The estate manager, Albert Hoelscher, became a civil defense warden, his home the district headquarters. Along the cliff, there were posts in the ground with time clocks to make sure the armed sentries made their rounds. The young sentries were a little goosey and shot at anything, recalled Barry Hoelscher, Barbara's older brother. The children were issued 1917-style steel helmets and gas masks. Anna was generous to the staff and showed concern for their safety. Each year during the war, she gave the Hoelscher family a $1,000 war bond and each of the children a $75 bond. She also outfitted the Hoelschers with a rifle, a .45-caliber pistol, and $10,000 in case they had to evacuate.

On February 23, 1942, a Japanese submarine surfaced off Santa Barbara and began to fire shells at the Ellwood Oil Field and its fuel storage tanks, about ten miles west of Bellosguardo. Though little damage was done, fear of a Japanese attack bordered on hysteria. A week later, President Franklin Roosevelt authorized the removal and internment of Japanese Americans living on the Pacific coast. A government pass was needed to get through the barbed wire checkpoint on Cabrillo Boulevard near the Clark estate. Curtains had to be closed at sundown because of the blackout. Streetlights were painted over, and cars had to drive with only their parking lights on, so as not to help the unseen enemy spot the silhouette of an American ship near the shore. Anna grew suspicious of outsiders and at one point mistook a kelp cutter boat for a Japanese submarine.

Because of the ever-present danger of invasion, Anna sought a refuge away from the coast for herself and Huguette, and, more important, for the staff. She bought a 215-acre ranch in the Santa Ynez Valley, twenty-two miles northwest of Santa Barbara. Called Rancho Alegre ("cheerful ranch"), it included a ranch house, a sloping meadow for horses and deer, a swimming pool fed by a mountain stream, and open views of Figueroa Mountain. Guests at the Clark ranch could ride horses, including a recalcitrant brown stallion named Don Antonio and the pure white Lady, who had been known in town as a flag bearer in parades.

Although the Japanese surrendered after the United States dropped atomic bombs on Hiroshima and Nagasaki in August 1945, the closed-off feeling never left Bellosguardo. Anna was rattled when one night the electricity failed, leaving the entire estate in the dark. After that episode, whenever Anna and Huguette planned a visit of only a week or two, they would sleep at the Biltmore, saying they didn't want to trouble the staff to open up the house.

Anna was getting older, and may have wearied of the long train rides. Anna and Huguette made their last trip west sometime around 1953.

While the Chrysler convertible and the Cadillac limousine stayed in the garage, Anna gave the Rolls-Royce to the chauffeur, Armstrong, who hadn't used it in quite a while, except to have fun by putting on his white gloves for picking up an embarrassed Barry Hoelscher, the estate manager's son, after classes at Santa Barbara High School.

FIRST-CLASS CONDITION

AFTER ANNA DIED in 1963, leaving Bellosguardo and Rancho Alegre to Huguette, the daughter issued new instructions to the staff. No longer was the house to be kept in readiness for the arrival of the Clarks under a forty-eight-hour rule.

When John Douglas came on as estate manager in 1983 after Albert Hoelscher died, he was given only two instructions: Keep everything in "first-class condition" and in "as original condition as possible."

When El Niño storms uprooted a half dozen hundred-foot trees at Bellosguardo in the 1980s, the gardeners planted replacements and sent photos to New York. Huguette sent word that one of the new trees wouldn't do; it was too small. The tree was taken out, and a mature tree was planted. She declared that tree also too small. Finally, on the third try, she said it would have to do.

When painters finished work on the back of the service wing, Douglas sent photos of the work to New York. He received a quick reply, through Huguette's attorney. The painting was fine, but "Mrs. Clark would like to know what happened to the doghouse that the Pekingese used." The Pekingese had died many years earlier. Douglas asked if Mrs. Clark wanted the doghouse in place even if there was no dog. Her attorney responded that Mrs. Clark was well aware that the dog was no longer there but wanted to be sure its house was still on the property. It was.

Huguette insisted that an archway leading through a dense hedge of Monterey cypress be kept just as she remembered it. She sent word after seeing a photo that she "would like to know if the small oak tree that was outside her bedroom window could be replanted."

One Clark relative recalled being shocked, on a rare visit to the main house, when a housekeeper barked, "Who moved that chair?" The housekeeper moved it about four feet back to its spot.

Her mother was gone, and Huguette would have to live with that, but her mother's house could be preserved indefinitely.

. . .

Not even for kings would Huguette allow Bellosguardo to be disturbed.

She turned down the entreaties of an agent for Mohammad Reza Pahlavi, the shah of Iran, when he wanted to buy the property in January 1979, in the last days before he fled the Islamic Revolution. Even after his death, the shah, the last king of Iran, couldn't meet the admission standards for the Montecito neighborhood. His sister wrote to the Santa Barbara Cemetery asking to buy space for a family mausoleum but was refused.

Huguette wouldn't give permission for the Hollywood billionaire Marvin Davis to land his helicopter for a tour of Bellosguardo in 1989, when he was offering $30 million to $40 million for the estate.

Newspapers offered reports that the Beanie Babies tycoon, Ty Warner, had raised the possibility of paying $100 million for Bellosguardo, but Huguette wasn't interested.

The Santa Barbara Museum of Art asked her in 1991 and 2004 to donate the home but got nowhere. Her attorney Don Wallace said she did seriously discuss leaving the home to the nearby Music Academy of the West. She said it would be nice to have chamber concerts at Bellosguardo again, but she was concerned about cars spoiling the grounds.

When the mayor of Santa Barbara asked Huguette twice to consider giving Bellosguardo to a foundation, she said that she would consider it. In a handwritten note to Mayor Sheila Lodge in 1997, Huguette wrote, "My answer to you about Bellosguardo, is the same as it was in the year 1993 but if some day I should have a change of mind I shall let you know."

Historians and journalists sent letter after letter, usually trying to get interviews by promising to avoid too much mention of her father's electoral scandal. In a typical letter, a graduate student in history, Jeanette Rodda, wrote to Huguette in 1988, "The scandal, of course, cannot be ignored but I believe I effectively reinterpret and underplay several unfortunate incidents." Huguette's attorneys forwarded these letters to her, but the supplicants got nowhere.

. . .

Anna had visited her mountain refuge outside Santa Barbara, Rancho Alegre, only occasionally and Huguette perhaps not at all. After Anna died, Huguette soon donated Rancho Alegre to the Boy Scouts in her mother's memory. She attached one condition: The kindly ranch manager, Niels "Slim" Larsen, and his wife, Oda, would be allowed to move into the ranch house, staying as long as they wished. Today many community groups use Rancho Alegre for retreats, and the Outdoor School of Santa Barbara, run by the Scouts, serves four thousand children a year through Huguette's generosity.

Before Oda Larsen died in 2001, she said she recalled talking only once to Huguette, on the phone. Huguette asked her two questions:

"What color is the swimming pool?"

"Are there any gazelles on the property?"

. . .

In the sixty quiet years at Bellosguardo after Anna and Huguette's last visit, the furniture has been covered. Anna's harps were laid on their sides to protect them from damage in case of an earthquake. The floral Aubusson rugs of raspberry and pink were wrapped in paper and labeled with photographs of the contents, each bundle dated and signed by a member of the staff.

The furniture at Bellosguardo remained covered during the nearly sixty years when Huguette no longer visited. Her instructions to her staff were to change nothing and to keep everything in "first-class condition."

Not everything on the Clark estate has stayed in first-class condition, however. The passage of time has been enough to bring about changes. The bathrooms throughout the house haven't been updated since the 1930s, and warning signs in some read "DO NOT FLUSH." Although seamstresses were brought from Holland in the 1950s to repair the Louis XV upholstery on the sofa and chairs in the sitting room, in recent years some of the cushions have rotted.

The extensive landscaping once required between twelve and twenty gardeners and two full-time plumbers to keep the grounds irrigated. In recognition of the water shortages that plague Santa Barbara, the twelve hundred rose plants were carefully removed and their location mapped so the garden could be re-created if Huguette desired. Now there are only four gardeners, and the rest of the staff consists of a houseman, two part-timers for bookkeeping and filing, and the estate manager.

IN CONVERSATION WITH HUGUETTE

We discussed several times Huguette's memories of Bellosguardo. I asked why she didn't visit. Didn't she want to see the house and gardens again, to enjoy the view of the Pacific?

"Well," she said, "when I think of Santa Barbara, I always think of times there with my mother, and it makes me very sad."

• • •

Huguette kept in touch with Santa Barbara from New York. Until her death, the staff sent monthly dues to the Valley Club, though she hadn't been there for sixty years, and annual checks to the Santa Barbara Museum of Art, along with contributions to music institutions and police and fire charities.

She received clippings of news from Lorraine Hoelscher, second wife of the longtime estate manager, who kept the books at the estate, and from the chauffeur's widow, Alma Armstrong, both of whom received

Still in the garage at Bellosguardo, under an ornate light fixture, are two of Anna and Huguette's automobiles, including a 1933 Cadillac seven-passenger limousine with a gilded hood ornament and a 1933 Chrysler Royal Eight convertible. Both have license plates from 1949.

pensions until they died. When maid Sylvia Morales retired in 1993 after thirty years of cleaning the estate manager's house, Huguette approved a pension at 92 percent of her regular pay.

Beginning in 1987, Huguette spent nearly a million dollars on an eight-hundred-foot rock seawall to protect the cliff and, as a consequence, the main driveway, which is the only way for fire trucks to reach the house. This project destroyed a beautiful cliff face and removed a line of Monterey cypress trees along the cliff top. In exchange for permission to build the wall, Huguette allowed the city to designate most of the estate as a landmark, limiting its future development and perhaps its resale value.

John Douglas, who never met her in the twenty-eight years he managed her most valuable property, talked with her on the phone only twice. During those conversations, as he described any improvements on the estate, Huguette replied politely, "Yes, Mr. Douglas." But when she heard of work to keep the property just as it had always been, as it was in her mother's time, she exclaimed, "Isn't that wonderful!"

CHAPTER NINE

LE BEAU CHATEAU

JUST AS ANNA HAD her emergency retreat in California at Rancho Alegre, Huguette added her own country refuge in the leafy Connecticut suburbs. It was called Le Beau Château. The castle takes its name from an old French children's song, the music for a circle game in which two concentric circles of children alternate singing verses. Here's one translation of the refrain:

> *Oh! My beautiful castle!*
> *My auntie turns, turns, turns.*
> *Oh! My beautiful castle!*
> *My auntie turns, turns beautifully.*

The verses follow, with a new beginning line modifying each round:

> *Ours is more beautiful!*
> *We will destroy it!*
> *How will you do that?*
> *We will take your girls!*
> *Which one will you take?*
> *We will take this one!*
> *What will you give her?*
> *Beautiful jewels!*
> *We don't want any!*

In 1951, the Clarks' chauffeur drove Huguette and Anna out to New Canaan, a Connecticut suburb an hour north of New York City. Huguette later explained to her man Friday, Chris Sattler, that it had been her mother's idea to have a refuge for family and friends in case of a Russian attack on New York. (This was, after all, during the Cold War, which had heated up with North Korea's invasion of South Korea in 1950.)

In appearance, Le Beau Château is an echo of the château de Petit-

Bourg from the Clarks' happy summers in France. Huguette bought the property, expanded the house, and bought more land for a buffer, eventually owning fifty-two acres, twenty-two rooms, and more than fourteen thousand square feet of emptiness. She never moved a stick of furniture into the house during the six decades she owned it.

The senator's daughter was buying the house of a senator. The château was built in 1938 by David Aiken Reed, former Republican senator from Pennsylvania. Reed was best known for the Immigration Act of 1924, which tried to keep Jews and Asians out of the United States, with the goal of "keeping American stock up to the highest standard."

New Canaan is one of the most affluent communities in the nation, with little notice taken of quiet wealth. Nearby neighbors now include musician and actor Harry Connick, Jr., and others not far away during Huguette's ownership were architect Philip Johnson in his Glass House, *NBC Nightly News* anchor Brian Williams, and singer-songwriter Paul Simon.

Huguette bought the Connecticut estate, Le Beau Château, in 1951, the year she turned forty-five. Her annual property tax bill reached $161,000, but she never moved in. It was maintained but unfurnished for more than sixty years. She was nearly one hundred before she agreed to put it on the market.

As the years passed and the mysterious property remained unoccupied, neighbor children sneaked through the woods to peek at the house, and townspeople passed around legends about the missing owner. Her fiancé had built the house for her, one story went, and after he died at sea on the honeymoon, she couldn't bear to move in. Another story had Huguette's father paying the fiancé a million dollars to go away.

. . .

Le Beau Château would have been a pleasant hideaway for enjoying her Impressionists, for listening to violin sonatas and partitas, and for painting portraits quietly into old age. As one enters on the long driveway, deer bound out of the woods. The balcony of the magnificent bedroom with its double-height window is only twenty steps from the woods near a waterfall on a trout brook. But Huguette had her own private castles and dollhouses to attend to in New York.

The spiral staircase was grand, but for sixty years no wedding photos were taken there. The water heater in the basement, the length of a Rolls-Royce limousine, never heated water for a bath. An old green Jag-

Huguette's enormous bedroom at Le Beau Château is quiet, except for the sound of a waterfall on a trout brook running through the nearby woods.

uar belonging to the caretaker was parked in the garage. The combination to the walk-in safe was lost long ago.

This Connecticut home was never maintained with the care lavished on her Bellosguardo. There were no memories to preserve. In California, the annual salary of estate manager John Douglas reached $110,000 plus use of the beach house. But at Le Beau Château, caretaker Tony Ruggiero got the use of a guard cottage and only $16,800. Huguette did keep paying the property taxes—they eventually reached $161,000 a year—and in 1997 she spent hundreds of thousands of dollars on repairs and painting.

Today the white paint is peeling off the red brick on the back of the house. The New England stone walls are collapsing. The tennis court is so overgrown that it's easy to miss. And creeping vines have the kitchen shutters firmly in their grasp.

Le Beau Château has served for years now as an informal wildlife refuge for turkeys; deer; screech owls, barred owls, and great horned owls; goshawks, sharp-shinned hawks, and Cooper's hawks; an occasional bald eagle; yellow-spotted salamanders; rare box turtles; and red and gray foxes. Chimney swifts nest in the stacks. The caretaker's son

When Huguette built a two-story addition at Le Beau Château in 1951, the stairway received a touch of whimsy: paintbrushes.

rehabbed injured and orphaned animals: raccoons, cottontail rabbits, deer. When Huguette's attorney Don Wallace once came out for a tour, a goose named Curly untied his shoes.

The only personal touch in the twenty-two rooms is in the wing Huguette had constructed in the early 1950s. A graceful wooden staircase leads from the thirteen-hundred-square-foot bedroom up to a loft, a painter's studio with sinks for washing brushes. On the staircase, every other baluster holding up the handrail is hand-carved in the shape of an artist's brush.

THE VIRGIN

A S SHE APPROACHED HER FIFTIES and her mother grew frail, Huguette bought not only Le Beau Château but also major pieces of art and musical instruments, showing her father's eye for betting on winners.

In May 1955, she added her third violin by Stradivari. These violins were hers, not among the four that Anna was lending to the Paganini Quartet. Huguette's new violin was not just any ordinary Stradivarius. This was perhaps the finest violin in the world not in a museum. Huguette selected the violin herself, making sure to negotiate a discount.

Made in 1709 in Cremona, Italy, this is the great Stradivarius violin, the one used by experts to date the beginning of his finest years. Aficionados can distinguish this violin at a great distance by sight, as easily as an electric guitar fan would know Keith Richards's 1953 Fender Telecaster, "Micawber." A purchaser in Paris in the mid-1800s, seeing that the violin had never been opened for repair, exclaimed, *"C'est comme une pucelle!"* (It's like a virgin!), and thereafter it was known as "La Pucelle," meaning "the maid" or "the virgin." That purchaser not only gave it a name but immediately added a distinctive carved wooden front-piece representing Joan of Arc, "the Maid of France." The asking price for La Pucelle in 1955 was $55,000 at the famed Rudolph Wurlitzer Company on Forty-Second Street, but Huguette inquired what discount she could receive for paying cash. She was told 5 percent. A week later, when the bill of sale was drawn up, she had negotiated the discount to 10 percent, making the final price $49,500, or about $450,000 in today's dollars, for one of the finest violins ever made.

Huguette took great care of La Pucelle, making sure it was serviced annually. In the 1950s and 1960s, it was one of her few regular adventures away from 907 Fifth Avenue. But when she played the violin, she used a lesser Strad from 1720, which she called her Traveler.

In the same period, she expanded her collection of Impressionist paintings, which already included two Renoirs, *In the Roses* and *Girl with Parasol,* Manet's *Peonies,* the Degas *Dancer Making Points,* and two by Monet, a Water Lilies and *Poplars on the Epte.* She added a third Renoir, the spectacular *Girls Playing Battledore and Shuttlecock,* depicting fashionable young women playing badminton in the French countryside: vivid blue and yellow against a green countryside. No doubt she had seen it at the Metropolitan Museum of Art in 1937, when she had lent one of her own paintings to the museum for a Renoir show. It has many figures (similar to *The Bathers*) and is from his greatest period: The dealers call it a perfect Renoir. She asked the Knoedler gallery to send it over, and after a week she decided to keep it, paying the list price of $125,000.

Not all her fine paintings were French. She owned two by the American painter John Singer Sargent: In *Rooftops of Capri,* a young woman dances the tarantella to entice an older man, and in *Girl Fishing at San Vigilio,* the fisherwoman seems far overdressed for the occasion.

Huguette also bought Apartment 12W, which was her own residence, and also 8W, her mother's, as the building at 907 Fifth Avenue converted from rentals to co-op apartments at the end of 1955. She paid less than $120,000 for the pair, or about $1 million in today's dollars.

In each of these purchases, Huguette proved to be a shrewd investor.

"DID YOU EVER REPLACE SNOOPY?"

THROUGH ALL THE YEARS, among all her secrets, Huguette had kept up a friendship with a man who was about her age and living in France, a man other than Etienne. She was not one to let things go, not one to end an old friendship.

In the spring of 1964, she sent this friend a telegram at his home on the French Riviera, consoling him on a loss:

Dear Bill, received your letter with sad news about Snoopy. Having had dogs I know what the heartbreak is. All my best wishes for a good Easter under the circumstances. Affectionately, Huguette.

This Bill was her former husband. Though they couldn't make it through the honeymoon, the former Mr. and Mrs. William Gower carried on an affectionate correspondence for decades.

Two years after Huguette divorced him, Bill Gower remarried, choosing in 1932 another daughter of a wealthy politician from the western states. Constance Toulmin was the child of George White Baxter, former territorial governor of Wyoming. She already had two failed marriages. Bill and Constance had no children together, but they raised her daughter from an earlier marriage, Cynthia, who drove an ambulance in the Second World War. Bill was unable to fight in that war, having developed an awkward gait since his track team days, so he put his legal training to work as the American Red Cross delegate to Europe, briefing Churchill and Eisenhower. After the war, Bill ran the Paris office of the company that published *Look* magazine. Here he was in his element, hobnobbing with society figures, including author Somerset Maugham.

"Everything was sketchy with my uncle," recalled his niece, Janet Perry. He was a womanizer, a gregarious big talker, irrepressibly lovable. He sent his niece a huge framed photograph of himself, too large to display, but she put it out on the piano when he came to the New York area to visit. He always had tickets to the newest hit play, a table at the finest restaurant. "He was a huge name-dropper, but he really knew all the people."

Through all the years after their divorce, Bill and Huguette stayed in touch. He sent her birthday wishes. She kept him up on family news and illnesses. Their warm correspondence shows a relationship completely at odds with the Clark family suggestion that she had been traumatized by her brief marriage.

In February 1964, she checked on his health and suggested he visit her on his next trip to America:

> *Dear Bill, Thank you for your letter. Photographs very lovely. Anxious to hear the results about your foot. When are you thinking of coming to the states? Be sure to let me know in advance so I will be in New York. With affection, Huguette.*

She made plans to meet him a few weeks later, after his arrival at New York's oldest private club:

> *Thanks for your letter. So glad about the foot. Will call Union Club on 3rd or 4th of March. Bon voyage. Affectionately, Huguette.*

She checked on him that August:

> *Cher Bill, Wondering what you are doing today. We are having marvelous weather. How is it over there? Did you ever replace Snoopy, not in your heart but in your household? Bien affectueusement, Huguette.*

And the following year, in 1965, she worried after he took a spill at age sixty:

> *Dear Bill, am anxious to know how you are and if you have fully recovered from your fall. So do let me hear from you. With much love, Huguette.*

Bill's wife, Constance, had died in 1951, and he retired in 1960 to the coastal resort town of Antibes on the French Riviera. He owned a classic, antique-stuffed Mediterranean house, which he called La Sarrazine. His yard had a huge mirror at one end to make the estate look twice as large.

Huguette wrote checks to Bill, $3,000 at a time, well into the 1970s. He died of consumption, or pulmonary tuberculosis, in December 1976 in Antibes, at age seventy-one. His ashes were buried beside his parents in North Elba Cemetery outside Lake Placid, New York, in a shady spot with a mossy headstone.

Even until her death, eighty-three years after their brief marriage, Huguette still had in her apartment her Cartier gold wedding band with its thirty-two small diamonds, as well as her Tiffany wedding presents with the monogram "H.C.G."

SPOOKY

THOUGH SHE NOW OWNED a country house in Connecticut, in addition to her apartments in New York and the California estate, Bellosguardo, Huguette's staff was dwindling. As old employees died or retired, she didn't hire new ones. She apparently wasn't comfortable interviewing new people. After her mother died, and then her Aunt Pauline, who had also resided at 907 Fifth Avenue, Huguette was the only resident of the forty rooms there.

One of her last full-time caretakers, Delia Healey, was an Irish immigrant six years older than Huguette. During the 1960s until the late 1970s, Delia's main duties were threefold.

She brought in fresh bananas every morning and made Huguette's lunch, usually crackers with sardines from a can.

She looked after Huguette's collection of French dolls, carefully washing and ironing their clothes. She also ran out to buy new dolls as soon as they became available at FAO Schwarz.

She managed the recording of TV shows for Huguette to watch, particularly cartoons, so that Huguette could study the individual frames of animation. (In the 1960s, Huguette kept a library of French films, stored on early reel-to-reel tape, which she studied frame by frame.) Huguette purchased a newfangled Sony video recorder for recording the shows and had it delivered to Delia's apartment. Delia's assignment at one point was not only to record but also to transcribe every word of every episode of *The Flintstones*.

Delia's grandchildren remember Huguette as kind and generous. In 1975, she sent them Home Pong, an early videogame. She also sent them a custom-made dollhouse from Germany, which had exquisite detail, including toilet seats that went up and down and human figures that matched each member of their family. They recalled being surprised, a few weeks later, when Huguette sent the dollhouse back to Germany for repairs, because she said the floors needed to be refinished.

After seventy-nine-year-old Delia became too infirm to take the train into the city from Larchmont, in Westchester County, Huguette sent a driver in a town car to pick her up every morning. Never at ease with strangers, Huguette was forestalling having to hire someone new. When Delia died in 1980, her family was surprised to learn that Huguette was not an older woman but was actually younger than she.

With no more full-time staff, Huguette called on a circle of part-time helpers. Out in Yonkers, New York, several evenings a week in the 1980s, the phone would ring at the home of Huguette's antiques dealer, Robert Samuels. His daughter, Ann Fabrizio, remembers Huguette's small voice insisting that he come right away to fix some item in her mother's apartment: an inlaid table that had cracked, a chair that needed to be reupholstered, new cases for the dolls. In twenty-five years of fixing and furnishing her apartments, Samuels never talked face-to-face with her.

In 1970, Huguette had a staff of eight. By 1990, she had only one part-time maid and a handyman to maintain her forty-two rooms at 907 Fifth Avenue.

Then there was a frightening incident at the apartment. Huguette described a day in the late 1980s when a water delivery boy, or someone pretending to be a delivery boy, came to 8W. Huguette was up in 12W, getting something for one of her art projects. When she came back downstairs, she found the maid locked in the bathroom, with no sign of the delivery boy.

As Huguette described it much later, "It was spooky."

CHAPTER TEN

DOCTORS HOSPITAL

MADAME PIERRE

H UGUETTE CLARK had been outliving her doctors.

When the cancers on her face ate away at her lip, nearly causing her to starve in March 1991, it was her friend Suzanne Pierre whom she finally called with an SOS. Suzanne was the wife of Huguette's longtime doctor, Jules Pierre, but he was quite elderly and no longer seeing patients. After he retired, Huguette had seen Dr. Myron Wright, but he died in 1990. Huguette didn't find a new doctor, so her skin cancers had gone untreated.

Madame Pierre called Dr. Henry Singman, who was seeing some of her husband's former patients. The internist that evening discovered Huguette, an "apparition" in her own apartment, and persuaded her to go to the hospital immediately. And that's how she began her long seclusion, choosing Doctors Hospital because it was near Suzanne's Upper East Side apartment.

Though everyone said Suzanne Pierre was Huguette's best friend, Suzanne knew her place in the pecking order. "Her dolls," Madame Pierre said, "are her closest companions."

Suzanne and Huguette loved to converse in French. Suzanne was fifteen years younger than Huguette, born in France in 1921. Her first marriage ended quickly in divorce. She left her nine-month-old son with his grandparents in Brittany and went to work. She rarely saw her son until he was a young man.

Suzanne came to the United States in 1948 and eventually married Dr. Jules Pierre, a Frenchman, an officer in the Legion of Honor, and president of the Federation of French War Veterans. Dr. Pierre was the physician for Anna and Huguette.

Madame Pierre and Huguette became friends. She visited 907 Fifth Avenue regularly. Over time, she began to act as sort of a social secretary and assistant for Huguette, a buffer against the world.

. . .

On a stormy afternoon in March 2010, serving hot tea and cookies for a visitor in her tasteful apartment at 1075 Park Avenue, eighty-eight-year-old Suzanne Pierre was dressed in a sharp blouse and jacket with a pearl stickpin. She said she couldn't explain why Huguette was a recluse. In the years after Huguette's mother had died, Suzanne said, she tried to get Huguette to join her for afternoons out.

"I would ask her to go out to lunch, but she preferred to stay in. She would say she has a little cold."

Huguette did not want to see outsiders, even relatives, Madame Pierre said. "She thought they were just after her money. She didn't trust people."

Believed to be a self-portrait, this unsigned painting shows Huguette Clark in her twenties. At a time when most women painted with pastels, Huguette was a serious art student, mixing her own oil paints.

This painting by Huguette captures her view down Fifth Avenue in the snow, toward the Empire State Building. It emphasizes the cold, moist air in the blue-gray night, contrasted with the warmth inside her room, lit by the glow from a Japanese lamp.

*Huguette's art teacher, Tadé Styka, painted this portrait of her painting a
nude male model at the Styka studio on Central Park South.*

Huguette painted this tiny painting of a geisha bathed in gold, paying special attention to the colors and the exquisite detail in the fabrics. She studied Japanese culture and collected elaborate kimonos and hairpieces. But visiting Japan was a different matter.

Huguette poses uncomfortably in furs, a cloche hat, and her emerald and diamond bracelets after her wedding to Bill Gower in 1928, when she was twenty-two. This photo appears to be from her honeymoon trip and was republished in newspapers in 1930, when she divorced him. She would live until 2011 but no newer photo was published during her lifetime.

Bellosguardo, the Clark summer estate in Santa Barbara, California, was pur-chased by former senator Clark in 1923. His widow, Anna, had this mansion built in the early 1930s. She and her daughter Huguette stopped visiting in the early 1950s, although today it remains fully furnished and carefully preserved. Huguette, who inherited Bellosguardo in 1963, insisted that it be kept unchanged, in "first-class condition."

Bellosguardo, at lower right, sits in privacy on a mesa by the Pacific Ocean, above Santa Barbara's East Beach. The pond at right is the Andrée Clark Bird Refuge, created by Huguette as a memorial to her sister. When this photo was published on a picture postcard, Huguette's property manager bought up every copy to protect her privacy.

In a photo from about 1940, the library at Bellosguardo is dominated by a portrait of Huguette's sister, Andrée, over the mantel. The painting and the library are still as they were then, but now with the furniture covered.

The bedroom at Bellosguardo of Huguette's mother, Anna, features one of her ornate pedal harps, her bed with damask upholstery on the footboard, a John Singer Sargent painting of a dancer enticing a man on a rooftop in Capri, and photos of her daughters, Andrée and Huguette.

Although Huguette's sister, Andrée, did not live to see Bellosguardo, she is present everywhere. The Clarks named this Tudor playhouse Andrée's Cottage in honor of their daughter, who died at sixteen. W.A. and Anna also donated land in New York for the first national Girl Scout camp, named Camp Andrée Clark.

Just as her mother bought a California ranch as a refuge during World War II,
Huguette during the Cold War bought this Connecticut retreat, Le Beau Château,
on fifty-two acres in New Canaan. It sat empty for more than sixty years, with vines
eventually growing through the shutters outside the kitchen windows. When she
finally offered it for sale, it led to the disclosure of her reclusive life.

HADASSAH

F
ROM DAY ONE at Doctors Hospital, Huguette had private nurses twenty-four hours a day. The nurse on the day shift, assigned randomly to Huguette in the spring of 1991, was Hadassah Peri. She would work for her "Madame" for twenty years, becoming, it seems probable, the wealthiest registered nurse in the world.

Doctors Hospital was not the place that a New Yorker with a life-threatening illness normally would select. It was better known as a fashionable treatment center for the well-to-do, a society hospital, a great place for a face-lift or for drying out. Michael Jackson had been a patient, as had Marilyn Monroe, James Thurber, Clare Boothe Luce, and Eugene O'Neill. The fourteen-story brick structure on the Upper East Side of Manhattan, between Eighty-Seventh and Eighty-Eighth streets by a bend in the East River, gave the impression of being an apartment building or hotel, with a hair salon offering private appointments in patient rooms and a comfortable dining room where patients could order from the wine list if the doctor allowed. When it opened in 1929, it had no wards and no interns, allowed no charity care, and included hotel accommodations for family members of patients. In its early days, it was often used as a long-term residential hotel or spa, and finally in the 1970s it added modern coronary units and intensive care.

Huguette checked in to a room on the eleventh floor with a lovely view down to a city park and Gracie Mansion, the Federal-style home that is the official residence of the mayor of New York.

After living mostly alone at home for so many years, now Huguette was in a hospital with its constant noises and staff coming and going. At first she was a difficult patient, swathed in sheets and refusing to let anyone see her. A nurse wrote in the chart that she was "like a homeless person—no clothes, not in touch with the world, had not seen a doctor for 20 years, and threw everyone out of the room."

A week into her stay, Huguette was evaluated by a social worker, who filled out the standard initial assessment. The patient, just short of age eighty-five, was scheduled for surgery to remove basal cell tumors and to reconstruct her lip, right cheek, and right eyelid. She had been "managing poorly at home—reclusive—not eating recently" and was dehydrated. Her only support system was her friend Suzanne Pierre, "helping with her affairs," and a maid—no family. Her mental status was always awake and alert, but she was skittish: "Patient refused to speak with social worker. Patient has not been to doctor in many years—had refused medications in past. Patient anxious and uncooperative at times."

Her plans after treatment? "Spoke with friend, Mrs. Pierre—feels patient will need convalescent care in facility but does not want to go to nursing home which she feels would be depressing. . . . Patient may need to go to a hotel with a nurse to recuperate."

As for financial problems, "none noted."

Huguette did not move on to a hotel. Within just over two months, she was an indefinite patient, a tenant, with Doctors Hospital charging her $829 a day. Eventually the rent rose to $1,200, or more than $400,000 a year.

Huguette had a series of surgeries in 1991 and 1992, with Dr. Jack Rudick removing malignant tumors and making initial repairs to her face. She was healthy, though she still needed a bit of plastic surgery, especially on her right eyelid. "It is not necessary," she told her doctors. "I am not having any surgery. I don't like needles." She was not badly disfigured by the cancer. And there might have been another reason, Dr. Singman speculated. "This she has steadfastly put off," he wrote in her chart in 1996, "I presume to avoid the final treatment and then possible discharge home."

A board-certified specialist in internal medicine, cardiology, and geriatrics, Dr. Singman assured her that she could have round-the-clock nurses at home, and he would visit daily. "I had strongly urged that she go home," he said. She was, however, "perfectly happy, content, to remain in the situation she was in." When one of the first night nurses kept urging her to move back home, Huguette fired her. In the end, Dr. Singman accepted her decision, writing in her chart in 1996, "I fervently believe that this woman would not have survived if she had been discharged from the hospital."

Dr. Singman's backup, internist Dr. John Wolff, said he agreed. Huguette "was so content and so secure in the environment. There's no question in my mind that's really where she chose to be." He brought her flowers on her birthday and liked to stop in. "She was a lovely woman, and we would talk. Her mind was clear. There was no confusion about her. Very warm, gracious, sweet, gentle, interested in other people, independent, guarded."

Huguette was hardly ever sick. She refused to take a flu shot—she didn't believe in medicine, she told her nurses, and felt that "nature should take its course." Her only persistent medical issues were mild: osteopenia, a decrease of calcium in the bones not advanced enough to be called osteoporosis; a slightly elevated systolic blood pressure (150/80); and two nutrition issues, a mild electrolyte disorder and a mild salt depletion. Her illnesses passed quickly, usually with her refusing antibiotics. She had a bout of pneumonia, the seasonal flu, and a surgery to check out a suspicious lump that was benign.

In other words, from age eighty-five to well past one hundred, a stage when most people need elaborate pillboxes marked with the days of the week, Huguette was remarkably healthy, requiring no daily medications other than vitamins. Yet she was living in a hospital.

. . .

Dr. Singman said Huguette at first was "extremely frightened" of new people. She refused most medical treatments unless her day nurse, Hadassah, was there to hold her hand and talk calmingly. Hadassah and Huguette had a bond from the beginning, with Hadassah able to read Huguette's feelings and help her overcome her distress. When they couldn't reach Hadassah, the other nurses would sometimes pretend that they were talking with her on the phone, telling Huguette that Hadassah said that she had to eat now or she should allow them to check her blood pressure.

"You have to convince her," explained Hadassah later. A small, compact woman with warm, dark eyes and black hair flecked with gray, Hadassah described patience as the key to her chemistry with Huguette. "You have to explain it to her, you have to educate her who is coming, what is that for—at times we have some difficulty."

Hadassah Peri was born Gicela Tejada Oloroso in May 1950 to a politically prominent and eccentric family in the Philippine fishing town of Sapian. Gicela received a nursing degree before immigrating to the United States in 1972. She worked first at a hospital in Arkansas, then moved to New York in 1980. She passed her New York exams as a licensed practical nurse, then a registered nurse, and started working as a private-duty nurse. Born a Roman Catholic, she had married an Israeli immigrant and New York taxi driver, Daniel Peri, in 1982, converting to his Orthodox Judaism and using the name Hadassah Peri, although she didn't change her name legally until 2011. Even today, she is a bit embarrassed about her English, though it's quite good, despite some confusion over pronouns: "Madame love his favorite shoes."

When she was assigned to Huguette, the Peris owned a small apartment in Brooklyn. They had three children born in the 1980s, two boys and a girl.

Private-duty nurses are temp workers, always hoping for a long-term assignment. Taking a day off means having a replacement nurse, one who might step into the regular role. So despite the Orthodox prohibition against working on Saturday, and despite having three school-age children, for many years Hadassah worked for Huguette from eight A.M. to eight P.M., twelve hours a day, seven days a week, fifty-two weeks a year. She was up and out of the house before her children left for school and home close to bedtime. It would be several years before she took a day off. Hadassah was paid $30 an hour, $2,520 a week, $131,040 a year, but she described her self-sacrifice for Huguette as extreme. "I give my life to Madame," Hadassah said.

· · ·

The private hospital room was perfectly ordinary, a small room for one patient with a hospital bed, recliner, chest of drawers, bedside table, small refrigerator, TV, radio, closet, small bathroom. "She like a simple room," Hadassah said.

Once an outdoorsy youth, Huguette now didn't want any daylight. The cancer had left her eyelid unable to close properly. She kept her shades drawn, though she often asked her nurses about the weather, and she did look out on the Fourth of July to watch the fireworks. The room wasn't entirely dark, with an overhead light usually on, and Huguette had a reading lamp as well. Drawings by the nurses' children and doctors' grandchildren sometimes were hung on the walls. The door was closed, and Huguette would see only the visitors she knew. Dr. Singman called it a cocoon, a safe place, but not unpleasant.

The doctor said he asked Huguette once to see a psychiatrist, not because he thought she was mentally ill but because he thought talking with another doctor might help persuade her to return home. She declined to discuss it, and neither the doctor nor the hospital ever mentioned it again.

"The woman was an eccentric of the first order," Dr. Singman said, but "she had perfect knowledge of her surroundings, she had excellent memory . . . a mind like a steel trap. . . . At that point she was perfectly happy, content, to remain in the situation she was in. . . . The hospital setting . . . was a form of security blanket for her. . . . I didn't think there was going to be any great help from a psychiatrist to change her attitude about what she was doing. . . . The woman was perfectly conversant at all times, never demonstrated any . . . disturbances of her mind. . . . I didn't think her behavior was that of one suffering from a psychiatric illness." At most, said her doctor, she showed "eccentricity and neurotic behavior"—not exactly distinguishing characteristics in New York City.

Huguette dressed in hospital gowns, hardly ever wearing her clothes from home. When she was cold—and she was often cold—she would wear layered sweaters, always white button-front cashmere cardigans from Scotland, her only hint of luxury.

. . .

The daily routine began with Huguette drinking two cups of warm milk that the night nurse, Geraldine Lehane Coffey, had left for her. Hadassah would arrive with *The New York Times*. (Huguette always read the obituaries, as older people do, followed the progress of wars and weather emergencies, and delighted in finding stories about Japan and royalty.) Hadassah would greet Huguette and give her kisses. Huguette could walk to the bathroom by herself and give herself a sponge bath. Then Huguette would blow into the incentive spirometer, the little plastic tube where each deep breath makes the plastic ball rise, which helped ward off pneumonia. Huguette could make the ball go up five times, sometimes eight times. She would do coughing and deep-breathing exercises. Then it was time for breakfast: oatmeal and eggs, pureed, and her French coffee with hot milk, or café au lait.

Most of Huguette's diet was liquid, taken through a straw because of the wound to her lip. Dinner was usually a soup that Hadassah had made at home, such as potato leek, made with eggs to provide protein. At night she would ask the nurse for a warm glass of milk before bed. Between meals, she drank Ensure nutritional drinks. For a special treat, Madame Pierre brought her steamed artichokes or asparagus with a rich hollandaise sauce, made in the classic French fashion with egg yolks and fresh butter, because Huguette said she couldn't stand hospital food.

After breakfast, it was time for Huguette's morning walk, three or four times around the room. She and Hadassah called this their "walk in Central Park." Then it was personal time for Huguette. She made phone calls on her Princess telephone with the lighted dial, calling Madame Pierre sometimes three to five times a day. "Mrs. Clark liked to speak French with my grandmother," said Suzanne's granddaughter Kati Despretz Cruz, "because she didn't want her nurses to understand what they were talking about."

Huguette called her coordinator of art projects, Caterina Marsh, in California to make changes in a Japanese castle. She read *The New York Times* and followed the financial markets on CNN. "She would watch the stock," said one of the night nurses, Primrose Mohiuddin, "and she would say to me, 'Oh, NASDAQ has gone down. That's terrible!'" She paid particular attention to news of presidents and royalty. "When President Clinton was in trouble," her assistant Chris Sattler said, "she was asking Mrs. Pierre and me about the Monica Lewinsky thing. She didn't get it, and she wanted us to explain it to her. And we sort of let it go, if you know what I mean."

She kept a few personal items in shopping bags on the floor by the window. Her address book and recent correspondence. A deck of cards.

Dr. Singman taught her solitaire and bought her a book of rules of card games, which she used to learn many variations. Because Huguette kept information about herself tightly controlled, on a need-to-know basis, Dr. Singman knew little of her art projects and her correspondence with friends in France. To his view, solitaire was her main activity. "She was a wiz," he said. "She could shuffle a deck like I haven't seen anybody except in a gambling house."

She no longer painted but would watch her videotapes of cartoons, studying the animation and enjoying the stories. She liked to make flip books of still images captured from videotapes, so she could see the animated stories in her hands. Her favorite cartoons were *The Flintstones, The Jetsons, The Smurfs*, and a Japanese series called *Maya the Bee*. These cartoons came in particularly handy when Huguette tired of a conversation with a doctor or hospital official. She'd start up *The Smurfs* as if to say, *No, I've made up my mind*.

And she would look at her photo albums, which contained snapshots from her early days with her father, mother, and sister. She'd show her nurses and doctors the photos: Andrée on a bicycle. Huguette on a horse at château de Petit-Bourg outside Paris. (She told them how the Germans had burned the house down.) The girls visiting their father's copper mine in Butte. One of herself at her First Communion, and also surrounded by dolls on the porch of her father's first mansion, in Butte, where she remembered the pansies on the stoop. Anna smiling as she sat on a park bench during a summer sojourn in Greenwich, Connecticut. Huguette's Aunt Amelia, her mother's sister, standing on the grand marble staircase at the old Clark mansion on Fifth Avenue. The rooms and gardens at Bellosguardo. Anna and W.A. on the beach at Trouville, laughing. Little Huguette in her Indian costume and headdress, hugging her father.

She would talk, Hadassah said, mostly about "her dear father, her dear mother, her dear sister, Aunt Amelia." Huguette liked to tell the nurses about the summers at the beach in Trouville, how her father built the beautiful Columbia Gardens so the people of Butte could have something to enjoy, how Duke Kahanamoku carried her on his shoulders on a surfboard. And she would share somberly how her sister had died on the trip to Maine. "She talked dearly about that," Hadassah said. "Talked all the time about her sister and parents. Yes, that affected her very much."

Huguette's eyesight had declined, but she was able to read with eyeglasses and then a magnifying glass until past age one hundred. Her hearing was poor in the right ear, but she could hear well out of her left if one talked right at it, and she refused a hearing aid. She didn't deny that her hearing was poor, but she didn't want anything put into her ears, nothing like her mother's primitive squawk box. Hadassah bought a telephone with big numbers and adjustable volume, but Huguette refused to use it, saying she could hear fine with the regular phone.

Doctors and nurses described Huguette as a woman who knew her own mind. "She was remarkably clear," said Karen Gottlieb, a floor nurse who brought her warm milk at bedtime. "Clear in her wants, and things she didn't want. Yes meant yes, and no meant no." Gottlieb said that she never saw any family try to visit, that Huguette's real family seemed to be Hadassah.

The regular hospital staff rarely saw Huguette. One exception was in 2000, when Hadassah herself was in the hospital for back surgery. Huguette arranged for Hadassah to be in a room just down the hall, two or three doors away. Huguette then went to visit Hadassah, dressing up in street clothes and walking down the hall. She wore her favorite Daniel Green shoes.

"That's one day everybody in the floor almost dropped dead," Hadassah said. "They saw Madame coming out of the door with heel shoes."

. . .

Hadassah described Huguette as "a beautiful lady. Very loving. Very respectful. Love people. Very refined lady. Very cultured. Good heart—good soul and good heart. Never hurt anybody. Very, very generous, Madame."

Dr. Singman said he saw that Hadassah and Huguette were very close. "Hadassah was very good to her and was a good nurse for her and worked hard with her."

Huguette's first question in the morning would be "When is Hadassah coming?" She would call nearly every night to make sure Hadassah got home safely and to be reassured that Hadassah would be coming in the next day. Sometimes she'd call just as Hadassah got home, and the answering machine would pick up first. Here is a recording from about 2007, when Huguette was 101. We hear Huguette's sweet, high-pitched

French, and Hadassah's Filipino accent, shouting to make sure she is heard.

HADASSAH: Madame, I love you.

HUGUETTE: I love you, too. Good night to you.

HADASSAH: Have a good night.

HUGUETTE: Have a good night.

HADASSAH: Thank you, Madame.

HUGUETTE: Will I see you tomorrow?

HADASSAH: Yes, Madame.

HUGUETTE: Thank you.

HADASSAH: I love you.

HUGUETTE: I love you, too.

HADASSAH: Good night.

HUGUETTE: Good night, Hadassah.

A REASONABLE PRICE

H UGUETTE KEPT HER LOCATION SECRET for nearly twenty years, never telling any relative or anyone outside her inner circle that she was in the hospital. All of her outgoing correspondence showed 907 Fifth Avenue as her return address.

Though she was no longer living in Apartment 8W, Huguette set to work remodeling it—not to modernize it, but to furnish it so it looked more like her old apartment, 12W. Her main focus was on making her bedroom identical to her mother's old bedroon from the 1920s, which remained undisturbed in the apartment upstairs.

For fifty dollars in tips, she could easily have gotten the doormen to carry the bedroom furniture from the twelfth floor to the eighth. But then, well, the furniture would no longer be in 12W.

Instead, Huguette approached a French furniture company, the renowned Pernault Workshops, with a request that it find original French pieces of the Louis XV period. Yes, the company explained, it might be able to find matching furniture, but the cost would be "staggering." A rolltop desk in the Louis XV style could cost 10 million francs, or about $1.8 million. An alternative plan was offered by Pernault, one that could be accomplished for "a reasonable price." It could make reproductions. Huguette agreed.

The invoices from 1991–92 show the enormous expenditures for "the making and delivering of the copies of your own furniture." For a Louis XV dressing table with three oval mirrors, a three-drawer commode table, two bedside tables, and a rolltop desk, all in solid oak, lavishly engraved and gilded, with floral inlaid wood and bronze trim, Mrs. Huguette M. Clark paid 2,497,000 francs, or $445,893. And those are 1991 dollars, equal to nearly $800,000 today.

This was merely the beginning. For her bedroom, she ordered green silk draperies and a sumptuous green silk damask bedspread with matching cover for a bolster pillow, in a pattern showing Japanese musicians, just like her mother's. These items cost 897,000 francs, or $160,178. The

Louis XV mantelpiece in the bedroom of Apartment 12W was removed, copied, and reattached, with the copy installed in Apartment 8W.

All told, over three years, she spent $4.3 million on the renovation, equal to more than $7 million today. Without updating the bathrooms or kitchens.

For nearly two decades, you could walk into the bedrooms of 12W and 8W, both overlooking the corner of Fifth Avenue and Seventy-Second Street, and see the same oak furniture, the same elaborate mantel, the same luxurious green silk damask bedspread. Aside from a slight difference in the placement of the doors and the radio cabinet in the closet, you couldn't begin to guess what floor you were on.

During that time, Huguette never spent a night there, never walked into either bedroom, seeing the results of the renovation only in photographs brought to her hospital room.

CHRIS

HUGUETTE, who could have anything money could buy, had found one of the keys to true contentment: a personal assistant to help with her art projects and hobbies. Chris Sattler was Huguette's greatest luxury. With an oval door-knocker beard and the sturdy build of a linebacker, the father of two young daughters spent his late forties and his fifties arranging Huguette's dolls.

The son of a family that did high-end painting and construction, Chris first visited her apartment at 907 Fifth Avenue as a volunteer in the 1970s, helping bag three hundred Christmas gifts. He said Huguette ordered the gifts each year from Au Nain Bleu and then had them delivered, anonymously, to an orphanage in Greenwich Village. In the mid-1990s, after Huguette had moved into the hospital, Madame Pierre arranged for Chris to create an inventory of everything in Huguette's apartments. In 2000, Huguette called to offer him a full-time job as her personal assistant.

Every workday for a dozen years, Chris began his morning by walking through each room of Huguette's three apartments at 907 Fifth Avenue. With forty-two rooms, not counting the bathrooms, that was quite a chore. The daily walk was necessary, especially in the twelfth-floor dining room, where a portrait of a rose-cheeked girl dressed in a striped shirt with a bow tie and holding a parasol was signed "Renoir." Across from it hung one of Monet's Water Lilies, which hadn't been seen in public since Huguette bought it in 1930. Beside the fireplace was another Monet, of poplar trees by the Epte River. This wasn't the best place to keep the paintings, because old pipes up on the roof frequently leaked.

The median size of a new home in the United States in 2010 was 2,169 square feet. Huguette had 15,000 square feet that she used as a warehouse, a lending library for her projects.

Only a few rooms were still set up as Huguette had left them, with furniture arranged for regular occupancy: the dining rooms in both apartments, her mother's bedroom in 12W, and Huguette's identical bedroom in 8W.

To keep Huguette's documents in order, Chris found a use for Huguette's third apartment, 8E, which she bought in 1963, protecting her borders so she had no neighbors on the eighth floor. (She was preparing to move down to her mother's old apartment.) But what to do with another five thousand square feet, the size of a basketball court? Chris sorted her financial records, using the unused servants' bedrooms for different years.

In 12W, the living room, with its dark Jacobean wood walls and wood beam ceiling, was filled with rows of simple wooden bookcases with floor-to-ceiling shelves full of items from Japan. Each shelf was carefully labeled and numbered: musical instruments, kimonos, wigs, hair ornaments, traditional footwear, fans, silk costumes, butterflies, art books. A large painting of a geisha with a dragonfly hairpin was hidden behind a three-part Japanese screen with dragons and swans. A Japanese castle with a moat sat on a table by the Steinway grand piano.

One bedroom, an artist's studio, was crammed with easels, canvases, and frames. Paintings included those of a Japanese doll, a self-portrait of the blond artist in a string of pearls, a harlequin, a doll in wooden shoes, and several female nudes.

In a sitting room, there was a filing cabinet full of childhood mementos next to another one with bank statements from the 1970s. Boxes on shelves were marked "personal correspondence."

Shelves in cedar closets were filled with hatboxes, satin bed jackets, and dozens of boxes of shoes, many variations on the same styles: pumps from the Bonwit Teller department store of the 1930s and 1940s, casual slippers with a felt lining from Daniel Green. The white, glass-front kitchen cabinets displayed silver and fine china from the 1920s, and there was an old black Garland six-burner stove. The coat closet was stuffed with pink women's housecoats and white cashmere cardigan sweaters, still in the package, as though the owner were away for a weekend.

. . .

Being Huguette's personal assistant really meant that Chris, with an undergraduate degree in history and literature from Fairfield University in Connecticut, found himself enrolled in the Huguette Marcelle Clark Graduate School of Japanese History.

Huguette called each morning from the hospital room, telling Chris which items she needed him to bring over for the day's project. He kept a diary to record every day's assignment. He answered her calls on one of the vintage black phones with a rotary dial and labeled with old-style phone numbers: BUtterfield 8 1093 and BUtterfield 8 3453.

One morning in 2003, when Huguette was ninety-seven, she rattled off to Chris six books on Japanese theater history, calling each one by title. She was deep into a two-month project on Kabuki, creating a mock-up of a theater to be sent to the elderly artist in Japan, who would make a tabletop theater to her specifications. Everything had to be perfectly to scale and historically accurate. Her instructions for Chris:

Find all the ladies-in-waiting of medium size.
Find all the emperors in casual attire.
Find all the court ladies who are playing cards.

Huguette sent Chris searching through hundreds of boxes of dolls and figurines, looking for a particular Japanese historical character. Just as Americans would know a figure of Abraham Lincoln immediately from his top hat and beard, Huguette would know the figures from the Tokugawa shogunate, specifically those from the 1770s.

Chris also had to find figures for the audience members, then the right scenery to go with them. "I wasn't an expert on Kabuki theater," Chris said. "I tried my best."

When he thought he had it all just right, he would measure the scenery, pose the figures in scenes from twelve or fourteen different plays or stories she selected, photograph it all from every angle, often including a ruler to show the measurements, and take the hundreds of snapshots to Huguette at the hospital.

"Chris," she would say, "that has nothing to do with it." That was her gentle rebuke, a polite way of saying he had it all wrong. He'd mixed up a shogun with a daimyo. He'd placed a major character at the back of the stage.

Finally, when she approved a set of photos, he would bring the full setup to the hospital room, all the delicate scenery and rare figures, just one time, for her to hold them and arrange them for a few hours or a couple of days. "Then," Chris recalled, "she would be in heaven there for a while." To her doctors, Huguette appeared to be merely playing with dolls. "But that wasn't it," Chris said.

He would finally ship a full set of designs and photos to Mrs. Marsh in California, and she would send them along to the artist in Japan. In a couple of years, the finished model would come back, at a price of $50,000 to $80,000. Huguette would give it a look, then it would go into storage at 907 Fifth Avenue. By then, she would have started half a dozen other projects. She went through a French Revolution phase and a religious house phase. She had Chris give photos of Bellosguardo, her Santa Barbara house, to a French designer so that he could make a miniature Bellosguardo as a French château dollhouse.

"I never saw her unhappy," Chris said. "She never appeared bored."

Not all the art projects were highbrow. Huguette gave Chris strict instructions about how to arrange her expensive antique Barbie dolls at the apartment for photo sessions. "She liked to have them set up in a certain way, certain poses." Chris had to "dress and undress them in certain ways, have the furniture set up a certain way." He would photograph the dolls in these scenes. It was too confusing, Chris said, to have too many dolls at the hospital, so she usually wanted him to bring only the photos.

Chris stopped himself in the telling, protective of Huguette, realizing that he may be creating a certain impression. Clarifying, he said people might assume "because she liked these Barbie dolls, that there was something wrong with her. If you could have spoken with her, you wouldn't think that. The most important thing here is that people respect Madame Clark."

. . .

Chris also would bring Huguette her French magazines and newspapers: *Paris Match* for the European news and celebrities, *Point de Vue* for news of the royal courts of Europe. She had a soft spot for royalty, swooning over old photos of Grace Kelly, following closely the Japanese tizzy in the 2000s over the lack of a male heir to the Chrysanthemum Throne, and expressing sorrow for France's last queen, Marie Antoinette.

Every day, Chris brought her French baked goods, usually brioche, the classic sweet bread made from flour, yeast, egg, butter, and milk. It seems like a simple recipe, but it's tricky. The key is to chill the rich, buttery dough so it becomes elastic. "Believe me," Chris said, "there is only a very small amount of stores in New York that sell fresh brioche and madeleines."

Chris also brought the mail from the apartments: bank statements and such, but what Huguette asked for was the auction catalogs for antique dolls and the new toy catalogs from Au Nain Bleu in Paris.

Auction days for Huguette were "like a day at the racetrack," Chris said. After every auction, her attorneys would write her a letter informing her that she had won. Like her father, Huguette was always the highest bidder. One attorney learned this lesson when he failed to win for her an antique Japanese painted screen; he ended up having to buy it with her money from the winning bidder at a higher price.

And yet, when the dolls arrived and she would get a good look at them, she would often give them away to a doctor's grandchild. Some of the dolls, she never unpacked. "She loved the auctions, the thrill of the auction," Chris said. But she already had plenty of dolls.

Chris said he counted at one point 1,157 dolls in her apartments, including more than 600 antique Japanese dolls, more than 400 French and German dolls, and dozens of the highly prized mechanical automatons: a nurse, a dwarf, clowns, giraffes, parrots, marionettes. One automaton owned by Huguette, made by the Jumeau Company in 1880, was a nineteen-inch girl who had blond hair and was wearing an ivory French frock. When a lever was pulled, the girl fanned herself and raised a book of fables to read.

She had modern dolls, too: Barbie teenage fashion dolls from the 1950s on and Family Corners multiracial dolls from the 1990s. And she had the accessories, carefully organized by Chris on numbered shelves:

Shelf 771 in her apartment was packed with minuscule lawn chairs and umbrellas. Shelf 772 had bedroom wardrobes and kitchen stoves.

Chris was fiercely protective of Huguette's privacy, screening her mail according to her instructions. Letters from friends went straight through. Others he would ask her about or send to the lawyers. He screened visitors, too. When one of her old friends started asking questions about the value of her estate, "Mrs. Clark didn't like it," Chris said, and that friendship cooled. Even Chris could overstep the bounds of Huguette's privacy. Once he used his cellphone to take a photograph of Hadassah at the hospital. When he asked to take a photo of Huguette, he said, "Madame flatly refused."

As for why she chose to abandon luxuries to stay in the hospital, Chris said that he, even after sixteen years of taking care of her precious possessions, "was never able to figure it out."

Huguette trusted Chris with the keys to her dear possessions: her castles and dolls and books, not to mention millions of dollars' worth of rare paintings and violins. He described himself as "pathologically honest." She paid him $90 an hour, a figure he suggested and she approved. In 2006, for example, he was paid $187,920, plus $18,000 for health insurance, $9,000 for his two daughters' tuition to Catholic schools, and a $60,000 Christmas gift. Chris brought his wife and children to visit her once in the hospital, and she seemed to enjoy the conversation.

"She was," Chris said, "a sweetheart."

NINTA

T HE RECIPIENT of Huguette's greatest charity was a memory from her childhood.

Her governess, Madame Sandré, had a daughter, Ninta, who was just six months older than Huguette. Like Huguette, Ninta had an artistic spirit, studying dance in the 1920s with the celebrated Japanese dancer and choreographer Michio Itō and performing to Chopin at Carnegie Hall. Her Broadway debut at age twenty-five was reviewed by *The New York Times* less than eagerly: "Nearly all the numbers were extremely brief, occupying less time in some instances than the costume changes that preceded them. Miss Sandre has an agreeable manner and a youthful freshness, but she is scarcely ready as yet to subject her work to comparison with the standards of the metropolitan dance field."

Ninta worked for the Clarks off and on as a cook, and taught dance and French at a private school in Flushing, Queens, but later she was off on her own in New York City. By the time she was about eighty years old, Ninta had fallen on hard times. Living in Astoria, Queens, she had dementia and was often found digging through trash bins on the street.

One evening in January 1987, before Huguette moved to Doctors Hospital, eighty-two-year-old Ninta was picked up by New York police and taken to Bellevue Hospital. She had Huguette's home phone number in her possession, and Huguette was called. In turn, Huguette called her doctor, Myron Wright, arranging for him to take care of Ninta. At first Huguette paid for round-the-clock nursing care for Ninta at home, then for an apartment, then for Ninta to move into Amsterdam Nursing Home. She paid Ninta's medical bills and sent flowers to Ninta's nurses. Huguette had supported other friends and former employees, but this was a great deal more. For thirteen years, Huguette paid more than $200,000 a year for Ninta's care. She also bought Ninta's co-op apartment, although Ninta never recovered enough to return to it.

Huguette's go-between for these arrangements was Dr. Wright's office manager, Lyn Strasheim. Huguette called often, courteous but insis-

$329,000 A MONTH

Huguette Clark entered Doctors Hospital on March 26, 1991. The following expenditures, as documented in periodic reports sent to Huguette by attorney Don Wallace, cover a period of just over three and a half years, or forty-three months, from May 1991 through December 1994. Each dollar in 1992 had the buying power of about $1.70 today, so her monthly costs would be about $560,000 in 2013 dollars.

EXPENSE	TOTAL	PER MONTH
Medical expenses and payroll taxes	$2,226,745	$51,785
Le Beau Château, Connecticut	$146,377	$3,404
Bellosguardo, California	$1,725,945	$40,138
Servants' wages at Fifth Avenue	$12,080	$281
Household bills at Fifth Avenue	$62,167	$1,446
Apartment renovation at Fifth Avenue	$4,306,121	$100,142
Apartments for employees	$605,211	$14,075
Doll purchases and castles	$954,277	$22,192
Insurance and storage	$149,746	$3,482
Federal and state income taxes	$1,959,851	$45,578
Federal gift taxes	$738,599	$17,177
New York State gift tax refund	−$274,910	−$6,393
Connecticut real estate taxes	$156,791	$3,646
Miscellaneous	$487,354	$11,334
Gift: Ninta Sandré's medical care	$769,580	$17,897
Gift: Ninta Sandré's apartment	$17,504	$407
Gifts: Hadassah Peri	$455,100	$10,584
Gifts: Beth Israel Medical Center	$285,000	$6,628
Gift: Trust for Museum Exhibitions	$110,892	$2,579
Gift: Corcoran Gallery of Art	$50,000	$1,163
Gift: Music association, Santa Barbara	$10,000	$233
Transfer to her personal checking account (mostly for more gifts)	$1,200,000	$27,907
Total	$14,167,346	$329,473

tent, wanting to know how Ninta was eating, what clothing she needed. She sent Ninta a television and French magazines, even though Ninta could no longer read or talk. Strasheim said Huguette never seemed to comprehend the severity of Ninta's dementia. "Mrs. Clark wanted everything and anything done for her. Ninta had no quality of life, no pleasure in eating, no enjoyment of TV. She couldn't get her hair cut because she behaved badly at the salon. When you explained that to Mrs. Clark, her solution to everything was to fix it, hire more staff, spend more. She thought that everything came with a price, that if you just paid more, everything could be solved."

Strasheim said Huguette was similarly unrealistic about her own situation. "Dr. Wright said her reaction to her mother's passing was quite irrational, and he thinks that led to her being so much of a recluse. She never really dealt with it. Dr. Wright tried many times to tell her she needed to get out, she needed sunlight, vitamin D. She had a way of switching that off. She didn't want to see the ugliness of things around her. She could divert the conversation in a million ways: 'I'm very busy right now, it's a busy time of year, but I will get back to you on that.' She was a shy ten-year-old throughout her life."

Ninta Sandré died in March 2000. Huguette did not attend the funeral Mass. She sent Lyn Strasheim $50,000.

Strasheim said she once visited Huguette unannounced at Doctors Hospital, but Hadassah shooed her away. Huguette "looked like a bag woman. In a teeny, tiny little room, all the shades drawn."

Y OU DIDN'T HAVE TO BE a longtime friend or employee of Huguette's to benefit from her generosity. In fact, you didn't have to
know her at all.

A lawyer showed up at Gwendolyn Jenkins's apartment, way out in
Queens, bearing a mystery. It was 1982. The lawyer said he had a letter
for her, but he wouldn't let her open it unless she promised to keep a secret. "This lawyer told me not to tell no one. He made me swear."

Yes, she said, she went to church every Sunday and Bible study on
Wednesdays. She wouldn't tell. The lawyer handed over the letter that
changed her life.

Gwendolyn was a nurse's aide, a fifty-seven-year-old immigrant
from Jamaica, living in a working-class area off Jamaica Avenue. Early
every morning, she had taken the Q2 bus and the F train into Lower
Manhattan, to Greenwich Village, more than an hour and a half each
way. Even in the snow, she had walked the last blocks to an apartment at
1 Fifth Avenue, an Art Deco building overlooking Washington Square
Park. Her patient was Irving Gordon, a Madison Avenue stockbroker,
who had recently died of cancer.

And now this lawyer was at her door, with his black-rimmed owl eyeglasses and every hair in place, saying his name was Don Wallace, trying to explain that he didn't know Gwendolyn, that he didn't know
Irving either, but he had a client whose investments Irving had handled.
Word of this nurse's aide and her dedication had gotten around.

"I was telling my daughter that night," Gwendolyn recalled in her
Jamaican accent, "I couldn't believe how this woman, an older woman
she was, had written such a nice card, a proper note. She thanked me for
taking care of poor Mr. Irving. And she included a 'little gift,' she said,
a check for three hundred dollars! I couldn't believe it. I was going to tell
them all about it at Bible study. I've been blessed!

"And my daughter, she said, 'You'd better sit down, Mother, and let me read this letter over to you. This check is for *thirty thousand* dollars!'"

The check was written out with a blue felt-tip pen in a distinctive handwriting, an artist's script, with every lowercase letter formed slowly, precisely, the same height. Gwendolyn didn't recognize the name. "Never met her. Never heard of her."

Gwendolyn used the check to move south, putting a down payment on a house outside Atlanta, her retirement home. No more Q2 bus to the F train in the snow.

Thirty years later, when asked by a reporter who had a copy of the canceled check for $30,000, Gwendolyn reluctantly confirmed the story. Still, she was mindful of her vow, protective of her benefactor's privacy.

Gwendolyn Jenkins still has the thank-you card in her bedroom, tucked away in her hosiery drawer, and she's not going to tell anyone who sent it.

AN ABSOLUTELY RIDICULOUS SITUATION

THOUGH HE NEVER SAW his client's face, attorney Don Wallace would scold her from time to time via letters and phone calls.

"Every year since you have been in the hospital, now for almost three years," he wrote to Huguette in September 1994, "your total expenses for each year have exceeded your total income for each year. This is an absolutely ridiculous situation." He cited her unoccupied three apartments, her Connecticut house, "which has never been occupied," and the "completely wasted expense" of Bellosguardo, which she had not visited in more than forty years. He urged her to sell all of her properties. She also had expenses for the storage of dresses at Bonwit Teller and an automobile stored out in Westchester County, which she no longer called a driver for. As Wallace put it, "None of these expenses benefit you in any way."

She went right on spending, soon drawing up plans for an $87,000 teahouse to be made by the artist in Japan and giving him, over a period of five years, gifts totaling $290,000.

Huguette had a fairy-tale checkbook, one that was refilled whenever it ran out of magic beans. She had been careful with her checking accounts, well into her seventies, balancing her checkbook and marking a balance after each check. The overdrafts had started around 1985, when she was nearly eighty. She wasn't out of money; she just didn't bother to tell her attorney or accountant that she had written checks.

For the next twenty-five years: Huguette would write the checks. The bank would call the attorney to say the account was overdrawn. And the attorney would transfer in money from another account, $50,000 or $100,000 at a time, guessing blindly at how much she might spend in the next few weeks. Irving Kamsler, the certified public accountant that Wallace had brought on in 1979 to handle Huguette's finances, said Huguette knew the value of money but thought the checks would be covered without her involvement. And they were. Although this arrangement troubled her bankers, who had never met Huguette, they never charged her an overdraft free.

Huguette was not poor. She was never poor. But what worried Wallace was that she was starting to eat into her savings.

Most of her income came from dividends paid by blue chips, stocks in the solid cornerstones of American industry: AT&T, American Airlines, Conoco, Exxon, General Electric, General Motors, Gulf Oil, RCA, Texaco. Her smallest were shares in two of her father's old companies, Tonopah Banking Corporation and Clark Holding Company, which were no longer paying dividends. She engaged in no tax shelters or other schemes, paying more than 40 percent of her income in federal taxes through most of the Carter and Reagan years. (Ronald Reagan's Tax Reform Act of 1986, which cut income tax rates on the highest earners, saved Huguette about $1 million a year.) Her income had its ups and downs with the stock market, but it was generally increasing, as shown on her tax returns: $725,734 in 1975, $1,000,010 in 1979, $3,092,147 in 1981, $5,827,446 in 1987.

Her spending, however, was increasing even faster, even from a hospital bed. During the 1970s, she had given away only about $35,000 a year, much of that to Etienne's family, but her generosity increased when Ninta Sandré went into the nursing home in 1987 and accelerated again when Huguette herself went into the hospital in 1991. By the mid-1990s, she was giving away nearly a million dollars a year.

Each spring, her money men chased after her, seeking the information needed to report her gifts to the IRS. As the giver, Huguette owed the gift tax. It was a puzzle. Her attorney and accountant knew every penny spent on her properties and medical care, because they paid those bills. But for her personal account, which she used for most of her gifts, they had only the check numbers and amounts as listed on her bank statements. Well into the 2000s, her money men didn't know the names of the recipients, because only she received the canceled checks, and she refused to give them up.

. . .

For a banker's daughter, Huguette was not much interested in investing her capital either. Summit Bank of New Jersey held millions for her in an uninvested account. For example, on February 4, 1997, Huguette's balance in that account was $5,899,133, earning nothing. The bankers, fearing they'd be sued for acting irresponsibly, wrote to her repeatedly, pleading with her to put the money in an interest-bearing account. Her attorneys and accountant urged the same, time after time. She told them she'd think about it, but she did nothing. Perhaps she preferred to keep the money where she could get at it quickly.

If she had put that $5,899,133 balance into a one-year certificate of deposit, then earning 5 percent, she would have earned $294,957 in interest, nearly enough to pay for a Louis XV rolltop desk.

HUGUETTE RECEIVED a plea for help in 1988 with a familiar postmark—Butte, Montana—and bearing the name Clark. Though the letter was too polite to say so, it was raising a philosophical question: Do children owe an obligation to the place where their parents got their start?

W.A.'s youngest son, Francis Paul Clark, known as Paul, was just sixteen when he died in March 1896. He was a student at Phillips Academy in Andover, Massachusetts, preparing to attend Yale University. Paul was a shy boy, whose hobby was writing to famous artists to ask for their autographs. He died from a bacterial infection, erysipelas, which causes a painful rash known as Saint Anthony's fire. W.A. was in Paris and came back to New York for the funeral. Paul was entombed at Woodlawn Cemetery alongside his mother.

As a memorial, W.A. donated $50,000 for the Paul Clark Home, which opened in Butte in 1900. The Associated Charities of Butte took care of children in the handsome three-story brick home on Excelsior Street, less than a mile from the Clark mansion where Paul had grown up. W.A. also left the home an endowment of $350,000 in his will.

Anna visited the home with young Andrée and Huguette and gave money for a grand piano for the children to play. She left the home $5,000 in her will, one of her smallest bequests.

The Paul Clark Home wasn't strictly an orphanage; it also took in children whose parents were still living but couldn't care for them anymore. In addition, the home provided free medical care for any child from Butte and day care for children of working mothers. It was not in a bad part of town; directly across the street were three identical homes for managers of Clark's mines.

In 1988, the Paul Clark Home reached a crossroads, and the board of directors reached out to W.A.'s surviving daughter, Huguette, who was born ten years after Paul died. During the 1960s, it had been converted into a home for developmentally disabled young adults, whom the state was moving out of institutions. Now this Clark legacy needed a new mission, and it had bills to pay. The trust set up by W.A. in his will was providing only $29,000 of the $60,000 budget each year, and the home's board hoped to raise $200,000 for a renovation. W.A.'s will had set up the home to exist for as long as his children and grandchildren should live. Well, his grandchildren were nearly all dead, but his daughter lived on. Was it Huguette's wish, the home's attorney asked, that it continue?

Huguette sent back, through her attorney, questions about the home's finances, but she didn't send any money.

In December 1988, the Paul Clark Home was converted into a Ronald McDonald House, providing a temporary home for families who have a child or family member in the hospital. So it continues today.

The home is still a comfortable spot, with a reading room and a sun parlor. And one can still see, in the upstairs dormitory, the charming bathrooms with little sinks all in a row at a child's height, twenty for boys and twenty for girls, with numbered cubbies for their toiletries and beautiful rows of lockers made of oak.

Huguette received similar letters over the next few years from the YWCA of Los Angeles, where the $25,000 left by W.A. for a women's home was not enough for its upkeep. This home was a memorial to her grandmother, Mary Andrews Clark. Huguette again asked questions but sent nothing.

. . .

On May 18, 1993, Huguette was a bidder at a Sotheby's auction for two antique French dolls. The first, in Lot 219, was a Jumeau triste pressed bisque doll, circa 1875, with a dimple in the chin, fixed brown glass paperweight eyes, pierced ears, blond mohair wig, in cream lacy overdress with Eau-de-Nil silk below and cream lacy and silk bonnet. The estimate was $12,000 to $15,000. She authorized her attorney to bid up to $45,000, but got it for $14,933.

The second, in Lot 244, was a Thuillier pressed bisque doll, circa 1885, with fixed blue glass paperweight eyes, pierced ears, blond mohair wig, in pink silk dress with cream lacy overdress and matching straw bonnet. The estimate was higher, $18,000 to $27,000, and she craved this one even more, authorizing a bid up to $90,000. She won it at $14,054.

On that day, not so different from many other days, Huguette spent $29,000 on two dolls, but she had been a lucky bidder. She had authorized her attorney to bid up to $135,000, twice the annual budget of the Paul Clark Home.

WANDA

====

FTER HUGUETTE was no longer taking painting lessons from Tadé Styka and he had moved on to his own marriage during World War II, she kept up a lively correspondence with Tadé and his new wife, Doris. When the Stykas had their only child, a daughter born in 1943, Huguette became godmother to the girl, Wanda Magdaleine Styka. Like her mother, Huguette kept the thread of relationships alive from generation to generation.

Wanda always called Huguette by the French word for godmother, Marraine. "She really is adorable," Huguette wrote to Doris. "I find her more so each time I see her."

Sometimes Huguette offered to babysit when Wanda's parents went to the movies, and the families exchanged gifts and talked on the phone. But even with these dear friends, her visits were few. "Mrs. Clark," Doris wrote in July 1948, "it has been so very long since we have seen you. We do hope to be given the pleasure of a visit from you soon. But if you find it difficult to venture out in this steaming weather—may Wanda and I now or soon accept the invitation you so sweetly offered, so long ago, to visit you one afternoon—for just a little while?"

Huguette sent Wanda a baby carriage, her first bicycle, and a cashmere cardigan in ecru. She paid for air-conditioning so the Stykas wouldn't have to suffer from the heat. And later she sent checks, $50,000 and $60,000 at a time. Huguette and Anna sent Doris and Wanda a new television in August 1948, just in time to watch Milton Berle take over as the regular host of the *Texaco Star Theater* on Monday nights. That same month, Huguette did arrange a visit, giving Wanda a new doll and a proper wardrobe for it. "As we think of what you have done and are doing for Wanda," Doris wrote, "with no thought of glory for your dear self, the overwhelming sense of gratitude we feel is really too deep for words."

After Tadé died in 1954, Huguette's generosity filled the breach, supporting Doris and Wanda and paying for Wanda's continued education at an elite Catholic high school for girls. The Stykas became an oddly reclusive pair themselves, living in a hideaway 1837 farmhouse in a river valley between the Berkshire Hills and the Taconic Range in southwestern Massachusetts. Wanda had no siblings and never married. It was just mother and daughter alone together in the mountains, just like Anna and Huguette alone together on Fifth Avenue.

Like Huguette, Wanda lost her father when she was young. She lived with her mother until Doris's death. She lived alone thereafter. She had very little contact with any of her relatives.

Wanda, too, showed an artist's sensibility, combined with a meticulous nature. Working as an art curator and archivist, she wrote regularly to Huguette, describing her work in a striking and imaginative handwriting that Huguette showed off to her doctors at the hospital. It was an artist's handwriting, carrying earnest messages of her love for Huguette, along with news of the holidays and the passing seasons. Wanda often included photos of herself, at Huguette's insistence. These photos show a short woman with her hair pulled back and parted in the middle, a bundle of positive energy posing dramatically among the peonies or the yellow roses flanking the stone steps to the Styka home. Wanda was living the quiet life, like her godmother, but in a beautiful place.

Mother and I send streams and streams of fondest good wishes for a deeply happy Thanksgiving Day. . . .

Mother and I love June for its warmth and blossoms but most of all because it is your month. . . .

Snow lies all about us, as the chance of having an Indian Summer fades. . . .

We greet you most affectionately, and our wishes are with you for all that is happy and beautiful. Mother sends her fondest love, and you always have, dearest Marraine, All my most Devoted love, Wanda.

Huguette told her staff that she *loved* Wanda, a word she didn't use with many people.

Chris Sattler suggested that Huguette invite Wanda to the hospital, but she said she didn't want Wanda to see her that way or that she couldn't entertain properly there.

In fact, though they talked often on the phone, Wanda said she never knew Huguette was in a hospital. She had figured out, however, that Huguette was no longer at 907 Fifth Avenue. After her mother died in September 2003, Wanda tried to call Huguette at the BUtterfield 8 numbers at the apartments. When she didn't get an answer, she called Madame Pierre, asking her to tell Huguette of her mother's death. Huguette returned the call to offer her condolences.

Then Huguette called again, with urgent advice for Wanda. Huguette insisted that Wanda not live alone. With her mother gone, Huguette told Wanda that she wasn't safe by herself in her retreat in the woods. She insisted that Wanda send her a map of the property showing the proximity of neighbors.

Wanda never found out where Huguette was living. Madame Pierre told Wanda that she could reveal Huguette's location, but at the same time she said she was afraid to tell, because Huguette might not like it. Wanda later said that she had replied, "Well, then don't." She said she didn't need to know. "My godmother was very private, and I always respected that."

Wanda traveled to Manhattan from time to time and would tell Huguette all about her trips, but she didn't press for an invitation to visit. She said she just didn't want to impose on Huguette.

Wanda said she must have seen Huguette for the last time at her father's studio just after he died in 1954. Huguette was forty-eight, and Wanda was eleven. Wanda still kept in touch with her godmother for more than half a century. "If there ever was anybody in the world who ever loved Mrs. Clark just for her love," Chris Sattler said, "it was that lady."

IT JUST SNOWBALLED

HUGUETTE'S GIFTS to her nurse Hadassah began almost immediately after she moved into Doctors Hospital.

The first large one came in September 1993, after there was a flood in the basement of the Peris' building. Hadassah mentioned to Huguette that all three of her children had asthma. The next day, Hadassah recalled, Huguette suggested they move. The Peris found a house nearby, on Shore Boulevard, and bought it, with Huguette giving Hadassah $450,000. They kept the previous apartment, too.

That year, her accountant, Irving Kamsler, expressed concern to her attorney Don Wallace that Huguette was "vulnerable to the influence of people around her evidenced by her extraordinary gifts to her nurses and their families." Any sob story would have her reaching for her checkbook.

Huguette started giving the Peris gifts at Christmas, $40,000 for Hadassah and $40,000 for her husband. Hadassah said she would say, "Madame, you have given us so much." Huguette was generous to other employees as well, but the gifts to Hadassah accelerated. She paid for twenty years of schooling for the three Peri children, from preschool through high school at the Yeshivah of Flatbush, then through college and graduate school. She paid for their medical bills, piano lessons, violin lessons, and Hebrew lessons, their basketball and summer camps in upstate New York. When the Peris had some trouble with back taxes, she paid for that.

Huguette wrote more than three hundred checks to Hadassah over the twenty years she was in the hospital. Some of these checks, Hadassah said, were not for her but for other staff members. Huguette would make the gifts through Hadassah to protect her privacy. For instance, Huguette gave $25,000 to Ruth Gray, the hospital kitchen worker who brought her meals. Sometimes she'd give Hadassah two checks a day— $45,000 in the morning, $10,000 in the afternoon.

"Sometimes I would say, you gave me a check already today. She

*Huguette Clark's dear Frenchman and childhood friend, Etienne
de Villermont, shown here in France, brought his daughter,
Marie-Christine, to visit Huguette in New York. The girl's toy
donkey, Cadichon, was one of many gifts she received from
Huguette. Etienne and Huguette corresponded for decades, and
he visited her many times, even with his wife. He wrote to her in
1966: "In spite of our separate lives, my heart always beats with
you. The years will always live . . ."*

On a single day in 1993, when Huguette was eighty-six, she bought these two French dolls from the late 1800s (a Jumeau, left, and a Thuillier). She paid nearly $30,000 for the pair, but had authorized her attorney to bid up to $135,000. She was nearly always the highest bidder.

Huguette designed and commissioned many tabletop reproductions of Japanese buildings: castles, tearooms, houses, temples. "She was just a delightful person," said Caterina Marsh, her go-between with the artists in Japan. "She developed an incredible knowledge about the art and culture of Japan. It was astonishing what she knew, all the legends and folklore. To me, she was the last of an era."

Trying to count all of Huguette's dolls in her three apartments, her personal assistant came up with 1,157, including more than 600 antique Japanese dolls. She loved the tiny hina dolls, which in Japan are displayed during a festival every March. "They are hard to get," she said. "They are very lovely dolls, you know."

A dedicated amateur photographer with a collection of high-end cameras, Huguette in her middle years posed regularly for simple self-portraits taken with her Polaroid instant cameras. Regularly on Easter and Christmas, she would pose for such snapshots in her apartment on Fifth Avenue.

After moving into a hospital in 1991, Huguette spent $445,893 for a French company to make these reproductions of the antique furniture that was upstairs in her late mother's former bedroom. If you walked into Huguette's bedroom in Apartment 8W, or her mother's in 12W, you would have had a hard time telling the difference. She never returned to this room or saw any of this furniture, except in photos.

2383

DATE May 1st 2000

62-23/311
20531482

PAY TO THE
ORDER OF Mrs. Hadassah Peri $5,000,000 no/100

Five million no/100 _____ DOLLARS

JPMorgan   Morgan Guaranty Trust
Company of New York
Checking Account

MEMO _____   Huguette M. Clarke

⑂031100238⑂   205 31 482⑂ 2383

One of three $5 million checks that Huguette wrote to her private-duty nurse, Hadassah Peri, who received more than $31 million from her, not counting millions more in her will. Hadassah worked for Huguette for twenty years, including every day for nearly a decade. She said, "I give my life to Madame."

*Huguette lost this $10 million Degas ballerina, which was
stolen from her apartment while she was in the hospital
and turned up on the wall of a noted collector. She refused
to sue to get it back, because the publicity would threaten
her privacy. She sold this Stradivarius violin for $6 mil-
lion so that she could give more gifts. In 1955, she had
bought the violin, known as "La Pucelle" (meaning "the
virgin"), but she preferred to play a lesser Strad.*

*After Huguette died, her jewelry fetched $18 million at auction. This
Art Deco diamond and gem charm bracelet by Cartier from about
1925, with themes of love, sold for $75,000.*

*Her pair of emerald, natural pearl, and diamond
ear pendants, by Cartier, from the early twentieth
century, sold for $85,000.*

*Her Art Deco diamond bracelet, by Cartier, circa 1925, sold
for $480,000.*

*Her Art Deco emerald and diamond bracelet, by Cartier,
circa 1925, sold for $90,000.*

At top is the view Huguette abandoned when she moved to a hospital from her apartment building at 907 Fifth Avenue, including the sailboat pond in Central Park in the foreground. At bottom is the view from Huguette's last regular hospital room at Beth Israel Medical Center. From her window in room 3K01, one can see no sky at all, only the facing wall of another wing of the hospital, and the air-conditioning units.

HUGUETTE'S CHARITY

Following are Huguette's gifts for the year 1991, as listed on her federal gift tax return.

EXPENSE	TOTAL
Ninta Sandré, nursing home care	$223,510
Dr. Jules Pierre and Madame Suzanne Pierre	$114,000
Mr. and Mrs. Sautereau (friends in France)	$60,000
Elisabeth de Villermont (Etienne's widow)	$29,000
Marie-Christine (Etienne's daughter)	$10,000
Hadassah Peri (day nurse)	$32,000
Geraldine Lehane Coffey (night nurse)	$18,000
Doris and Wanda Styka (friend, goddaughter)	$22,000
Anna E. LaChapelle (cousin)	$10,000
Mrs. Walter Armstrong (chauffeur's widow)	$16,000
Other former employees and their children	$68,000
Total	$602,510

would say, 'You have a lot of expense, you can use it.' I accepted the check because we have a lot of bills. Madame is very generous, and we don't force her to give us—we don't ask for it. That's how she is, very generous, not only me, thousands of people, a lot of people."

. . .

Huguette also kept buying homes for the Peris.

In August 1999: $149,589 for a second apartment in their old building in Brooklyn, the one with the flood. The Peris' older son, Abraham (or Avi), moved in there.

In 2000: $775,000 for a house in Brooklyn, so Hadassah's brother and his family would have a place to stay when they visited. It's worth about $1.7 million today. But the brother moved to California, and the house has remained vacant ever since she bought it.

Yes, Huguette's nurse has her own empty mansion.

The generosity continued.

In December 2000: $885,000 for an apartment for Hadassah's children at the Gatsby, a prewar building on East Ninety-Sixth Street in Manhattan.

In August 2001: $1,475,097 for a second unit in the Gatsby, because Huguette said Hadassah should have a nicer view of Central Park.

And, the last, in August 2002: $599,000 for a house on the New Jersey shore, near Long Branch, so the family could take vacations together and so they would have a refuge in case of a terrorist attack, as Huguette had bought her own safe house in Connecticut.

The Peris, a family of five, now owned seven residences—all but the first apartment had been bought by Huguette. The total that Huguette gave to Hadassah for real estate was $4.3 million. Some of the money was characterized as a loan, which Huguette forgave without any payments being made.

"I told Madame I have many houses already," Hadassah said. "Just to maintain this houses means a lot of money." Huguette responded by also paying the common charges and taxes for the apartments.

. . .

The entire Peri family wrote frequent thank-you notes "to our dear Madame Clark." They said they thought of her like a grandmother or fairy godmother.

"All these luxuries me and my family enjoyed could never be in reality if not for your support, both spiritual and financial," the family wrote in a card in March 1998. "I could never forget these wonderful things you have shared to us. I pray to God, that you will be rewarded with good health and long life. Respectfully and gratefully, Daniel, Hadassah, Avi, David and Geula Peri."

In other notes, the children told Huguette that their tuition and fees continued to rise.

Huguette also bought the Peris a used Dodge Caravan minivan, then a new Isuzu. From the gift checks they received from Huguette, the Peris bought a series of other new cars, each one about twice as expensive as the last: a 1998 Lincoln Navigator luxury SUV for $48,000 in cash, a 1999 Hummer for $91,000 in cash, and finally a 2001 Bentley. And not just any Bentley, but an Arnage Le Mans, one of only 150 in the world, for which they paid $210,000 in cash. The former taxi driver Daniel Peri was now driving a Bentley.

Hadassah said the Bentley was a burden. The fastest four-door sedan in the world wasn't a practical car in Brooklyn. "To tell you the truth, we never enjoy this car. So expensive to repair. You cannot drive it anywhere. You scared somebody going to bang it. . . . It's hell. My kids don't enjoy it. You are scared somebody going to steal it. I don't know why we buy this stupidity, you know." She said she prefers to drive the Lincoln.

Those automobiles were not enough. In 2001, seventeen-year-old Abraham added to a birthday card he sent to Huguette a thinly disguised plea for new wheels:

> *Dearest Madame, I would like to thank you from the bottom of my heart for all the help you have given us. My development from a child to a young adult, during the past 17 years of my life would not be possible without your care, love, and support. I am graduating from high school on Sunday, June 10, and will be entering New York University in the fall. I am proud to tell you that I am old enough to drive. When I had my orientation at NYU, I had to drive my mother's car, since the van was stolen. With a big family, it is difficult to commute with only one car.*

Huguette wrote him a check for $5,000.

The Peri children ran errands for Huguette, finding Japanese art books she asked for and ordering jewelry from Gump's San Francisco, which she liked to give away to the children of doctors and nurses. Huguette regularly wrote checks to the Peri children. From 1996 through 2011, Abraham received $628,250; his sister, Geula, $621,250; and his younger brother, David, $706,550.

Hadassah and Huguette had their spats. In late 2004 they had a serious disagreement, and Hadassah finally took some time off. There was a long discussion among Huguette and her circle about whether she should fire Hadassah. But soon Hadassah was back.

Huguette showed great empathy for any problem Hadassah's family had. She paid $35,000 in medical bills for Hadassah's older son. She gave them money for Hadassah's brother, who had trouble finding work, and

HUGUETTE'S GIFTS TO THE PERIS IN A SINGLE YEAR

Just in the year 2003, Huguette wrote thirty-five checks totaling $955,200 to Hadassah and her family, on top of Hadassah's salary.

January 3	$45,000 (son David)
January 13	$45,000
January 13	$10,000
January 13	$8,000
January 13	$40,000 (son Abraham, or Avi)
January 13	$20,000 (daughter Geula)
January 14	$35,000 (David)
February 4	$30,000
February 4	$8,000
February 4	$40,000
March 5	$35,000
March 13	$8,000
April 15	$35,000
May 3	$15,000 (David)
May 3	$15,000 (Geula)
May 9	$30,000
May 9	$30,000
May 12	$25,000
July 8	$75,000
July 18	$25,000
July 25	$35,000
August 5	$40,000
August 5	$6,000
September 8	$20,000 (Abraham)
September 8	$20,000 (David)
September 8	$15,000 (Geula)
September 14	$7,000

September 24	$35,000
October 1	$15,000
October 27	$10,000
November 3	$45,000
December 1	$8,200
December 3	$35,000
December 21	$45,000
December 21	$45,000 (husband Daniel)

paid for breast cancer treatment for his daughter. And when the Peris were audited by the IRS, Huguette paid the $300,000 bill for that, too.

. . .

Madame Pierre was protective of Huguette, expressing concern to her granddaughter about the gifts Huguette was giving to Hadassah and others. "My grandmother felt that Madame Clark was being solicited by everyone that had any contact with her," Kati Despretz Cruz said. "Everyone was crying their tale of woe to her." But Suzanne would never have mentioned this concern to Huguette, Kati said, for that would have been impolite.

The Pierres also were recipients of Huguette's generosity. Huguette had regularly given Suzanne checks for $20,000 or $50,000 as gifts, disguised as payment for secretarial services, but in her nineties she stepped up her giving.

Huguette, who had met Suzanne's great-grandson, had grown up in a household afraid of a possible kidnapping. She told Suzanne that the boy was so cute that someone might try to kidnap him. She said it wasn't safe for him and his mother to be living on the second floor of their apartment building on the Upper East Side. She insisted they trade up to an apartment on a higher floor, paying the $610,000 difference.

On the very same day, Huguette bought two more apartments in the building, one for her day nurse, Hadassah, and one for her night nurse, Geraldine Lehane Coffey, so they could live closer to the hospital. Geraldine, who came to America from Ireland and is a licensed practical nurse, received a bit more than $1 million in gifts from Huguette over the years. "I respected her very much. She respected me," Geraldine said. "I felt she was very smart, she was strong, she was intelligent, well-traveled. She was a very nice lady." Geraldine worked seven nights a week, eleven P.M. to seven A.M., at the same salary as Hadassah: $131,040. She said Huguette cut her own hair, bathed herself, and was so healthy that often there was no need to take her temperature. "There was very little nursing to do."

The gifts also caused concern among Huguette's advisers, accountant Irving Kamsler and her new attorney, Wally Bock. (He took over after her longtime attorney Don Wallace had a heart attack in 1997. Wallace died in 2002.) Despite their concerns, Bock and Kamsler were only advisers, always deferential in their conversations and letters. "Certain questions were not asked of Mrs. Clark, or her motives questioned," Bock said. "She knew what she wanted to do, she made up her mind what to do, and normally you couldn't change her mind anyhow, and she would get angry if you persisted." Besides, he thought of Hadassah as loyal and devoted to Huguette, and it appeared Huguette was not being pestered for gifts, but would instead seize on any opportunity to be generous.

Bock explained:

Somebody would come in and say, "Oh, dear, my sister needs an operation and I can't afford it." She would say, "Well, I'll pay for it."

I discussed it with her, and her question was, "Can I afford it?"

And I would say yes. I would say, "But why don't you put it into a will rather than giving it now?"

And she said, "I want to see people enjoy the gifts that I give while I'm alive." Mrs. Clark was a very smart and astute woman who made up her own mind, decided what she wanted to do, when she wanted to do it. She didn't ask permission.

Hadassah said she never asked for any of these gifts. She said she would mention that tuition would be expensive for her daughter at grad school, and then Huguette would insist on paying for it. "Sometimes she gives you checks, you will be amazed, it is not the amount you want, it is more than the amount you want. And it happens many, many times. That's how Madame is. . . . Madame insist we have to get this. . . . I did not ask for it."

Hadassah disputed the idea that mentioning family issues was her way of asking Huguette for gifts. "For twenty years what do you do if you stay in the room? We always talk about our lives, we talk about anything, you know, and she always ask my family. . . . Daily talk, of course. It is like a family. I am the nurse of Madame, I am very their friend, I dedicate my life to Madame. For almost fourteen years I stayed more in Madame room than in my house. I work twelve hours. . . . My husband is a mother and father while I'm working with Madame. Family vacation, I miss, when the kids were growing up. Because she never wants me to take off. She is uncomfortable with other people. I gave my life for her."

Hadassah's husband, Daniel, received $1,503,813. He ran errands for Huguette and stayed home with the kids while his wife worked seven days a week. With the money his wife was making, he said, they were in too high a tax bracket. "Figure it out. I have to stop working, because whatever I make is going to pay taxes and that's it."

Kamsler and Bock cautioned Huguette repeatedly about making excessive gifts, citing the federal gift taxes that would be due. Bock warned Huguette in a letter: She had "failed to understand the consequences of your continued course of action." But Bock hardly saw her. Communicating with his client was like the children's game of fishing, where the player throws a line with a clothespin attached over a curtain. Usually when he pulled the line, she didn't bite, or she would say she'd think about it.

. . .

Before he died in 1992, Dr. Jules Pierre wrote a private letter to his former patient Huguette. In French, he outlined his financial situation. With scant income from a dwindling trust and Social Security, he told Huguette that his wife, Suzanne, would soon be a widow and would probably be unable to keep their Park Avenue apartment. He asked Huguette to lend her money until she could sell the apartment.

"Please believe me when I say that I know what I am talking about when I think about the serious problems that my wife will have to face," Dr. Pierre wrote. "Please receive, dear Madame and great friend, my very affectionate thoughts. Your faithful friend—ever grateful for everything you do for us. Pierre."

His request was answered seven years later, in 1999, when Huguette arranged, through her attorney, to sell two paintings at Sotheby's so she could offer more gifts to her friends. One was Monet's *Three Poplars in Gray Weather*. It brought $10 million, which Huguette gave to Madame Pierre.

Talking about Huguette in her apartment on a Saturday afternoon in 2010, Madame Pierre was easily distracted by the television, and the conversation lagged. As she was looking at photos of Huguette, her face brightened. In the kitchen, her caretaker explained that Madame Pierre had Alzheimer's disease, as her son confirmed.

Because of Huguette's generosity, Suzanne Pierre could afford round-the-clock care until she died in February 2011 at age eighty-nine. Because of Huguette, Suzanne had been able to remain in her home until the end.

. . .

Huguette offered the second painting, Cézanne's *Earthenware Jug*, to Hadassah. The nurse said she didn't have any use for an old painting, so Huguette included it in the 1999 sale at Sotheby's. It sold for $15 million, and Huguette said she wanted to give it all to Hadassah.

Huguette's lawyer and accountant were aghast. The tax implications were astounding. Giving away $25 million to Hadassah and Madame Pierre would cost Huguette another $28 million in taxes. Bock and Kamsler told Huguette she would have to sell other assets just to pay the taxes, so she improvised.

She immediately gave Hadassah two checks for $5 million each—along with an IOU, in the form of a third check, also for $5 million, undated.

"She told me to hold it," Hadassah said, until the Connecticut property was sold. Bock and Kamsler weren't told about this check, but Hadassah made an unusual note of it in Huguette's medical chart, citing the $5 million that "she promised."

Huguette also may have profited from this transaction. She did not like hiring new people. An employee carrying a well-worn, undated check for $5 million would be unlikely to seek other employment.

. . .

Huguette's man Friday, Chris Sattler, also started receiving gifts. He said Huguette instructed him to open the large safe in the walk-in closet in Apartment 12W. He had to get a locksmith to drill the lock. There he found her stash of everyday jewelry. He brought the boxes from Cartier and Van Cleef & Arpels to the hospital in a shopping bag. Huguette enjoyed looking it all over and gave him a piece. Then she gave Hadassah a piece, "and it just snowballed," Chris said.

Chris, who is Catholic, received from Huguette a crucifix, a $7,000 Cartier antique diamond and ruby cross pendant on an Art Deco diamond and platinum chain, and other pieces, in all worth $27,000. He said he didn't think to refuse the gifts, which were documented through Huguette's attorney after an appraisal.

To Hadassah she gave eighty-four pieces of jewelry, appraised at $667,300, as well as two antique harpsichords, a clavichord, and fifteen antique dolls.

And to Hadassah's younger son, David, Huguette gave an even larger gift. When he had been a schoolboy, David played the violin for Huguette in her room. "And Madame said, 'Someday I have something for you, but you are too young,'" Hadassah said. "'When you are responsible to have, I have something for you.'" Now she gave him her third-best violin by Stradivari, worth about $1.2 million.

"I told Madame, he doesn't play anymore," Hadassah said, "but she insist he will go back to learn again. . . . I think one time she told me she played the violin for twenty-one years, but she never really like it, but she just did it for her mother."

Counting all the gifts, Hadassah and her family received at least $31,906,074.81 in cash and property from Huguette while she was alive.

Of course, one must keep that amount in perspective. If Huguette were willing to keep selling property, she could have afforded ten Hadassahs.

Hadassah was asked whether she questioned the ethics of accepting large gifts from her patient. Hadassah showed no hint of embarrassment or doubt, only entitlement, saying she didn't know of any rules, and besides, she was an independent contractor, not a hospital employee. "I cannot recall any paper that I am not allowed to receive any such gift."

What about the ethics of the nursing profession?

"Never come to my mind."

I T WAS TIME to dig in their heels. On October 26, 2001, Huguette's advisers wrote separate letters to her, a coordinated warning about her excessive generosity. Her significant gifts in the past year had depleted her cash, and her income was no longer sufficient to pay her expenses.

"You will have to seriously consider," attorney Bock wrote, "the sale of additional assets in order to raise the cash necessary to meet all of these obligations."

Five days later, Bock sent his client a solicitation for a gift.

Wallace "Wally" Bock, born in 1932, is a quiet Orthodox Jewish American with ties to Israel that reach back long before there was a State of Israel. His parents, before World War I, were among the founders of the Mizrachi religious movement in the United States to build a Jewish state. His mother was personal secretary to the world leader of that movement. His brother was imprisoned by the British for helping transport Jewish immigrants to Palestine.

Now Bock's daughter and her husband were making a return to Israel (in Hebrew, *aliyah,* or "ascent"). They were living with Wally's grandchildren and a great-grandchild in an Israeli settlement town called Efrat, in the Judaean Mountains of the disputed West Bank, just south of Jerusalem. The town was raising money for a sophisticated, state-of-the-art security system, including technology to monitor suspicious vehicles and alert military forces.

Though Bock had never met his client, Huguette called often to issue orders, and whenever she saw Mideast turmoil on CNN or in *The New York Times,* she would call to check on his family.

Bock sent Huguette the town's fund-raising brochure for the security system. He explained that there had been several shooting attacks on the town and that one of its synagogues had been desecrated. "As you well know," Bock wrote to his client, "I have never sought help from you for myself personally or for any cause that I may have been involved in. However, in view of your expressed interest in what is happening in

Israel and your concern for my family there, I am taking the liberty of asking your financial assistance in this project. I will of course leave it to your discretion as to the amount, if any, that you may wish to contribute."

Huguette had made gifts to her previous attorneys. She gave Don Wallace $130,000 in French mechanical dolls, so many that he had to build extra shelves in his house. When Wallace's secretary wrote to Huguette, saying she was moving to Europe to launch a singing career, Huguette sent her a check for $10,000. But Bock had never received a gift, other than a dollhouse for a granddaughter. Bock later said that he had expected Huguette might donate $5,000 or $10,000.

Huguette filled in an amount on the second page of the solicitation, signed it, and sent it back. She had written in the entire amount the town was trying to raise, $1.85 million.

Bock paid out the money slowly over the next three years, writing checks to the town's sponsors, the Central Fund of Israel and the American Friends of New Communities in Israel. He said he had to fend off efforts by some in the town to use the money for other than its intended purpose.

Bock went to Efrat in 2008, speaking at the dedication of the Efrat Emergency Command and Rescue Center. "So there I was," he told the gathering, "an Orthodox Jew, seeking a contribution from a non-Jewish millionairess, for a project to provide a security system for this place called Efrat, which she had never heard of, in a country called Israel, which she read about in the papers but was not too familiar with. Fortunately, she knew that I had a daughter living in Israel, and every time there was a terrorist incident she would call me to make sure that my family had not been affected."

A plaque reads: "The security system for Efrat has been made possible by the generosity of Madame Huguette M. Clark. May the Almighty bless her with good health and long life." Bock said that at first Huguette had insisted on anonymity, as she always did, but that she had relented as the dedication neared.

Chris Sattler said Huguette expressed pride in the donation to Efrat. "She said she bought the fence to keep the bad people out."

. . .

Huguette was just two miles from the World Trade Center on September 11, 2001, when Islamist terrorists killed nearly three thousand people in the United States. She had a personal connection to one who died: The son-in-law of her California attorney was killed on hijacked American Airlines Flight 77, which struck the Pentagon. Although she had never talked with her attorney, James H. "Jim" Hurley, Jr., in the thirty-five years he had handled her business in Santa Barbara, Huguette wrote a note of condolence.

After September 11, as the news was filled with instances of deadly anthrax and other powdered substances being sent to prominent people, Huguette was insistent that she not receive anything else through the mail. From then on, she received no mail or packages directly from the few people who knew she was at the hospital. All mail had to be sent to 907 Fifth Avenue, where Chris Sattler would open it and deliver it, or be delivered by courier from Bock's office. Bock said Huguette often seemed to draw her fears from the day's news.

Despite her fears, just two days after the September 11 attacks, ninety-five-year-old Huguette was thinking of others. She called her goddaughter, Wanda, in Massachusetts to assure her that she was fine in New York City. They discussed the horrible events, and Huguette remarked to Wanda how glad she was that her shades were drawn most of the time.

CASHING OUT

To RAISE CASH for the accelerating gifts, Huguette had to sell some of her collections and property.

In 2001, she sold her best Stradivarius violin, La Pucelle, which she had bought in 1955 and carefully maintained.

In April 2003, she sold Renoir's *In the Roses*, which had been the very first portrait by Renoir to enter a collection in the United States. The portrait shows a stockbroker's wife with a plunging neckline seated on a bench in a rose garden. The Las Vegas casino magnate Steve Wynn bought the painting for $23.5 million. This Renoir, while in the hands of the Clarks, had not been seen by the public since 1937.

IN CONVERSATION WITH HUGUETTE

In November 2003, Huguette made an unintended call to my number. She apparently called me by mistake while trying to reach someone else. The call was placed station-to-station collect. She was briefly confused, but after she realized whom she had reached, we talked for about five minutes. I'm not surprised by the mistaken call. I've done that myself. But to this day I am perplexed: Why would one of the richest women in the world be placing a collect call to anyone?

In 2005, Huguette put her Connecticut refuge, Le Beau Château, on the market. Documents show that Huguette was well aware of each of these sales, authorizing them and even directing how La Pucelle should be sold.

The London violin expert and dealer Charles Beare had written to Huguette many times since the 1980s asking about La Pucelle. Finally in 2001 Wally Bock told him that Huguette had consented to sell it. At first Bock planned to let Sotheby's auction off the violin. The estimate was

$2 million to $3 million. Huguette insisted instead that Bock go through a dealer, because such instruments bring higher values in private sales.

There was one hitch: Huguette refused to let La Pucelle leave the apartment to be seen by potential buyers. She didn't say why, but that wouldn't make it easy to sell the violin.

Beare, however, had a regular customer, and the dealer knew just what to tell him. He called David Fulton, a software millionaire in the Seattle area. A former concertmaster, Fulton had merged his Fox Software database company into Microsoft and was now using his fortune to collect the world's finest violins.

Beare remembers telling Fulton, "I have in hand the very best Strad that will ever be available to you, almost certainly the finest Stradivari that's not in a museum and certainly the best preserved. This is the last chance you'll ever have to get a fiddle this great. Are you interested?"

Fulton couldn't travel then to New York, but he agreed to buy La Pucelle at the asking price, sight unseen.

There was another hitch. Beare said the confidentiality agreement proposed by Bock was so onerous that not only would it forbid him to disclose whom he had bought the violin from, or even the seller's gender, but it would prevent him from revealing that he owned the violin at all. He could not play it in the presence of anyone, ever.

Fulton responded that either the violin was for sale or it wasn't. A less restrictive arrangement was negotiated: Fulton agreed to a ten-year ban on revealing the previous owner.

Beare went to 907 Fifth Avenue to pick up the violin for Fulton. He was allowed in the side service entrance and up the freight elevator to Huguette's kitchen. And there, on a stainless steel counter, in a leather case, was La Pucelle, with its famous frontpiece of Joan of Arc. Chris Sattler also showed Beare the well-worn Strad that Huguette called her Traveler, explaining that she had kept La Pucelle untouched.

La Pucelle is indeed an extraordinary instrument, said the acclaimed violinist James Ehnes, who played a sad, sweet tune with a French name, "Salut d'Amour," for the instrument's first recording, in 2007. "It really has an amazing purity of tone," Ehnes said. "But purity with incredible breadth as well. I think that it's like a beam of light that is very strong and very wide. . . . I've never seen another violin like it."

Huguette was disappointed in the selling price. She'd said the violin might be worth $10 million. La Pucelle had cost her $49,500 in 1955, equivalent to about $327,000 in the inflated dollars of 2001. But she was entirely right about keeping it out of the auctions. She received $6 million, at that point a record price for a Strad, multiplying her investment eighteen times.

CHAPTER ELEVEN

BETH ISRAEL MEDICAL CENTER

SHAKEDOWN

HOW TANTALIZING this eccentric patient was for the leaders of a nonprofit hospital dependent on fund-raising. Here was a woman, well into her nineties, with something more than $300 million, and she was living in their hospital.

The hospital's doctors and managers could have treated the patient and sent her home, then follow up with a request for a donation. But they allowed her to stay in the hospital for twenty years, repeatedly coming back to her for larger and larger donations. They knew who was living in the darkened hospital room: the girl who could spin straw into gold.

A month into her stay, Dr. Henry Singman alerted the brass at Doctors Hospital that his patient "was quite wealthy, the scion of a multimillionaire copper industrialist." When the doctor told Huguette that it was costing him $20,000 to paint his house, a few days later she gave him a check for $20,000. When an air ambulance from Italy cost him $65,000 after he broke his hip, Huguette gave him that amount. Singman proposed to help the hospital develop an "appropriate cultivation approach" to seek donations. When a woman from the development, or fund-raising, staff met with Huguette, Dr. Singman introduced her as a member of the "public relations" staff.

Doctors Hospital soon became part of Beth Israel Medical Center, in 1991, becoming known colloquially as Beth Israel North. The hospital president, Dr. Robert Newman, took the lead in internal discussions about how to persuade Huguette to give the hospital some of the wealth she so obviously was not using. In a memo to the fund-raising staff, he stated bluntly, "Madame, as you know, is the biggest bucks contributing potential we have ever had." A specialist in treating addiction and well known for establishing methadone clinics, Dr. Newman started visiting Huguette three months after she checked in.

The hospital worked on Huguette from the classic donor-development playbook.

Step one: research.

At the New York Public Library, officials researched W. A. Clark, trying to estimate how many millions Huguette may have had. From her advisers, the hospital learned that she hadn't signed a will.

Step two in the playbook: strategic cultivation. Show the donor that you know her and care about her.

Dr. Newman sent Huguette cashmere sweaters, balloons, and gourmet chocolates from Paris. He had lived in Japan for three years, so they had much to discuss, and his wife, who is Japanese, visited Huguette several times. He introduced Huguette to his mother, who was in her nineties and had lived in France for many years. The mother wrote to Huguette and visited her in the hospital. They watched ice-skating on TV together, as Huguette explained the backstories of the Olympic figure skaters in their princess costumes. Huguette also shared a Smurfs television special with her. "I kid you not!" Dr. Newman wrote to colleagues. "My mom spent 30 minutes watching the Smurfs celebrate Christmas; she deserves a medal."

In January 1994, Dr. Newman wrote to Huguette:

Dear Mrs. Huguette: I took the liberty of sending a copy of your very kind season's greetings card to my mother in Nice. She frequently asks about you. My mother is an avid amateur graphologist, and I want to share with you her comments on your handwriting. "The most remarkable and admirable handwriting! I am greatly impressed by so much willpower, clear thinking and an orderly mind. Amazing." Clearly, I'm a tiny bit biased, but in my humble view my mother is very rarely wrong; certainly, I agree with her fully in this particular judgment. All the best, Robert Newman.

Huguette appeared to enjoy the visits by the hospital staff and insisted that they send her photographs of their children and grandchildren. She remembered their names and asked about their activities.

Behind her back, hospital officials made fun of Huguette for her delight in cartoons and dolls. They advised anyone soliciting her to keep the focus on donations, "even if she changes the subject to Smurfs or

Flintstones." When she complained that the hospital had included her name on a list of benefactors, piercing her veil of privacy, one hospital official quipped that they should give her "one Smurf to make amends."

Step three in the development playbook: solicitation. Make specific appeals based on the donor's interests. Huguette seemed to take the most interest in making gifts that honored her doctors. When she gave $300,000 for a cardiac lab, the hospital put Dr. Singman's name on it in appreciation for helping raise the money from his patient. She gave $80,000 to the hospital as a tribute to both Dr. Singman and her surgeon, Dr. Jack Rudick. In her first decade in the hospital, she gave $940,000.

Hospital leaders sought advice from Dr. Rudick, who urged them to make larger, specific requests, because "she has no 'concept' of money."

Dr. Rudick followed his own advice, borrowing $1 million from his patient. Though he signed promissory notes agreeing to pay the money back with interest, he made no payments. When Rudick asked for another $500,000, he told Huguette he wouldn't be able to continue as her doctor otherwise. Her attorney, Bock, called this "almost blackmail," warning Huguette that Dr. Rudick was misleading her by claiming that he needed the money to open an office in the city, when in fact he was retiring. She was not resentful, signing documents forgiving his loans entirely. Dr. Rudick denied this account, saying he never misled Huguette or even asked her for the money. He said that he and Huguette agreed from the beginning that the $1 million was actually a gift, though it was described as a loan in the documents.

Her nurse, Hadassah Peri, encouraged Huguette to make gifts to the hospital. The hospital waived some of Hadassah's fees when she had back surgery.

Hospital officials said they had no idea that Huguette was giving gifts to her doctors or nurses. Internal emails show that gifts to Hadassah, who was not a hospital employee, were discussed at a 1998 meeting in the office of the board chairman, shipbuilding tycoon Morton Hyman.

Hospital correspondence shows that officials were disappointed with their own results. "I think her gifts," Dr. Newman said, "considering what she could have given, considering what other people had given, . . .

had been relatively, relatively modest." He lamented in an email to fund-raising staff, "Without knocking her past gifts, the potential has been overwhelmingly unrealized."

. . .

Hospital officials knew from Huguette's advisers that she had not signed a will. Dr. Newman urged her to sign one, then sent his mother to share with her "the great joy and spiritual satisfaction of preparing her will."

Hospital officials considered having their legal department scope out what would happen to Huguette's money at her death if she died without a will. There was a problem, however. One official raised in a memo the fear that if the hospital leaders asked for advice from their own lawyers, "they might push the question of whether she should even be living in the hospital."

Indeed, Huguette was hidden away from hospital inspectors, according to two former employees at Doctors Hospital, a nurse and a social worker. The Joint Commission, which accredits hospitals, made regular visits to Beth Israel to ensure it met standards. One of its standard investigative techniques was to choose a "tracer" patient, going through all of a patient's file, evaluating each department that had worked on that patient's case. Patients with long stays might attract particular attention, as Huguette did on at least one occasion. With more than twenty thousand pages of medical records, Huguette would have been the ultimate tracer. The nurse and social worker said that her name was left off the daily patient census and they were told to hide her file when inspectors came. In later years, every new page in her hospital chart was stamped with an admission date of January 1, 2003, which was nearly twelve years after her actual date of admission. As one fund-raising official noted in the file, "If we were forced to 'evict' her, we'd certainly have no hope of any support."

The hospital encountered financial difficulties, spurred on by a couple of high-profile malpractice cases in obstetrics. By 1995, Moody's Investors Service had lowered the hospital company's bond rating, and in 2000 dropped the rating again as its liquidity reached "an extremely low level," with only six days' worth of cash on hand. Beth Israel in 1997 became part of a hospital super-company, Continuum Health Partners,

with Dr. Newman the CEO over Beth Israel, as well as St. Luke's–
Roosevelt and the New York Eye and Ear Infirmary.

Huguette came to the hospital's rescue. In 2000, when Hyman asked
her for a donation, she decided to give a painting by Edouard Manet, *Peonies in a Bottle*. Sotheby's appraised it at $6 million, and she instructed
Chris Sattler to deliver it to Dr. Newman's apartment, insisting as always
that her gift be anonymous. Yet the hospital was foiled again. Only
$3.5 million was bid at Christie's in November 2000, including the com-
mission for the auction house; the hospital declined to sell it at that price.

In Huguette's hospital room, Dr. Newman discussed with her what to
do with the painting. It was mid-November 2000, as the disputed presidential election between George W. Bush and Al Gore remained in
doubt. Huguette lamented the "terribly confused political situation,"
telling Dr. Newman she was strongly for Gore. (She was a Democrat,
just like her father, though in the intervening years the Republicans and
Democrats had switched sides on nearly every political issue.) She also
spoke of the volatile situation in the stock market, which was falling, and
of the generally poor results in art auctions. The Picasso that had recently sold for $50 million, she told Dr. Newman, was "ugly." When he
stressed that the hospital needed the money from the Manet painting,
Huguette urged him to wait until the political situation resolved and to
see what the market was doing before making any decisions. He said
waiting could cost the hospital money if art prices continued to decline.

But the hospital did wait, to keep her happy. The next summer, it tried
the auction again, accepting the same $3.5 million that had been bid pre-
viously and pocketing $3.1 million after paying the commission. Hu-
guette's market advice had not been bad: Though the price hadn't gone
up, it hadn't declined either.

· · ·

It was time for the hospital to go for the big score.

In March 2004, Dr. Newman proposed to Huguette that she transfer
$106 million of her wealth to the hospital. His pitch emphasized that she
would be the beneficiary, receiving "an unconditionally guaranteed
cash payment" of $1 million per month for life. That number seemed to
catch her ear, and she said she would think about it.

Of course, Huguette would have had to hand over all her stocks and bonds, as well as the Connecticut house and perhaps a few more paintings. Dr. Newman emphasized how such a gift would be a blessing, "freeing you from the considerable burden" of having to arrange the sale of property herself.

The type of contract proposed by Beth Israel is called a charitable gift annuity, which universities and other nonprofits tout to their donors, sometimes without fully explaining the pitfalls. Huguette was nearly ninety-eight years old, with a life expectancy of only 2.9 more years, based on actuarial tables, not on her medical history. According to the proposal she was given, for every million she gave the hospital, she would receive about $100,000 back each year, for a total of $310,750 over those 2.9 years of remaining life. She'd get a charitable deduction of $718,010 for the rest.

Was this a good deal? There were more cons than pros to the proposal.

The annuity would serve Huguette's desire to support Beth Israel, and would have provided her some income and a tax deduction. But an annuity is a very unusual financial instrument for a person of her age, and a charitable gift annuity is a blunt instrument for someone of Huguette's high net worth. It wasn't the most flexible way for her to donate to the hospital or to solve her cash flow problems. She would have no say in what happened to any property that she gave to the hospital, which it could sell as it wished.

And the deal was irrevocable. If the hospital, already in trouble financially, filed for bankruptcy, she might not get anything back. If she later became dissatisfied with the way the hospital was treating her, that would be too bad; the hospital would already have her money. And there was an inherent risk in trusting her healthcare to an institution that would enjoy the benefit of stopping paying her money as soon as she died.

Huguette didn't fall for the proposal.

The hospital may have been somewhat relieved that she hadn't jumped at its offer. Huguette would, in fact, blow away the actuarial charts, living 7.2 years more. Over that time, for every $1 million she would have given the hospital, the hospital would have paid her back nearly $800,000, diminishing the gift.

· · ·

A crisis presented the hospital with one more chance to strike Clark copper. In early 2004, there were rumors that the Doctors Hospital building would be closed. A developer wanted to buy the hospital and tear it down to put up a high-end apartment building. Dr. Newman suggested to the chairman, Hyman, that they use this opportunity to get a "super-mega gift" from Huguette.

On May 11, 2004, Dr. Newman and Hyman visited Huguette. Dr. Newman wrote a note documenting his visit. He told Huguette that Beth Israel was almost sure to sell the building and that offers were in hand. The hospital wasn't for sale, wasn't being shopped around, but these offers were just too lucrative to ignore. Beth Israel would have to sell the hospital, and the patients would have to move.

Huguette asked to see a copy of the hospital's financial statement. And she said she didn't want to move.

There was one way she wouldn't have to move, Hyman told Huguette. "A contribution in the neighborhood of $125 million would obviate the need to sell."

The next day, in her medical chart, Dr. Singman wrote, "Expressing concern about having to leave her room here in the hospital." Hadassah explained Huguette's anxiety: "She don't want changes. She used to that place. She loved that place. She liked the place. It is comfortable, she knew all the people there, all the nurses, and she is really happy in that place."

Huguette's choices as presented by Hyman and Dr. Newman were clear: If she did nothing, she would have to move. If she gave the hospital $125 million, or bought the building for that amount, she could stay.

This was a shakedown. On the street, such a payment is called protection money. In nonprofit hospital management, it's called major donor development.

· · ·

Beth Israel staff, from janitors to doctors, receive annual notices of the hospital policy on conflicts of interest. Gifts from patients are strictly forbidden. Accepting a tip is grounds for termination. Yet Huguette's doctors and nurses were receiving millions in checks, and now the hospital's leaders were holding up one of their most vulnerable patients for $125 million.

Beth Israel officials won't answer questions about the hospital's efforts to procure gifts from Huguette, or about their decision to let a healthy woman live in the hospital for twenty years. Attorney Marvin Wexler offered a general statement that the hospital acted in its patient's best interests. Indeed, Huguette thrived at the hospital much more than she had in her last years at home. "The indisputable reality is that Beth Israel rescued Mrs. Clark from a secluded and extremely unhealthy existence that endangered her life," Wexler said, "and then provided her a well-attended home where she was able to live out her days in security, relative good health and comfort, and with the pleasures of human company."

Huguette's reply to the $125 million request was "That's a lot of money." Hyman and Dr. Newman assured her they'd "never abandon her and that somewhere in the Continuum empire she'd find a home if she needed." She told Dr. Newman that she would have to talk with her lawyer, that she'd have to think about their request.

Yet her answer gave them hope. Dr. Newman wrote to his staff that he'd gotten a similar answer when he'd asked her for a painting: "She came through with the Manet. So we'll see this time."

She did consider it. Two days later, she called Bock to ask if she could sell her Connecticut home to "buy Beth Israel." He told her the property, worth perhaps $20 million, wouldn't bring nearly enough for that.

She could have raised the money. She had more than $150 million in stocks, bonds, paintings, jewelry, and cash, in addition to more than $150 million in real estate. But she withstood the pressure. The shakedown failed. As desperately as she wanted to stay in the hospital, in that very room, she agreed to move.

Indeed, Huguette's last donation to Beth Israel was in 2002, not counting money she left in her will. For the last nine years of her life, she repeatedly said no to its implorations. She gave nothing when Dr. Newman wrote her a letter asking for an annual donation in 2003. She gave nothing when he wrote again in 2004. She said no when they asked her to buy the building in 2004. She gave nothing when the new president of the hospital wrote to her in 2007 asking for $255,000. Beth Israel's leaders had tried their best to exert their influence on Huguette Clark, but W.A.'s daughter stood firm.

· · ·

So Huguette would move. But where?

Her first rule: no nursing homes. She told Dr. Newman that she didn't want to go downtown to Beth Israel's main hospital. She preferred to remain close to Madame Pierre on the Upper East Side. She sent her attorney and accountant to scour the city for other hospitals. Beth Israel officials did as Huguette asked, reaching out to those other hospitals to try to arrange a room for her. Huguette considered Mount Sinai, where her mother had died, up Fifth Avenue from her apartments. If she moved there, however, she would have to switch caregivers. Dr. Singman told her he "would have to discontinue my care for her" if she moved to Mount Sinai—it was too far from his home, he said. In fact, Mount Sinai is on the Upper East Side, the same as Doctors Hospital, and was only five minutes farther from his home in SoHo.

Hadassah told her the same: If she went to Mount Sinai, she'd have to get a new team.

The next day, she relented, agreeing to move down to the main Beth Israel hospital. She moved in July, just before Doctors Hospital closed. The next year, it was torn down to make way for multiple-story condo buildings.

The medical records show that Huguette was anxious leading up to the move, but Hadassah talked her through it.

A MORNING OUTDOORS

NOT ONCE in twenty years did Huguette take a walk or a ride in a wheelchair out to the parks near her hospital rooms. "We told her," Hadassah said, "we can have some fresh air outside. . . . We have a wheelchair for you. Refused." Her friend Madame Pierre said she urged Huguette to go out, but Huguette always changed the subject.

Huguette went outside the hospital a few times to see doctors and dentists, especially in the early years. But she was mostly in excellent health and was able to get her teeth cleaned inside the hospital.

Her last time outdoors was the day she transferred from the closing Doctors Hospital down to the main Beth Israel. It was a Tuesday morning, July 27, 2004, when Chris Sattler helped her into the ambulance for the five-mile trip from the Upper East Side. She didn't take a long look at the old site of the Clark mansion or her apartments on Fifth Avenue or the Spence School. She didn't see the Empire State Building or Central Park. She didn't see a single bit of New York City on the fifteen-minute ride. The entire time, her eyes were covered, Chris said, by those big patches that patients wear after eye surgery.

. . .

In her chart on the day of the transfer, Dr. Singman summarized her for the staff at Beth Israel: "She is terribly insecure, and a hospital room is her home from whence she rarely leaves." He added one more note: "At present patient not pleased with her new surroundings, and is considering leaving."

She didn't leave, and now she had six nurses to watch over her. Hadassah cut back to an eight-hour shift, so more nurses were added. But because Huguette didn't do well with new people—"She have to know you first," Hadassah said—the nurses started doubling up, two per shift, so she would always see a familiar face if someone needed to leave early or take a day off.

Huguette's room no longer had a view of the river. Her new room looked out on apartment buildings. She talked about how much nicer Doctors Hospital had been, though her shades were drawn most of the time anyway. Her new room was larger, a double room, though occupied by one patient. It was on the tenth floor of the hospital's main circular building, called Linsky. Room 10L04 was decorated in standard late-century hospital tans and browns: wood closet of cheap laminate, tile floor, sink, bathroom, standard hospital bed with curtain for privacy, schoolhouse wall clock, modern armchair, nightstand with three drawers, fluorescent lighting.

Huguette had fewer visitors at Beth Israel than at Doctors. It was much farther from the apartment of Madame Pierre, who now visited only about every four to eight weeks. Though they still spoke on the phone every day, by 2005 Madame Pierre was showing the beginnings of Alzheimer's, so their conversations became shorter.

Despite having fewer visitors, over these years Huguette became more open with strangers, more conversant. As she passed her hundredth birthday, in 2006, she began to leave her door open more often. She allowed her attorney Bock to visit, as Don Wallace never could. She shared French pastries and childhood stories with the nurses and other staff.

"She started coming out of her shell," Chris said. Her time in the new hospital "re-socialized Mrs. Clark. She became less of a recluse." She even made a new friend, visiting a woman who was a patient down the hall. Chris said Huguette "enjoyed the traffic of humanity for the first time in fifty years."

Once a year, Huguette also allowed doctors and nurses from the floor to come into her room for little birthday parties for her. There was a little gathering for her one hundredth birthday on June 9, 2006. Attorney Bock was there, and accountant Kamsler, Chris Sattler, and Madame Pierre.

Someone brought a SpongeBob SquarePants balloon. The hospital delivered a huge cake. As birthday presents, Huguette wrote out checks to her nurses. A week later, Huguette asked a nurse if she could put more air in the balloon.

H UGUETTE SEEMED TO FEAR one thing most of all: publicity. In this
she favored her mother more than her father.

The jewelry that W. A. Clark gave to Anna when he was courting her, when he married her, while they raised a family, all that jewelry
was entrusted by their daughter Huguette to First National City Bank,
where the family banked for more than fifty years.

In the 1980s, a blue diamond and other pieces of Anna's jewelry disappeared from the securities department at Citibank, as it was now
called, either lost or stolen. Citibank made just the right threat: The
bank insisted that it couldn't pay any more than $3 million without in-
volving the insurer, Lloyd's of London, where such a large loss might
bring publicity. Huguette accepted in 1991 a $3 million settlement, much
less than the jewelry's appraised value.

Then, in 1994, when Huguette was in the hospital, Citibank did it
again. The rest of Anna's jewelry was in a safe-deposit box, No. 883.
The trust department at Citibank was paying the bill for the box, but an
interoffice address changed, and the bill fell delinquent. Bank officers
cut open the box and sold the contents as abandoned property to a liqui-
dator at rock-bottom prices.

Anna's gold wedding band, gone. Her 2 gold lockets. Her tortoiseshell combs with 320 diamonds. Her Cartier 2-strand pearl necklace
with the 7-carat diamond clasp. Her 3-strand cultured pearl and jade
bead necklace with two 4-carat diamonds by Cartier. Her bracelet with
36 sapphires and 126 small diamonds. Her 5 small gold bracelets. Her
Cartier diamond and rock crystal hairpin with 64 diamonds. Her 3-stone
diamond ring. Her pearl ring. Her 18-carat-gold-mesh purse with 5
inset emeralds and the matching gold-mesh change purse. Her Cartier
gold watch with 30 carats of diamonds. Her Cartier bracelet with 22
carats of diamonds. Her Cartier necklace with 60 carats of diamonds
and 40 carats of emeralds. Her 20 gold safety pins. And 30 other pieces.
All gone.

The loss "has been devastating," attorney Don Wallace wrote to Citibank, relating her "anxiety and pain." This time Huguette didn't know what to do. At first she wanted all her mother's jewelry back. Citibank traced some pieces to a dealer in Europe, but they had been resold. The bank trotted out its successful threat again: Further efforts to hunt down the jewelry could bring public attention.

So Huguette wouldn't sue, wouldn't risk having her name in the newspapers. Valuing her privacy more than money, she had no leverage. She relented, demanding $6 million while protesting that the jewelry was worth $10 million.

The bank chairman, John S. Reed, wrote her a note of apology but agreed to pay no more than $3.5 million. She took it. Before making the payment, Citibank insisted that she produce a statement from an independent physician attesting to her mental competence so she couldn't revoke the deal. After a few months, the bank accepted such a statement from her own physician, Dr. Singman.

Similarly, Huguette and her attorneys took no action, and did not call the police, when someone stole nearly a quarter of a million dollars from her in November 1991, after she went into the hospital. Her bank reported that someone cashed a check from an old unused account, getting away with $230,000. Another check for $650,000 was refused. Her attorney, Wallace, didn't call the police, but quietly closed the account.

· · ·

Huguette's gentle ballerina by Edgar Degas, *Dancer Making Points*, which she had bought with her mother in 1929, was stolen from her apartment wall in 1992 or 1993. Not wanting any publicity, she urged her attorney not to report the loss. She didn't file an insurance claim or call the police, but the building manager reported the theft anyway, and an FBI agent marched right into Huguette's hospital room for an amiable conversation. Wallace was shocked: The FBI had spent a full hour more with his client than he ever had.

Twelve years later, in 2005, the FBI discovered that Huguette's Degas pastel was hanging in Mission Hills, Kansas, at the home of the noted collector Henry Bloch, the "H" in the H&R Block tax preparation firm. He and his wife, Marion, had purchased the Degas ballerina unwittingly from an art dealer in Manhattan. Soon after the painting had disappeared, a well-dressed man with a European accent had walked into a small gallery, saying the Degas ballerina had been in his family for many years. The gallery owner bought it, no questions asked. Then the Blochs were told of the painting and had it shipped to Kansas, after having a museum director friend look over the painting's provenance.

Huguette wanted the painting back, of course. Instead of demanding their money back from the dealer and returning the painting, the Blochs claimed that, even if the painting had been stolen, it was abandoned property, because Huguette had not tried to find it. Besides, the Blochs had promised to give their entire collection of Impressionists, after their deaths, to Kansas City's Nelson-Atkins Museum of Art, where Henry Bloch had been chairman of the board. The museum was adding a Bloch Building to honor its longtime benefactors. Huguette did not want to sue. Any publicity about a stolen Degas could bring her life into the open.

To avoid any embarrassing public attention for either party, after years of discussions the attorneys agreed on an unusual solution. Huguette signed a deed giving the painting to the Kansas City museum. She, not America's tax expert, would receive the charitable deduction for the $10 million painting. To assure the museum that Huguette, who was now 102, was able to make such a decision, Dr. Singman signed a second statement attesting to her competence.

To make things tidy for the lawyers, the painting actually had to change hands. Outside the Bloch home on an October day in 2008, the Degas ballerina was the object of the following game of hot potato. The ballerina was taken down from the wall and handed to Huguette's attorney, Wally Bock. Bock was escorted by a former FBI agent to the driveway, where the director of the museum, Marc Wilson, was waiting in a limousine.

Bock handed the painting to the director of the museum, which was receiving it as a gift from Huguette.

And the museum director walked the ballerina back into the Bloch home, where it went in the same spot, above the sofa, between a Seurat and a Toulouse-Lautrec. The museum's executive committee had agreed to lend the painting to the Blochs. Although a stolen painting had been found on their wall, they got it back, for as long as they lived. The deal was so hush-hush that the museum's curators, and most of the museum's directors, didn't know they now owned the Degas. The museum did agree that it would consider lending the painting, up to twice within the next twenty-five years, to Huguette's favorite museum, the Corcoran Gallery in Washington.

The effect for Huguette, of course, was that she no longer owned her ballerina. She asked the Kansas City museum to take a photograph, at full size, so she would have a print to remember her by.

TWO WILLS

CHRIS SATTLER CALLED attorney Bock with disturbing news: "Mrs. Clark's condition seems to be deteriorating." It was February 15, 2005, and Huguette's cold had turned into pneumonia.

The same day, Hadassah followed up with her own call to Bock, asking about the $5 million "owed on her gift." She was referring to the $5 million she had not yet gotten from the sale of the Cézanne, the $5 million she was carrying around in an undated check. Huguette told Bock she wanted to give Hadassah the $5 million right away.

Huguette, at age ninety-eight and with pneumonia, still hadn't signed a will. This was the opening that her attorneys had been waiting forty years for.

. . .

When Huguette was young, she signed two wills, leaving everything to her mother. The last one had been signed in 1929, when she was Mrs. Gower.

After Anna died, Huguette's lawyers at Clark, Carr & Ellis, the old railroad firm, made a renewed push. In 1964, they sent over a draft will, leaving Bellosguardo to the Santa Barbara Foundation to support the arts, and $1 million to her friend Etienne de Villermont, among other bequests.

Every time the lawyers brought this up, she'd say, "Let's wait until after the holidays." Her objection seemed to be to the idea of having a will at all, or at least to having one *now*. Perhaps she found the subject too dark, or was suspicious of signing away her authority, as she refused repeatedly to sign any power of attorney.

Lawyer after lawyer tried every argument. They explained that she was in such good financial condition because her parents had made sound plans. They explained that her many friends were relying on her generosity and could be left with nothing.

Her attorneys' letters show that they assumed they were writing to an educated, intelligent person who knew what she wanted. Huguette was her father's daughter. The letters are businesslike, detailed, and respectful, leaving decisions to her.

Don Wallace reminded her that without a will, her money would go to her relatives from her father's first marriage. "You have never expressed any interest," he wrote, "in any of them having any part of your inheritance." She didn't sign, and she didn't say why.

. . .

By 1985, Don Wallace was fed up with his client. For more than a decade, Wallace had handled her purchases of dolls at auction, had delivered her anonymous gifts, had done all the little things that one didn't learn in law school. A fellow attorney recalled a meeting with Wallace in the 1980s. Huguette interrupted four times with telephone calls, and each time Wallace's end of the conversation went something like this: "Yes, Mrs. Clark. Yes, Madame. Yes, I will take care of it, Madame."

Wallace had learned to talk her through her quirks. What Wallace couldn't do was get her to sign a will.

Wallace summed up his exasperation in a "personal and confidential" letter to Huguette in March 1985. He summoned the names of her previous lawyers who had given her the same advice.

In the not too far distant future I will have been personally responsible for the handling of your affairs after Mr. Bannerman's death for almost nine years. While I enjoy being of assistance in connection with your sometimes complex business and personal affairs and I can honestly say that I have never found it dull, at the same time, it has been one of the most frustrating experiences I have ever had.

You have received and have ignored or avoided advice given to you almost every year from 1942 to date outlining all of the reasons why it is essential that you have a current, up-to-date will. I know as I have been trying with a total lack of success for almost nine years. Based on my personal knowledge, Mr. Bannerman, Mr. Winslow, Mr. Stokes, Mr. Ellis and others all gave you similar advice. All of them, now dead, were equally unsuccessful in persuading you to have a current, up-to-date will.

*Perhaps their failure should make mine seem less frustrating to me, but it
does not.*

*If I could have one wish granted this year it would be that you would
accept my advice and instruct me to prepare a will expressing your wishes
on how your property should be distributed.*

His wish was not granted that year. Nor for the next seventeen years,
as he continued to send pleading letters. Nor in his lifetime. When Don
Wallace died in 2002 without persuading Huguette to sign a will, he had
never met his client of twenty-six years. He had talked with her only on
the phone or through a closed door. Wallace's successor, Wally Bock,
had written her with the same wish. "Once again," he begged in 2000,
"I urge you to stop *thinking* about a Will and do something about it."

From time to time, the attorneys did get Huguette to revise her list of
beneficiaries, reflecting the pecking order of her current friendships. A
2001 list would have left 30 percent of her estate, after specific bequests
to employees and friends, to nurse Hadassah, 30 percent to goddaughter
Wanda, 15 percent to Etienne's daughter Marie-Christine, 15 percent to
establish the Bellosguardo Foundation for the arts in Santa Barbara, and
10 percent to Madame Pierre. But she signed nothing.

Often on afternoons in the early 2000s, Bock and Kamsler would
gather at Bock's office. Bock would pour a vodka for Irv and a double
Scotch for himself, and they would work on another draft.

Huguette said she'd be glad to talk about it after the holidays.

. . .

Now she had pneumonia. With her health in question, and with Hadassah
nagging for the promised $5 million, Huguette finally said she'd sign.

Bock and Kamsler took a draft to her hospital room on February 28,
2005, two weeks after she first fell ill. But Huguette didn't want to wait
until she died to pay Hadassah the $5 million, so that day she approved
putting the Connecticut home on the market. She was ambivalent, however, about selling even a home she had never spent one night in. She
changed her mind several times in the following weeks. Huguette even
proposed letting Hadassah act as the real estate agent, so she could also
pocket the commission, but her advisers said that wasn't feasible. Then

Huguette proposed just giving the Connecticut house to Hadassah, but Kamsler told her that would be "a financial disaster" because of the gift taxes she would have to pay.

Beth Israel's administrators heard that a will was in the works. Putting on a full-court press, Dr. Newman visited Huguette three times that month.

· · ·

On March 7, now recovered from her pneumonia, Huguette signed a will, a simple document of barely three pages. Its main beneficiaries were people who were not named at all: her father's descendants from his first marriage. The will said she left her estate to her "intestate distributees." In other words, she left her money to the same people who would inherit it if she didn't have a will. Under New York law, if she had no children and no siblings and her mother had no other living children, the entire estate would go to her father's descendants. (Her mother had no other descendants.) So in this regard, the will changed nothing.

This document did, however, accomplish two goals: First, it left the $5 million to Hadassah, if she had not already received it from sale of the Connecticut property. Second, it named Bock and Kamsler as executors, putting the two men in line for automatic commissions under state law of roughly $3.1 million each. Someone would get the $6.2 million, and now it would be her longtime advisers, which is not unusual.

If Huguette didn't want to leave money to her relatives, why did she sign a will that specified just that result? Bock and Kamsler explained later that this will was intended to get the ball rolling, that Huguette asked that it be as uncomplicated as possible so she could rest easily that Hadassah would get the $5 million. She and her advisers agreed that they would return soon for the more difficult task of updating her list of beneficiaries. The first will, Bock said, was a "stepping stone."

On March 23, Kamsler sent Huguette a list of possible beneficiaries, based on previous lists, and on April 12 he amended the list in a meeting with her with a check mark or an X changing the future for her friends. Two names from earlier lists were noticeably absent. The first was Madame Pierre, who had already received $10 million from the Monet. The second was Etienne's daughter, Marie-Christine, who had corresponded less with Huguette in recent years. Hadassah's share doubled. Bock sent the draft will to Huguette by courier on April 15. Kamsler says he went to the hospital to read it to her and explain each provision.

Four days later, on April 19, just six weeks after she'd signed the first will, Huguette signed the second one. Her medical chart, with notes from various nurses and doctors, shows that Huguette's mind seems to have been clear and sharp throughout this period. The chart shows her conversing cheerfully, reading French magazines, walking easily without assistance, sitting up in a chair soaking her feet in soapy water, writing letters, approving the auction at Sotheby's of her devotional Book of Hours from the Middle Ages if it could fetch at least $100,000, reminiscing about how much she liked the old Doctors Hospital, writing $90,000 in checks to Hadassah and her family, giving $50,000 more to Dr. Jack Rudick, overdrawing her checking account again and again, enjoying visits with Madame Pierre, even giving herself a haircut.

She had no medical problem other than worsening hearing. On March 21 and 25, she refused a hearing aid, but she was still able to listen to programs on the radio. The visiting doctors, who were not otherwise involved in her treatment and who didn't benefit from either will, said later that she seemed mentally competent, answering their questions appropriately, but she willfully refused the hearing aid. Her eyes were worse now, and she used a magnifying glass to sign cards and checks. (She had started printing Hadassah's name on gift checks as "H. Peri.") On March 28, her weight was recorded as eighty-five pounds, including her hospital gown, slippers, and six layers of cashmere sweaters.

On April 12, the hospital's Catholic chaplain tried to visit on his rounds. Huguette had received prayer cards from friends, and she would say the Lord's Prayer before bedtime—in Spanish if one of the Latina cleaning ladies was there. But she refused to see the priest.

. . .

A nurse on the hall in the 10 Linsky section at Beth Israel was on his way to help a patient with a tracheotomy tube when Hadassah Peri called him into Room 4. He was needed for just a minute to witness the signing of a document. It was April 19, 2005, and the copper king's daughter was about to sign her last will and testament.

If one were teaching a law school class in estates and trusts, demonstrating how not to handle the signing of a will for an elderly client with hundreds of millions of dollars, this ceremony would be Exhibit A.

Along with the nurse from the hall, the other witness was attorney Bock's secretary. The entire event took five minutes at most. Huguette sat on the side of the bed. Another lawyer from Bock's firm presided, asking Huguette to confirm that she intended this to be her last will and testament. Bock's secretary recalled that Hadassah helped Huguette hold the pen to direct where to sign but said there was no sign of any distress or coercion. Other witnesses said they didn't recall Hadassah helping her hold the pen.

This was a more complete document than the earlier one, encompassing seven pages. The key paragraph was this: "I intentionally make no provision in this my Last Will [and] Testament for any members of my family, whether on my paternal or maternal side, having had minimal contacts with them over the years. The persons and institutions named herein as beneficiaries of my Estate are the true objects of my bounty."

The will directed that a Bellosguardo Foundation be created as a charity "for the primary purpose of fostering and promoting the Arts." This foundation would receive her estate in Santa Barbara, as her attorneys had suggested for decades and as Santa Barbara's mayor Sheila Lodge had proposed to her in 1993 and 1997. To the foundation, she also left all but one of her paintings, including her own works and the masterworks she still owned, and her books and musical instruments. As foundation trustees, the document named her executors, again Bock and Kamsler, and a third trustee, her California attorney, Jim Hurley. These men would have the sole authority to pay themselves fees in perpetuity.

Next came the specific bequests to the people closest to her: $100,000 to her doctor, Henry Singman; $500,000 to her personal assistant, Chris Sattler; two years' pay to the manager at Bellosguardo, John Douglas; one year's pay to the caretaker at Le Beau Château, Tony Ruggiero; $25,000 to her handyman at Fifth Avenue, Martin Gonzalez (who would die before her); $500,000 to accountant Kamsler; $500,000 to attorney Bock (he would have to give 80 percent to his law firm under his partnership agreement); and all her dolls and dollhouses to Hadassah Peri, "my nurse, friend and loyal companion."

The Corcoran Gallery received a single painting, the Monet from the Water Lilies series, the one Huguette had bought just before her divorce. Though the painting was not one of Monet's monumental murals, it has been appraised for $25 million.

Of whatever remained, Huguette left 60 percent to Hadassah, 25 percent to Wanda Styka, and 15 percent to the Bellosguardo Foundation.

Huguette initialed every page with her felt-tip pen and signed the last page in a cursive immediately recognizable as belonging to the same girl who had signed the address book at her half-brother Will's Mowitza Lodge in 1916, only a bit shakier.

To Beth Israel, despite all its efforts and high hopes for tens or hundreds of millions, the will left only $1 million. Within two months, she lost her room with a view and was forced to move to the third floor. Hospital officials have said they had no idea whether Beth Israel was in Huguette's will and made the switch only because her floor was being renovated.

Her new neighborhood was called 3 Karpas, a depressing stretch of hallway normally used for patients undergoing physical rehabilitation. Then she was moved again, within that section. Her last regular hospital room, 3K01, was at the end of the corridor, next to the janitor's closet and the emergency exit. It was a double room, twenty-two feet by fourteen feet, made for two patients but occupied by only Huguette.

With all the potential views in the world at her disposal, from Paris to the Pacific, she now had a view without a single tree. She could see no sky at all, only in the background the gray-and-tan brick walls of the neighboring wing of the hospital, and in the foreground a maze of industrial compressors and valves, a grim twenty-first-century landscape of air-conditioning units.

You could say that it no longer mattered: In her second century, her eyesight was failing, and she insisted that a special shade be installed, a blackout shade so no daylight could creep in. But it mattered to her. Huguette often mentioned to her staff how much nicer the view had been at Doctors Hospital, with the river and the mayor's mansion below.

After the will was signed, as Bock's secretary tells the story, they went down the block to a restaurant, where Bock and Kamsler had a drink to success.

CHAPTER TWELVE

WOODLAWN CEMETERY

MARCH 1968. That's the last time any Clarks recall seeing their dear Tante Huguette.

In front of the golden altarpiece of St. Thomas Church on Fifth Avenue, sixty-one-year-old Huguette walked up after the funeral Mass to offer her condolences. This was the same church where her sister Andrée's funeral had been held in 1919. Today's deceased was their half-niece, Katherine Morris Hall, for whom Huguette had been a bridesmaid at this altar in 1924. After a respectful moment, Huguette quietly left the church, without being introduced to the younger relatives.

That's the last time, that is to say, any Clarks saw Huguette while she was awake.

It was more than forty years later, in 2009, when two of Huguette's relatives showed up unannounced at her hospital room. They had discovered something their 102-year-old aunt didn't know: Her accountant was a felon.

As the relatives started to do more research, they had good reason to suspect that Huguette's money was being stolen, and even to doubt whether she was alive.

. . .

The family's first hint of a problem came from the Corcoran Gallery of Art, the museum that holds her father's art collection and where Huguette exhibited her own work in 1929. Huguette had been a regular donor of $50,000 to $100,000 a year, stepping up to support Clark-related projects. She gave $200,000 for the seventy-fifth anniversary of the W. A. Clark Collection and major support for the $1 million restoration of the Salon Doré, the gilded French room from her childhood home, the Clark mansion at 962 Fifth Avenue.

The first grand art gallery in Washington, the privately supported Corcoran was perpetually in straitened circumstances, dwarfed by the

Smithsonian Institution's nineteen museums and galleries, which allowed free admission and received millions in federal support. The Corcoran stepped on its reputation in 1989 with Robert Mapplethorpe's *The Perfect Moment,* an exhibit by the late photographer including homoerotic and sadomasochistic content. Artists canceled exhibitions, and donors pulled back. Over the next ten years, the museum regularly ran deficits.

In 1999, the Corcoran announced a bold plan to reverse its decline. It would raise money for a $200 million addition designed by the noted architect Frank Gehry, whose well-known projects had raised the profile of institutions such as Spain's Guggenheim Museum Bilbao. Gehry proposed to update the Corcoran's image with an annex featuring flowing metal panels, like enormous billowing sails or ribbons of silver. This addition would adorn the Corcoran's 1897 Beaux Arts building, which faces across Seventeenth Street toward the South Lawn of the White House and the Ellipse, where the National Christmas Tree is decorated. Gehry's design would radically change the look of the neighborhood. The museum sought a major donation from Huguette, suggesting $10 million. She sent nothing.

A few years later, in 2003, Corcoran leaders were shocked to read in the newspapers that Huguette had sold Renoir's *In the Roses* for $23.5 million. In talking with Huguette's aide, Chris Sattler, the Corcoran staff learned that Huguette had considerable expenses and had sold the painting because she needed the cash. Why would Huguette Clark be broke?

The Corcoran's president and director, David C. Levy, wrote with concern to Huguette's half-great-grandniece, Carla Hall Friedman. After giving $1 million over the decade of the 1990s, Huguette had stopped, cold turkey. Her donation for 2003: $1,000. Carla, a great-granddaughter of Huguette's half-sister Katherine, was a member of a Corcoran committee, an informal advocate for the W. A. Clark Collection. She had never met Huguette, though she lived in Manhattan, but they knew of each other. Huguette had been a bridesmaid for Carla's grandmother and had sent Carla a wedding present of money back in the 1970s, to which Carla replied with a thank-you note, of course. Carla had sent Christmas cards to Huguette, and Carla's mother, Erika Hall, had spoken with Huguette on the phone, and sent flowers at Christmas.

Huguette's relatives were beginning to be concerned about more than her declining support of the Corcoran. Agnes Albert, Huguette's niece, had told her children before she died in 2002 that attorney Bock had rudely told her that she was not to contact Huguette directly anymore. After years of warm relations with Anna and Huguette, Agnes was shocked by this, her children say. Agnes had warned that Huguette must be "in bad hands." Bock said he doesn't recall this conversation, but his instructions from Huguette hadn't changed: Don't give out her number, don't say where she is, and take a message, no matter who is calling.

Similarly, cousin Paul Newell's contacts with Huguette ended abruptly. In March 2004, she invited him to make a private visit to Bellosguardo, and then he never heard from her again. Their last conversation had been as friendly as ever, and he said she sounded in good health and good spirits. He continued to call Bock as before, asking for Huguette to return the call. He heard nothing. He grew suspicious, thinking that either she had fallen ill or their communications were being blocked. Attorney Bock's time logs show that he continued to pass on Newell's messages.

Bock denies blocking anyone. Huguette was free to make any phone calls she wanted from her hospital room. He said he merely explained to the relatives that Huguette had gone into a reclusive phase, that she seemed to be returning fewer calls. His guess was that she was embarrassed about her worsening hearing loss, and at age ninety-seven she was no longer comfortable talking on the phone. This also was during the time when Huguette was wrestling with the decision about moving from Beth Israel North to South, but of course the relatives knew none of this. They didn't even know she was in a hospital.

The Corcoran's director, Levy, wrote to Carla, warning that the attorney could be blocking Huguette from making donations. The Corcoran and the relatives were unaware that Huguette's unbridled generosity to individuals had caused her cash-poor situation. Levy warned darkly that something "insidious" might be going on. Carla offered to help the Corcoran. Though Carla expressed to her family that she was appalled by the Gehry plan, she offered to write to Huguette to talk it up, stressing how it would make room for more of her father's art to be displayed. Carla speculated to Levy that her elderly aunt probably had "little or no understanding" of Gehry's post-structuralist design.

IN CONVERSATION WITH HUGUETTE

Huguette told me that she had indeed studied Gehry's design but wasn't pleased with the way it clashed with the traditional Corcoran building and the Clark Wing. She said, "I think it's kind of fussy."

The Gehry plan was in trouble. "Barring the emergence of an angel bearing $100 million," *The Washington Post* reported, "it appears that the Corcoran's Gehry dream is unlikely to come true." Huguette would not be that angel. The Corcoran board scuttled the Gehry plan in 2005, and Levy resigned. Losing millions each year, the museum laid off staff, closed two days a week, and began to sell off some of the W. A. Clark Collection, including his prized majolica and Persian rugs, and other treasures from Huguette's childhood home.

. . .

A new idea for cultivating ties to the Clark family came from the Corcoran's new director, Paul Greenhalgh, who offered to host a proposed Clark family reunion. It was at this reunion the relatives learned about criminal charges against Huguette's accountant.

More than seventy-five members of the family gathered at the Corcoran in October 2008, including descendants not only of the senator but also of his siblings. It was less a reunion than an introduction: Most of the far-flung relatives had never met. They arrived from France, England, California, New York. There were Republicans and Democrats and independents, Protestants and Catholics, Jews and Buddhists and atheists. Two had been classmates at the same prep school without knowing they were cousins.

It was a grand affair. The Clark relatives bonded as they toured the Salon Doré, studied Boutet de Monvel's six paintings of Joan of Arc from W.A.'s billiard room, and posed for photos with W. A. Clark by standing with his portrait by William Merritt Chase.

They also heard a presentation from a Clark-friendly graduate student who had written his master's thesis on the wrongs that history had done to W.A.'s reputation. The scholar assured the Clarks that the senator had never been convicted of a crime and hadn't been thrown out of the Senate but had resigned—all true, but skirting the less pleasant part of the story. His Senate trial, the Clark relatives were told, had been a parody of justice and jurisprudence. Clark's reputation had suffered, the scholar assured them, because Roman Catholic religious fervor colored the accounts of historians, who sided with the Irish Catholic Marcus Daly over the Scotch-Irish Presbyterian Clark. And besides, the scholar explained, all elections on the frontier were bizarre. The presentation was focused on burnishing, not examining, their relative's legacy.

Huguette was often mentioned. Carla had written to her, through attorney Bock, seeking $22,000 to pay the costs of the reunion, and Huguette had sent $10,000 for the steak banquet. Carla made effusive remarks thanking Huguette. Large photos of her and Andrée were included in a display. Many of the Clarks signed a card for her.

"Dear Tante Huguette," wrote Ian Clark Devine, her half-great-grandnephew. "Thank you for helping the whole family gather for the first time. A glorious weekend. Merci."

None of this was enough for Huguette's invited representative at the reunion, her accountant, Irving Kamsler. He made a scene, complaining to Carla that insufficient attention was being paid to Huguette's status as the senior family member. He made quite an impression.

After the second day of the reunion, one relative shared with others the headline she found when she typed Kamsler's name into Google: "Porno sting nabs temple president."

Irving H. Kamsler had been arrested on September 6, 2007, in Nassau County, New York. He had resigned his position as president of his Reform Jewish synagogue in the affluent Riverdale neighborhood of the Bronx. The fifteen-count indictment alleged that on five different days in 2005 and 2007, when he was between fifty-eight and sixty years old, he had tried to entice a thirteen-year-old girl and two fifteen-year-old girls via AOL instant messaging, describing sex acts and saying he wanted to meet with them for sex. Kamsler was using the AOL screen names Taxirv and IRV1040 (from his first name, Irv, and the accountant's usual tool, the IRS income tax form).

The thirteen-year-old was not, as IRV1040 soon learned, a middle-school-aged girl who wanted to date sixtyish accountants. She was an adult, volunteering as an investigator for the Long Island Society for the Prevention of Cruelty to Children. The fifteen-year-old girls were adult investigators from the Nassau County District Attorney's Office.

Kamsler was indicted on six felony counts of attempting to disseminate indecent material to minors and nine misdemeanor counts of attempting to endanger the welfare of a child. He admitted to police that he was IRV1040 and that he had discussed sex acts, but he said he had thought he was in an adult chat room and was just "pretending" to talk with girls. Although at first he pleaded not guilty, Kamsler changed his plea to guilty on September 29, 2008. That was less than a month before he represented Huguette at the Clark reunion, while he was awaiting sentencing.

. . .

One of the relatives found something else on the Web. An estate lawyer in New Jersey posted on her blog a note about her friend, Irving Kamsler. At that time, the tax laws were in flux, with the estate tax scheduled to expire at the end of 2009 if Congress didn't step in. The topic was being discussed by every estate professional in the country: If a person died in 2008 or 2009, his or her estate faced a top tax rate of 45 percent. But if the person could hold out until 2010, the estate might pay nothing. That made 2010, or so the joke went, the perfect year to die. From the Web posting, it appeared that Kamsler had an idea how to put this joke into practice. The estate lawyer wrote:

> On that note, the other day I was talking to Irving Kamsler, a terrific CPA friend of mine, who shared some out-of-the-box thinking on a transaction he had done for a client. . . . My CPA friend had suggested that, as part of the planning process, the client should amend his health care directive/living will to provide that the client be kept alive by any artificial means necessary . . . thereby ensuring as much as possible that the appreciation on the assets would not be includible in his estate. As my friend and I continued talking, our thoughts turned to 2010, and the possibility of counseling clients to include similar language in their current health care directives instruction

that they be kept alive by any means necessary until January 1, 2010 (or maybe a few days later, just to be safe). This would effectively permit a client to achieve maximum estate tax savings, assuming the client might otherwise pass away before 2010.

The Clark relatives were unsettled. What sort of financial adviser would suggest such a strategy? What would W. A. Clark think if he knew that his youngest child's affairs were in the hands of such a man?

They had just signed a card for their dear 102-year-old Tante Huguette. But now they wondered, what if she were brain dead and hooked to a machine just to "achieve maximum estate tax savings"?

THE CLARK FAMILY BEGAN to mobilize. Some consulted a lawyer about cases of elder abuse. Others looked up property records. They learned that Huguette's Connecticut home was on the market. As Carla wrote, "I feel like we are all playing CLUE!"

They went back to Huguette's attorney repeatedly, having different relatives make attempts to get information, but he maintained her privacy. Bock told them she was healthy and lucid, in "amazing" condition for 102. He said they could send letters or photos to him, or they could send mail to her Fifth Avenue address if they liked.

Bock's time logs back up his story that he was doing what Huguette wanted. "11/26/08: Telephone call from HMC re: letter about Carla Hall email. Will not call Carla. Doesn't want to be involved with family at all. Handle as best I can. Verified with Hadassah and Chris."

The family by this time had figured out that Huguette was at Beth Israel, though they had no idea of the cancer that had originally caused her to go to the hospital. Her half-grandnephew André Baeyens had heard through Madame Pierre that she was at Doctors Hospital, which had become part of Beth Israel. One phone call to Beth Israel's main hospital told them that she was on the third floor there. Not so hidden after all.

Carla knew she was taking a risk going to the hospital. On December 6, she wrote to the Corcoran's director, whom she was keeping informed, "I feel it is important to continue my relationship with Bock because the more we can interact, the more the information seeps out. To confront him right now would not serve our investigation. And it could alienate Huguette."

. . .

The next day, Carla went down to Beth Israel anyway, along with her cousin Ian Devine. They had only recently realized they were cousins, after working together as marketing experts for the same corporate clients, even sending their children to the same school. Ian lived a mile away from Huguette but had never met her: A mile in crowded Manhattan can be a great distance. He recalled sending a couple of holiday cards to Huguette in the 1970s but said he got no reply. He is a wealth management consultant, describing his expertise as helping families "prepare for the responsibilities of wealth," "create connections among the next generations," and "build sustainable family structures for communication and collaboration."

At Beth Israel, the two amateur detectives naturally looked for Huguette first in the "deluxe patient care unit," which offers luxury suites and gourmet meals for higher-paying patients. Huguette was not in this VIP section, which is named for the chairman of the board, the shipbuilder Morton Hyman, who had been meeting with Huguette to seek her donations. Instead, the nurses sent them down the hall to the drab 3 Karpas.

Carla and Ian spoke with the weekend nurse, Christie Ysit, who told them that Huguette was asleep. Carla asked to be able to give Huguette a blessing, and the nurse allowed them inside the darkened room. Carla and Ian stood at the foot of Huguette's bed. The shades were drawn, but in the dim light they could see a small Christmas tree. They saw no machines, no artificial life support, nothing out of the ordinary—aside from their wealthy aunt asleep in this sparse room. Carla recalled, "She was sleeping peacefully in her bed." They left after about a minute.

In the hallway, nurse Christie told them that Huguette was alert, of normal mental and conversational ability, and healthy enough to walk without assistance. She said Huguette was in control of her affairs, knew of the family reunion, but didn't want anyone to know she lived at the hospital. To find out anything more, she said, they'd have to come back the next day, when Hadassah would be there.

The next day, Ian and Carla arrived at the room bearing flowers. They were met in the hallway by an angry and agitated Hadassah Peri, who insisted they leave immediately. They heard Huguette call out to Hadassah, asking something they couldn't quite make out. Hadassah insisted they leave, and they did.

Though they hadn't talked with Huguette, Carla and Ian said they had succeeded in their mission. Ian wrote to the family:

Our impression is that she is as healthy as can be expected for a 102-year-old. She seems to receive adequate care. . . . All in all, our impression was that Tante Huguette is well and, according to her caregiver, displays a level of mental and conversational ability that is normal for a woman her age. . . . The attendants seemed open, honest and reliable, and both care genuinely for Madame Clark. . . . After speaking with the attendants, we believe that Tante Huguette is mentally competent and capable of making her own decisions. . . . Huguette seems to have chosen on her own not to continue to have relationships with her relatives. She is comfortable with her attendants, her lawyer and accountant, and does not wish to be contacted by others.

The nurse's notes in the medical chart show that the night before the first visit, Huguette was "alert and very responsive." After she heard about the visit, she was "agitated and not oriented to time" and kept asking if it was bedtime. Dr. Singman called in an order for Ambien, a sedative. Early the next morning, before the second visit, she again was disoriented and delusional (perhaps a side effect of the Ambien) and sat on the floor of her room while being helped to the bathroom, apparently thinking she had reached the bathroom.

Hadassah wrote in the chart that Huguette called Suzanne Pierre twice after the visits "stating to respect her privacy and not to divulge any information to her family members which she never see these people in her entire life. It's only now they are trying so hard to get too close to Madame which Madame was so upset about all their inquiries."

Hadassah and Huguette both called Bock to complain about the visits. "Telephone call from Mrs. Clark," Bock's logs show. "Make sure none of her money goes to any one in her family. Wants to make sure that Hadassah gets the $5 M she promised her." Inside Huguette's hospital room, the family visits weren't seen as expressions of concern but as attempts to get her money.

Bock sent Carla a stern warning to stay away from Huguette. "Neither she nor I understood your reasons in attempting to meet with her. Whatever the reasons she asks that it not be repeated either by you or any other 'well meaning' family members. If this conduct persists she has instructed me to arrange with the hospital administration to have any further intruders removed by security." Carla met with Bock, who tried to reassure her that Huguette was well cared for. In his office, Carla wrote out an apology to Huguette. Bock passed it on.

Ian Devine reassured his cousins, "We need not apologize" for the visit. "It was motivated solely by love and concern for her well-being; it was our familial obligation to determine for ourselves her health and happiness."

A day later, Hadassah wrote in the chart that Huguette was relaxed, "in very good mood. Asking about my family and what kind of weather we're having."

. . .

The family was still concerned about Kamsler, who was awaiting sentencing. Bock assured them that Kamsler was never alone with Huguette. Still, the family pressed Bock to force Kamsler to resign as her accountant. Bock said Kamsler worked for Huguette, not for him.

Kamsler reached a plea deal with the prosecutor, pleading guilty in January 2009 to a single felony: attempting to disseminate indecent material to minors. He got no jail time, five years of probation, a $5,000 fine, one hundred hours of community service, and a listing on the state's registry of sex offenders.

The felon was allowed to continue working as a certified public accountant. At first the judge on Long Island said in court that a felony conviction would result in the loss of Kamsler's license. But Kamsler's attorney said this was not a financial crime and Kamsler should be allowed to make a living. It was his first contact with the criminal justice system, and he was in treatment with a clinical social worker specializing in sex therapy. His attorney also told the judge that it was important that Kamsler was not accused of meeting with the girls, though the record showed that Kamsler had indeed proposed such meetings. The district attorney didn't take a position for or against Kamsler's request, and the judge granted him a "relief from civil disabilities," which state officials interpreted as sufficient to let him keep his CPA license after he served three months of a two-year license suspension and paid a $2,500 fine.

Kamsler's full statement to the court, when his time came to show remorse, was simply this: "I just want to apologize to the Court, to my wife, to my family for what I have done, and the aggravation, and thank the court very much for their consideration and assistance in this."

A month after his plea, as the Clark relatives kept pressing Bock, Kamsler met with Huguette and gave her a letter:

Dear Mrs. Clark: I recently visited with you and explained my legal situation concerning my pleading guilty to a single felony charge involving the use of my computer to attempt to communicate with minors, who in fact were not minors but were undercover agents. Although I do not believe that I had committed any crime, I accepted this plea in order to put this incident behind me and enable me to not have to put my family through the risks and agonies of a trial, as well as the high financial costs involved. The judge believed that this in no way should affect my ability to serve my clients and continue as a professional. He therefore granted me a Certificate of Relief from Civil Disabilities.

You have indicated that you want me to continue to serve as your accountant and representative and as one of your Executors and Trustees and in any other capacity that you decide. Please indicate your agreement by signing below.

Kamsler, in line for more than $3 million in fees when this elderly client died, had waited a year and five months to tell her about his arrest on sex charges, and even then his letter didn't disclose that he had explicit sex talk with people who had told him they were underage girls, or that he'd talked with them about meeting him, or that he was charged with multiple offenses over several years, or that he was undergoing sex therapy, or that he would remain a registered sex offender.

To pacify the relatives, Bock sent them a copy of the letter, signed by Huguette. He vigorously defended Kamsler, his co-executor of Huguette's estate, saying the accountant "had been changed" by the therapy and was the "victim" of a sting operation, as though he had been entrapped by police into doing something he didn't want to do.

The relatives were less than pacified. Kamsler the victim! They discussed whether Huguette could possibly have understood what had happened, but they were stymied. They feared that Bock was failing to protect Huguette from Kamsler, but they also considered that Bock could be protecting her from change, which they thought she feared, based on their knowledge of how she dealt with Bellosguardo.

One relative who is an attorney, half-grandnephew Paul Albert, urged the family to be cautious:

> Huguette has not asked for our intervention in her financial affairs. She has chosen to be a recluse her entire life and to cut herself off from her family. One of the foreseeable consequences was that she put herself in danger of being taken advantage of. But this was her choice and as long as she is competent I feel uncomfortable in interfering with it. She has a right to privacy. . . . It's possible that Bock is actually doing a good job on her behalf. We just don't know.

. . .

By early 2009, Huguette's eyesight was quite dim, and she stopped using her magic bottomless checkbook. She implored Bock to complete her promise to Hadassah from the sale of the Cézanne. That February, Bock wrote a third $5 million check to Hadassah. To cover the check, Huguette had to borrow. Although Huguette was nowhere near broke, in terms of total assets, she didn't have enough cash. Bock and Kamsler arranged for her to get a line of credit at JPMorgan Chase.

In exchange for the "good" $5 million check, Hadassah handed over to Bock her marker, the undated $5 million check that Huguette had written.

With the "fussy" Gehry plan for the Corcoran now dead and buried, and the new director pledging a "new approach" of respecting the W. A. Clark Collection, Huguette pledged in 2009 to give the museum $1 million in four installments. Her accountant, Irving Kamsler, delivered the first installment personally at the Annual Corcoran Ball, just after his sentencing.

THE DISTRICT ATTORNEY

THE ASSISTANT DISTRICT ATTORNEY held Huguette's hand and said hello, offering a greeting in French.

It was late summer 2010 at Beth Israel, after stories by NBC News raised questions about Huguette's orphaned houses, the men managing Huguette's money, the Stradivarius violin and the gifts to Hadassah. Huguette's photo from 1928 was in the tabloids and on the *Today* show. To protect her from prying eyes, attorney Bock arranged for her hospital room to be disguised with a fake room number and her medical records were stamped with the pseudonym "Harriet Chase."

The assistant district attorney was Elizabeth Loewy, chief of the Elder Abuse Unit of the Manhattan district attorney's office. Loewy had successfully prosecuted the son and attorney of heiress Brooke Astor in 2009 on charges of forgery and grand larceny from the heiress's accounts. Now Loewy was looking into the affairs of Huguette Clark, who had nearly three times as much money as Mrs. Astor.

At 104, Huguette was still able to walk and to feed herself, and she was still lucid nearly all the time, her medical records show. But since early 2007, she had had occasional hallucinations, a couple of times a year. Once, when she was one hundred, Huguette awakened with a night terror, reliving the torturous death of Joan of Arc. When she was 101, one night Huguette insisted that a tissue box was flying around the room, and she wouldn't get out of bed because it might fly into her. She talked again about the terrible way Joan was killed, burned at the stake.

The next day after these episodes, Huguette would be as conversant as ever. The doctors would say she had just been dehydrated, not at all unusual for an older patient, but now she was back to her cheerful self, commenting on events in the news. At age 101, she said she felt so sorry for the wife of New York governor Eliot Spitzer, who resigned after being caught paying a call girl.

About the same time as the assistant DA's visit, in September 2010 as the publicity about Huguette was reaching its height, the hospital arranged for a psychiatrist to see her for the first time in her nearly twenty years in hospital care. The doctor, evaluating Huguette's capacity to make medical decisions, wrote on her chart that she was in frail health with "periods of delirium," a confusion that comes and goes suddenly.

The assistant district attorney visited Huguette three times, seeing no evidence of dementia. She did see her frailty. Huguette didn't seem frightened at all and was responsive and friendly. Though nearly blind, she could hear well enough, could understand what Loewy was saying, and could speak clearly enough to communicate her answers. But the documents would have to tell whether Huguette's finances had been handled according to her wishes.

. . .

Two police detectives and a forensic accountant began to go over Huguette's checking accounts, the sale of the Renoir, the sale of the Stradivarius La Pucelle. The element in the news stories that most caught Loewy's eye was the curious case in which attorney Bock and accountant Kamsler ended up with the property of another former client. The elderly client was someone Huguette knew well: Don Wallace, her attorney for many years before his death in 2002 at age seventy-six.

Wallace's law partner and attorney was Wally Bock, who inherited Huguette as a client. And Wallace's accountant was Kamsler, Huguette's longtime accountant.

Wallace's goddaughter, Judith Sloan, said he had severe dementia in his later years, since his heart attack in 1997. He had no children, and she said earlier versions of his will had left the bulk of his estate to her and her brother, who was Wallace's godson. This included two properties: a $1.5 million weekend house with fourteen acres in the horse country of Dutchess County, New York, where he stored the dolls that Huguette gave him, and an upscale apartment in the Dorchester, on East Fifty-Seventh Street in Manhattan.

In a new will that Wallace signed in March 1997, a month after he returned home from a stay in the hospital, two new beneficiaries were added, to receive $50,000 each: Bock and Kamsler. In a 1999 revised will, the amounts doubled to $100,000 each, and Kamsler was also to receive Wallace's 1995 Mercedes-Benz E300D sedan. Under law, as executors, the men were entitled to a total of $368,000 in fees for being executors of his $4 million estate. The godchildren said they were called in to a meeting in 1997, where Kamsler and Bock told them brusquely that only the country house would go to them, while the city apartment would go to Bock and Kamsler.

If a lawyer who draws up a will receives a bequest in that will, New York law says this circumstance automatically raises a suspicion of undue influence. The probate court had the option to inquire into all of this, but no one challenged Wallace's will. After Wallace died in May 2002, Bock submitted a sworn statement to the court explaining that he and Wallace were not only law partners but also good friends. Wallace treated Kamsler, his accountant for twenty-five years, "as the son he never had." Kamsler said he had visited Wallace in the hospital and arranged home care, just as a child would do for a parent.

Bock explained, "I said to him that he was being overly generous, that he had done enough for me with various gifts given over the years. He insisted however, stating that the people he named as beneficiaries in his Will were 'his family' and that is what he wanted to do." As for the possibility that Wallace suffered from dementia, Bock wrote that although Wallace had been unable to work after January 1997, when pneumonia had led to coronary failure, "at all times, while there were limitations on his physical capabilities, his mental acumen never diminished."

Now, in 2010, eight years after Wallace's death, publicity about Huguette's empty mansions and sale of her property had put Bock and Kamsler on the radar of the district attorney. If these men had inherited money from one client, were they in line to inherit from another? What was the story behind the sale of Huguette's paintings and violin? Bock informed Huguette of the investigation into their handling of her affairs, and she signed another statement, agreeing to pay their legal fees for criminal defense attorneys.

Emboldened by news of the investigation, three of Huguette's relatives went to court in September 2010, seeking to have a guardian appointed to oversee Huguette's financial affairs. The three were Carla Hall Friedman, Ian Devine, and Karine McCall, representing three branches of W. A. Clark's children. They were convinced, Karine said, that Bock and Kamsler were taking advantage of Huguette. But they had no solid evidence of financial impropriety. The judge turned down the relatives without a hearing. Their hopes for a clear view of Huguette's situation would depend on the district attorney's office.

"THANK YOU FOR EVERYTHING"

———

Although Huguette had arranged for fresh flowers to be placed by the bronze doors of the mausoleum at Woodlawn Cemetery every week for forty-three years to honor her mother and father and sister, the last crypt had been filled in 1963 with her mother's casket. Huguette, who in life had more houses than she could use, who had spent so many hours building dollhouses, was in death going to be without a home.

Her attorney learned of this problem at about the time of Huguette's hundredth birthday, in 2006, when her Clark relatives were renovating the decaying mausoleum. Other descendants of W.A. were paying to restore the mausoleum and needed Huguette's consent. There was an additional need to add to the small endowment her father had left for the cemetery, and she agreed to put up the full $147,000. When the renovation was finished, the family held a picnic at the cemetery, on the grass beside the granite memorial to the senator. Of course, Huguette did not attend.

This effort brought to Bock's attention the fact that Huguette had no place to be buried. He'd never checked on this before. The cemetery staff suggested that her body could be cremated, but Huguette was upset by this idea, insisting that she be with her mother and father and sister. The cemetery proposed that she be buried in the ground near the mausoleum. No, she said, inside!

Any changes at the mausoleum required by law the approval of every living descendant of W. A. Clark. With urgency now, Bock rounded up their signatures from around the world, learning for the first time the names and whereabouts of all her living relatives. With approvals in hand, engineers found a solution in 2010: A new crypt could be built inside the mausoleum.

At age 103, Huguette finally had a place to be buried.

. . .

Huguette was laid to rest in the Clark mausoleum at Woodlawn Cemetery in the Bronx, along with her father, mother, sister, and relatives from her father's first marriage. Though every spot was filled by 1963, Huguette waited until she was nearly one hundred to have a place carved out for her under her mother's tomb.

Huguette had for decades, at least since 1989, refused to sign a living will or a do-not-resuscitate order, anything that would limit lifesaving efforts in an emergency. "She wanted to live as long as she possibly could," explained Geraldine, the night nurse. Huguette had named a medical proxy to speak for her with the hospital: her accountant, Irving Kamsler, who visited her every two to three weeks.

In late 2010, Huguette became more frail. When doctors found that she could no longer make her own decisions, Kamsler told them to follow her previously expressed wishes, to continue all lifesaving treatment.

In the spring of 2011, Kamsler got the call. Huguette had suffered heart failure, and was moved to intensive care.

So Huguette spent her last weeks as so many do, being fed through a tube, enduring IVs and scans and scopes.

Chris Sattler said she was able to speak the last time he saw her. "I said, 'I thank you for everything.' She says, 'No, Chris, I thank you.'"

She died early on the morning of May 24, 2011, two weeks short of her 105th birthday. Hadassah was by her side at the end. Huguette had long said she wanted no funeral, no priests, but in her final hours in the middle of the night, Hadassah, a Roman Catholic convert to Orthodox Judaism, called for a priest, who gave Huguette the last rites.

After a life lived in the shadows, the news stories had shoved Huguette back into the limelight. Her obituary appeared on the front page of *The New York Times,* just like her father's.

Her occupation, as listed on her death certificate, was "artist."

. . .

The Clark relatives pressed Bock to let them know about a funeral Mass or when she would be buried, but the attorney said her wishes were to have no ceremony.

Huguette's casket was carried up the steps of the Clark mausoleum at Woodlawn Cemetery and through the open bronze doors, joining her dear father, mother, and sister. The casket was placed on a shelf built under her mother's crypt. The two share a single tomb marker. The entombment was arranged before the cemetery's gates were opened for the day, to keep out relatives and cameras. The only attendants worked for the funeral home and the cemetery. This time no one read "Thanatopsis," including the passage "What if thou withdraw in silence from the living, and no friend take note of thy departure?"

A few weeks later, in California, at a Roman Catholic church near Bellosguardo, old friends and relatives gathered for a simple memorial service. Inside the gates at Bellosguardo, the work went on, gardeners and housemen preparing the Clark estate for another summer.

SURROGATE'S COURTHOUSE

CHAPTER THIRTEEN

SURROGATE'S
COURTHOUSE

JUSTICE

Nineteen of Huguette's closest relatives, her Clark relatives, went to court in 2012 to throw out her last will and testament. If the will were overturned, they would inherit her entire fortune, more than $300 million.

The nineteen relatives were W.A.'s great-grandchildren and great-great-grandchildren. To Huguette, eleven were her half-grandnieces and grandnephews, and eight were a generation further removed, her half-great-grandnieces and grandnephews.*

You could say that they had already gotten their share of the copper mining fortune of W. A. Clark. The millions had been divided equally among his five surviving children: Huguette and her four half-siblings from his first marriage. Each of W.A.'s five children who lived to adulthood had received one-fifth of his estate after his death in 1925: equal shares for May, Katherine, Charlie, Will, and Huguette. Huguette got her allowance for a couple of years, and eventually got something extra, inheriting Bellosguardo and the jewels and cash that her mother had received from her prenup. But W.A.'s plan, it seemed, was to treat each of his children equally.

None of that mattered, under the law. If the nineteen relatives could persuade a judge or jury in Surrogate's Court to overturn the will, they would be allowed to sell Bellosguardo, to sell the paintings, her castles, her dolls. Nothing would go to her nurse Hadassah Peri, her assistant Chris Sattler, her goddaughter Wanda Styka, nothing to the Corcoran museum or Beth Israel hospital—nothing to the people and institutions

---

* The nineteen included four descendants of W.A.'s daughter Mary Joaquina "May" Clark Culver—Edith MacGuire, Rodney Devine, Mallory Devine Goewey, and Ian Devine; nine descendants of his son Charlie Clark—André Baeyens, Patrick Baeyens, Jacqueline Baeyens-Clerté, Jerry Gray, Celia Gray Cummings, Alice Gray Coelho, Paul Francis Albert, Karine Albert McCall, and Christopher Clark; and six descendants of his daughter Katherine Clark Morris—Lewis Hall, Jack Hall, Carla Hall Friedman, Kip Berry, William Berry, and Lisa Berry Lewis. See the family tree on pp. x–xi.

she had supported while she lived. Not only would attorney Wally Bock and accountant Irving Kamsler not get their $500,000 bequests, but they would lose their $3 million commissions as executors, and the chance to reap fees as trustees of a new Bellosguardo Foundation.

The nineteen accused the attorney and accountant and nurse of fraud, and described Beth Israel as Huguette's jailer, keeping a scared, vulnerable old woman closeted as part of a plot to take her money. The doctors and hospital had treated Huguette's cancer, the family alleged, but hadn't treated an underlying psychiatric disorder that had caused Huguette to remain in her home with untreated cancer in the first place. The attorney for the nineteen, John R. Morken, wrote to his clients that their aim was not financial, but to ensure "that Huguette's true wishes are honored and that justice is done."

Fourteen of the nineteen acknowledged in court papers that they had never met Huguette. Of the other five, the last time each of them had met her was in 1957, 1954, 1952, 1951, and "during the second World War." A few of the relatives said they thought they had gotten a glimpse of her at the funeral for her half-sister's daughter, back in 1968. A few of the relatives did have limited contact with her. Eight of the nineteen said they had visited Bellosguardo in the 1940s, 1950s, or 1960s, usually when Anna and Huguette were not present. They had been awestruck by the beauty of the property, had played tennis, and sometimes got a peek inside the great house.

Ten of the nineteen said they had sent cards or letters to Huguette for Christmas or birthdays, and four had received some kind of reply. Most of these relatives were far younger than Huguette. She was born in 1906, and they between 1921 and 1964, so in some cases their parents had sent Christmas cards or lilies, or had received holiday phone calls from Huguette into the 2000s. Huguette on these calls was always very interested in their families, referring to the children and grandchildren by name.

But in the past half a century, these relatives had only occasionally reached out to their elderly aunt, and she had not reached out to them. After the terrorist attacks of September 11, 2001, Huguette did not call her relatives, as she called her goddaughter Wanda, to give reassurance that she was fine.

Of these nineteen, the one who came closest to having a relationship with Huguette was André Baeyens, her half-grandnephew, an elegant Frenchman who served as France's consul general in New York, as his father had before him. André approached Huguette in the late 1990s, after her friend Madame Pierre introduced herself at an event at the consulate. He was writing a book in French about Huguette's father, the senator. She engaged easily with André, calling him about ten or twelve times from her hospital room through the early 2000s, though as usual keeping control by not giving him her phone number or telling him she was in the hospital. He would call Madame Pierre, and Huguette would call him back. They never met. When André finished his book in 2005, a fond family memoir of "the senator who loved France," he sent it to Huguette and never heard from her again.

Huguette had been devoted to helping one of her cousins financially, but that was a LaChapelle cousin, on her mother's side of the family, not a Clark. She supported this California cousin, Annie, who called Huguette by her early nickname, Hugo. Huguette established a trust for Annie and paid her bills until Annie died in 1995, the last close relative in the LaChapelle line. There were no LaChapelles to fight over Huguette's estate.

The Clark relatives said they were always respectful of their elderly aunt's obvious desire for privacy and dignity, and didn't thrust themselves into her cocoon until they felt it absolutely necessary. When New York City went dark for three days in an electrical blackout in August 2003 and people were suffering from the heat, Clark relatives who lived within a mile of her apartment did not stop in to check on her. Some years later, one relative did have her attorney call Huguette's attorney: Niece Karine McCall had her counsel call in 2008 to ask whether she was in Huguette's will. Karine says she needed that information for tax and estate planning, as she was moving from England. Karine, who had met Huguette as a child but never established a connection, says she always had the impression Huguette was "mentally slow." She says she was shocked to learn that she was not going to inherit any of the Clark money from Huguette.

. . .

The nineteen Clarks seeking Huguette's fortune include an international campaigner for human rights for torture victims, and an organizer of legal services for people with HIV/AIDS. One is an honored diplomat who served as the French ambassador to South Korea. Many Clarks support symphonies and museums. In recent years, several in the family have donated to environmental causes, such as campaigning against fracking, a method of extracting natural gas that environmental groups say contaminates groundwater. In that way, Clark money is being used to protect the environment from the ravages of mining.

Although some of W.A.'s children and grandchildren squandered their money on racehorses and divorces, others worked hard, making quiet contributions on Wall Street or in hospitals. Some wrote children's books or translated Tibetan poetry. Others bred quarter-horses or sailed yachts.

While proud of their association with "the senator," the Clarks are aware that their family has suffered at least its share of dysfunction: generations of alcoholism, a long stay in a mental hospital, drug abuse, sexual abuse by a trusted family servant, numerous suicide attempts. All while keeping up the façade that everything was well at home. As one of W.A.'s descendants explained, all of the splendor of the mansions seemed so normal that "I didn't believe that people actually lived in those tiny houses that dotted the edge of our property."

One of W.A.'s descendants described the mixed blessing of inherited wealth: "I think having such wealth can lead some people to have a lack of self-worth because of not having developed a lucrative career of their own or even having investigated their own potential. Having an overabundance of wealth can make people insecure around others who have far less than they do, since the former might wonder if potential partners or even friends are 'only' after them for their money. Well-meaning people of excessive wealth can feel anxious about the lack of perfection of charities they support, and about the fact that even as willing patrons they are powerless to obliterate suffering—all the while knowing that any small amount of money that they might spend on themselves is still enough to change or even save some lives. Wealth can lead to guilt over the unfairness of people working endlessly for them who have never been included fully into the family. In sum, having immense wealth can lead one to feel isolated and to have a false sense of being special."

. . .

Most of the relatives saw Huguette's Fifth Avenue apartments for the first time in April 2012, when the administrator of her estate allowed them to take a tour. They marveled at the view of Central Park, the ornate woodwork, the outdated bathrooms.

Her apartments were vacant, ready for showing by a real estate agent. The only belongings of Huguette, aside from a few pieces of furniture and a Steinway piano, were several of her paintings the agent had hung to give the apartments a bit of her personality. The relatives saw up close the Japanese woman with a dragonfly pin smoking a cigarette, the woman cutting flowers. All the paintings bore Huguette's signature.

After the tour, several of the relatives commented that their Tante Huguette couldn't have done those paintings herself. It wasn't possible, they said. These must be the work of her painting instructor.

———

Two of Huguette's relatives didn't choose to play the inheritance Powerball lottery. One couldn't be found, and the other said she didn't want the money.

The twentieth descendant of Huguette's father was Timothy Gray, whose life story was one of rags to riches to rags to nearly riches. Born in 1952, he lived in several foster homes before being adopted at age five by one of Charlie Clark's daughters and her husband, a physician, becoming as a result a half-grandnephew of Huguette's. Tim had a troubled childhood verging into delinquency and was last seen by his family in 1990, not long after his mother Patsey's funeral.

When Huguette died twenty-one years later and it was time to alert all of her relatives of the filing of her will, private investigators were unable to find Tim. If the family was successful in overturning the will, he was in line for 6.25 percent of Huguette's estate. His take would be roughly $19 million, or about $6 million after all the taxes and estate expenses.

In late December 2012, Tim Gray, the adopted great-grandson of the copper king and railroad builder W. A. Clark, was found in the desolate mining and ranching town of Evanston, Wyoming, frozen to death under a Union Pacific Railroad viaduct. A boy and girl out sledding found his body. Tim was wearing a light jacket, and his shoes were off, though the temperature that week had dipped close to zero. He weighed only about a hundred pounds and looked homeless. Blood tests showed no alcohol or drugs, and the coroner listed the cause of death as exposure.

In his pocket, Tim had a 1905 Indian-head penny that his brother, Jerry, had given him when he took him in at age seventeen for a couple of years. And in his wallet was a cashier's check from the year 2003, his one-eleventh share of the disbursement of a trust left by his grandmother. The uncashed check was for $54,160.

Though Tim was dead, he remained a potential heir to Huguette's estate, because she predeceased him. If the relatives won their case or settled, a share would go to Tim's estate, and that share would pass to his heirs. If he had no spouse or children and left no will, his three siblings would divide his winnings.

Tim was not exactly homeless. He'd spent fifteen years in Evanston, the sort of town where people go when they don't want to be found. He had an apartment and a rented office downtown, where he worked on computer software projects, including voice recognition software, though he had no Internet connection and no phone. He was a loner, neither friendly nor unfriendly, working odd hours, eating alone at Mother Mae's Kitchen downtown, going to Alcoholics Anonymous meetings.

The owner of his apartment building said Tim spent only what he needed from the investment checks he received. He gave most of his money to charity, sponsoring children in Guatemala and handing cash to needy people in the neighborhood. He wrote to politicians, opposing the Bush tax cuts of the early 2000s as giveaways to the wealthy. He told the apartment building manager that he resented his Clark relatives, who he said had not made good use of their inheritances.

About a year before his death, Tim seemed to disappear. He stopped paying for the storage space in Utah where he left his cars. The owner of his building didn't rent out his apartment, knowing that Tim was good for the money. But Tim had staked out a prime sleeping spot under the viaduct, a corner of dirt that he and other men called Suite No. 3. There's no indication that he knew anything about his great-aunt Huguette or the money he stood to inherit.

Tim Gray left behind an apartment stuffed to the ceiling with scrap metal that he had been hoarding: rusted handsaw blades, automobile exhaust pipes, and wire, mostly aluminum and copper.

. . .

Huguette's twenty-first relative said she could not justify opposing her great-aunt Huguette's last will and testament.

This half-grandniece, Clare Albert, born in 1947, told lawyers that Bock and Kamsler seemed highly untrustworthy and she hoped the two men would not profit in any way from the estate. Nevertheless, Clare later said, she was reluctant to join the family's challenge, not finding enough evidence for her to swear that her great-aunt's will was invalid, that Huguette was mentally incompetent. "I do in fact believe," Clare said, "that my aunt well understood how she was dividing up her wealth, and that her final will represents her own intentions."

She continued, "In my view, it would be a terrible waste for the relatives to drain the Bellosguardo Foundation to the point of extinction and to deny the Corcoran its Water Lilies. More than half the wealth Aunt Huguette left to charities would now have to go toward paying huge estate taxes and the staggering commission for the relatives' own lawyer. The gain for any single member of the family would be small compared with the loss for these charities supporting the arts."

She concluded, "Altogether, I find the prospect of challenging my Aunt Huguette's will to be disrespectful of what could be her true wishes, an impolite act not in accordance with my values."

THE TAX BILL

HUGUETTE DIED owing the IRS $82 million in gift taxes, with the bill rising $9,000 per day from penalties and interest.

The tax bill was discovered because the judge decided that Bock and Kamsler needed a chaperone. In light of all the news coverage, the judge declined to let them administer Huguette's estate alone. The judge appointed a third financial watchdog, an official known as the New York County public administrator. That administrator's attorneys soon discovered that Huguette had not paid millions in gift taxes on her spree of generosity. One-quarter of her estate could be eaten up by the bill from the Internal Revenue Service.

Taxes on gifts are paid by the giver, not the recipient. No gift tax returns were filed for Huguette from 1997 through 2003, during which time she gave approximately $56 million in gifts. Some of her gifts were subject to another tax as well, the generation-skipping transfer tax, which must be paid when the recipient is much younger than the donor. The total due in taxes for all years was about $34 million, but that was just the beginning. Add on penalties of $16 million and interest of $32 million, for a total liability of $82 million.

Kamsler was responsible for the finances and was paid $5,000 a month for his accounting work. Records show that he warned Huguette repeatedly to stop making gifts because she didn't have enough liquid assets to cover the gift taxes. He never mentioned the generation-skipping tax, which came into play when she gave money to Hadassah and some others. The public administrator's lawyers also found that Kamsler prepared false gift tax returns claiming that the previous returns had been filed, and he lied to the IRS by claiming he didn't know about the $5 million given to Hadassah.

Bock said that when notices from the IRS came to him, he sent them to Kamsler, but Bock also had responsibility for taxes. His monthly invoices for $15,000 listed his duties, including filing estate and gift tax returns. When Huguette paid $1.85 million for the security system on

WHITTLING DOWN A FORTUNE

Huguette's estate was worth about $308 million before the payment of taxes. Following is a listing of her assets and how they were to be distributed according to her will.

Her largest assets:

- $84.5 million for Bellosguardo in Santa Barbara.
- $54.5 million for three apartments at 907 Fifth Ave., New York City.
- $14.3 million for Le Beau Château in New Canaan, Connecticut.
- $79.3 million in stocks, bonds, cash, and trusts, including $4 million in her checking accounts and $4,039 in unclaimed funds received from the State of New York.
- $75.4 million in personal property, including her $25 million Monet Water Lilies painting, $14.2 million in jewelry and furniture, $1.7 million in dolls and castles, and $34.5 million in paintings, books, and other property.

That $308 million would be whittled down pretty quickly. Here's an estimate of how it would get carved up if the will were carried out as Huguette signed it.

- $7.9 million to pay off a line of credit at JPMorgan Chase.
- $66.3 million for gift taxes, assuming the public administrator was able to reach a settlement with the IRS to eliminate the penalties.
- $6.3 million in executor commissions for attorney Bock and accountant Kamsler.
- $3 million in estate operating expenses for about three years while in court.
- $21 million estimated legal fees for attorneys representing the

public administrator, and attorneys for the presenters of the
will (attorney Bock and accountant Kamsler), and others.
- $23.6 million in estate taxes.
- $5.4 million in generation-skipping transfer taxes. (A bite
comes out of the bequests to younger beneficiaries.)

That would leave about $175 million after taxes to distribute to
beneficiaries. If Huguette's last will were upheld, it would be paid out
roughly like this:

- Bellosguardo Foundation: $123,751,465* (70.94 percent)
- Corcoran Gallery of Art: $25,000,000 (14.33 percent)
- Hadassah Peri, nurse: $15,287,554† (8.76 percent)
- Wanda Styka, goddaughter: $7,897,430 (4.53 percent)
- Beth Israel Medical Center: $1,000,000 (0.57 percent)
- Wally Bock, attorney: $500,000 (0.29 percent)
- Christopher Sattler, assistant: $370,370 (0.21 percent)
- Irving Kamsler, accountant: $370,370 (0.21 percent)
- John Douglas, manager, Bellosguardo: $162,924 (0.09 per-
cent)
- Henry Singman, doctor: $100,000 (0.06 percent)
- Tony Ruggiero, manager, Le Beau Château: $12,444 (0.01 per-
cent)

---

* Including $84.5 million in real property; $34.5 million in art, books, and
instruments; and $4.7 million in cash.

† Including an estimated $1.7 million in dolls.

the West Bank, a gift solicited by Bock in 2000, he did not tell her that she
already owed more than $5 million in taxes for gifts given that year and
that she had not filed gift tax returns from 1997 to 1999. Bock said he accepted Kamsler's assurances that he had taken care of any late filings.

When Kamsler was called to give a sworn deposition in the estate
case, he wouldn't answer questions about the gift taxes, exercising his

Fifth Amendment right against self-incrimination 192 times. He did say that he never lied or deceived Huguette and never stole from her.

Bock and Kamsler faced more trouble. The public administrator filed malpractice claims against them on behalf of Huguette's estate, and the judge suspended them as preliminary executors. Their $6 million in fees, the payday they had toasted that day in the restaurant in 2005, was gone.

. . .

The public administrator also aggressively went after the gifts themselves, demanding the return of more than $40 million to Huguette's estate. More than half of that amount had been given to Hadassah. If the administrator were successful, that also would reduce the gift tax bill: If there was no gift, there was no tax due. The administrator did not seek to recover gifts given to Madame Pierre and her family, Wanda Styka, or Chris Sattler, focusing on those whose financial or medical roles put them in confidential relationships.* Under New York law, any gift to a person in a confidential relationship is presumed to be the result of undue influence. The recipient has the burden of establishing that the gift was proper. The public administrator's office argued that Huguette's close circle of caregivers used their positions to exert influence and control over her, in effect looting her assets.

The problems for the public administrator were that most of these gifts were a long time ago, and Huguette had made the gifts herself, relentlessly writing the checks until her eyesight gave out. Defending Huguette's will, Bock's attorney, John D. Dadakis, said the legal challenge was an insult to Huguette. "To suggest that these gifts were not from Mrs. Clark's generous heart is to denigrate the person who gave these gifts, as well as the recipients who cared for her with their love," Dadakis wrote. "All of the records reflect that Mrs. Clark actively enjoyed her generosity and fully understood what she was giving."

---

* This effort created a mind-bending paradox. Unwinding, say, $10 million in gifts given to Hadassah could save the estate $20 million in taxes, interest, and penalties. And who would get that $30 million? Under the will, it would be part of the "residuary," the part distributed after specific bequests. That meant 60 percent of the money would go back to Hadassah.

L IKE A CONFIDENT TEENAGER at a carnival throwing three baseballs to knock over a tower of milk bottles and win a stuffed panda, the Clark family had three chances to win Huguette's fortune.

First, if the family could prove that both wills had not been legally signed and executed, they would inherit everything. If the family knocked out the last will, they could then go to work on the earlier will, which no one seemed to be able to find an original copy of anyway. Photocopies of wills are not often admitted. Even if the family got the later will thrown out but failed to throw out the earlier one, it still left nearly everything to the family except the $5 million to Hadassah.

The signing ceremony had certainly been faulty, especially considering that a challenge to the will by Huguette's distant relatives could have been anticipated. The defects were many. The will had been drawn up by one of the beneficiaries, attorney Bock. Another beneficiary, accountant Kamsler, was the only person who had any discussion with Huguette about her wishes, and he was a felon. At least one of the beneficiaries, Hadassah, apparently was in the room and, by one witness's account, was helping Huguette hold the pen. The ceremony was not videotaped or photographed. Though the patient was elderly with failing eyesight, the will was in regular-size type. The lawyer overseeing the signing, Bock's colleague, said he hadn't read the document and had no idea Bock was receiving a bequest. No independent doctor examined Huguette and swore to her competence. There was no discussion of the provisions of this will, or the existence of prior wills, or the fees that her executors would receive. The witnesses had no way of knowing whether Huguette knew what she was signing, or even whether this was Huguette, not an impostor.

Despite this slipshod handling of the procedure, the standards are so low that even an incompetently handled document could meet the minimum standards to be legally executed.

Second, the family could try to prove that Huguette was unduly influenced by her caregivers, that the will didn't represent her true wishes. The family argued that Huguette was so scared of going back to her apartment, so dependent on her nurses and advisers, that she couldn't resist their efforts to shape her decision.

Not all influence, however, is undue influence. To prove undue influence under New York law, the family must show almost to a certainty a "moral coercion, a powerful moral force that cannot be resisted," depriving the person of her own free will. If there are facts to show that the will was parallel with Huguette's wishes—love of her nurse and goddaughter, a desire to preserve Bellosguardo, a history of great generosity—it would be hard to distinguish undue influence from extreme eccentricity.

Even if the family could prove undue influence, that didn't mean they would get any money. A jury could throw out the will entirely, which would benefit the relatives. As an alternative, though it rarely happens, a jury could just as well excise only those beneficiaries it decided were taking advantage of positions of trust—possibly the nurse, doctor, attorney, accountant, and hospital. It's hard to see how any claim of undue influence could be leveled against the goddaughter, Wanda, who hadn't seen Huguette since 1954, or the Bellosguardo Foundation, which didn't even exist when Huguette signed the will. If other beneficiaries were knocked out, that would increase the shares going to Wanda and the foundation, not to the family.

Third, the relatives could try to prove that Huguette was incompetent, that she lacked the mental capacity to sign a will. If Huguette were incompetent, the relatives would win everything. The nineteen told the court, though none of them had seen her in more than forty years, that they were sure Huguette "was not of sound mind or memory and was not mentally capable of making a will."

One of the relatives assigned to Huguette a specific diagnosis. This half-grandnephew, Jerry Gray, is a psychotherapist, a licensed clinical social worker, and the founder of nonprofit groups that work around the world to help survivors of political torture bring their torturers to justice. Jerry saw Huguette only one time, the glimpse at a family gathering during World War II, when he was about nine and Huguette about thirty-seven. He was the one who said Huguette stared at him, saying nothing. Now, based on what he read in the media and in court papers, Jerry reduced his great-aunt to a diagnosis, which other Clarks said they found persuasive.

"Huguette was a schizoid personality disorder," Jerry testified, naming a mental condition in which a person has a lifelong pattern of social isolation and indifference to others, "possibly complicated later by paranoid ideation," he said, so she was "compelled by mental illness to isolate herself." He ticked off criteria in the diagnostic manual, saying this diagnosis clearly fit because Huguette "chose the solitary activity of playing with dolls all her life, apparently didn't have a sex partner, had no close friends as we measure friendships, and did not appear to want or need human relationships." Jerry contended that Huguette had "very few interests, if any," and clearly didn't understand what she owned, as shown by "living a reclusive life in a hospital, while you have enormous wealth and five residences you could live in." She displayed, Huguette's nephew summed up, "an irrational pattern of just throwing money away."

Proving incompetence is a high hurdle. The presumption that the signer of a will is competent, as one court put it, "cannot be destroyed by showing a few isolated acts, foibles, idiosyncrasies, moral or mental irregularities or departures from the normal unless they directly bear upon and have influenced" the writing and signing of the will. Even if the family proved that Huguette had some mental illness, that wouldn't bar her from signing a valid will. (An estimated one in six Americans would qualify for at least one personality disorder.) The mentally ill can sign a will during a period of lucidity. Under New York law, all that she would have had to understand when signing the will was what property she owned, her relationship to the beneficiaries, and that the will would hand over that property to them after she died. The law requires less evidence of competence to sign a will than it does to sign a contract.

The relatives could point to dolls and dollhouses, to Smurfs and SpongeBob, to extravagant spending on empty mansions, to the millions given away to Hadassah, to her self-exile at Beth Israel. But would that be enough to show that she was incompetent?

There was nothing in the medical record, nothing before Huguette signed either will, to indicate any mental confusion or dementia. The record does show decades of Huguette's not bending to the pleas of her attorneys or the hospital or the Corcoran.

The beneficiaries also had witnesses who knew Huguette, witnesses who did not benefit from the will, who could testify to her mental alertness and clear memory even years after the will was signed. They had, for example, the neurologist.

CUTE AS PIE

T WAS OCTOBER 25, 2005, six months after Huguette signed her last will. On that Tuesday morning, notes in her medical chart showed her to be in an "acute confusional state"—delirious, agitated. She was hearing piano music. A stroke was possible. Her doctor called for a specialist.

In her more than ten years at Beth Israel Medical Center, Dr. Louise Klebanoff had heard of the "little old lady who lived in the hospital." Now she was finally meeting her.

The neurologist nudged ninety-nine-year-old Huguette awake from her morning nap. The patient opened her blue-steel eyes, seeing an unfamiliar face. "Leave me alone," Huguette said irritably in her high French accent, and closed her eyes.

The doctor studied the chart and looked closely at the white-haired woman. Weighing barely eighty-five pounds, she was dressed in a housecoat and three white cashmere sweaters, and she had surprisingly soft, girlish skin and rosy cheeks. Skilled at cajoling older patients, Dr. Klebanoff gently persuaded Huguette to wake up and to play along with her mental status exam. She tickled her to test her sensory reactions. She gave her simple commands: Close your eyes. Hold up your arms. Wiggle your fingers.

Huguette complied, and the doctor moved up to more complex commands. Clap your hands three times and stick out your tongue.

"Leave me alone!" Huguette shouted, pulling the covers over her head.

This turtle wasn't coming out of her shell. Dr. Klebanoff said she'd come back tomorrow.

The next morning, Huguette brightened up immediately when she recognized the smiling doctor. She sat up in bed and stepped through the tests with ease. She knew who she was and where she was and when it was. Huguette was very hard of hearing, but she was attentive. Her speech was clear, her reflexes quick. Her lab results and chest X-ray were clean. She was normal in every way, neurologically.

"She seemed cute as pie," Dr. Klebanoff said later, "perfectly content."

Huguette just had a cold, the doctor wrote on the chart, and was dehydrated, causing a temporary electrolyte imbalance, which can bring on confusion or hallucinations. With her fluids back to normal, she was fine.

The women talked for another twenty minutes. Huguette gave the doctor a tour of her tabletop model castles from Japan with their brocade fabric interiors. She took out her photo album: Here was her dear mother, smiling shyly in an elegant summer dress. Her dear father, the copper king, looking proud in his dandyish white suit. Her dear sister with her bicycle in front of the family's summer castle outside Paris. Huguette showed the doctor her California house, a palace on a cliff by the Pacific, and her father's house, the largest in New York City, with a tower and 121 rooms, including one adorned with gold.

Taking all this in, the neurologist wasn't exactly sure how much to credit this tale of gold and copper, kings and castles. What did it indicate about the patient's neurological status?

Dr. Klebanoff turned to the nurse, Hadassah, and asked in a stage whisper: Is any of this stuff true?

Oh yes, Hadassah said. It's *all* true.

· · ·

Settlement negotiations in the battle over Huguette's estate began in late 2012. A settlement could dispose of the estate without a jury trial and could also clear away all the side issues, including the effort to recover Huguette's $40 million in gifts, as well as the malpractice claims against Bock and Kamsler. There were two opposing teams in the negotiations, at least on paper. On one side was the family. On the other was everyone else: Hadassah, Wanda, Chris, Beth Israel, the Corcoran, Bock, Kamsler, her property managers, and the largest beneficiary of all, an entity newly created, the Bellosguardo Foundation.

At first everyone gave only a little ground. The family began negotiations by asking for 75 percent of the estate. Others at the table, even those ostensibly on the side of Hadassah, took the position that the nurse had gotten an unseemly amount already, more than $30 million. If she would give up the $15 million or so that she would receive from the will after taxes, that money would go some distance toward a settlement offer to the family. Hadassah said no. Her attorney said she would give up half of her bequest if she could keep everything she'd already received. Her resolve seemed to be stiffened by Hurricane Sandy, which struck the East Coast in November 2012, damaging at least one of her homes and flooding her Bentley.

A new player at the table was the office of New York attorney general Eric Schneiderman. In theory, its role in the case was to protect the charities that might benefit from the will: the Corcoran Gallery, Beth Israel Medical Center, and the new Bellosguardo Foundation. That concern put the attorney general on the side of the will. But at the settlement negotiations, the attorney general's staff seemed more focused on the huge sums of money that Hadassah had gotten. That concern left the attorney general's office in a public relations bind: If it supported the will, Hadassah would get even more. In the summer of 2013, the attorney general began pushing for a settlement, supporting the will in general, supporting Huguette's wishes, but removing gifts to the nurse and others in confidential positions. That solution could make available millions to give to the relatives.

The Corcoran also complicated the scorekeeping by playing for the opposing team. Though Huguette's will left the museum Monet's Water Lilies painting, worth about $25 million, the Corcoran objected to the document, siding with the family's claim that Huguette "was not mentally capable" and that she had signed only under the influence of Bock, Kamsler, and Hadassah Peri.

This was most unusual. Why would the Corcoran, so desperate for cash that it had talked of moving out of Washington to the suburbs, oppose a will from a longtime donor who had left a Monet to the museum? One possible advantage for the Corcoran was that it was standing on the side of the living members of the Clark family, some of whom were already donors to the museum. The more money the Clark relatives won in a settlement or jury trial, the more they would be able to give to the Corcoran in the future. In testimony, family members swore that they had heard of no backdoor deal with the Corcoran, though Corcoran employees said that they had been assured that the Corcoran would not lose its Monet in a settlement.

The Corcoran's leaders explained that they had no choice but to oppose the will, because they couldn't be certain that Huguette was competent to sign it in 2005. Perhaps any incompetence was temporary. The museum didn't return the $500,000 it received from her after 2005,

In 1988, at age eighty-two, Huguette wrote to the mayor of Santa Barbara, Sheila Lodge. In her precise handwriting, she described how much she wanted to preserve Bellosguardo, the home her mother had built. "Dear Mayor Lodge, Your kind letter touched me deeply. It is most gratifying to me that you share my view on the beauty of Bellosguardo. My dear Mother put so much of herself into its charm and had the satisfaction of knowing that during the great depression, she was a bit helpful in giving much needed employment. I, in turn want to express to you, my grateful appreciation for the great help you are giving me in my endeavor to preserve Bellosguardo. With my sincere thanks to you.
Huguette Clark."

when she had paid out half of her $1 million pledge. Nor did they challenge her earlier $500,000 support for the renovation of the Salon Doré, her father's golden room, which the Corcoran now rents out to corporate clients at a rate of $25,000 per soirée.

. . .

Both the family and the beneficiaries had reasons to settle. Rolling the dice at a trial can mean losing everything. Both sides had already spent a great deal on pretrial research and legal fees. And a trial would be an exhausting endeavor, expensive for everyone, lasting weeks or months.

Another reason to settle was that most of the key witnesses wouldn't be able to testify to much at the trial. Through the "Dead Man's Statute," a quirk in New York law, beneficiaries of the will were barred from testifying about communications with Huguette. This law began with the common-law idea that a person with a financial interest shouldn't be encouraged to commit perjury by testifying about what a dead man said before death. So a trial wouldn't include much relevant testimony from Hadassah Peri or Chris Sattler or Dr. Singman. One option for attorney Bock and accountant Kamsler was to renounce their bequests, allowing them to fully testify in support of the will, though they would no longer stand to profit as beneficiaries. There was some doubt that a jury would let them inherit a dime anyway.

A final oddity in the negotiations was that the largest recipient in the will was not at the table. The family questioned whether the Bellosguardo Foundation was a genuine charity or just an excuse for Huguette's attorney and accountant to rake in fees as trustees. As evidence of this claim, the relatives pointed to how little money the foundation would end up with—only about $4.7 million in cash, as the will was written, not nearly enough to maintain the great house. The counterclaim was simple: If it were a fraud, wouldn't the attorney and accountant have put more money into it? The relatives also questioned how the foundation could be Huguette's intent. "She didn't have a charitable bone in her body," several relatives said, ignoring or unaware of Huguette's many years of donations to the Corcoran and to Beth Israel, her donation of Rancho Alegre to the Boy Scouts, her donation of the

Andrée Clark Bird Refuge, and her quiet charity to friends and strangers.

Hoping to bolster the plan for the nascent Bellosguardo Foundation, a group of arts foundations in California stood up to say they would welcome, and perhaps support financially, the new neighbor. However, when the Santa Barbara groups tried to send a lawyer to the settlement talks in New York, the Clark family's attorney, John Morken, refused to negotiate with him, saying if you love Bellosguardo that much, we'll let you buy it after we win.

The family had a reason to insist that Bellosguardo be sold: That's where most of the money was. As written, the will left 86 percent of the pot, after expenses and taxes, to charities, which don't pay taxes. The Bellosguardo Foundation was a charity, as were the Corcoran and Beth Israel. For every $10 million that went to the relatives instead of the charities, about $4 million more in estate taxes would have to be paid. In other words, to get an inch, the relatives had to ask for a mile.

. . .

There was a strong reason for all sides to settle: It would ensure that the lawyers got paid.

If one of the aims of Huguette's relatives was to keep the money out of the hands of her lawyers, their victory would nevertheless leave a large chunk of the estate in the hands of their own lawyer. Working on a contingency, as is standard, the family attorney would receive 33 percent of the first $50 million, and 30 percent of the next $50 million. At least sixty-two attorneys were named in court papers in this case, with dozens of others working behind the scenes, many of them in Manhattan, where it is not uncommon for experienced lawyers to bill at $1,000 an hour. Court dates and settlement conferences were attended by ten to twelve lawyers at a time, together running the meter in excess of $10,000 an hour.

Additional costs came from travel to take testimony from fifty witnesses, including an all-expenses-paid trip in 2012 for three attorneys to see half-grandnephew André Baeyens in Vienna. At age eighty-two, the elegant former diplomat was afflicted with aphasia, a brain disease akin to dementia. Despite the family's objection, André was subjected to two days of questioning in which he was unable to give even his home address. At least the attorneys were able to see the fountains of the Schönbrunn Palace at night.

THE PINK DIAMOND

To raise cash for the estate, the public administrator began selling some of Huguette's property, even before the legal battle was concluded. He was able to sell only the items that were not specifically bequeathed to anyone.

Her mother's jewelry was already long gone, sold off by Citibank, and the pieces in her safe at home had been given to Hadassah and Chris, but she had another stash of jewelry, still in their original 1920s boxes from Cartier and Tiffany—in a safe-deposit box. They had apparently not been worn since the 1930s.

After Huguette's jewels were displayed for a public viewing, the auctioneer at Christie's sold her nine-carat pink diamond ring for $14 million, as well as her twenty-carat rectangular diamond ring for $2.7 million; her Art Deco diamond and emerald bracelets that she wore on her honeymoon, for $90,000 and $480,000; her ruby, sapphire, and emerald gold bracelet for $220,000; and her charm bracelet, depicting themes of love—a girl watering a heart in a garden, a blindfolded lover choosing between two hearts—for $75,000. In all, the pieces brought $18 million, or so it first appeared. The purchaser of the pink diamond ring put out a press release announcing his purchase, then failed to come up with the money, so it was sold quietly for less.

...

The apartments at 907 Fifth Avenue also went on the market for a total of $55 million.

Apartment 12W sold for $25.5 million to hedge fund manager Boaz Weinstein. The apartment had proved to be a good investment for Huguette. Even accounting for inflation, her investment of $63,000 in 1955 had increased forty-seven-fold.

An oil sheik, the prime minister of the Persian Gulf nation of Qatar, bid $31.5 million for Apartments 8W and 8E, but the co-op board turned down his application. Too much traffic and security, the members said.

Eventually, 8W and a sliver of 8E were sold for $22.5 million to a quieter owner, private equity manager Frederick Iseman. The rest of 8E was still on the market in mid-2013.

In Connecticut, Le Beau Château had fetched an offer of $25 million while Huguette lived, but she wouldn't take it, because the appraisal had been a bit higher at $26 million. An accepted offer at $21 million required getting town approval to divide the fifty-two acres into ten lots, but then the market crashed anyway. The price fell from its height of $35 million to $24 million, fell after her death again to $17 million, then to $15.9 million. In the summer of 2013, it remained on the market, with neighbor Harry Connick, Jr., among the lookers.

The rest of Huguette's possessions—her paintings and books, her dolls and dollhouses and miniature castles—were in storage, awaiting a trial or settlement.

· · ·

The case was assigned in 2013 to a judge, Surrogate Nora S. Anderson, who the previous year had been censured for failing to report $250,000 in campaign contributions. She was acquitted by a criminal jury of two felony charges of filing false campaign reports, then was censured by the state judicial conduct commission. So the trial of the estate of Huguette Clark, whose father quit the U.S. Senate because of campaign finance irregularities, was being heard by a judge with campaign finance issues.

As of this writing in July 2013, the parties had not agreed to a settlement. Absent a deal, a jury trial was scheduled for September 2013 to divide the Clark copper fortune.

Two blocks away at the district attorney's office, the criminal investigation officially was "inactive." In nearly three years of digging, the district attorney didn't find justification to bring a criminal charge against anyone. Bock and Kamsler may have been enterprising, but the investigators found that the paper trail backed up their story. Huguette had authorized, in writing, the sale of the Renoir, the sale of the Stradivarius violin, the marketing of the Connecticut home, even the gift of the security system for the community in Israel where Bock's family lived. Nearly all of the hundreds of gift checks were written in Huguette's clear handwriting, right up until her eyesight gave out.

THE
CRICKET

A LIFE OF INTEGRITY

HUGUETTE CLARK LIVED a surprisingly rich life of love and loss, of creativity and quiet charity, of art and imagination. Though the platitude—money can't buy happiness—may be comforting to those who are less than well heeled, great wealth doesn't ensure sadness either.

Huguette suffered sorrows, yes, as happens when one lives more than a century—long enough to narrowly escape both the *Titanic*'s sinking and the collapse of the twin towers of the World Trade Center. She suffered the death of her dear sister, Andrée, and then of her father, W.A., and her mother, Anna. She persevered through divorce, cancer, mendacity. She lost her Degas ballerina, her mother's jewelry, her privacy.

Yet she did not have a sad life. Huguette focused on happy memories of good times with her close family, of playing hide-and-seek and listening to her sister's bedtime stories in the fairy-tale Clark mansion, of cleverly offering their banker father gold coins to escape from the German armies, of riding surfboards with Duke Kahanamoku at Waikiki Beach.

Huguette was not as she appeared to those who barely knew her. The story told by her relatives, the Clark relatives seeking her fortune, was that she was mentally ill, even intellectually disabled. In Paul Newell's years of conversations with her, however, right up to a year before the wills were signed, he found Huguette to be impressively lucid and cheerful, possessed of a keen memory. She remembered events from nearly a century earlier, and she remembered that he'd recently mentioned that his granddaughter was taking ballet lessons. In spite of her years in seclusion, her social skills appeared quite normal. If she was troubled or unhappy, she did a fine job of disguising it through years of conversation and correspondence. Eccentricity is not a psychiatric disorder.

Huguette was relentless and sophisticated in pursuing the arts—trained as a painter, self-taught as a photographer, a shrewd collector of Renoirs and Stradivaris. She explored Japan's culture and history—

language, hairstyles, fabrics—to lend authenticity to her castles and paintings. She kept alive, through her patronage and correspondence, an entire generation of the greatest illustrators in France, the ones she remembered from children's books and magazines. Before her eyesight failed, she read the classics, played the violin, learned chess in her eighties on one of her carved Japanese sets, conversed in French.

The family's story is that Huguette was controlled, was kept in a cocoon, that she must be a victim of fraud. And who didn't make the same assumption upon hearing about the wealthy woman who shut herself away in a hospital, giving millions to her nurse while her affairs were handled by an attorney and a felon accountant?

"Mrs. Clark," wrote attorney Peter S. Schram for the public administrator's office, "was completely dependent for her physical and emotional needs on a small group of individuals, who were her only contacts with the world outside of her hospital room."

Her only contacts? Though she lived alone, Huguette was not isolated. First, she had her nurses twenty-four hours a day, starting with Hadassah Peri. She also had her regular visitors: her friend Madame Suzanne Pierre, with her artichokes with hollandaise; her doctor Henry Singman, with his photos of his grandchildren; and her man Friday, Chris Sattler, with his French baked goods and their buttery smell from her childhood. And she had the children and grandchildren of her friends and doctors and nurses, who also visited on occasion.

Huguette had hundreds of other affectionate visitors, arriving in the mail. In exchange for the gifts she showered on the children and grandchildren of friends and employees, she asked only that the parents send photos of the children with their toys. These photos poured in by the hundreds: children with new bedroom furniture, children dressed as knights in suits of armor, children with guitars and electric pianos, train sets, castles, puppets, roller skates, and bicycles, all from their Tante Huguette.

For a recluse, Huguette had a lot of pen pals, her lifelong friends, most of them unknown to one another. She was a recluse in that she locked herself away from travel and sunsets and cafés, but a woman who leaves twenty thousand pages of affectionate correspondence is also a world traveler. And she was a faithful friend, maintaining warm, mostly long-distance, relationships for decades.

She had her Frenchman, Etienne de Villermont, with "the bond of love of half a life, which will never disappear." She had his wife, Elisabeth, their daughter, Marie-Christine, and many others in their extended family, all grateful for Huguette's sustained support, down to treats from their corner grocer in France.

And her gregarious ex-husband, Bill Gower, to whom she sent money and family news.

She had a loving, artistic goddaughter, Wanda Styka, who remained a faithful correspondent for sixty years.

And her artist friends in France: The whimsical Félix Lorioux with his comical gift-giving insects. The fantastic and erotic Chéri Hérouard, her magazine hunter. And Jean Mercier, Manon Iessel, and J. P. Pinchon, for whom she was "a good fairy" in their old age.

She had her telephone friends, including her cousin Paul Newell and her half-grandnephew André Baeyens. And her art helpers: Caterina Marsh, who was the go-between with her artist friend Saburo Kawakami in Japan. Her dollhouse repairman, Rudolph Jaklitsch, and his wife, Anna, who made the curtains. The staff at Au Nain Bleu and Christian Dior.

She had her longtime friends from her childhood, the ones she supported so generously into their old age: Ninta Sandré, the daughter of her governess, and many others who received her help. Even a stranger, Gwendolyn Jenkins, whose only connection to Huguette was that she took care of Huguette's stockbroker when he was ill.

She had her pen pals in Santa Barbara, keeping tabs on her mother's Bellosguardo and her sister's bird refuge: Alma Armstrong, the chauffeur's widow, who sent newspaper clippings. And the mayor, Sheila Lodge, whose long campaign to persuade Huguette to leave the Clark estate to the arts bore fruit in Huguette's will and the Bellosguardo Foundation.

Though many of those close to Huguette received large gifts, so much that one would naturally question their independence as witnesses to her competence, many doctors and nurses received nothing. Yet they tell the same story of a remarkable woman who knew her own mind. The audiologists tested her hearing and found her quite alert even at nearly ninety-nine. Dr. John Wolff visited frequently to bring Huguette flowers and to hear her stories. And the neurologist, Dr. Louise Klebanoff, found the little old lady in the hospital to be as "cute as pie."

An assistant district attorney, Elizabeth Loewy, met her obligation to check on Huguette's well-being. An FBI agent, investigating the theft of a Degas pastel, walked right into her hospital room.

. . .

Huguette's hobbies were not what most people would choose if they had unlimited wealth. She was unashamed about collecting dolls, building castles, and watching the Smurfs, just as other people like to collect stamps or can name the shortstop for the Boston Red Sox in 1967. Huguette took seriously Miss Clara Spence's admonition to "cultivate imagination"—even to the point of being concerned that "the little people are banging their heads!"

We will never know why Huguette was, as she might say, "peculiar." The people in her inner circle say they have no idea. Outsiders speculate. It was being the daughter of an older father! It was her sister's death! Or her mother's! The wealth! It was autism or Asperger's or a childhood trauma! Easy answers fail because the question assumes that personalities have a single determinant. Whatever caused her shyness, her limitations of sociability or coping, her fears—of strangers, of kidnapping, of needles, of another French Revolution—Huguette found a situation that worked for her, a modern-day "Boo" Radley, shut up inside by choice, safe from a world that can hurt.

Like her attention-grabbing father and her music-loving mother, both strong-willed and private in their own ways, Huguette was a formidable personality who lived life as she wanted, always on her own terms. Far from being controlled by her money men, she drove them to frustration. Though she was firm, she was always kind. It would have been easy for anyone born into her cosseted circumstances to have abused her power. Yet in all the testimony by fifty witnesses in the battle for her fortune, in all her correspondence, there is not a single indication that Huguette ever used her wealth to hurt anyone. That just wasn't her way.

Huguette had experienced the finest belongings and most luxurious travel. She had seen heart-stopping panoramas, owned great art, heard inspiring music. Yet in the end, she preferred to live in a hospital room, with her hollandaise and brioche and cashmere sweaters. Huguette had the courage—or Clark stubbornness—to be an artist at a time when that wasn't an approved path for a woman, to break away from a marriage she didn't want, to resist the manipulations of her hospital and her museum to get more of her money, to leave most of her estate to her friends and to a charity that honored her mother's memory. According to common belief, "just throwing money away" may be a sign of mental illness, but Huguette enjoyed giving gifts to the people she knew.

These were not acts of incompetence, but of self-expression and resilience. In her own way, she found what life may be, a life of integrity.

Huguette was a quiet woman in a noisy time. She had all the possessions that anyone could want, but she set them aside—all except her brioche and cashmere sweaters.

TO LIVE HAPPILY

ON MARCH 2, 2005, just a month before she signed her last will and testament, Huguette was sitting up in her hospital bed when Dr. Singman stopped by for a visit. She had a treat for him.

Huguette recited a poem. "Le Grillon" (The Cricket) was one of the old French fables from the book of morocco leather in her father's library at the Clark mansion on Fifth Avenue, where ninety years earlier Andrée had read to Huguette. This fable was written in the late 1700s by Jean-Pierre Claris de Florian. It is also sometimes called "True Happiness." Huguette knew it by heart.

THE CRICKET

A poor little cricket
Hidden in the flowery grass,
Observes a butterfly
Fluttering in the meadow.
The winged insect shines with the liveliest colors:
Azure, purple, and gold glitter on his wings;
Young, handsome, foppish, he hastens from flower to flower,
Taking from the best ones.
Ah! says the cricket, how his lot and mine
Are dissimilar! Lady Nature
For him did everything, and for me nothing.
I have no talent, even less beauty;
No one takes notice of me, they know me not here below;
Might as well not exist.
As he was speaking, in the meadow
Arrives a troop of children.
Immediately they are running

After this butterfly, for which they all have a longing.
Hats, handkerchiefs, caps serve to catch him.
The insect in vain tries to escape.
He becomes soon their conquest.
One seizes him by the wing, another by the body;
A third arrives, and takes him by the head.
It should not be so much effort
To tear to pieces the poor creature.
Oh! Oh! says the cricket, I am no more sorry;
It costs too dear to shine in this world.
How much I am going to love my deep retreat!
To live happily, live hidden.

Huguette, at ninety-eight years old, recited the childhood fable, from memory, three times.

In English.

In Spanish.

And, of course, in French.

Pour vivre heureux, vivons caché. To live happily, live hidden.

THE LIVES OF HUGUETTE CLARK and her mysterious family, hidden in the shadows for so long, are illuminated now by an array of human sources, private documents, and public records.

Our sources begin with Huguette herself, through her telephone calls with co-author Paul Newell. We also interviewed more than a hundred people—relatives, friends, employees, attorneys—who gave generously of their time and memories, sometimes with the understanding that we would not use their names. Their accounts are supplemented by the sworn testimony of fifty witnesses in the legal battle over Huguette's estate, including her goddaughter, personal assistant, nurses, and doctors, as well as the relatives seeking her fortune.

Luckily for us, Huguette kept nearly every important document in her life, and many papers that most of us toss out, even the first drafts of Christmas cards. We weren't able to see everything in her archives, but we were able to read some twenty thousand pages of her personal and financial correspondence, including four thousand pages we had translated from the French. We read thousands of pages of notes made by her nurses in her twenty years in the hospital. We read correspondence that Huguette received from her attorneys and accountants; her income tax returns, bank statements, and canceled checks; and bills of sale for artwork, musical instruments, and furniture back to the early 1900s, as well as more recent inventories of her property. We read historical papers, including sections of her father's journal and ledger from the 1860s and 1870s in Montana and genealogical entries in the Clark family Bible.

To understand the Clarks and their world, we examined more than five thousand previously unpublished photographs from Huguette's apartments, including those in her personal albums and snapshots of her dolls and dollhouses and her art projects. Perhaps more fascinating were her paintings, including those she owned, those she painted herself, and those painted of her by her painting instructor. Although private tours of her empty mansions were a window into her style and tastes during various periods, the detailed photographs, both historic and recent, in which one can see the books and sheet music on her shelves and the framed photos on her bedside table, brought those empty rooms to life.

Add to these the public records of her life: the 1900 Senate investigation and trial resulting in W. A. Clark's resignation from the U.S. Senate; the transcript of a 1920s court battle in Montana over W.A.'s estate; marriage and divorce certificates; burial records; property records; census rolls; passenger registries from ocean liners; passport applications; and hundreds of books, scholarly theses, and newspaper and magazine articles.

Also telling are the ephemera: a lock of her sister's hair, a harp composition of "Sleeping Beauty," and a menu in French from W.A.'s dinner celebrating his first election to the Senate. The menu, like the man, bears a permanent stain, a single drop of Bordeaux.

ACKNOWLEDGMENTS

MANY PEOPLE CONTRIBUTED to the Clark story, and we thank them for their extraordinary generosity.

Michael V. Carlisle of Inkwell Management was as helpful and encouraging as any agent could be, assisted by Lauren Smythe and Nathaniel Jacks.

Pamela Cannon, executive editor at Ballantine Books, reached out to encourage our plans to write about the Clarks, and edited this text with patience and good judgment. Anna Bauer designed the jacket. Others at Random House Publishing Group who helped get this book into your hands include Richard Callison, Susan Corcoran, Benjamin Dreyer, Toby Louisa Ernst, Michelle Jasmine, Barbara Jatkola, Ratna Kamath, Mark LaFlaur, Carole Lowenstein, Mark Maguire, Libby McGuire, Allison Merrill, Cindy Murray, Grant Neumann, Beth Pearson, Paolo Pepe, Quinne Rogers, Evan Stone, Simon M. Sullivan, Jennifer Tung, Betsy Wilson, Maralee Youngs, and Amelia Zalcman.

Paul Newell

IN MEMORY of Clark relatives no longer with us, I acknowledge important contributions by my cousins Mary Abascal, Anita Mackenzie, and their mother, Elizabeth Clark Abascal, as well as Anita's son, Sandy Mackenzie, all of whom knew and remembered well W. A. Clark, Anna Clark, and Huguette Clark. I appreciate these cousins for their personal recollections and for their sharing of archival photos, letters, and other documents.

I'm grateful especially to my dear father, Paul Clark Newell, who admired his famous uncle, wrote about him, and conserved the large accumulation of photographs and letters left by my grandmother Ella, who was W.A.'s youngest sister and who was caregiver to their mother in the years approaching her centennial birthday. My appreciation also to Agnes Clark Albert, whom I interviewed by phone in April 2000, at a time when she was the last surviving grandchild of Senator Clark.

Finally, I express my fond memories of my cousin Huguette Clark, with whom I was privileged to become acquainted as she entered her ninetieth year and with whom I often communicated by telephone and written correspondence. She was generous in sharing family photos and personal reminiscences of her father, her dear departed sister, Andrée, and her mother, Anna, who was her closest companion during Anna's long life.

Among living Clark cousins and their spouses, I thank a number of them for their kindness in sharing bits of family history and genealogical information, including André Baeyens, John Michael Clark, Lorilott Clark, Carla Hall Friedman, Erika Hall, Lewis and Gemma Hall, Margie Henry, Edie MacGuire, Helen Murray Miller, and particularly Beverly McCord, who created a Clark family tree at the dawn of the twenty-first century, a prototype that has been amended in the years following to confirm accuracy and to add the most recent generations. I thank my sister, Eve Newell, for many, many hours devoted to this genealogical mission, and her husband, Ron Forsey, for his implementation electronically of an updated family tree and for scanning and storing many documents and photo images, some of which grace the pages of this book.

Among institutions, I received invaluable help from the Corcoran Gallery of Art, with special thanks to Dare Myers Hartwell, conservator, and Marisa Bourgoin, formerly the archivist at that institution; and from the William Andrews Clark Memorial Library at the University of California, Los Angeles, with my gratitude for office space and archival storage made available to me. Much appreciation to the librarians and other staff at the Clark, and particularly to Suzanne Tatian, who provided me with useful counsel and assistance over the past eighteen years.

I received courteous and useful assistance from many other libraries and historical societies, including the Connellsville Area Historical Society in Pennsylvania; Thelma Shaw, Nora Meier, and Nancy Silliman at the Kohrs Memorial Library in Deer Lodge, Montana; the Montana Historical Society Research Center in Helena; Ellen Crain at the Butte–Silver Bow Public Archives in Butte; the World Museum of Mining in Butte; and the Jerome Historical Society in Arizona.

With gratitude for the support and encouragement received from my loving family, including parents with me in spirit, siblings, and wonderful progeny.

And with special admiration for my co-author, Bill Dedman, Pulitzer Prize winner, for his knack of putting a friendly face on history and for his uncommon prolificacy, born of years of delivering impressive copy in the face of inflexible deadlines.

Bill Dedman

THANK YOU to the many online readers who demanded we follow up to find Huguette and to make sure she was well cared for.

The editors at NBCNews.com (the former msnbc.com) said right from the start that they'd like to know what was up with those empty mansions, and allowed me time to work on this book. Investigations editor Mike Brunker is the patient editor every reporter imagines but doesn't believe exists. (He also is 2,411 miles away, which turns out to be exactly the right distance from your editor.) And thanks to the big bosses: Russ Shaw, Jennifer Sizemore, Greg Gittrich, Dick Belsky, Stokes Young, Jen Brown, Charlie Tillinghast, and Vivian Schiller. They supported this effort, even if they silently questioned the view, as one reader put it, "Well, if she had a doctor with only one patient, accountants and lawyers with only one client," then "certainly she can have one reporter. . . ."

Patrick McCord, the plot whisperer, offered valuable insights from the Editing Company in Westport, Connecticut.

Guillaine Dale Farrell translated from French four thousand pages of correspondence from Huguette's papers and was a patient translator of continuing conversations with contacts in France. In Paris, Ph.D. student Alexander Yarbrough from the University of Buffalo helped by tracing the history of Etienne de Villermont and the Allard family's interrupted path to nobility. Research assistants who contributed hundreds of hours to this effort were Michelle Crespo, Margaux Stack-Babich, Sara Germano, and Beau Caruso. Roland Jones helped with public records in New York, and Jacques Kauffmann in France.

Other researchers who have walked the Clark trail showed great kindness toward this project. Professor Keith Edgerton of Montana State University Billings, who graciously shared research files on W. A. Clark. Retired newspaperman Steven Shirley in Helena, who reached Huguette for a couple of chats on the phone, offered his memories and his extensive bibliography of Montana history. Don Lynch provided research on the *Titanic* and the Clarks. Author Brad Tyer, who surveyed the environmental damage in Montana. Documentary photographer Elijah Solomon, who looked into the circumstances of Timothy Gray's life and death. Others who offered information include Barney Brantingham of *The Santa Barbara Independent* and Gerry O'Brien, Carmen Winslow, Tim Trainor, and Roberta Stauffer of *The Montana Standard*.

Generous assistance came from experts in diverse special subjects. On psychiatry in geriatric patients, Dr. Benjamin Liptzin, professor and deputy chair of psychiatry at Tufts University School of Medicine and psychiatry chair at Baystate Medical Center. On the history of fashions, Nancy Deihl, a master teacher of costume studies at New York University. On the music of harpist Marcel Grandjany, Professor Kathleen Bride of the Eastman School of Music at the University of Rochester. On Huguette's paintings and the women artists of her time, Associate Professor Marice E. Rose of Fairfield University. On Japanese art and translation, postdoctoral teaching fellow Ive Covaci of Fairfield University. On New York architecture, attorney/architect Andrew Alpern. On charitable gift annuities, wealth management specialist Gavin Morrissey of Commonwealth Financial Network. On Huguette's Stradivarius violin, La Pucelle, collector David Fulton, dealer Charles Beare, and violinist James Ehnes. On Butte and its mining history, geologist and historian Richard I. Gibson. On Masonic history and the Vigilantes, Reid Gardiner and Daniel Gardiner of the Grand Masonic Lodge of Montana. On the French nobility, Professor Jonathan S. Dewald of the University of Buffalo. On the Clark pipe organ, author Jim Lewis. On medical ethics, Yale University senior scholar Daniel Callahan, president emeritus of the Hastings Center. For analysis of Huguette's tax returns, journalist David Cay Johnston. For information on copper-jacketed bullets, Dale Clingan. On the trees and plants at Bellosguardo from detailed photographs, Jessica Lawrence of Green Landscape Nursery in

Santa Clarita, California. On the Hawaiian language, Professor Puakea Nogelmeier of the University of Hawaii Manoa. And on Huguette's automobiles, Geoffrey Keller at Dragone Classic Motorcars in Westport, Connecticut.

Many members of the Clark family shared information, despite their attorney's repeated admonitions. We drew on the genealogical research on the family by Eve Newell, Colin Berens, and J. P. Canton and the resourceful research staff at Ancestry.com.

Many individuals who had contact with the Clarks provided invaluable information: Reminiscences of life at Bellosguardo in Santa Barbara came from Barbara Hoelscher Doran and Barry Hoelscher, among others. The son and grandson of Félix Lorioux, Jean-Loup Brusson and Fabrice Brusson, graciously shared information on his work and his patron Huguette. Ann Raynolds and Leontine "Tina" Lyle Harrower described their godmother, Anna Clark. John Taylor still has the Rolls-Royce that Huguette and Bill Gower took on their honeymoon, his father having purchased it after the Clark chauffeur sold it to a dealer. Janice Benatz shared information on Clarkdale, Arizona; Ann Fabrizio on her father, Robert Samuels, and the work of French & Company, which redecorated Huguette's apartments; Jeff Southmayd on his great-grandfather, Nathan Leroy Southmayd, who may be the man in the middle of the photo of three miners on page 24; Mary Muir on one of Huguette's paintings found in a London shop; and Stephen Gruse on W. A. Clark, Jr. And then there's Michael Nygaard, the ultimate Huguette fan.

One of the pleasures of this hunt has been the chance to work with so many noteworthy institutions. Very special thanks to Art Loss Register, London (Chris Marinello); Associated Press, New York (Carolyn McGoldrick); Barbara Cleary's Realty Guild, New Canaan, Connecticut (Barbara and Brian Cleary); Brown Brothers, Sterling, Pennsylvania (Linda Tyler); Brown Harris Stevens, New York (John Burger, Kristin Clark, Leslie Coleman, Amy Gotzler, Mary Rutherfurd, Danielle Wagner, Hall Willkie); Butte Silver Bow Arts Foundation, Butte, Montana (Glenn Bodish, Gretchen Miller); Butte–Silver Bow Public Archives, Butte (Ellen Crain, Irene Scheidecker, Harriet Schultz); Christie's, New York (Jaime Bernice, Erin McAndrews); Clarkdale

Historical Society & Museum, Arizona (Mary Lu Estlick); Copper King Mansion, Butte (Erin Sigl, Pat Sigl, John Thompson); Corcoran Gallery of Art, Washington, D.C. (Marisa Bourgoin, Melanie Feaster, Ila Furman, Kristin Guiter, Dare Myers Hartwell, Anna Kuehl); County of Santa Barbara, California (Beverly Curren); Dunbar Historical Society, Pennsylvania (Donna Myers); Durand-Ruel & Co., Paris (Paul-Louis Durand-Ruel); Fairfield University, Connecticut (Professor Joel Goldfield); Girl Scout National Historic Preservation Center, New York (Pamela Cruz, Yevgeniya Gribov, Michelle Tompkins); Harry S. Truman Library and Museum, Independence, Missouri (Randy Sowell); Iowa Wesleyan College, Mount Pleasant (Lynn Ellsworth, Jay Simmons); Jerome Historical Society, Arizona (Allen Muma); the Joint Commission, Oakbrook Terrace, Illinois (Elizabeth Zhani); Lewis & Clark Fort Mandan Foundation, Washburn, North Dakota (Nicolette Borlaug, Joseph Mussulman); Mark Twain Papers, University of California, Berkeley (Neda Salem); Montana Historical Society Research Center, Helena (Rebecca Kohl, Delores Morrow, Zoe Ann Stoltz); Montecito Historical Archives of the Montecito Association, California (Dana Newquist, Guy Webb); Museum of New Zealand Te Papa Tongarewa, Wellington (Jennifer Twist); Museum of the City of New York (Nilda Rivera, Lindsay Turley); Nassau County District Attorney's Office, Mineola, New York (Carole Trottere); NBC News InfoCenter, New York (Donna Mendell); Nelson-Atkins Museum of Art, Kansas City (Kathleen Leighton, Toni Wood); New Canaan Historical Society (Janet Lindstrom); New York County District Attorney's Office (Erin Duggan); New York Department of Education, Office of the Professions, Albany (Jane Briggs); New-York Historical Society (Robert Delap, Eleanor Gillers, Marybeth Kavanagh, Jill Slaight, Joe Festa); *The New York Times* and Redux Pictures (Rosemary Morrow, Jeff Roth); Nippon Music Foundation, Tokyo (Kazuko Shiomi); Onyx Classics, London (Matthew Cosgrove); Paul Clark Home, Butte (Corri Evans, Betty Ostoj); Pearl S. Buck Family Trust, New York (Craig Tenney); Princeton University's Seeley G. Mudd Manuscript Library, Princeton, New Jersey (Christa Cleeton, Charles Greene, Anna Chen); Santa Barbara Historical Museum (Michael Redmon); Santa Barbara Trust for Historic Preservation (Anne Petersen); Save Our Seminary,

Silver Spring, Maryland (Bonnie Rosenthal); Sotheby's, London and New York (Blair Hance, Virginia Harley); the Surrogate's Court, New York City (Suzan Tell, Eugene McCusker, Omar Colon, Marcia Goffin, Diana Sanabria); Tokyo String Quartet (Louise Beach); United Daughters of the Confederacy, Richmond, Virginia (Jane Durden); University of Montana, Missoula (Kathy Zeiler); University of Nevada, Las Vegas (Su Kim, Kelli Luchs); University of Virginia Law School Foundation, Charlottesville (David Ibbeken); Wildenstein & Company, New York (Joseph Baillio); William Andrews Clark Memorial Library, University of California, Los Angeles (Gerald Cloud, Rebecca Fenning Marschall); World Museum of Mining (Dolores Cooney, Tina Davis, Tom Satterthwaite).

Advice and assistance with photographs came from John Makely, Jonathan Sanger, David Britt-Friedman, Jim Seida, Meredith Birkett, and Damon Kiesow. We acknowledge the granting of publication rights by Cris Molina, Buddy Moffet, David Fulton, Patrice Gilbert, and Stefen Turner.

Thank you to early readers for suggestions on the manuscript: JoNel Aleccia, Andrew Alpern, Ted Anthony, Linda Dahlstrom, Steven Epley, Gene Foreman, Tish Fried, Don Fry, Lisa Holewa, Tom Johnson, Dave Kindred, Lenette Kosovich, Claire Viguerie Layrisson, Andrew Meyers, and Leslie Spangler.

I thank co-author Paul Newell for his good humor, gentlemanly spirit, and respect for the truth.

Deepest thanks go to my family for enduring the latest Huguette stories, and for their loving support: my mother, Bobbye Schroeder; my brother, Scott Dedman; my son, Justin, and daughter-in-law, Brittany; my wife, Pam Belluck; and our girls, Arielle and Jillian.

NOTES

Abbreviations

HMC PAPERS: The unpublished correspondence and financial records of Huguette M. Clark, reviewed by the authors.

HMC MEDICAL RECORDS: The medical records from Huguette Clark's twenty-year stay at Doctors Hospital and Beth Israel Medical Center.

DEPOSITIONS: Sworn testimony from the several proceedings related to the estate of Huguette M. Clark, Surrogate's Court of the State of New York County, County of New York, case 1995-1375A. Most of the testimony has not been filed with the court, but all of it has been reviewed by the authors.

Introduction

xiv THERE WAS AN ODD NOTE: The zoning attorney for Huguette Clark, Edward Mellick, said at a meeting of the New Canaan Planning and Zoning Commission on December 18, 2007, that the Clark home "has never been lived in." (In fact, it was occupied until 1951, when Huguette bought it.) She was seeking approval for a subdivision into ten lots, to make it easier to sell the property. The minutes are available online at http://ebookbrowse.com/plan-zone-comm-minutes-071218-pdf-d121148791.

xv ACCORDING TO THE INTERNET CHATTER: See, for example, Edhat Santa Barbara, http://www.edhat.com/site/tidbit.cfm?id=1215&tid=1394&art=13051.

xvii THE NEW YORK TIMES CALCULATED: "Fortunes Which Exceed a Hundred Million Dollars," The New York Times, February 24, 1907. "John D. Rockefeller's fortune, according to Frederick T. Gates, his almoner, 'cannot exceed $250,000,000 to $300,000,000.' This statement was made last week on Mr. Rockefeller's own estimate. While this figure indicates a smaller sum than Mr. Rockefeller has been popularly supposed possessed of, it leaves him still the richest man in America, although many believe Senator William Clark may prove eventually to be the richest man in the United States. . . . A recent estimate of Senator Clark's fortune at something over

$150,000,000 was considered not excessive." The *Times,* after W.A.'s death, settled on the figure of $250 million as an estimate of his estate. For tax purposes, the total came in at about half that amount, with Arizona valuing his properties there at $80 million, Montana $40 million, New York $10 million, and California $1.5 million.

xvii ANNA LaCHAPELLE CLARK: The name is sometimes spelled La Chapelle, or LaChappelle, but family documents consistently show LaChapelle.

xvii ONE-FIFTH OF THE ESTATE: Last will and testament of W. A. Clark, Surrogate's Court of the State of New York County, County of New York; available online at NBCNews.com, http://msnbcmedia.msn.com/i/msnbc/Sections/NEWS/William_Clark_Will.pdf.

xviii IN RESEARCHING STORIES: The reports on Huguette by msnbc.com, NBCNews.com, and the *Today* show are collected at http://nbcnews.com/clark/.

xix NEW YORK TABLOIDS: See, for example, Doug Auer, Laura Italiano, and Dan Mangan, " 'Princess' of Beth Israel," *New York Post,* August 27, 2010.

xix FRONT PAGE OF *THE NEW YORK TIMES:* Margalit Fox, "Huguette Clark, Reclusive Heiress, Dies at 104," *The New York Times,* May 24, 2011.

An Apparition

xxv DR. HENRY SINGMAN: Dr. Singman described his visit to 907 Fifth Avenue on March 26, 1991, in a note in Huguette Clark's medical chart on April 30, 1996. This note was filed with his affidavit in Surrogate's Court, May 24, 2012.

Still Life

xxvii "ON 29 NOVEMBER 2001": Photograph, HMC papers.

xxvii ARMSTRONG FILLED THE QUIET AFTERNOONS: Walter Armstrong's bagpipe playing was remembered by Barry Hoelscher, son of the estate manager, in an interview with Dedman, February 27, 2012.

xxvii HUGUETTE PAID HIM HIS FULL SALARY: HMC papers.

xxvii TWO OF THE AUTOMOBILES: Photographs, HMC papers.

Chapter 1: The Clark Mansion, Part One

3 ARRIVED IN NEW YORK HARBOR: See, for example, *The Anaconda Standard,* "Former Senator Clark and His Daughters," July 6, 1910, and *Grand*

Rapids Press (Michigan), "Children Speak No English: Former Senator Clark Had Them Educated in France," July 28, 1910.

3 BORN IN PARIS: Huguette was born in the elegant sixteenth arrondissement of Paris, an area known as Passy.

3 FRANCE'S BELOVED NOVELIST: All of Paris had turned out for Hugo's funeral in 1885.

3 "LET ME THINK IT OVER": Coffey deposition.

4 HIS NEW YORK APARTMENT: The Clark apartment was in the Navarro Flats, the Spanish-themed apartment buildings at 175 West Fifty-Eighth Street.

4 "WHEN THIS MODERN PALACE": Progress on the construction of the Clark mansion was reported regularly in newspapers and magazines around the world. See, for example, "The Most Remarkable House in the World," *The Straits Times* (Singapore), May 19, 1906; "The Astonishing Story and First Photographs of America's Costliest Palace," *The World Magazine*, September 24, 1905; "New York's Most Expensive Private Mansion," *The New York Times*, May 31, 1908; "Costly Furnishings of an American Palace," *Michigan Artisan*, June 10, 1908; and "$125,000 Pipe Organ to Soothe Former Senator Clark," *The San Francisco Call*, June 11, 1911. W.A. had bought the corner lot in 1895; see "Senator Clark's New Home Causes a Suit," *The New York Times*, December 11, 1901, which describes a disagreement over architects' fees. Construction had begun by February 1899; see "W. A. Clark's New House," *The New York Times*, February 6, 1899.

5 THEY WENT COASTING: Photos and letters, HMC papers.

5 REPORTERS WHO TOURED THE HOME: Details of the home are drawn from photographs and many newspaper and magazine articles. See, for example, "Senator Clark's Home," *The New York Times*, February 28, 1904.

5 LITTLE-KNOWN FIRM: The first architects on the Clark mansion were from the firm of Lord, Hewlett & Hull.

5 TO HURRY ALONG THE WORK: "Senator Clark's New Home Causes a Suit," *The New York Times*, December 11, 1901.

7 "I AM NOT MUCH OF A CHURCHMAN": W. A. Clark to W. M. Bickford, letter, March 13, 1915. He was being asked to donate to another church building. "I have, I think, helped to build every church in Butte and a number of others in the state. As you well know, I am not much of a churchman, and I think the superabundance of churches results in an unjust burden upon the resources of the community in maintenance thereof."

7 JOAN OF ARC: The son of artist Louis-Maurice Boutet de Monvel described how the planned paintings for Domrémy became a Clark commission, in "Maurice Boutet de Monvel," by Bernard Boutet de Monvel, introduced by Stéphane-Jacques Addade, Part 3; available online at http:www.stephane -jacques-addade.com/en/maurice-boutet-de-monvel-3/by-bernard-boutet -de-monvel-part-3.

9 SALON DORÉ: The room was decorated with mirror-paneled doors, garlands, and "trophy panels," vertical decorations derived from the practice of hanging captured weapons from a tree or standard on a battlefield. The original panels represented victory, love, music, and the arts and sciences, and W.A. added panels for theater and sports. Overhead, a canvas ceiling was painted with putti, the clever, chubby figures of winged male children, frolicking amid stately figures representing the seasons and the arts.

9 VAINGLORIOUS FRENCH NOBLEMAN: The comte d'Orsay, with designs by the architect of the Arc de Triomphe.

9 "AS THE SENATOR AND MRS. CLARK": "New York's Most Expensive Private Mansion: For the First Time a Detailed Description Is Given of Senator Clark's Fifth Avenue Palace, a Residence Remarkable Among American Homes," *The New York Times,* May 31, 1908.

10 THE FAMILY OF FOUR: U.S. Census, New York City, 1920.

10 SET OF CHINA, COSTING $100,000: "$100,000 Dinner Service," *The New York Times,* December 6, 1901.

11 DICKENS AND CONAN DOYLE: The books from W.A.'s library are detailed in an auction catalog for a sale on January 29, 1926, by the American Art Association, New York.

12 A BOOK OF THE GREAT HOUSES: Huguette had a copy of Michael C. Kathrens's *Great Houses of New York, 1880–1930* (New York: Acanthus Press, 2005), published in her ninety-ninth year.

12 P. T. BARNUM: "The House of Senator Clark," *Architectural Record,* January 1906, 27.

12 "THESE OPINIONS HAVE BEEN PARROTED": Christopher Gray, "Huguette Clark's 'Worthless' Girlhood Home," *The New York Times,* June 2, 2011.

Chapter 2: The Log Cabin

15 WHEN THE SLIGHTLY BUILT MAN: A photograph by International News Service of the April 1914 Easter Parade on Fifth Avenue is contained in the *New York Times* archives.

16 HE CHEERFULLY TOOK CENTER STAGE: W.A.'s singing of "The Star-Spangled Banner" is recorded, for example, in *Proceedings and Debates of the Constitutional Convention Held in the City of Helena, Montana, July 4th, 1889, August 17th, 1889* (Helena: State Publishing, 1921), 974.

18 HAUL FARM PRODUCE: Elizabeth Clark Abascal, unpublished memoir.

18 WHO WERE LEAVING BY FLATBOAT: Connellsville's role as a departure point is described by the Connellsville Area Historical Society in "Con-

nellsville History," http://connellsvillehistoricalsociety.com/connellsville
_history: "Early settlers went into the boat and barge construction business
in the late 1700s as more people moved west. People headed toward the
Youghiogheny River at Stewart's Crossing, after crossing the Allegheny
Mountains, to continue their westward travel by water."

19 SCOTCH-IRISH HERITAGE: The longtime proper use of the term "Scotch-
Irish," not Scots-Irish, is described, for example, in Wayland F. Dunaway,
The Scotch-Irish of Colonial Pennsylvania (Chapel Hill: University of North
Carolina Press, 1944). They are known in Great Britain as Ulster Scots.

19 "WHAT FUN WE HAD": Abascal memoir.

20 HE HELPED HIS FATHER BUILD: Abascal memoir.

20 MORE THAN 160 YEARS: The Clark home was still standing outside Dunbar
as late as 2013, confirmed by matching current photos with historic ones.

20 "SUCH GOOD COMMON SENSE": Ibid.

21 "ABOUT GROWN UP": Abascal memoir.

21 CHOOSING BRAINS OVER BRAWN: Clark established the dates for his education and early travels in "Early Days in Montana: Being Some Reminiscences Dictated by Senator William A. Clark and Written Down by Frank
Harmon Garver," typewritten pages in the collection of the Montana Historical Society Research Center.

21 ONE-ROOM SCHOOL: In 1859–60, W.A. taught in a one-room school in
north-central Missouri, near Milan, where his older sister, Sarah, had
moved.

21 "YOUNG MAN, YOU ARE": Abascal memoir.

21 IN 1860, HE ENROLLED: Records of Iowa Wesleyan University, now Iowa
Wesleyan College, were provided by archivist Lynn Ellsworth. The freshman curriculum included Cicero's orations and the poetry of Virgil and
Ovid, in Latin; the histories of Herodotus and Homer's *Iliad*, in Greek;
higher algebra and geometry; English language and grammar; and the customs, beliefs, and mythology of the ancient world. The readings for the first
year of law study were Blackstone's *Commentaries*, Vattel's *The Law of Na-
tions*, Smith's treatise on constitutional law, Story on promissory notes and
bills of exchange, Edward on bailments, and Story's *Commentaries on Equity
Jurisprudence*.

21 IOWA WESLEYAN UNIVERSITY: Now known as Iowa Wesleyan College.

21 HE DROPPED OUT OF SCHOOL: The records of Iowa Wesleyan University
show W. A. Clark enrolled in both general freshman studies and the law
department in 1860–61. In several of his later public speeches, he described
attending a second year, though the university catalog for 1861–62 is lost.
He is not listed among the graduates for any year and is not known to have
described himself as a graduate. Nearly sixty years later, in response to a

University of Montana request for a financial contribution, W.A. offered his assessment of the value of a college education. Writing on October 10, 1921, to associate W. M. Bickford in Montana, he said, "I have never been fully impressed with the idea of indiscriminate college education for young men. A great many of them are not qualified to take on a classical education. The result is that after graduating they feel as though they should adopt some profession, which in many cases they are unable to succeed in. . . . Young men who are better fitted for business than for a professional life should not spend so many years pondering over Latin and Greek, but would profit much more by a business education for which they are better adapted. Personally I do not feel inclined to be very liberal in promoting the cause of education, when there are so many people starving or at least suffering for the necessaries of life."

21 "SIT AROUND IN OFFICES": W. A. Clark to W. M. Bickford, letter, October 28, 1921. The full passage: "No one appreciates the importance of educational advantages more than myself, but the important part of it is obtained in the common schools. The colleges and other institutions of learning are going too far, in my opinion. I think 50% of those attending educational institutions, having the professions in view, would be better off with a common school education that would enable them to earn a living, rather than to sit around in offices and wait for clients."

22 THE CONFEDERACY BEGAN DRAFTING: The history of the Confederate and Union drafts is described, for example, in Jennifer L. Weber, "Service Problems," Opinionator (blog), *The New York Times*, March 8, 2013, http://opinionator.blogs.nytimes.com/2013/03/08/service-problems/.

22 AFTER W.A. DIED: The apparently false claim regarding W.A.'s Confederate war service, often repeated, was made by William D. Mangam in *The Clarks: An American Phenomenon* (New York: Silver Bow Press, 1941), which was originally published as *The Clarks of Montana* in 1939. (Changes between the editions are minor. For example, Anna became "good looking.") It has often been said that W.A.'s heirs tried to buy up all the copies of the book, though we've seen no substantiation of that. Mangam's bitter tell-all presents an interesting challenge, because he clearly held great animus toward W. A. Clark and his former law school classmate and employer, W.A. Jr. At the same time, he was privy to certain letters and documents during his long employment by the younger Clark. We have tried to check his claims and have relied on him only as a source for material he quotes and as an indicator of the stories passed around by the Clark family.

22 NO W. A. CLARK OF HIS AGE: In 2013, the staff of Ancestry.com searched muster rolls and other service records from Pennsylvania, Iowa, and Missouri and found no one matching W.A.'s age and county serving on either the Union or Confederate side.

22 HE RECALLED HEARING: W. A. Clark, Address to the Semi-Centennial Celebration of the Grand Lodge of Montana (Virginia City, 1916).

22 W.A. CHOSE THREE BOOKS: W. A. Clark, Address to the Society of Montana Pioneers (Livingston, September 5–7, 1917).

23 IN THE SOUVENIR PHOTOS: This photograph (see page 24) was handed down through the Clark and Newell families with the oral tradition that the man on the right is W.A. There is considerable circumstantial evidence to support this claim. Paul Newell found the photo among his parents' family memorabilia. Paul's grandmother, W.A.'s sister Ella Clark Newell, cared for their mother in her old age. The photo bears on the back the imprint of Reed & McKenney, Photographers, with studios in Central City and Georgetown, Colorado. One inscription indicates that it was received in February 1870. The facial features appear consistent with those in other photos of W.A. and with how he might have looked at about age twenty-four. A separate copy of the photo was handed down through the Southmayd family, with the matching oral tradition that the man in the center is Nathan Leroy Southmayd and the man on the right became a U.S. senator.

23 HIS PASSPORT APPLICATIONS: An 1889 passport application obtained via Ancestry.com describes W.A. as being five feet nine inches. He was listed as an inch taller in 1894, then back down to five eight and a half in 1909, and five feet nine in 1914. These descriptions were written in by the clerks; perhaps he didn't give false information, but just looked taller than he was.

23 FIVE FEET FIVE: Testimony of Charlie Clark and others in the Montana probate trial in 1926, after W.A.'s death (In the matter of the estate of William A. Clark, deceased, case 7594, District Court of the Second Judicial District, Silver Bow County, Montana, 1926. Transcript in the Newell family collection, referred to hereafter as "1926 probate transcript"). Charlie testified, "My father was a man about five feet five to five feet five and a half in height; I don't think he ever weighed 130 pounds in his life, and in the latter years of his life he declined to about 108 pounds."

23 HIS HANDS WERE CONSTANTLY: Ibid. Charlie testified, "He was very wiry, nervous, untiring physically. . . . His hands were what would be described as a nervous type, constantly in motion."

23 "WITH THREE OTHERS": Clark, Address to the Society of Montana Pioneers (1917). In "Early Days in Montana," Clark said he first stopped at Breckenridge, then went on to Central City. His friend from Iowa Wesleyan, James Rand, got him a job on the windlass, where he worked from September 1862 to May 1863.

23 NOW MONTANA: It wasn't easy to say what part of America this Bannack was in. The gold rush had birthed the town of Bannack, named for the Bannock people, a Native American tribe that had fished for salmon and hunted buffalo in the western mountains for at least ten thousand years. Bannack

was located on leftover land that had been acquired from France in the massive Louisiana Purchase (1803). Just west of the Continental Divide, it was originally part of Louisiana Territory. In 1812, it became part of Missouri Territory, in 1821 it became an unorganized area with no name at all, and in 1861 it was absorbed by Dakota Territory. After gold was discovered there, it passed to the new Idaho Territory in 1863. The following year, the new boomtown of Bannack, with nearly ten thousand people, briefly became the capital of another new territory, Montana.

23 "THE REPORT GOT": Clark, "Early Days in Montana" and Address to the Society of Montana Pioneers (1917).

23 "OUR MOTTO THEN": Clark, Address to the Society of Montana Pioneers (1917).

25 "SAW THE NEWLY MADE GRAVES": Ibid.

25 "THIS WE BEGAN": Ibid. Also described briefly in Clark, "Early Days in Montana."

25 "WE FOUND SOME STAMPEDERS": Clark, Address to the Society of Montana Pioneers (1917).

26 "UPON MY ARRIVAL": Ibid.

26 "DURING OUR PROSPECTING TRIP": Ibid.

26 "THERE I FOUND": Clark, Address to the Semi-Centennial Celebration of the Grand Lodge of Montana.

27 "THE THIRD DAY": Clark, Address to the Society of Montana Pioneers (1917).

27 BRIGHAM YOUNG: Clark described having a later opportunity to talk with Brigham Young, a fellow Mason, in Salt Lake City in 1867 in Address to the Society of Montana Pioneers (Deer Lodge, 1923).

28 W.A. SAW THE BODY: Clark, "Early Days in Montana."

28 "I HAVE THOUGHT IT A MYSTERY": Clark, Address to the Society of Montana Pioneers (1917).

29 THE MASONIC LEADER: Paris Pfouts was the head of the Virginia City Masonic lodge when W.A. joined in the winter of 1863–64, and during the same period was the first chosen leader of the Vigilance Committee. See Paris Swazy Pfouts, *Four Firsts for a Modest Hero: The Autobiography of Paris Swazy Pfouts* (Grand Lodge of Ancient Free and Accepted Masons of Montana, Helena, 1968).

29 "WE WILL NOT SAY": Cornelius Hedges, past grand master of the Masonic Lodge in Montana and longtime grand secretary, set down his description of the Vigilante history in "Freemasonry in the State of Montana," in John Milton Hodson, William H. Upton, Jonas W. Brown, and Cornelius Hedges, *Masonic History of the Northwest* (History Publishing, 1902). This chapter is available online at http://www.freemason.com/library/norwst29.htm. The

Masonic connection to the early Vigilantes has been debated, but contemporaneous accounts by Masons, including Hedges and Clark, show they took great pride in the connection.

29 "THEY HAD UNDOUBTED PROOF": Clark, Address to the Society of Montana Pioneers (1917).

29 "WHILE I HAD CONSIDERABLE KNOWLEDGE": Clark's memories of the Vigilante days were included in his Address to the Semi-Centennial Celebration of the Grand Lodge of Montana, in which other speakers also laid out the history of the Masonic involvement in forming the Vigilantes (records of the Grand Lodge of Ancient Free and Accepted Masons of Montana).

30 "THERE WAS NO LACK": Clark, Address to the Society of Montana Pioneers (1923).

30 "TRADED TOBACCO": Clark, "Early Days in Montana."

30 RATES OF ABOUT 2 PERCENT: Clark, Address to the Society of Montana Pioneers (1923).

30 "WITH EVERY DOLLAR I HAD": Clark described these days in "Early Days in Montana."

30 EARN A BIGGER PROFIT: Clark described this contract in his Address to the Society of Montana Pioneers (1923).

31 "I WAS ENTERTAINED": 1926 probate transcript.

31 "MASSACRE AT FT. PHIL KEARNEY": This massacre became known as the Fetterman Fight. It took place along the Bozeman Trail in northern Wyoming, near the Montana border, and was part of Red Cloud's War, a series of conflicts between the U.S. Army and Native Americans.

31 "THE WEATHER IS VERY COLD": 1926 probate transcript.

32 "CLEAR AND COLD MORNING": Ibid.

33 "ARRIVED IN HELENA": Ibid.

33 "SENT A PROPOSAL": Ibid.

Chapter 3: The Copper King Mansion

35 COPPER KING MANSION: Known then as simply the Clark home, it became a school and convent in the 1930s, and since the 1990s has been a bed-and-breakfast called the Copper King Mansion.

37 "WHO WAS DEAR TO ME": W. A. Clark, Address to the Society of Montana Pioneers (Deer Lodge, 1923).

37 "WOOED AND WON": Ibid.

37 THEIR NEW HOME: Ibid.

38 DONNELL & CLARK: Ibid.

38 "WHEN WE FIRST KNEW HIM": *Missoula Gazette*, 1888.

38 THE FEDERAL CENSUS: Accessed via Ancestry.com.

38 HORSE-DRAWN BUGGY: Charlie Clark testimony, 1926 probate transcript. W.A. described his experience in his Address to the Society of Montana Pioneers (1923).

39 "TO SOUND THE ALARM": Ibid.

39 FIRST NATIONAL BANK: Clark, Address to the Society of Montana Pioneers (1923).

40 W.A. LEARNED HOW TO FIELD-TEST: Clark, Address to the Society of Montana Pioneers (1923).

41 WHEN FARLIN GOT OVEREXTENDED: Michael P. Malone, *The Battle for Butte: Mining and Politics on the Western Frontier, 1864–1906* (Seattle: University of Washington Press, 1981), 17.

41 BUTTE WOULD PRODUCE: The output of the Butte mines was calculated by geologist Richard I. Gibson, who provided the estimates in interviews with Dedman in August 2012.

41 "RICHEST HILL ON EARTH": The five thousand miles of horizontal tunnels under the Butte hill have yielded about 100 tons of gold, which is nothing compared with its 24,000 tons of silver, which again is nothing compared with its 11.5 million tons of copper. Those aren't the quantities of raw ore removed, but of pure metal extracted. And that's not to mention the vast quantities of zinc for brass, manganese for stainless steel, lead for bullets, cadmium for batteries, sulfuric acid for drain cleaner, and selenium for dandruff shampoo.

44 PANIC ROOM: One can see the panic room on a tour of the Copper King Mansion bed-and-breakfast in Butte, http://www.thecopperkingmansion.com.

44 "I MUST SAY THAT THE LADIES": *Proceedings and Debates of the Constitutional Convention Held in the City of Helena, Montana, July 4th, 1889, August 17th, 1889* (Helena: State Publishing, 1921).

45 SHE CONTRACTED TYPHOID FEVER: Helen Fitzgerald Sanders, *A History of Montana*, vol. 1 (Chicago: Lewis, 1913).

45 OFFICIALS HAD ASSURED FAIRGOERS: *The Official Directory of the World's Columbian Exposition, May 1st to October 30th, 1893* (Chicago: W. B. Conkey, 1893.

45 W.A. DEMONSTRATED HIS LOVE: W.A.'s care in designing the mausoleum is shown in his detailed correspondence with Paul Bartlett, at the Library of Congress.

46 HIS FIRST PROTÉGÉE: Kathlyn Williams described her association with W.A. in a fan magazine interview in 1912 (*New York Clipper*, April 20, 1912; reprinted in *Taylorology*, no. 48 [December 1996]).

46 STARRING IN MORE THAN 170 FILMS: Kathlyn Williams starred in the first cliffhanger serial, *The Adventures of Kathlyn* (1913), and the first film version

of the gold rush drama *The Spoilers* (1914), in a role Marlene Dietrich later played in the talkies.

46 "TOOK A GREAT INTEREST": Ibid.

46 IN 1893 OR 1894: Anna's introduction to W.A. is set in 1893, the year she turned fifteen, in William D. Mangam, *The Clarks: An American Phenomenon* (New York: Silver Bow Press, 1941), 94–95. Mangam sides with the story of Anna first approaching banker James A. Murray, who sent her to Clark.

47 ANNA EUGENIA LaCHAPELLE WAS BORN: Anna's birth certificate spells the name phonetically as "Lashpell." Located through Ancestry.com.

47 ANNA WAS THE OLDEST: U.S. Census, Calumet, MI, 1880.

47 THE LaCHAPELLES RENTED OUT: U.S. Census, Butte, MT, 1900.

47 ANNA'S MOTHER, PHILOMENE, COULD SPEAK: Ibid.

48 STUDYING THE CONCERT HARP: Anna's harp teacher was Alphonse Hasselmans, a Belgian-born French harpist who trained the most well-known harpists of his day.

48 COURT RECORDS IN BUTTE: Search conducted for authors in 2013.

48 SHE HAD A PUCKISH: Paul Newell discussed Anna's stay in Paris with Anita Mackenzie and Mary Abascal, who were there with their mother, Elizabeth Clark Abascal, W.A.'s sister.

48 HER UNUSUAL EYES: The Abascal sisters described Anna's heterochromia iridum, having eyes of different colors, blue and brown. Anna's passport application from 1920, via Ancestry.com, confirms that she had "different coloring in eyes," which are described as blue gray.

48 "MOST INTERESTING LADY IN WASHINGTON": W.A., serving in the Senate in Washington, was also sponsoring Anna's sister, Amelia, at the National Park Seminary, a girls' finishing school in the suburb of Forest Glen, Maryland. See "She May Marry Senator Clark," *The Denver Post*, March 26, 1900. This article misidentifies Anna as "Miss Ada La Chappelle."

48 HATTIE ROSE LAUBE: "Senator Clark to Wed Again? Bride-Elect Said to Be Miss Laube, an Effective Campaign Speaker," *The New York Times*, April 13, 1901.

48 THE PATERNITY SUIT: "Senator Clark in Breach of Promise Suit," *The New York Times*, April 19, 1903. The case is Mary McNellis v. William A. Clark, Supreme Court, City and County of New York, March 1901. See also "She Asks $150,49 of Senator Clark," *New York Herald*, April 19, 1903.

49 BRACELET WITH 36 SAPPHIRES: Anna's jewelry is described in detail in HMC papers.

50 THERE HE TOURED: A history of W.A.'s acquisition of the United Verde mine and details of the operation appeared in a company-sponsored series of articles in *The Mining Congress Journal*, April 1930. W.A. described the New

Orleans exposition in his Address to the Society of Montana Pioneers (1923).

51 EIGHT MILLION POUNDS: Clark, Address to the Society of Montana Pioneers (1923).

51 "THIS WAS ONE": Ibid.

52 HIS BROTHER ROSS SOON FOLLOWED: The first of W.A.'s siblings to move to Los Angeles were his unmarried sisters Anna Belle and Ella, who accompanied his mother, Mary, in 1880. They lived initially at Hill and Spring streets and subsequently in Mary's spacious but unpretentious Victorian home at 933 South Olive Street. W.A.'s other sisters, Sarah, Elizabeth, and Mary Margaret, followed with their families. Ross and his family arrived in 1892, and he founded Citizens Bank there. Joseph left W.A.'s employ as superintendent of the Butte mines and took up residence in Portland, Oregon.

53 MONTANA RANCH: Portions of the Montana Ranch were developed and sold later, including the Douglas Aircraft factory and residential properties near Long Beach. The remainder was sold to developers after World War II for the creation of the planned city of Lakewood. Rancho Los Alamitos became part of the city of Long Beach.

54 CLARK OUT FRONT AS PRESIDENT: Clark and Harriman remained railroad partners until Harriman died in 1909. Clark sold his railroad interests in 1921.

57 THE CLARKS DONATED: The home in Los Angeles was operated by the YWCA until it was damaged in the 1987 earthquake, but it continues today, beautifully renovated, as housing for low-income residents—and a film location for movies and television shows.

57 "AMONG THE MORE VIVID": Paul Clark Newell, Sr., "Senator and the Train," *Air California Magazine*, May 1977.

59 "THEY'RE MARRIED": *The Anaconda Standard*, July 19, 1904.

59 LOUISE AMELIA ANDRÉE CLARK: The place of Andrée's birth is uncertain. Mangam places it at "a sumptuous villa on Cape Matifou, overlooking the beautiful Bay of Algiers on the Mediterranean" (*The Clarks*, 97). A Girl Scout publication lists the Bay of Algiers as well. A ship's registry from 1914 on the SS *France* via the Statue of Liberty Ellis Island Foundation lists it as San Luca or San Lucia, Spain.

59 "HE LEARNED THAT HIS EARLY AFFECTION": *The Butte Miner*, July 13, 1904.

60 "MRS. CLARK DID NOT CARE": Ibid.

60 "A LINE ONLY": Katherine's letter to Will is quoted in Mangam, *The Clarks*, 101–2.

61 "IT HAS BEEN STATED": *The Butte Miner*, July 13, 1904.

61 THERE WAS SPECULATION: A second pregnancy, of a boy who lived but an hour after birth, is described in Mangam, *The Clarks*, 100.

61 NOT EVERYONE BELIEVED: As to the reality or fiction of the date of the marriage, Mangam (*The Clarks*, 114–15) wrote that W.A. gave an interview to his own newspaper, *The Butte Miner*, in June 1901 about his European trip the previous month, and his description of his itinerary didn't place him anywhere near Marseille.

61 THE CLARK FAMILY BIBLE: In the possession of Paul Newell.

62 "NO RECORD OF SAID MARRIAGE": 1926 probate transcript.

62 ANNA WAS NOW WRITING LETTERS: HMC papers.

Chapter 4: The U.S. Capitol

65 HE BEGAN A PUBLIC CAMPAIGN: Associated Press, "Clarks and Schwabs Challenge the '400,'" *Evening Times* (Grand Forks, ND), August 23, 1906.

65 "THIS CARD WILL ADMIT": This card is in the Metropolitan Museum of Art archives. The Clarks and the newspapers generally gave the address of the mansion as 962 Fifth Avenue, though the entrance was on Seventy-Seventh Street. The address is listed as "1 E. 77th Street" on Clark passport applications and in city building records, but the Fifth Avenue name carried prestige.

66 "MY FATHER'S GREAT JOY": "Clark Family Bewail Refusal," *The Spokesman-Review* (Spokane, WA), May 6, 1925. The history of W.A.'s art collection, including the panels of Joan of Arc by Louis-Maurice Boutet de Monvel, is described in several publications from the Corcoran Gallery, including Laura Coyle and Dare Myers Hartwell, *Antiquities to Impressionism: The William A. Clark Collection* (London: Corcoran Gallery of Art, 2001), and Yellowstone Art Center, *The William A. Clark Collection: Treasures of a Copper King* (Billings, MT: Yellowstone Art Center, 1989).

67 BUT SUCH DISHES: W.A.'s collection of pottery is described in Wendy M. Watson, *Italian Renaissance Maiolica from the William A. Clark Collection* (London: Scala Books, 1986).

69 W.A. HAD BEEN INDUCED: W.A.'s hiring of Duveen is described in Meryle Secrest, *Duveen* (New York: Alfred A. Knopf, 2004).

70 THE FINEST ORGAN: The organ's history is told in David Lennox Smith, *Murray M. Harris and Organ Building in Los Angeles, 1894–1913* (Richmond, VA: Organ Historical Society, 2005), 77–80. Smith includes the estimate of $120,000, which apparently included the elaborate case and decorations, citing the Clark organist, Arthur Scott Brook: "Senator Clark spared no ex-

pense.... Consequently, the effect is the most exquisite ever produced. It is the largest and most wonderful chamber organ in the world, excepting none. It is difficult to say just what it cost, but it must have been about $120,000." The Clark pipe organ is also described in many news articles of the day, including "W. A. Clark Has Test of $120,000 Organ," *The New York Times*, June 10, 1911. The elaborate instrument included a choir organ with twelve stops, a great organ with thirteen, swell organ with nineteen, solo with six, echo with twelve, and pedal organ with ten stops.

70 MORMON TABERNACLE CHOIR: "Mormons at Clark Mansion," *The New York Times*, November 9, 1911.

70 THEIR OWN CHURCH ORGANIST: The Clark organist was church musician Arthur Scott Brook, who had helped design the Clark pipe organ.

71 "HE IS SAID TO HAVE BOUGHT": *Mark Twain in Eruption*, ed. Bernard De Voto (New York: Harper and Brothers, 1940).

72 MARCUS DALY: Though the Clark-Daly battles are well remembered as part of Montana's "War of the Copper Kings," no one has been able to determine how the feud began. It seemed to start as a business feud, but it soon became personal and political. This oft-told tale of political warfare is most vividly explored in Michael P. Malone, *The Battle for Butte: Mining and Politics on the Western Frontier, 1864–1906* (Seattle: University of Washington Press, 1981).

72 "THE CONSPIRACY": W. A. Clark to Martin Maginnis, letter, November 19, 1888.

73 "THE MOST ESSENTIAL ELEMENTS": Edwin Wildman, *Famous Leaders of Industry: The Life Stories of Boys Who Have Succeeded* (Boston: Page, 1920). W.A. went on to say, "Then there must be unflinching courage to meet and overcome the difficulties that beset one's pathway."

74 "OVERTHROWING THE POWER": W.A.'s testimony is in U.S. Congress, *Report of the Committee on Privileges and Elections of the United States Senate Relative to the Right and Title of William A. Clark to a Seat as Senator from the State of Montana*, 56th Cong., 1st sess., 3 vols. (Washington, DC, 1900).

74 "NOBODY COULD EXPECT": Ibid. By "these people," W.A. was referring not just to Daly but to John D. Rockefeller's Standard Oil trust, which was trying to buy Daly's Anaconda Copper Mining Company and consolidate the copper industry under a national trust, squeezing Clark's purse considerably. That marriage happened the following year, in April 1899, beginning a period of corporate warfare for which the Senate campaign was merely a proxy.

74 "I HAVE NOT THE SLIGHTEST": Ibid.

75 SEAL THEM INSIDE: One often-published photograph from the Library of Congress shows thousand-dollar bills sticking out of an envelope bear-

ing the initials "WAC." This photo does show evidence from the Senate trial, and appears in high school history textbooks in Montana and many popular histories as proof of the complicity of candidate W. A. Clark of Butte, the banker. Yet, as the scheme was designed, it was the recipient of the bribe that wrote the initials. Testimony showed that these were the initials of a different W. A. Clark, of Virginia City, a lawyer and state legislator, the supposed intended recipient. The scheme may have been reckless, but no one was foolish enough to write the candidate's initials on envelopes full of cash.

75 "THERE SEEMS TO BE NO END": U.S. Congress, *Report of the Committee on Privileges*.

75 "EVERY MAN WHO VOTES": W.A.'s campaign manager, John B. Wellcome, was disbarred. See "Wellcome Is Disbarred," *The New York Times*, December 24, 1899.

76 "A DAMNABLE CONSPIRACY": *The Butte Miner*, January 11, 1899.

76 "HIS VINDICATION": *The Butte Miner*, January 27, 1899.

76 "THEY SIMPLY FELL": *The Anaconda Standard*, January 27, 1898.

77 CAVIAR À LA RUSSE: The menu from W.A.'s dinner party is in the collection of the Montana Historical Society Research Center, http://cdm16013 .contentdm.oclc.org/cdm/compoundobject/collection/p267301coll1/id/4518/ rec/8. Apparent typos on the menu have been fixed here: "ris de veau" was printed as "ris de vean," and what appears to be "salade Laitue" was "al ade Isaitue."

78 "VOICE OF THE PEOPLE": *The Butte Miner*, January 29, 1899.

78 "THEY TOOK": *The Anaconda Standard*, January 27, 1899.

79 THE EVIDENCE THAT HURT: Details of the changed financial status of these legislators come from U.S. Congress, *Report of the Committee on Privileges*.

80 WHEN IT CAME HIS TURN: Ibid.

80 "ABOUT EVERY SIX MONTHS": Ibid.

80 "A MAN DOES NOT FORFEIT": Ibid.

80 "CANNOT BE OVERLOOKED": W. A. Clark to John S. M. Neill, letter, April 11, 1900, Montana Historical Society Research Center.

81 "THE FRIENDS OF SENATOR CLARK": U.S. Congress, *Report of the Committee on Privileges*.

81 "THE ELECTION TO THE SENATE": Ibid.

81 "HIS FACE WAS SOMEWHAT FLUSHED": *New-York Tribune*, April 11, 1900.

82 "THE MOST DEVILISH": U.S. Congress, "Resignation Remarks of Senator W. A. Clark," *Congressional Record*, 56th Cong., 1st sess., vol. 33, May 15, 1899.

82 A. E. SPRIGGS: Lieutenant Governor Spriggs not only later became governor on his own, but in 1911 he was W.A.'s point man in Guatemala, a poor

country that gave Clark's mining company free rein to use all the country's public resources.

83 "CLARK RESIGNS; THEN APPOINTED": "Clark Resigns; Then Appointed; Vacancy Hardly Made When Lieutenant Governor Names Him to Fill It; Daly Caught Napping; His Friend the Governor Leaves the State, and Senator's Supporter Comes into Power; All a Series of Surprises," *New York Herald*, May 16, 1900. See also "Clark Gives Up Seat in Senate; but His Appointment to Post He Resigned Is Announced," *The New York Times*, May 16, 1900, and "Trickery in Montana," *The New-York Tribune*, May 16, 1900.

83 "CHAS IS WITH ME": W. A. Clark to W. M. Bickford, letter, October 17, 1908.

83 CHARLIE DARED NOT ENTER: Charlie's château, at 321 West Broadway, is now the home of the Butte Silver Bow Arts Foundation, which offers tours. As in his father's mansion, the top floor was devoted to a ballroom.

84 "I HAVE CANVASSED": W. A. Clark to John S. M. Neill, letter, April 28, 1900. Montana Historical Society Research Center.

84 "THE APPOINTMENT BY THE GOVERNOR": W. A. Clark to John S. M. Neill, letter, May 17, 1900. Montana Historical Society Research Center. The letter was written on U.S. Senate stationery.

84 "CONTEMPTIBLE TRICKERY": "Gov. Smith Talks," *The New York Times*, May 17, 1900.

84 "THIS MAN, CLARK": *The Helena Independent*, May 16, 1900.

84 LONG-LASTING EFFECTS: In 2012, more than a century after the Clark case, the U.S. Supreme Court loosened restrictions on campaign donations, allowing individuals and corporations to once again spend millions of dollars on elections, often without reporting the source of these funds. The Court's ruling overturned a Montana law passed in 1912 to rein in the role of money in politics. That law, the Corrupt Practices Act, banned contributions by corporations in elections. Personal contributions were limited to $1,000. Exactly one hundred years later, Supreme Court justices affirmed, by a ruling of 5 to 4, that limits on campaign spending are limits on free speech, a violation of the First Amendment. In response to that ruling, Montana attorney general Steve Bullock lamented, "The integrity of our system and the voices of Montanans, whatever their political views, are too important to be drowned out by modern-day copper kings." Steve Bullock, "Montana—Big Sky, Clean Politics," *Los Angeles Times*, op-ed, June 15, 2012.

85 SEVENTEENTH AMENDMENT: The weaknesses and unintended consequences of the Seventeenth Amendment are discussed in Jay S. Bybee, "Ulysses at the Mast: Democracy, Federalism, and the Sirens' Song of the Seventeenth Amendment," *Northwestern University Law Review* 91, no. 2

(Winter 1997), available at http://scholars.law.unlv.edu/facpub/350. Paradoxically, this amendment may also have increased the role of money in elections. Scholars have described this amendment as giving more power to corporations and the wealthiest citizens. How could that be? To be elected to the Senate, candidates now had to persuade thousands or millions of people across an entire state to vote for them, making elections more expensive, especially in the television age. As a result, only those with great personal wealth or access to corporate money could expect to reach the Senate. Today, as in Clark's day, the U.S. Senate remains a club for millionaires. No longer checked by "instructions" from state legislatures, senators are also more likely to serve for life than they were before passage of the amendment. "It is as difficult for a poor man to enter the Senate of the United States as for a rich man to enter the kingdom of heaven," Representative John Corliss of Michigan said in 1898. The newspaper *Roll Call* found in 2010 that fifty-four of the one hundred senators reported a net worth over $1 million. Jennifer Yachnin, "Senate Procures Influx of Millionaires," *Roll Call*, October 28, 2010.

85 "LIFE WAS GOOD": Malone, *The Battle for Butte*, 200.

85 "MY CLOSEST AND MOST VALUABLE": *Autobiography of Mark Twain*, ed. Harriet Elinor Smith et al. (Berkeley: University of California Press, 2010), 1:192.

85 "AS FINE A PIRATE": Ida M. Tarbell, *All in the Day's Work* (New York: Macmillan, 1939), 10.

85 ONE OF THE GREAT STOCK SWINDLES: The Amalgamated stock scam is described in Thomas W. Lawson, *Frenzied Finance: The Crime of Amalgamated* (New York: Ridgway-Thayer, 1905).

86 "FOR A WEEK NOW": *Mark Twain's Correspondence with Henry Huttleston Rogers, 1893–1909*, ed. Lewis Leary (Berkeley: University of California Press, 1969).

86 THE MAN WHO HATCHED THE PLAN: Lawson, *Frenzied Finance*.

86 "YOU KNOW HOW TO MAKE": *Mark Twain's Correspondence with Henry Huttleston Rogers, 1893–1909*.

87 "I AM IN FAVOR OF GIVING TO WOMEN": *Proceedings and Debates of the Constitutional Convention Held in the City of Helena, Montana, July 4th, 1889, August 7th, 1889* (Helena: State Publishing, 1921).

87 "TRUE OR FALSE": Victor Hugo, *Les Misérables* (New York: Carleton, 1863), 1.

88 "IN REARING THE GREAT STRUCTURE": U.S. Congress, "Resignation Remarks of Senator W. A. Clark."

89 "MY HOUSE IN NEW YORK IS NOW OPEN": "Society Not Worth While," *The New York Times*, February 10, 1912.

89 "I AM NOT LIKELY": Ibid.

Chapter 5: The Clark Mansion, Part Two

93 A PHOTO OF ANDRÉE: See, for example, "Senator Clark and Family Leave for the Coronation," *Oakland Tribune,* June 4, 1911.

94 11B, RUE DES ROCHES NOIRES: From a letter addressed to Andrée Clark, HMC papers.

95 "SOCIALISTS IN GERMANY": Quoted by Baeyens, *Le sénateur qui aimait la France.*

95 PARADE OF A THOUSAND ANARCHISTS: "Anarchists Spread Alarm in 5th Ave.," *The New York Times,* March 22, 1914.

95 THE VIOLIN FOR HUGUETTE: Huguette's violin teacher was the Parisian master André Touret, a member of the Capet String Quartet, one of the leading chamber groups of the time.

96 THE GIRLS SIGNED WILL'S GUEST BOOK: The book is in the William Andrews Clark Memorial Library at UCLA.

97 "TAP 'ER LIGHT": One can see details of mine operations on underground tours at the World Museum of Mining in Butte, http://www.miningmuseum .org. Tom Satterthwaite led a tour for Dedman in October 2011.

97 A WALKING STICK: On display at the World Museum of Mining.

98 FRANK LITTLE WAS FOUND HANGED: "I.W.W. Strike Chief Lynched at Butte," *The New York Times,* August 2, 1917.

98 "MY DEAREST LITTLE MOTHER": Andrée Clark to Anna Clark, letter, August 27, 1918, HMC papers.

100 "SHY AND TIMID": Alma Guy, interview with an unnamed writer for the Girl Scouts, Girl Scout National Historic Preservation Center archives.

100 "TOO DEMOCRATIC": Ibid.

101 "I HAVE MADE EVERYTHING": Copies of Andrée's letters are in the Girl Scout National Historic Preservation Center archives.

101 "SCOUTING REALLY MADE": Guy interview.

101 "PROBABLY TUBERCULAR MENINGITIS": Andrée's death certificate describes the quick course of her illness over four days. Maine death records, 1617–1922, via Ancestry.com.

102 "WAS MOST BEAUTIFUL": W. A. Clark to W. M. Bickford, letter, August 13, 1919.

102 "YET NOT TO THINE": William Cullen Bryant, "Thanatopsis," in *Thanatopsis and a Forest Hymn* (Boston: Joseph Knight, 1893).

102 "MRS. CLARK HAS": Clark to Bickford, August 13, 1919.

103 "SCOUTING HAS BEEN A HAND": Andrée's diary is quoted in Scouting publications in the Girl Scout National Historic Preservation Center archives and in Leslie Paris, *Children's Nature: The Rise of the American Summer Camp* (New York: NYU Press, 2008).

103 HUGUETTE STOOD GRIMLY: Photographs of the presentation of the deed are in the Girl Scout National Historic Preservation Center archives.

103 CAMP ANDRÉE: The history of this camp is told in Paris, *Children's Nature: The Rise of the American Summer Camp,* and in "The Story of Camp Andrée," an updated, unsigned narrative in the Girl Scout National Historic Preservation Center archives.

105 AGNES HAD BEEN TOLD: Karine McCall interview with Dedman, July 6, 2012, and McCall deposition.

105 CLASSES AT MISS SPENCE'S: The school's story is told in Mary Dillon Edmondson, *Profiles in Leadership: A History of The Spence School, 1892–1992* (West Kennebunk, ME: Phoenix, 1991).

106 "I BEG YOU TO CULTIVATE": Ibid.

106 "MISS HUGUETTE CLARK": "Social Notes," *The New York Times,* May 4, 1922.

107 LOUISE WATT: Her niece, Natalie Dejoux, was interviewed by Dedman, May 24, 2013.

107 DOROTHY WARREN: Her recollections were relayed to Dedman by her friend Andrew Alpern.

111 "THEY TAKE GREAT DELIGHT": W. A. Clark to W. M. Bickford, letter, August 26, 1921. In her conversations with Paul Newell, Huguette described two trips to Hawaii with her parents, in 1915 and 1921.

111 UP TO FIVE MILES: W.A. described his daily walks in a letter to W. M. Bickford, August 16, 1921.

111 SMOKING HIS CIGARS: In a letter to W. M. Bickford dated December 29, 1921, W.A. thanked Bickford for a gift of cigars to go along with his Pennsylvania rye. He wrote, "You know I am very fond of the weed."

112 LAID ROSES AT: Huguette had a photograph of W.A. at the Arc de Triomphe (HMC papers), which was published in Baeyens, *Le sénateur qui aimait la France.*

112 "EX-SENATOR CLARK": "Ex-Senator Clark, Pioneer in Copper, Dies of Pneumonia: Taken with a Cold a Few Days Ago, He Succumbs Suddenly Here at 86; Family at His Bedside; He Had Been Actively Directing His Business Affairs Until He Became Ill; His Career Picturesque; Went to Montana with Ox Team and Acquired One of Biggest Fortunes in America," *New York Times,* March 3, 1925. *The New York Sun* on the same day offered a hopeful view of his legacy: "Ex-Senator Clark will be remembered not for his stormy political record or the other events of his later life, but as one of the foremost figures in the development of the West."

112 MORE THAN THREE HUNDRED: "Clark Rites amid His Art Treasures," *The New York Times,* March 7, 1925.

113 W.A.'s WILL LEFT: Last will and testament of W. A. Clark, Surrogate's Court of the State of New York County, County of New York; available online at

NBCNews.com, http://msnbcmedia.msn.com/i/msnbc/Sections/NEWS/ William_Clark_Will.pdf.

116 EVEN CLARK'S *HOPE VENUS:* W.A.'s sculpture is now described by the Corcoran Gallery as "after Antonio Canova," a copy executed by an English artist after Canova's death. It appears in David Finn, *Sculpture at the Corcoran: Photographs by David Finn,* with Susan Joy Slack (Washington, DC: Ruder Finn Press, 2002), 33–37. This book also includes other pieces from the Clark Collection mentioned here: *Eve,* by Rodin, 76–79; *Prometheus Attacked by the Eagle,* by Charles-Alexander Renaud, 32; and *Odysseus Bending His Bow* (or *Soldier Drawing His Bow*), by or after Jacques Bousseau, 24–27.

116 PEOPLE WROTE TO THE MET: Letters are in the files of the Metropolitan Museum of Art. One writer, Julius Meyer, suggested, "Could not the Museum buy the Clark mansion, call it the Clark Annex, accept the collection, leave it where it is and, by thus keeping it all together, get around all the difficulties arising from stipulations of the will?" If the Met had followed that advice, the Clark mansion might still be open for public tours today. Another letter writer, Edward N. Perkins, deplored "the practice of seeking to employ generosity or public spirit as the vehicle of vanity."

116 THE MET SAID NO: "Clark Art Rejected by Metropolitan Because of Terms," *The New York Times,* April 21, 1925. In an editorial, the *Times* applauded the Met, saying, "In refusing Senator Clark's art treasures the Metropolitan Museum suffers a great and in many ways an irreparable loss, but maintains its dignity and its integrity" ("Not a Necropolis," April 22, 1925).

117 THE CORCORAN QUICKLY: The path that W.A.'s art took to the Corcoran Gallery is described in Coyle and Hartwell, *Antiquities to Impressionism.*

117 COOLIDGE OPENED THE W. A. CLARK COLLECTION: The Clark Wing, with its dark English paneling, wide marble staircase, and rotunda dome reminiscent of the Clark mansion, is still open today. It holds W.A.'s statue of Eve by Rodin, Fortuny's *The Choice of a Model,* William Merritt Chase's portrait of Clark, the *Hope Venus* (listed as "after Canova"), and rooms full of majolica, lace, and rugs. The Corcoran in 2013 sold a single Clark Persian carpet for $30 million.

119 HUGUETTE AND HER HALF-SIBLINGS: The fate of the Clark mansion was covered extensively in the newspapers. See, for example, "Clark Home Sold Under $3,000,000," *The New York Times,* February 2, 1927.

119 MANY MANSIONS YIELDED: Some of the Fifth Avenue mansions from this era survive, including homes owned by Henry Frick at Seventieth Street, James B. Duke at Seventy-Eighth, Payne Whitney at Seventy-Ninth, and Andrew Carnegie at Ninety-First.

119 AT AUCTION, THE CLARK HEIRS: "$70,721 in Two Sales of Senator Clark

Art," *The New York Times*, January 12, 1926. See also "Rug Brings $16,000 at Clark Art Sale," *The New York Times*, January 13, 1926, and "$9,600 Tapestry Sold at Clark Auction; Day's Sale at Ex-Senator's House Brings in $53,469—Total to Date Is $446,410," *The New York Times*, January 14, 1926.

120 BEFORE THE PINCH BARS: The tours were described in "View Clark Home, Due to Be Wrecked," *The New York Times*, February 23, 1927.

120 NO ONE THOUGHT: The fate of the Clark pipe organ was described in "Sad Fate of Famous Organ," *The New York-Tribune*, June 26, 1932, and in Harris, *Organ Building in Los Angeles*, 79–80.

Chapter 6: 907 Fifth Avenue, Part One

126 NEIGHBORS INCLUDED W. C. DURANT: " 'Upstairs, Downstairs,' Apartment Style," Christopher Gray, *The New York Times*, April 5, 2012.

126 SO SHE WENT SHOPPING: Receipts for Anna's furniture purchases, HMC papers.

127 A SECOND APARTMENT: There has been uncertainty about which apartments the Clarks held at which times in 907 Fifth Avenue. What seems clear from documents and witnesses is that mother and daughter moved into the twelfth floor in late 1925, that Anna moved to the eighth floor sometime after, and that Huguette took that eighth-floor apartment after her mother died, while keeping 12W. Best evidence: A letter to Huguette from her attorney Frederick Stokes in late 1955, when she purchased 12W after the building became a co-op, says she had been occupying that apartment under a lease. Building records show Huguette bought 8W in 1956 and 8E in 1963. In 1964, a letter to Huguette from her decorator shows that she was fixing up her "new apartment" on the eighth floor. Both of Anna's goddaughters, who visited in the 1930s and 1940s, refer in interviews to Huguette being upstairs. We don't know what apartment the Gowers took or planned to take after the wedding, or when Anna moved from 12 to 8, or when Huguette acquired 8E. All mysteries.

128 CHER MAÎTRE: Huguette addressed Styka with this salutation in her letters, HMC papers.

128 CZECH-POLISH FAMILY OF PAINTERS: Tadé's father, the painter Jan Styka (1858–1925), was known for his enormous paintings, particularly those with religious themes, including *Golgotha* and *Crucifixion*. Born in Poland, the son of a Czech officer, he ended up in France. Pronounce the family name however you like. It started in Czechoslovakia and Poland as STEEK-uh, but the family changed it in France and America to STICK-uh, before some in the family relented to the Americanized STYK-uh. Jan's son Adam (1890–1959)

was known for vivid scenes of the people of Morocco and the Sahara. Tadé (1889–1954) favored more traditional portraits of prominent men and women.

128 GYPSY ROSE LEE: She described the episode in her biography, *Gypsy: Memoirs of America's Most Celebrated Stripper* (Berkeley, CA: Frog Books, 1957), p. 258.

128 HARRY TRUMAN SAT: The Harry S. Truman Library and Museum includes correspondence documenting Styka's painting of the president's portrait, which White House staff considered a way to curry favor with Polish American voters.

128 WOMEN AT THE TIME: Professor Marice Rose at Fairfield University helped assess Huguette's painting style in relation to that of other women artists of the time.

129 HER PAINTINGS, OFTEN LIFE-SIZE: The authors viewed many of Huguette's paintings.

129 HUGUETTE'S SHELVES WERE STACKED: Photographs, HMC papers.

130 "YOUNG LADY OF A GOOD FAMILY": HMC papers. Several letters from artists in Japan show Huguette's search for appropriate names for the women in her paintings.

131 "SORROW AND JOY": Translation by postdoctoral teaching fellow Ive Covaci of Fairfield University.

131 SEVEN OF HER PAINTINGS: "Exhibition of a Group of Paintings by Huguette Clark," Corcoran Gallery of Art, Washington, D.C., April 28, 1929, through May 12, 1929.

131 "HER PAINTINGS RECEIVED": Associated Press, news brief, *Evening Tribune* (San Diego), September 4, 1931.

131 PRINTED AS HOLIDAY CARDS: Copies of Christmas cards with Huguette's paintings are in HMC papers and were an exhibit to the testimony of Celia Tobin Gray Cummings, September 12 and 14, 2012, Depositions.

131 THE DELICATE BAREFOOT GEISHA: Bill Dedman purchased the painting on eBay in 2010.

131 HUGUETTE'S MOST AFFECTING PAINTING: This painting was published when Huguette's apartments went on sale in 2012 ("Selling the Hideaways of a Reclusive Heiress," *The New York Times*, March 11, 2012).

132 THIS VIEW DISAPPEARED: The bricked windows in Huguette's apartments can be seen today. The 1959 date of construction of 900 Fifth Avenue is from "New Respect for White Brick Buildings," *The New York Times*, May 25, 2008.

134 A NEWSPAPER CARTOON IMAGINED: The undated cartoon has this caption for four panels: "A Day in the Life of Little Huguette Clark. This Drawing Shows Her Having Breakfast in Bed. Here She Steps into Her Limousine, Bound for a Shopping Tour, to Spend Some of Her $333 a Day. In the Eve-

ning She Dons Gorgeous Clothes and Sets Out for the Opera, or—She Attends a Debutante's Dance Where, Because of Her Wealth and Beauty, She Is the Center of Attention."

136 GOWER HAD PRESENTED A PAPER: William B. Gower, "Depletion of Mines in Relation to Invested Capital" (paper presented at Conference on Mine Taxation, Annual Convention of the American Mining Congress, Denver, November 16, 1920).

137 BRIDESMAID FOR HER HALF-NIECE: "Miss Morris to Wed J. H. Hall, Jr.," *New York Evening Post*, January 9, 1924.

139 "WHY AMERICA'S $50,000,000": This syndicated feature was published in many newspapers, including *The Hamilton* (Ohio) *Evening Journal*, June 28, 1930.

139 "HUGUETTE REFUSED": William D. Mangam, *The Clarks: An American Phenomenon* (New York: Silver Bow Press, 1941).

139 "IT DIDN'T STAY LONG": Hadassah Peri testimony, August 13, 14, 15, and 17, 2012, Depositions.

141 "RENO AGOG": The full headline in the *Los Angeles Times*, April 17, 1930, was "RENO AGOG OVER CLARK KIN'S MOVE: Wife and Daughter of Late Senator Take Floor of Hotel for Summer."

141 THE DEED WAS DONE: Reno, Nevada, Second Judicial District Court, divorce decree, William Gower and Huguette M. Clark Gower, August 11, 1930.

141 HUGUETTE SAILED AGAIN: Passenger records via Ancestry.com show that Huguette and Anna sailed to Hawaii from San Francisco on the SS *Malolo* on August 26, 1939.

143 "DADDY CLARK": Will's letters to George Palé were provided by Palé's grandson, Stephen Gruse. Letters are also available from the Montana Historical Society Research Center, http://mhs.mt.gov/research/default.asp.

144 "MR. CLARK TOLD ME": George John Palé described Will Clark and the adoption plan in an affidavit in regard to the estate of W. A. Clark, Jr., County of Los Angeles on August 27, 1935, a year after Will died. Montana Historical Society Research Center, http://mhs.mt.gov/research/default.asp.

145 REMEDIATION OF THE WATERSHED: The environmental devastation and halting cleanup of the Clark Fork is described in Brad Tyer, *Opportunity, Montana: Big Copper, Bad Water, and the Burial of an American Landscape* (Boston: Beacon Press, 2013).

146 "THE CUMULATIVE SENTIMENT HERE": Keith Edgerton to Dedman, February 26, 2010.

146 "THOSE MEN, THOSE BRAVE PIONEERS": *Proceedings and Debates of the Constitutional Convention Held in the City of Helena, Montana, July 4th, 1889, August 17th, 1889* (Helena: State Publishing, 1921), 476. As chairman of the convention, W.A. was speaking against taxation on mines. The full quota-

tion is as follows: "So I say to you, gentlemen, to whom it may seem an un-fair and unjust discrimination in favor of this industry, that if you will study it as we have done, that you can arrive at no other conclusion than that it is the only method whereby the state can secure from this species of property a reasonable and just revenue, and at the same time protect those men, those brave pioneers, who have come out here and have made the wilderness blos-som as the rose, and opened up these great mountains and brought their hidden wealth to light; yea, I say it is the duty of the members of this con-vention to throw such safeguards around this industry as are proper and just; this great industry that is the foundation of almost all the prosperity of this country; this industry that has made possible the building of railroads into this country; that has made this city of Helena, of which all Montanans are proud; that has built up the city of Butte and has made all the valleys and mountains of Montana productive."

147 ANNA BEFRIENDED OTHER CHILDREN: This section is based on Tina Lyle Harrower and Ann Ellis Raynolds interviews with Dedman, beginning April 2012.

147 CALLED ANNA "LANI": Lani actually means "heavens" or "heavenly," and sometimes "sacred chief" or "noble person." It may have been a word Anna picked up on her visits to Hawaii.

149 DEMOCRATS FOR WILLKIE: Associated Press, "Republicans Show Fund of $2,993,991," *The New York Times*, November 2, 1940.

152 "SHE HAS NEVER BEEN ABLE": Jerry Gray described his visit to Bellos-guardo and his parents' comments in his testimony on November 13, 2012, Depositions.

152 A PHOTOGRAPH SURVIVES: A copy of this restaurant photograph was an ex-hibit to the testimony of André Baeyens, October 8 and 9, 2012, Depositions.

153 SHE KNEW THE NAMES: See, for example, the testimony of Erika Hall, mother of Carla Hall Friedman, October 3, 2012, Depositions: "She would ask about every child. She would ask about the story that I told in my Christ-mas letter. She knew every child by name. She knew—she would ask how the children are, what they were doing."

153 "DEAR PAUL. YOUR KIND LETTER": Huguette's condolence card was an ex-hibit to the testimony of Paul Albert, November 13 and 14, 2012, Deposi-tions.

153 "AUNT HUGUETTE WAS VERY SHY": Jacqueline Baeyens-Clerté, testimony, October 9, 2012, Depositions.

153 SHE SENT FLOWERS: Receipts for Huguette's flower purchases, HMC papers.

154 TAKING AFTERNOON LESSONS: The Clark connections to Marcel Grand-jany were described by Grandjany's protégée, Kathleen Bride, a harp pro-fessor at the Eastman School of Music, and by Grandjany's son, Bernard, in

interviews with Dedman, July 2010. Bride provided copies of unpublished and unrecorded works that Grandjany dedicated to the Clarks.

154 MARCEL GRANDJANY: Grandjany was a former student of Anna's first teacher in Paris, Alphonse Hasselmans.

155 "WAS STRANGELY WITHDRAWN": Anna's concertgoing and his introduction to Huguette are described by Henri Temianka in *Facing the Music: An Inside View of the Real Concert World* (Sherman Oaks, CA: Alfred, 1980).

155 "YOU SEE CÉZANNE'S PORTRAIT": The incident with the portrait of Madame Cézanne was described by Karine McCall in her interview with Dedman, and she wrote a brief unpublished essay about that afternoon. The painting *Madame Cézanne in a Red Dress* is described in John Rewald, *The Paintings of Paul Cézanne: A Catalogue Raisonné*, with Walter Feilchenfeldt and Jayne Warman, 2 vols. (London: Thames and Hudson, 1996, 1997), and in the online catalog of the Museu de Arte, São Paulo, Brazil.

155 ANNA AND HUGUETTE HAD LONG SPONSORED: Anna's sponsorship of the Loewenguth String Quartet is described in HMC papers and in letters from Artine Courbalk to Félix Lorioux. Courbalk's correspondence about the Clarks to Lorioux was supplied by Lorioux's son, Jean-Loup Brusson, and grandson, Fabrice Brusson.

156 "DEEP INTO THE STRINGS": Temianka, *Facing the Music*.

157 "ROBERT," ANNA SAID: McCall essay.

157 FOUR REMARKABLE INSTRUMENTS: Temianka describes the history of the Paganini Strads in *Facing the Music*. Anna's will left the instruments to the Corcoran Gallery. The Corcoran held the instruments until 1994, when, citing "extreme" financial pressures, it sought Huguette's permission to sell the quartet. Again she chose the generous course, approving the sale. Japan's Nippon Music Foundation paid a record $15 million, tripling the Corcoran's endowment in one stroke. The Paganini Strads were played for the next nineteen years by the Tokyo String Quartet, which ended its run in 2013, leaving the Strads to find new players.

157 SOLD MADAME CÉZANNE: Anna's brooding portrait of Madame Cézanne ended up in the São Paulo Museum of Art in Brazil.

157 "NOW, ROBERT": McCall essay.

159 "WITH THE IDEA OF MARRYING SOMEONE RICH": Associated Press, "Heiress Hunt Is Told by Duke of Leinster," *The New York Times*, October 15, 1936. The suicide and financial troubles of Edward FitzGerald, the seventh duke of Leinster, are described in his son's obituary, "The Duke of Leinster," *The Telegraph* (London), December 7, 2004.

159 SPEAKING SIXTY YEARS LATER: Thomas Darrington Semple, Jr., described his sixteen first dates in an interview with Dedman, August 26, 2010. Semple died on January 6, 2011.

Chapter 7: 907 Fifth Avenue, Part Two

163 A FRENCH BOOK: Tryphosa Bates Batcheller, *La France au soleil et à lómbre* (New York, Paris: Bretano's 1944), 52.

164 NEWSPAPER FRONT PAGES: "Heiress to Marry," *The Light* (San Antonio, Texas), February 26, 1936, p. 1. The column appeared in some papers on February 25.

164 WALTER WINCHELL: "On Broadway," syndicated column, *Syracuse Journal*, March 3, 1936.

164 ETIENNE WAS BACK IN WINCHELL'S: "On Broadway with Walter Winchell," *The Brownsville Herald* (Texas), May 31, 1939, p. 4.

164 HELPED ETIENNE FIND A POSITION: "Copper Company Formed to Operate in Vermont," *The New York Times*, April 17, 1942.

165 THE MARQUISE DE VILLERMONT: H. I. Marsh to Huguette Clark, February 22, 1956, letter, HMC papers.

165 OLD SPANISH DAYS: "Society Rallies to Fiesta Gayety at Santa Barbara," *The Los Angeles Times*, August 11, 1941.

166 "I JOIN YOU THROUGH MY THOUGHTS": Etienne de Villermont to HMC, May 21, 1965, letter.

167 HUGUETTE SENT MONEY: HMC papers.

169 "TO MY DARLING MOTHER": This photo of Huguette in a Japanese print dress was shown at Christie's, New York, when Huguette's jewelry was sold in 2012.

169 HUGUETTE BOUGHT FOR HERSELF AND FRIENDS THE LATEST CAMERAS: HMC papers.

169 "ONE FLOODLIGHT, OPENING 4": Many examples of these photographs are in HMC papers.

169 SAT FOR PHOTOGRAPHS AT HOME: Copies of at least a dozen of these portraits are in HMC papers.

169 ONLY ONE YEAR DID HER MOTHER: This photo of Anna standing with her back to the camera is in HMC papers.

170 ANNA EUGENIA LACHAPELLE CLARK: "Mrs. Anna Clark, Senator's Widow; Art Patron, Whose Husband Left $250 Million, Dies," *The New York Times*, October 12, 1963.

170 MOST OF THE BEQUESTS: Last will and testament of Anna E. Clark, Surrogate's Court of the State of New York County, County of New York; available online at NBCNews.com, http://msnbcmedia.msn.com/i/msnbc/Sections/NEWS/Anna_Clark_Will.pdf.

171 "MY DEAR FRIEND": Villermont to HMC, October 14, 1963, letter, HMC papers.

173 SHE REMEMBERS VISITING: Marie-Christine's memories are from an interview with Dedman, via translator, August 2, 2012.

176 ETIENNE WAS NOT A MARQUIS: The Allard family story is told in a detailed book by a relative, Guillard Allard: *Une Famille Normande, de 1550 à nos Jours: Ascendance et Descendance de Jacques Allard, Conseiller du Roy, Seigneur de Sotteville, du Val et de Villermont.* (Self-published, Normandy, 1973)

176 ETIENNE'S OBITUARY: *Le Figaro*, April 13, 1982, p. 28. The full obituary translates as: "Madame Etienne Allard de Villermont, Miss Marie-Christine Allard de Villermont, The Count and the Countess de la Chevardiere de la Grandville, Madame Dominique Allard de Villermont, His children and grandchildren, Madame Henri Allard de Villermont and his sons, Mister Emmanuel Jullien de Pommerol, His children, grandchildren and great-grandchildren, Sorrowfully announce the return to God of Mister Etienne ALLARD de VILLERMONT on Maundy Thursday, furnished with the sacraments of the Church. The religious ceremony will take place in the church Sainte-Philomène du Cannet, this Tuesday 13 April, at 10:15am. The burial will take place in the cimetière monumental de Rouen, Thursday 15 April at 11:30am. A Mass will be celebrated for him this same Thursday 15 April, 1982, at 6:45pm in the church Saint-Pierre du Gros-Caillou, Paris (7th arrondisement), chapel of the Holy Virgin." Also, a brief notice appeared in *Nice-Matin*, April 11, 1982. In the second, his name is listed as Etienne Allard de Sotteville; this surname has been used by some members of the Allard family.

177 THE HOUSE OF CHRISTIAN DIOR: This story of Huguette's visit to the French consulate was told by Jacqueline Baeyens-Clerté in her testimony, October 9, 2012, Depositions.

178 "RUMPELSTILTSKIN HOUSE JUST ARRIVED": HMC to Edith von Arps, cable, October 6, 1964, HMC papers.

178 RUDOLPH JAKLITSCH, BORN IN AUSTRIA-HUNGARY: Rudolph's daughter, Linda Kasakyan, interview with Dedman, May 29, 2012.

179 "THE LITTLE PEOPLE ARE BANGING": Ibid.

179 "THANK YOU FOR YOUR KIND LETTER": HMC to Manon Iessel, cable, August 16, 1962, HMC papers.

179 "RECEIVED THE WALL AND GARDEN": HMC to Au Nain Bleu, cable, June 14, 1963, HMC papers.

180 "FOR THE LOVELY PASTRY SHOP": HMC to Au Nain Bleu, cable, May 7, 1956, HMC papers.

180 "RECEIVED YOUR NICE LETTER": HMC to La Maison Christian Dior, cable, August 9, 1962, HMC papers.

180 RUDOLPH, HER DOLLHOUSE CABINETMAKER: Kasakyan interview.

181 CAREFULLY REDRAFTING EACH ONE: HMC papers. Huguette kept even the drafts of her cards and grocery lists.

181 "I DON'T LIKE HOLIDAYS": HMC medical records.

181 HUGUETTE KEPT SENDING THE CHECKS: HMC papers and Kasakyan interview.

182 A RARE TYPE OF CEDAR: Caterina Marsh interview with Dedman, May 18, 2012.

182 A DOLLHOUSE-SIZE CASTLE: HMC papers and photos.

182 HUGUETTE CORRESPONDED WITH THE JAPANESE ARTIST: HMC papers.

182 CHANGING TRAINS FOUR TIMES: Caterina Marsh to Huguette Clark, May 11, 1987, HMC papers.

182 THE MEASUREMENTS IN HER DETAILED DESIGNS: Marsh interview.

182 SHE ACCEPTED AN ADDITIONAL CHARGE: HMC papers.

182 "SHE KNEW WHAT SHE WANTED": Marsh interview.

183 "SHE HAD A VERY HAPPY VOICE": Ibid.

183 "IT SEEMS THE ARTIST": Caterina Marsh to HMC, letter, HMC papers.

183 THE CASTLE PROJECTS CONTINUED: HMC papers.

183 HUGUETTE WASN'T HAPPY WITH HIS WORK: Marsh interview.

185 SHE SAID ONE OF HER FAVORITE MOVIES: HMC papers.

185 HUGUETTE SAID HER FAVORITE NOVEL: HMC conversation with Newell, April 10, 2002.

185 "WE ARE ALL TAKEN BY CUSTOMS": Marsh interview.

186 LORIOUX WAS AN EARLY INSPIRATION: Among the many online introductions to the work of Félix Lorioux, see http://animationresources.org/?p =2272. See also Jean de La Fontaine, *Fables of La Fontaine*, illust. Félix Lorioux (1927; repr., New York: Dover, 2012), in French and English.

187 PICASSO, WHO RIFFED ON: Lorioux's illustrated version of *Don Quixote* was published in 1930 by Hachette. Picasso's *Don Quixote* was sketched in 1955.

187 "RARE BIRD": Artine Courbalk's correspondence about the Clarks to Félix Lorioux was supplied by Lorioux's son, Jean-Loup Brusson, and grandson, Fabrice Brusson.

187 THROUGH COURBALK, HUGUETTE COMMISSIONED: Lorioux's letters to Huguette are in HMC papers.

187 ONE HAND-PAINTED BIRTHDAY CARD: Copies of these Lorioux cards are in the authors' possession, supplied by a dealer in Paris.

188 "OUR BENEVOLENT FAIRY": Félix and Lily Lorioux to HMC, letter, April 29, 1959, HMC papers.

188 "DEAR MADAME, VERY SAD": HMC to Lily Lorioux, cable, September 29, 1964, HMC papers.

188 FÉLIX LORIOUX WAS NOT THE ONLY: The extensive contacts between Huguette and the other illustrators in France can be found in HMC papers and are described in Courbalk's letters.

188 "YOU KNOW HOW LOYAL": HMC to Pinchon, letter, undated draft, HMC papers.

188 CLOSEST TO HÉROUARD: His real name was Chéri-Louis-Marie-Aimé Haumé (1881–1961).

188 INCLUDING A FEW OF HIS "DARING" ONES: Hérouard to HMC, letter, November 13, 1959, HMC papers.

189 "IN SPITE OF THEIR FRAGILE STATE": Hérouard to HMC, letter, October 12, 1957, HMC papers.

189 "THE FAIRY TALE CONTINUES": Pinchon to HMC, letter, April 15, 1953, HMC papers.

190 HUGUETTE WOULD CALL: Brusson family interviews and letters with Dedman, via translator, January–March 2013.

190 THE LORIOUX FAMILY HAD INVITED: Huguette's stated fear of another French Revolution was described by the Brussons in interviews.

Chapter 8: Bellosguardo

193 A DETAILED REPORT OF MISINFORMATION: The myths told on the trolley tour are described in James H. Hurley to Donald L. Wallace, December 2, 1986, HMC papers.

193 THE NAME BELLOSGUARDO: The Montecito Historical Archives of the Montecito Association have rich information on the Bellosguardo history. (The Clark estate is actually inside the city limits of Santa Barbara, but just barely.) An overview of Bellosguardo history is given in David F. Myrick, *Montecito and Santa Barbara*, vol. 2, *The Days of the Great Estates* (Glendale, CA: Trans-Angelo Books, 1991), 384–92.

194 "MY DEAR MOTHER": Sheila Lodge provided a copy of this June 10, 1988, note from Huguette. (See the handwritten note on page 344.)

195 MADE SOCIAL CONNECTIONS: One of Anna's musical friends in the 1940s was Ganna Walska, the owner of the Lotusland estate in Montecito. Walska was a Polish opera singer of uncertain talent whose career was fostered by her older husband, industrialist Harold Fowler McCormick, a story that Orson Welles said helped inspire part of the screenplay for his 1941 film, *Citizen Kane*.

195 AFFLUENT COMMUNITY OF MONTECITO: Montecito has long been the summer home of wealthy families seeking seclusion. It is now populated by the likes of actress Drew Barrymore, former vice president Al Gore, author T. C. Boyle, Google executive chairman Eric Schmidt, and media entrepreneur Oprah Winfrey.

195 THE MAIN DRIVEWAY ASCENDS: Descriptions of the exterior and interior of Bellosguardo are from Paul Newell's tour in 2004 and from detailed photographs taken after Huguette died in 2011, Estate of Huguette M. Clark.

197 THE CLARKS DIDN'T BUILD: Photos of Andrée's Cottage, when it was Geraldine's Cottage, appear in Robert S. Birchard, *Silent-Era Filmmaking in Santa Barbara* (Charleston, SC: Arcadia, 2007).

197 THEIR DAUGHTER, GERALDINE: Geraldine "Gerry" Graham became well-known as a model for portrait artists and for her string of attachments to prominent men, not the least Edward, Prince of Wales, years before he'd heard of Wallis Warfield Simpson.

198 ANN'S TRIP CAME: Ann Ellis Raynolds interviews with Dedman, beginning in April 2012.

199 HUGUETTE HONORED HER SISTER: Some have said that Anna made the donation for the bird refuge, but Huguette's papers and documents at the Montecito Historical Archives make clear that Huguette wrote the check from her own funds, although Anna may have worked behind the scenes to make the refuge happen.

200 "WOULD ARRIVE ON SUCH SHORT NOTICE": Barbara Hoelscher Doran offered her memories in "Behind the Gates of Bellosguardo," *Santa Barbara Magazine*, Winter 1996, and in interviews with Dedman, 2010–13.

200 HER PHOTO ALBUMS: HMC papers.

201 "HUGUETTE WANTED MY MOTHER": Barbara Hoelscher Doran interviews.

203 "TURNING THE COLOR": HMC to Tadé Styka, letter, December 3, 1941, HMC papers.

203 THE YOUNG SENTRIES: Barry Hoelscher described his memories of Bellosguardo in interviews with Dedman, beginning February 2012.

204 SHE BOUGHT A 215-ACRE RANCH: The date of the purchase of Rancho Alegre is given in Anna's will as July 14, 1943.

204 RANCHO ALEGRE: The ranch had a pedigree Anna could identify with, having been the weekend getaway of a former U.S. senator, Thomas M. Storke, owner of the *Santa Barbara News-Press*. The ranch served a useful purpose, providing milk and eggs for the Hoelschers and other staff, with the milk churned into butter at the Petan Dairy on Santa Barbara's Eastside.

205 "FIRST-CLASS CONDITION": John Douglas described his instructions and the episodes with the tree replacement and doghouse in his testimony, October 12, 2012, Depositions.

205 "WHO MOVED THAT CHAIR?": Several relatives described the episode of the maid who was upset by a chair having been moved at Bellosguardo. One was Paul Albert in his testimony, November 13 and 14, 2012, Depositions.

206 THE SHAH OF IRAN: The efforts by the shah (January 1979) and Marvin Davis (1989) to buy Bellosguardo are described in letters to Huguette from her California attorney, James Hurley, HMC papers.

206 "MY ANSWER TO YOU": Sheila Lodge provided the text of this April 9, 1997, note from Huguette.

206 "THE SCANDAL, OF COURSE": Jeanette Rodda to HMC, letter, November 8, 1988, HMC papers.

207 "WHAT COLOR IS THE SWIMMING POOL?": Oda Larsen interview with Newell in late 1995 or early 1996.

209 "YES, MR. DOUGLAS": Douglas deposition.

Chapter 9: Le Beau Château

214 EVENTUALLY OWNING FIFTY-TWO ACRES: New Canaan property records show Huguette completing the purchase in August 1951, then adding land to expand the property to fifty-two acres from the original forty-two. In 1952, she had the roof raised and added a wing that measures twenty-three feet by twenty-five feet. It has a large public room on the first floor, a bedroom above with a cathedral ceiling, and an artist's loft.

214 DAVID AIKEN REED: Senator Reed's construction of the house and its features were described in detail in newspaper articles, including "Senator Reed Builds Home in New Canaan," *The New York Times,* August 7, 1938.

214 "KEEPING AMERICAN STOCK UP": George M. Stephenson, *A History of American Immigration: 1820–1924* (New York: Russel and Russel, 1964).

216 SHE SPENT HUNDREDS OF THOUSANDS: 1997 estimates and work orders, HMC papers.

218 THE FINEST VIOLIN IN THE WORLD: The history of La Pucelle is described by David Fulton in an unpublished manuscript of a memoir.

218 THE ASKING PRICE: Documents on Huguette's purchase of La Pucelle, HMC papers.

218 SHE EXPANDED HER COLLECTION: Documents on Huguette's purchases of art and of Apartment 12W, HMC papers.

220 "DID YOU EVER REPLACE SNOOPY?": Huguette Clark to Bill Gower, August 1946, cable, HMC papers.

220 "EVERYTHING WAS SKETCHY": Janet Perry interview with Dedman, May 31, 2012.

222 ANTIBES: Gower's home in Antibes was painted by artist Felix Kelly, *La Sarrazine, Antibes,* 1968, sold at Christie's, London, November 6, 1998, listing at http://www.christies.com/lotfinder/LotDetailsPrintable.aspx?intObjectID=1365867.

222 HE DIED OF CONSUMPTION: The cemetery files of the Town of North Elba, near Lake Placid, New York, give information about Gower's death and burial.

222 A MOSSY HEADSTONE: Bill Gower's whereabouts have tormented researchers for years. He was hard to find because he used two middle names. His full name was William MacDonald Levenson Gower. When he married Huguette, he was known in the papers as William MacDonald Gower, then

in the Social Register as William M. L. Gower. Finally, in his professional life, he switched to William L. Gower.

223 DELIA HEALEY: Delia Healey's grandchildren Chris Santorsola and Patrick Brady described her work for Huguette in interviews with Dedman, beginning March 2010.

224 OUT IN YONKERS: Ann Fabrizio described her father, Robert Samuels, and his work for Huguette in interviews with Dedman, beginning March 2010. His work is documented in letters and receipts in HMC papers.

224 ONLY ONE PART-TIME MAID: The dwindling of Huguette's staff is shown in expenditure reports, HMC papers.

224 "IT WAS SPOOKY": Hadassah Peri described what Huguette told her of this incident with the delivery boy in her testimony, August 13, 2012, Depositions.

Chapter 10: Doctors Hospital

227 MADAME PIERRE CALLED: Suzanne Pierre's role in contacting Dr. Singman is told in his affidavit, filed in Surrogate's Court, May 24, 2012.

227 "HER DOLLS," MADAME PIERRE SAID: Suzanne Pierre interview with Dedman, March 13, 2010.

228 "I WOULD ASK HER TO GO OUT": Ibid.

228 "SHE THOUGHT THEY WERE JUST": Ibid.

229 DOCTORS HOSPITAL WAS NOT THE PLACE: The reputation of the hospital as catering to the elite is described, for example, in "These Days, You Have to Be Ill to Get into Doctors Hospital," *The New York Times*, December 27, 1970.

229 "LIKE A HOMELESS PERSON": HMC medical records.

230 "MANAGING POORLY AT HOME": The social worker's assessment is in HMC medical records.

230 "THIS SHE HAS STEADFASTLY": HMC medical records.

230 "I HAD STRONGLY URGED": Dr. Henry Singman, HMC medical records.

230 "PERFECTLY HAPPY, CONTENT": Dr. Henry Singman, testimony, August 16 and 20, 2012, Depositions.

230 HUGUETTE FIRED HER: The later night nurse, Geraldine Lehane Coffey, described this incident in her testimony: "Huguette told her, I do not want Angela to work for me any more because I don't feel comfortable, she wants me to go home. Because they wanted Mrs. Clark to go home, but she didn't feel ready to go home." Coffey testified July 9 and September 4, 2012, Depositions.

231 "WAS SO CONTENT": Dr. John L. E. Wolff, testimony, September 13, 2012, Depositions.

231 Huguette was hardly ever sick: HMC medical records.

231 "extremely frightened": Ibid.

231 "You have to convince her": Hadassah Peri, testimony, August 13, 14, 15, and 17, 2012, Depositions.

231 Gicela Tejada Oloroso: Peri's birth name, date of birth, and place of birth are given on a name change petition, Civil Court of the City of New York, October 24, 2011, in which she changed her name legally to Hadassah Peri, the name she had been using for years.

232 She passed her New York exams: Peri described her work and family history in her deposition. Her status as a registered nurse is confirmed in New York State records.

232 "I give my life to Madame": Hadassah Peri deposition.

232 "She like a simple room": Ibid.

232 look out on the Fourth of July: Coffey deposition.

233 "The woman was an eccentric": Singman deposition.

233 The daily routine began: The typical day is described in the depositions of several nurses, as well as in the daily nurses' notes in HMC medical records.

234 "walk in Central Park": Chris Sattler, testimony, August 23 and September 6, 2012, Depositions.

234 "Mrs. Clark liked to speak French": Kati Despretz Cruz, testimony, September 6, 2012, Depositions.

234 "She would watch the stock": Primrose Mohiuddin, testimony, September 17, 2012, Depositions.

234 "When President Clinton": Sattler deposition.

235 "She was a wiz": Singman deposition.

235 "her dear father": Hadassah Peri deposition.

235 Huguette's eyesight had declined: Her physical condition and response to her hearing loss are described in depositions and HMC medical records.

236 "She was remarkably clear": Karen Gottlieb, testimony, July 10, 2012, Depositions.

236 "That's one day": Hadassah Peri deposition.

236 "a beautiful lady": Ibid.

236 "Hadassah was very good": Singman deposition.

237 "Madame, I love you": The tape of this conversation, captured on the answering machine at the Peri home, was played during Hadassah Peri's deposition. Based on when the machine was purchased, Peri estimated it occurred around 2007.

238 Huguette approached a French furniture company: HMC papers.

240 Chris first visited: Sattler described his work history and his routine in his deposition.

242 FIND ALL THE LADIES-IN-WAITING: Sattler kept a time log of his daily activities for Huguette, entered as an exhibit to his deposition.

242 "I WASN'T AN EXPERT": Sattler deposition.

242 "CHRIS," SHE WOULD SAY: Ibid.

243 "THEN," CHRIS RECALLED: Ibid.

243 AT A PRICE OF $50,000: Correspondence from G. T. Marsh and Company is in HMC papers and exhibits to Caterina Marsh, testimony, July 2, 2012, Depositions.

243 "I NEVER SAW HER UNHAPPY": Sattler deposition.

243 "SHE LIKED TO HAVE": Ibid.

243 "BECAUSE SHE LIKED": Ibid.

244 "BELIEVE ME": Ibid.

244 "LIKE A DAY AT THE RACETRACK": Sattler deposition.

244 "SHE LOVED THE AUCTIONS": Ibid.

244 CHRIS SAID HE COUNTED: Ibid.

245 "MRS. CLARK DIDN'T LIKE IT": Ibid.

245 "WAS NEVER ABLE TO FIGURE": Ibid.

245 "SHE WAS," CHRIS SAID: Ibid.

246 STUDYING DANCE IN THE 1920S: Ninta Sandré is listed in *The New Yorker,* April 14, 1928, as presenting a dance recital with Michio Itō at the Princess Theatre, and her debut at a Broadway theater was reviewed in "Ninta Sandre Offers Program of Dances," *The New York Times,* May 3, 1931.

246 ONE EVENING IN JANUARY 1987: Ninta's later years were described by Lyn Strasheim, who worked for Dr. Myron Wright, in an interview with Dedman, July 5, 2012.

247 $329,000 A MONTH: The authors compiled Huguette's expenditures for these months from regular reports made to her by attorney Donald Wallace, HMC papers.

248 "MRS. CLARK WANTED EVERYTHING": Strasheim interview with Dedman, July 5, 2012.

248 "LOOKED LIKE A BAG WOMAN": Ibid.

249 A LAWYER SHOWED UP: Gwendolyn Jenkins described Don Wallace's visit in an interview with Dedman, May 29, 2012.

251 "EVERY YEAR SINCE": Don Wallace to HMC, letter, September 30, 1994, HMC papers.

251 CAREFUL WITH HER CHECKING: Copies of Huguette's bank books, HMC papers.

251 OVERDRAFTS HAD STARTED: A Don Wallace letter to Huguette Clark, in February 1985, warned about overdrafts and asked her to warn him whenever she wrote a check over $5,000, HMC papers.

252 MOST OF HER INCOME: Huguette's tax returns, HMC papers.

253 HUGUETTE'S BALANCE IN THAT ACCOUNT: Repeated letters from Summit

Bank and Huguette's advisers urging her to move the money into an interest-bearing account are in HMC papers.

254 HUGUETTE RECEIVED A PLEA: Letters from the Paul Clark Home are in HMC papers.

254 AS A MEMORIAL: The Paul Clark Home gave the authors copies of documents on its early days, and the authors toured the home.

255 HUGUETTE RECEIVED SIMILAR LETTERS: HMC papers.

255 HUGUETTE WAS A BIDDER: Letters informing Huguette about this auction and many others in which she won the bid are in HMC papers.

255 TWO ANTIQUE FRENCH DOLLS: These two dolls are in the Sotheby's catalog *Important Dolls, Teddy Bears, Toys and Automata, London, Tuesday 18th May 1993* (London: Sotheby's, 1993), lots 219 and 244.

257 "SHE REALLY IS ADORABLE": Huguette Clark to Doris Styka, December 29, 1944, exhibit to Styka deposition.

257 "IT HAS BEEN SO VERY LONG": Doris Styka to Huguette Clark, July 23, 1948, Styka deposition exhibit.

257 "AS WE THINK OF WHAT": Doris Styka to Huguette Clark, August 19, 1948, Styka deposition exhibit.

258 ART CURATOR AND ARCHIVIST: Wanda was for many years the archivist at Chesterwood, the Massachusetts country home, studio, and gardens of sculptor Daniel Chester French, best known for *The Minute Man* in Concord, Massachusetts, and the seated Abraham Lincoln at the Lincoln Memorial in Washington, D.C.

258 "MOTHER AND I SEND STREAMS": Styka deposition exhibit.

259 WANDA TRIED TO CALL HUGUETTE: Wanda Styka told this story in her testimony, August 1, 2012, Depositions.

259 "WELL, THEN DON'T": Ibid.

259 "IF THERE EVER WAS ANYBODY": Sattler deposition.

260 HUGUETTE'S GIFTS TO HER NURSE: The gifts to Hadassah Peri are detailed in the petition of the New York County Public Administrator's Office to recover gifts made from Huguette's accounts. An amended petition was filed on November 30, 2012, in Surrogate's Court of the State of New York County, County of New York, case 1995-1375A. (Referred to hereafter as "public administrator's petition.") This petition is available online at http://msnbcmedia .msn.com/i/msnbc/Sections/NEWS/clark_petition_for_clawback.pdf. Many of the same documents are included in HMC papers.

260 "VULNERABLE TO THE INFLUENCE": Public administrator's petition.

260 "MADAME, YOU HAVE GIVEN US": Hadassah Peri deposition.

260 "SOMETIMES I WOULD SAY": Hadassah Peri deposition.

261 HUGUETTE'S GIFTS FOR THE YEAR 1991: Her gifts are listed on her federal gift tax return for 1991, HMC papers.

261 HUGUETTE ALSO KEPT BUYING: Public administrator's petition.

262 "I told Madame I have many": Hadassah Peri deposition.

263 "To tell you the truth": Hadassah Peri deposition.

263 "Dearest Madame, I would like": Abraham Peri to HMC, birthday card, 2001, HMC papers.

264 Huguette's gifts to the Peris: Public administrator's petition.

265 "My grandmother felt": Cruz deposition.

265 the boy was so cute: Cruz described this apartment purchase in her deposition.

266 more than $1 million in gifts: Coffey deposition.

266 "I respected her very much": Coffey deposition.

266 "There was very little nursing": Coffey deposition.

266 "Certain questions were not asked": Wallace Bock, testimony, March 22 and 23 and July 24–26, 2012, Depositions.

266 "Somebody would come in": Ibid.

266 "Sometimes she gives you checks": Hadassah Peri deposition.

267 "For twenty years": Ibid.

267 With the money his wife was making: Daniel Peri, testimony, September 24, 2012, Depositions.

267 "failed to understand the consequences": Public administrator's petition.

267 "Please believe me": Dr. Jules Pierre to Huguette Clark, March 8, 1992, letter, HMC papers.

268 the full $10 million: The gift to Suzanne Pierre is described in HMC papers and in Suzanne J. Pierre v. Commissioner of Internal Revenue, U.S. Tax Court, 2010, which Madame Pierre won. See http://www.ustaxcourt .gov/InOpHistoric/pierre.TCM.WPD.pdf. As though it were an everyday occurrence, documents say, "Petitioner had been a widow for many years when she received a $10 million cash gift from a wealthy friend in 2000."

268 Talking about Huguette: Pierre interview.

268 "She told me to hold it": Hadassah Peri deposition.

269 "it just snowballed": Sattler described the opening of the safe and the distribution of the jewelry in his deposition. The gifts are detailed in public administrator's petition.

269 "And Madame said, someday": Hadassah Peri deposition.

269 at least $31,906,074.81: This total for gifts to the Peris is from public administrator's petition.

270 "I cannot recall any paper": Hadassah Peri deposition.

270 "Never come to my mind": Ibid.

271 "You will have to": The October 26, 2001, letters from Bock and Kamsler are cited in public administrator's petition.

271 "As you well know": Bock to HMC, letter, October 31, 2272, HMC papers. This letter was also an exhibit to his deposition.

272 SHE GAVE DON WALLACE $130,000: The total value of dolls that Wallace received from Huguette is listed in the accounting of his estate in Surrogate's Court. A copy of the file is available online at http://msnbcmedia.msn .com/i/msnbc/Sections/NEWS/wallace_probate.pdf.

272 WALLACE'S SECRETARY WROTE: Series of letters from Gloria Parker to Huguette Clark, 1992, HMC papers.

272 "SO THERE I WAS": Wallace Bock, prepared text of remarks, Efrat, Israel, July 29, 2008.

272 "THE SECURITY SYSTEM FOR EFRAT": Photograph.

272 "SHE SAID SHE BOUGHT": Sattler deposition.

273 HUGUETTE WAS JUST TWO MILES: Her condolence note to James Hurley for the loss of his son-in-law, Chandler R. "Chad" Keller, is in HMC papers. See Keller's biography at the National 9/11 Pentagon Memorial, http:// pentagonmemorial.org/explore/biographies/chandler-r-keller.

273 DEADLY ANTHRAX: Huguette's fears of an anthrax attack were described by Bock in his deposition.

273 SHE CALLED HER GODDAUGHTER: Styka deposition.

275 "I HAVE IN HAND": The transaction for La Pucelle was described by violin dealer Charles Beare in an interview with Dedman, February 27, 2012. The buyer, David Fulton, also told the story in interviews and emails with Dedman, and in an unpublished manuscript of a memoir.

275 AGREED TO BUY LA PUCELLE: Fulton didn't realize at the time of the purchase that he had a connection to the Clarks. Fulton's father had been a manager at W.A.'s United Verde copper mine in Arizona.

275 AN EXTRAORDINARY INSTRUMENT: There is a popular misconception that a fine violin has to be played regularly to be kept in fine condition. The less stress on the instrument, the better. There's a good reason that Huguette would have preferred her less expensive Strad. As David Fulton, who purchased La Pucelle, explained in an interview with Dedman, "La Pucelle, as it was set up when it came to me, is perfectly fine for most pros to play but, for an amateur, even a skilled amateur, it would probably be set up a little differently. The fact that Huguette preferred her early Strad is somewhat indicative. Early Strads are lighter in tone and generally easier to play, more approachable for an amateur. I doubt Huguette was a particularly strong player, though doubtless she was fairly competent. My conclusion from all this is that La Pucelle was essentially untouched while Huguette owned it, in a time capsule really. I'd guess she didn't particularly enjoy playing it. That is confirmed by the condition, setup, strings, and the accessories that were in the case when the violin came to me. This was a stroke of great good fortune for the violin. . . . People who buy big, important instruments are often dismayed to discover that they can be very demanding to play. . . . I think Huguette must have had trouble taming it."

275 "IT REALLY HAS AN AMAZING PURITY": Violinist James Ehnes provided this description of La Pucelle through his publicist in August 2010.

Chapter 11: Beth Israel Medical Center

279 "WAS QUITE WEALTHY": Dr. Henry Singman, testimony, August 16 and 20, 2012, Depositions, and public administrator's petition.

279 "MADAME, AS YOU KNOW": Singman deposition.

280 DR. NEWMAN SENT HUGUETTE: Dr. Robert Newman, testimony, August 9, 2012, Depositions.

280 THE MOTHER WROTE TO HUGUETTE: The visits by Dr. Newman's mother and the two women's time watching skating are described in HMC papers.

280 "I KID YOU NOT!": Public administrator's petition.

280 "DEAR MRS. HUGUETTE": Newman to HMC, letter, January 1994, HMC papers.

281 "EVEN IF SHE CHANGES": Public administrator's petition.

281 "ONE SMURF TO MAKE AMENDS": Ibid.

281 "SHE HAS NO 'CONCEPT' ": Ibid.

281 HE MADE NO PAYMENTS: The public administrator's petition gives details on the Rudick loan documents, which turned into a gift.

281 DR. RUDICK DENIED THIS ACCOUNT: Dr. Jack Rudick, testimony, September 19, 2012, Depositions.

281 WAIVED HADASSAH'S FEES: Singman deposition.

281 "I THINK HER GIFTS": Newman deposition.

282 "WITHOUT KNOCKING HER PAST GIFTS": Ibid.

282 "THE GREAT JOY AND SPIRITUAL SATISFACTION": Public administrator's petition.

282 "THEY MIGHT PUSH THE QUESTION": Ibid.

282 HUGUETTE WAS HIDDEN AWAY: The former employees were interviewed by Dedman in July 2012.

282 THE JOINT COMMISSION: The routine practice of the Joint Commission was described by spokeswoman Elizabeth Zhani in an email to Dedman, July 26, 2012.

282 "IF WE WERE FORCED": Public administrator's petition.

282 ENCOUNTERED FINANCIAL DIFFICULTIES: Moody's Investor Service, "Moody's Downgrades Bonds for Beth Israel Medical Center in New York City," press release, 1995, http://www.thefreelibrary.com/Moody's+Downgrades+Bonds+for+Beth+Israel+Medical+Center+in+New+York...-a017424498, and "N.Y.'s Beth Israel Medical Center Takes Rating Hit from Moody's," *The Bond Buyer,* June 16, 2000.

283 SHE GAVE A PAINTING: Details of the sale of the Manet painting are in HMC papers. Letters show that Beth Israel showed the painting at a benefit on November 5, 2000, and it failed to sell on November 8.

283 "TERRIBLY CONFUSED POLITICAL SITUATION": Huguette's advice to delay the second attempt to sell the Manet is described in an affidavit by Marvin Wexler, attorney for Beth Israel Medical Center, in reply to the public administrator's petition.

283 "AN UNCONDITIONALLY GUARANTEED CASH PAYMENT": Newman to HMC, letter, HMC papers. The letter is also in the public administrator's petition.

284 "FREEING YOU FROM": Ibid.

284 THERE WERE MORE CONS: The proposed charitable gift annuity was evaluated for the authors by wealth management specialist Gavin Morrissey of Commonwealth Financial Network.

285 "A CONTRIBUTION IN THE NEIGHBORHOOD": Dr. Newman described this meeting in notes to the Beth Israel development staff, described in the public administrator's petition. It's also discussed in his deposition and in Morton Hyman's testimony, October 10 and 11, 2012, Depositions.

285 "EXPRESSING CONCERN": HMC medical records.

285 "SHE DON'T WANT CHANGES": Hadassah Peri, testimony, August 13, 14, 15, and 17, 2012, Depositions.

286 HOSPITAL POLICY ON CONFLICTS OF INTEREST: The Beth Israel policy was an exhibit to the Hyman deposition. It says, in part, "Gifts of money (including gift certificates) are never acceptable."

286 "THE INDISPUTABLE REALITY": Hospital attorney Marvin Wexler made this comment in an affidavit filed in opposition to the public administrator's petition, January 15, 2013.

286 "THAT'S A LOT OF MONEY": Dr. Newman described his conversation with Huguette in an email to a hospital development official, May 12, 2004, which was an exhibit to his deposition.

286 "NEVER ABANDON HER": Ibid.

286 "SHE CAME THROUGH": Ibid.

286 HUGUETTE'S LAST DONATION: Her resistance to further implorations is described by Wexler in his affidavit.

287 "WOULD HAVE TO DISCONTINUE": Singman deposition.

287 HADASSAH TOLD HER THE SAME: Hadassah Peri deposition.

288 "WE TOLD HER": Ibid.

288 CHRIS SATTLER HELPED HER: Sattler described the morning trip with Huguette in his testimony, August 23 and September 6, 2012, Depositions.

288 "SHE IS TERRIBLY INSECURE": HMC medical records.

288 "SHE HAVE TO KNOW YOU FIRST": Hadassah Peri deposition.

289 ROOM 10L04 WAS DECORATED: Observation by Dedman.

289 "She started coming out": Sattler deposition.

289 There was a little gathering: Several of the participants described in depositions the birthday party. Nurse Erlinda Ysit described the balloon in her testimony, August 22, 2012, Depositions.

290 Anna's jewelry disappeared: The jewelry losses are described in a series of letters from the bank and from Huguette's attorneys in HMC papers.

291 "has been devastating": Ibid.

291 wrote her a note of apology: Ibid.

291 an independent physician: Letter from Don Wallace to Huguette Clark, October 13, 1994, relaying the offer from Citibank. A Wallace letter from February 1995 shows that Dr. Singman signed a statement of competency.

291 someone stole nearly: November 1991 letter from Don Wallace to Huguette Clark, HMC papers.

291 Huguette's gentle ballerina: The theft of the Degas painting, the FBI investigation, and the settlement agreement are described in letters in HMC papers.

294 "Mrs. Clark's condition": Sattler's call is noted in attorney Bock's time logs, files of Collier, Halpern, Newberg, Nolletti & Bock, in White Plains, New York.

294 they sent over a draft: HMC papers.

295 "You have never expressed": Wallace to HMC, letter, March 7, 1985, HMC papers.

295 "In the not too far distant": Ibid.

296 he had never met his client: Wallace's goddaughter, Judith Sloan, described his frustration at never meeting Huguette in an interview with Dedman, August 2010.

296 "Once again," he begged: Bock to HMC, letter, September 20, 2000, HMC papers.

296 A 2001 list: HMC papers.

296 Bock and Kamsler took a draft: The men discussed this visit in their testimony: Wally Bock, March 22 and 23 and July 24–26, 2012, Depositions; Irving Kamsler, May 8 and 9 and July 17–19, 2012, Depositions.

297 Dr. Newman visited: Newman deposition.

297 On March 7, now: A copy of this first will is available online at http:// msnbcmedia.msn.com/i/msnbc/Sections/NEWS/huguette_clark_earlier_will _from_msnbc.com.pdf.

297 automatic commissions: Under New York law, each executor would receive 5 percent on the first $100,000, 4 percent on the next $200,000, 3 percent on the next $700,000, 2.5 percent on the next $4 million, and 2 percent on the balance. The commission is paid on assets other than real property and tangible personal property. Assuming Huguette had $154,257,899 in as-

sets subject to a commission, Bock and Kamsler would each have received $3,119,158.

297 BOCK AND KAMSLER EXPLAINED: Bock and Kamsler depositions.

297 KAMSLER SENT HUGUETTE A LIST: Kamsler deposition.

298 HUGUETTE SIGNED THE SECOND ONE: The second and last will is available online at http://msnbcmedia.msn.com/i/msnbc/Sections/NEWS/huguette _clark_will_from_msnbc.com.pdf.

298 SHE REFUSED A HEARING AID: These details from the period between the two wills are in HMC medical records.

300 HAD A DRINK TO SUCCESS: Bock's secretary, Danita Rudisill, was a witness to the will signing. She testified about the trip to the restaurant in her deposition on July 30, 2012. Bock, in his deposition, said he didn't recall drinking after the will was signed.

Chapter 12: Woodlawn Cemetery

303 MARCH 1968: Lewis Rutherford Morris Hall said in documents that he was not introduced to Huguette at his mother's funeral in 1968, but that Huguette was pointed out to him. John Hudson "Jack" Hall III, grandson of the deceased, said in documents and a deposition that he saw Huguette or was told that she was leaving the funeral. Jack Hall testimony, November 12, 2012, Depositions.

304 IN TALKING WITH HUGUETTE'S AIDE: Correspondence among relatives and between relatives and David Levy at the Corcoran Gallery is in the Surrogate's Court record as an exhibit to several depositions, particularly that of Carla Hall Friedman, who testified on September 18 and October 1 and 8, 2012, and in answers to interrogatories.

305 AGNES ALBERT: Karine McCall testified about her mother, Agnes, being told by Bock not to contact Huguette directly (Karine McCall testimony, September 14 and 20, 2012, Depositions).

305 SOMETHING "INSIDIOUS": David Levy to Carla Hall Friedman, email, December 6, 2004.

305 SHE OFFERED TO WRITE TO HUGUETTE: Carla Hall Friedman to David Levy, email, December 5, 2004.

305 "LITTLE OR NO UNDERSTANDING": Ibid.

306 "BARRING THE EMERGENCE": "Corcoran Director Quits; Trustees Shelve Gehry Plans," The Washington Post, May 24, 2005.

306 HOST A PROPOSED CLARK FAMILY REUNION: Carla Hall Friedman to HMC, letter, September 4, 2008. A reunion had been discussed among family members. Carla explained to Huguette that the new director of the

Corcoran, Paul Greenhalgh, "suggested that the Corcoran host a Clark
Family reunion with a dinner for us in the Salon d'Ore." The salon proved
to be too small for the dinner, which was held in another space at the Corcoran.

306 A CLARK-FRIENDLY GRADUATE STUDENT: Stanley Thomas Pitts, "An Unjust Legacy: A Critical Study of the Political Campaigns of William Andrews Clark, 1888–1901" (master's thesis, University of North Texas,
2006).

307 SEEKING $22,000: Carla Hall Friedman to HMC, letter, September 4,
2008, exhibit to interrogatories, Surrogate's Court. "The remaining cost of
event [*sic*] will be approximately $20,000–22,000 for our expanding group.
We would be most grateful, if you would consider generously underwriting
as much of this cost as is possible for you."

307 "DEAR TANTE HUGUETTE": The signed card is in evidence in Surrogate's
Court, submitted along with answers to interrogatories.

307 HE MADE A SCENE: Friedman deposition.

307 "PORNO STING NABS TEMPLE PRESIDENT": *The Riverdale Press* (Bronx,
NY), September 20, 2007.

307 KAMSLER HAD BEEN ARRESTED: A copy of Kamsler's entire court file at
County Court of the State of New York, Nassau County, including the indictment, affidavits from investigators, and a transcript of Kamsler's guilty
plea, is available online at http://msnbcmedia.msn.com/i/msnbc/Sections/
NEWS/clark_kamsler_court_file.pdf.

307 THE FIFTEEN-COUNT INDICTMENT: IBID.

308 KAMSLER WAS INDICTED: Ibid.

308 HE ADMITTED TO POLICE: Ibid.

308 CHANGED HIS PLEA TO GUILTY: Ibid.

308 "ON THAT NOTE": The blog posting has since been removed, but the estate
lawyer in New Jersey confirmed that she posted it and that she knew Kamsler from professional conferences.

310 "11/26/08: TELEPHONE CALL": Wallace Bock telephone logs, Collier,
Halpern, Newberg, Nolletti & Bock, in White Plains, New York.

311 "PREPARE FOR THE RESPONSIBILITIES": Ian Devine described his professional expertise on LinkedIn.

311 CARLA AND IAN SPOKE: Friedman deposition and Ian Devine, testimony,
September 10 and 11, 2012, Depositions.

312 "OUR IMPRESSION": Ian Devine to relatives, email, December 9, 2008.

312 "ALERT AND VERY RESPONSIVE": HMC medical records.

312 "AGITATED AND NOT ORIENTED": Ibid.

312 "STATING TO RESPECT HER PRIVACY": Ibid.

312 "TELEPHONE CALL FROM MRS. CLARK": Bock telephone logs.

312 "Neither she nor I": Bock to Friedman, email, December 8, 2008, in responses to interrogatories, Surrogate's Court.

313 "We need not apologize": Devine to Friedman, email, December 8, 2009, in responses to interrogatories.

313 "in very good mood": HMC medical records.

313 Kamsler reached a plea deal: Nassau County court file.

313 "it was important": Ibid.

313 after he served three months: Records of the Office of the Professions, New York State Education Department, show that two years after his guilty plea, and after the publicity about the Clark case, Kamsler was found guilty of professional misconduct in an administrative proceeding by the Board of Regents, which oversees professional licenses. The action on February 8, 2011, was based on his conviction for sending information to a person he believed to be a minor in an attempt to invite sexual conduct. The records are available online at http://www.op.nysed.gov/opd/feb11.htm#kams.

314 "I just want to apologize": Nassau County court file.

314 "Dear Mrs. Clark": Kamsler to HMC, letter, February 20, 2009. Kamsler filed a copy of this letter in court along with her last will and testament, in support of his claim that he was entitled to be an executor, even as a felon. A copy is available online at http://msnbcmedia.msn.com/i/msnbc/Sections/NEWS/clark_kamsler_letter.pdf.

314 "had been changed": Bock to Friedman, letter, March 6, 2009, in responses to interrogatories.

315 "Huguette has not asked": Paul Albert to Ian Devine, March 19, 2009, letter, Surrogate's Court. Also discussed in Albert's testimony, November 13 and 14, 2012, Depositions.

317 "periods of delirium": HMC medical records.

317 The element in the news stories: This episode is described in Bill Dedman, "Who Is Watching Heiress Huguette Clark's Millions?," msnbc.com, September 8, 2010, http://www.nbcnews.com/id/38733524/ns/business-local_business/. Donald Wallace's estate papers are on file at Surrogate's Court in lower Manhattan and available online at http://msnbcmedia.msn.com/i/msnbc/Sections/NEWS/wallace_probate.pdf.

318 probate court had the option: The office of the New York County Public Administrator was alerted to the Wallace estate, as required by law when heirs are unknown or someone is survived only by distant relatives (cousins, in Wallace's case). The public administrator's outside counsel on the Wallace estate, Peter S. Schram, examined the documents and found no grounds to question the validity of the will. Wallace estate file.

318 "as the son he never had": Ibid.

318 "I said to him": Ibid.

318 "AT ALL TIMES": Ibid.

320 HUGUETTE HAD NO PLACE TO BE BURIED: The negotiations over the Clark mausoleum and finding a place for Huguette there are described in letters made available by the relatives in the estate case.

321 REFUSED TO SIGN A LIVING WILL: HMC medical records and Irving Kamsler, testimony, May 8 and 9 and July 17–19, 2012, Depositions.

322 "I THANK YOU FOR EVERYTHING": Chris Sattler, testimony, August 23 and September 6, 2012, Depositions.

322 SHE DIED EARLY ON THE MORNING: Obituaries include Bill Dedman, "Huguette Clark, the Reclusive Copper Heiress, Dies at 104," msnbc.com, May 24, 2011, http://www.nbcnews.com/id/39006900/ns/business-local_business/, and Margalit Fox, "Huguette Clark, Reclusive Heiress, Dies at 104," *The New York Times,* May 25, 2011.

322 THE ENTOMBMENT WAS ARRANGED: See "Family Excluded from Huguette Clark Burial," msnbc.com, May 26, 2011, http://www.nbcnews.com/id/43166747/ns/business-local_business/.

Chapter 13: Surrogate's Courthouse

325 PERSUADE A JUDGE OR JURY: If a New York resident dies without a will or the will is overturned, the money goes first to a spouse and children or grandchildren. If there are none of those, the parents inherit, then the siblings. Huguette was survived by none of these. Next are the nieces and nephews descended from the siblings, and Huguette did have those on her father's side of the family. Huguette's thirteen half-grandnieces and grandnephews who were alive when she died would each receive 6.25 percent of her estate, and in cases where that level of relative died after Huguette, their children, her eight half-great-grandnieces and great-grandnephews, would each receive 2.34375 percent. Two of those twenty-one relatives, a grandniece and a grandnephew, did not join the lawsuit filed by the nineteen others.

326 "THAT HUGUETTE'S TRUE WISHES": John R. Morken to Clark family members, letter, September 30, 2011.

326 THEY HAD NEVER MET HUGUETTE: The nineteen Clark relatives described their contacts with Huguette in answers to interrogatories as well as in depositions.

326 THE LAST TIME: Paul Albert said he last saw her in 1957, Karine Albert McCall in 1954, Jacqueline Baeyens-Clerté in 1952, and Patrick Baeyens and Jerry Gray during the war years of 1941–45.

327 OF THESE NINETEEN: André Baeyens described his discussions with Huguette in an interview with Dedman, June 6, 2010, as well as in previous

conversations with Newell and in answers to interrogatories in the estate case.

327 "THE SENATOR WHO LOVED FRANCE": The book, *Le sénateur qui aimait la France,* was published in 2005 by Scali.

327 SHE SUPPORTED THIS CALIFORNIA COUSIN: HMC papers.

328 "I THINK HAVING SUCH WEALTH": Several relatives described in interviews and emails with Dedman the traumas and difficulties suffered by the Clark family.

329 SAW HUGUETTE'S FIFTH AVENUE APARTMENTS: Relatives described the tour in interviews.

330 IN LATE DECEMBER 2012: The death of Timothy Gray was reported in Bill Dedman, "Potential Heir to $300 Million Clark Copper Fortune Found Dead, Homeless," msnbc.com, December 30, 2012, http://openchannel .nbcnews.com/_news/2012/12/30/16238005-potential-heir-to-300-million -clark-copper-fortune-found-dead-homeless.

331 TIM WAS NOT EXACTLY HOMELESS: Apartment owner George Riker and commercial building owner Rick Sather interviews with Dedman, February 22, 2013. Documentary photographer Elijah Solomon unearthed details about Tim Gray's life in Evanston, Wyoming, and published photos in "The Winter of Timothy Gray," January 2013, http://www.elijahsol.com/ stories/the-winter-of-timothy-henry-gray/.

332 "I DO IN FACT BELIEVE": Clare Albert interview with Dedman, February 2013.

333 THAT ADMINISTRATOR'S ATTORNEYS: The New York County public administrator is Ethel J. Griffin, who was appointed by Surrogate Kristin Booth Glen as temporary administrator of the Clark estate. The private attorneys hired by the public administrator to handle the legal work are Peter S. Schram, of Schram & Graber, who had been involved in the Wallace case, and the firm of Milbank, Tweed, Hadley & McCloy.

333 NO GIFT TAX RETURNS: The attorneys for the public administrator laid out the tax deficiencies in court papers. The attorney's petition is available online at http://msnbcmedia.msn.com/i/msnbc/Sections/NEWS/huguette _clark_public_administrator_petition.pdf. See also Bill Dedman, "Tax Fraud Alleged in Estate of Heiress Huguette Clark; accountant resigns," msnbc.com, December 21, 2011, http://openchannel.nbcnews.com/_news/ 2011/12/21/9615401-tax-fraud-alleged-in-estate-of-heiress-huguette-clark -accountant-resigns, and Bill Dedman, "Judge Bounces Attorney and Accountant from Estate of Heiress Huguette Clark," msnbc.com, December 23, 2011, http://openchannel.nbcnews.com/_news/2011/12/23/9659274-judge -bounces-attorney-and-accountant-from-estate-of-heiress-huguette-clark.

333 KAMSLER WAS RESPONSIBLE: HMC papers and public administrator's petition.

333 BOCK SAID THAT WHEN NOTICES: Wally Bock, testimony, March 22 and 23 and July 24–26, 2012, Depositions.

335 WHEN KAMSLER WAS CALLED: Irving Kamsler, May 8 and 9 and July 17–19, 2012, Depositions.

336 THE PUBLIC ADMINISTRATOR ALSO AGGRESSIVELY WENT AFTER: Public administrator's petition. See also Bill Dedman, "Staff Bled $44 Million in Gifts from Heiress Huguette Clark, Suit Says," msnbc.com, May 23, 2012, http://openchannel.nbcnews.com/_news/2012/05/23/11824035-staff-bled -44-million-in-gifts-from-heiress-huguette-clark-suit-says.

336 "TO SUGGEST THAT THESE GIFTS": John Dadakis, statement to press, May 22, 2012.

338 A SPECIFIC DIAGNOSIS: Jerry Gray described his diagnosis in his testimony, November 13, 2012, Depositions.

339 "HUGUETTE WAS A SCHIZOID": Ibid.

339 THE DIAGNOSTIC MANUAL: The diagnostic criteria for schizoid personality disorder are listed in *Diagnostic and Statistical Manual of Mental Disorders*, 4th ed., text revision (Washington, DC: American Psychiatric Association, 2000), 694–97, summarized as "A pervasive pattern of detachment from social relationships and a restricted range of expression of emotions in interpersonal settings, beginning by early adulthood and present in a variety of contexts, as indicated by four (or more) of the following: (1) neither desires nor enjoys close relationships, including being part of a family; (2) almost always chooses solitary activities; (3) has little, if any, interest in having sexual experiences with another person; (4) takes pleasure in few, if any, activities; (5) lacks close friends or confidants other than first-degree relatives; (6) appears indifferent to the praise or criticism of others; (7) shows emotional coldness, detachment, or flattened affectivity." The manual cautions, on page xxxi, that it classifies disorders (schizoid personality disorder), not people (a schizoid). It cautions, on page xxxii, that "the valid application of the diagnostic criteria included in this manual necessitates an evaluation that directly accesses the information," as in a direct examination of the patient. And the manual offers a cautionary statement, on page xxxvii: "The proper use of these criteria requires specialized clinical training that provides both a body of knowledge and clinical skills."

339 "AN IRRATIONAL PATTERN": Ibid.

339 "CANNOT BE DESTROYED": Estate of Wright, 7 Cal. 2d 348 (1936). The California Supreme Court, in a ruling often cited in New York and other states, reversed the order of the trial court denying admission of a will to probate. The witnesses had expressed the view that the testator was of unsound mind, because the testator was queer; he did not have in mind the legal description of his property; he had had a serious operation; his

living quarters were dirty; he gave a witness a fish soaked in kerosene; he insisted on buying furniture not for sale; he turned the hose on children; he was drunk much of the time; an accidental injury to his head seemed to change him; he ran out of the house only partly dressed; he picked up articles from garbage cans and hid them around the house; he put paper flowers on rosebushes; he left home without explanation; he recovered gifts from donees without explanation; he falsely told of fictitious gifts to donees; he failed to acknowledge his grandson; he held his breath and appeared to be dead; he malingered in the use of a wheelchair; he kept bottles under his bed; he failed to buy medicine; he failed to keep engagements; and he was unkindly. The court said, "The foregoing sets forth the full strength of contestant's case. Tested by the decisions of this court the judgment is wholly without evidentiary support. There is no evidence that testator suffered from settled insanity, hallucinations or delusions. Testamentary capacity cannot be destroyed by showing a few isolated acts, foibles, idiosyncrasies, moral or mental irregularities or departures from the normal unless they directly bear upon and have influenced the testamentary act."

341 IT WAS OCTOBER 25, 2005: Dr. Louise Klebanoff described her two visits with Huguette in her testimony, August 31, 2012, Depositions. Her visits are also recorded in HMC medical records.

343 THE CORCORAN ALSO COMPLICATED: The Corcoran Gallery's opposition to the will was filed on April 16, 2012.

345 "SHE DIDN'T HAVE A CHARITABLE BONE": Several relatives made this comment in interviews with Dedman.

346 THE ELEGANT FORMER DIPLOMAT: André Baeyens, testimony, October 8 and 9, 2012, Depositions. According to the transcript, the attorneys traveling to Vienna were Angelo M. Grasso, representing Hadassah Peri; John R. Morken, representing the nineteen family members objecting to Huguette Clark's will; and Stacie P. Nelson, representing Wally Bock, the presenter of the will. The family opposed forcing Baeyens to testify.

348 HEDGE FUND MANAGER BOAZ WEINSTEIN: Weinstein, known as one of the quantitative traders, or quants, on Wall Street, had just made far more in a well-publicized trade. When JPMorgan Chase, Huguette's bank, lost billions in 2012 because of bad bets by a trader known as "the London Whale," Weinstein was the largest winner on the positive side of those trades.

349 A JURY TRIAL: Updates on the estate contest can be found at http://NBCnews.com/clark.

Epilogue: The Cricket

358 HUGUETTE RECITED A POEM: Dr. Henry Singman testified about Huguette reciting the poem in three languages in his testimony, August 16 and 20, 2012, Depositions.

358 "THE CRICKET": This translation of "Le Grillon" is adapted, with a few modifications to modernize, from *Douze Fables: Avec Traduction Littérale Allemande et Anglaise En Regard Suivies Du Vocabulaire*, Frédéric Edouard Sillig (Vevey, Switzerland: F. Recordon, 1858), 55–59.

SELECTED BIBLIOGRAPHY

Legal Documents and Official Records

Civil War muster rolls and service records from Pennsylvania, Iowa, and Missouri. Searched by staff of Ancestry.com.

Iowa Wesleyan University, now Iowa Wesleyan College, catalogs and enrollment records.

Los Angeles, affidavit of George John Palé regarding W. A. Clark, Jr., August 27, 1935.

Maine death records, 1617–1922, via Ancestry.com.

Montana, District Court of the Second Judicial District, Silver Bow County, 1926, case 7594, in the matter of the estate of William A. Clark, deceased, Alma E. Clark Hines, Effie I. Clark McWilliams, and Addie L. Clark Miller, plaintiffs, v. Anna E. Clark, Huguette Marcelle Clark, Mary C. de Brabant, Katherine L. Morris, Charles W. Clark, William A. Clark, Jr., et al. A transcript in the Newell family collection includes testimony and transcriptions of documents, including portions of the journal of W. A. Clark.

Montana, District Court of the Second Judicial District, Silver Bow County, last will and testament of William A. Clark, Jr., 1934.

New Canaan, Connecticut, assessor records, zoning records, and minutes of the Planning and Zoning Commission, relating to 104 Dan's Highway.

New York, County Court, Nassau County. People of the State of New York v. Irving H. Kamsler, case 00532N-2008.

New York, Surrogate's Court of New York County, case 1995-1375A, the estate of Huguette M. Clark, 2011–. Beyond the material filed in court, the authors have reviewed the deposition testimony of more than fifty witnesses.

New York, Surrogate's Court of New York County, the last will and testament of Anna E. Clark, 1963.

New York, Surrogate's Court of New York County, the last will and testament of William Andrews Clark, 1925. Copy at http://msnbcmedia.msn.com/i/msnbc/Sections/NEWS/William_Clark_Will.pdf.

New York City Office of the City Register, property records related to 907 Fifth Avenue.

New York Department of Education, Office of the Professions, disciplinary record of Irving Kamsler. License no. 030909, calendar no. 25303, action date February 8, 2011.

Passenger ship records, via Ancestry.com.

Passport applications, W. A. Clark, Anna Clark, and Huguette Clark. W.A.'s application is available through Ancestry.com. Anna and Huguette's are among Huguette's papers.

Proceedings and Debates of the Constitutional Convention Held in the City of Helena, Montana, July 4th, 1889, August 17th, 1889. Helena: State Publishing, 1921.

Reno, Nevada, Second Judicial District Court, divorce decree, William Gower and Huguette M. Clark Gower, August 11, 1930.

Rouen, France, records for the Cemetery Monumental, tomb of Etienne A. de Villermont.

Santa Barbara County, California, marriage license for William Gower and Huguette Marcelle Clark, August 18, 1929.

Santa Barbara County, California, Treasurer–Tax Collector, records relating to 1407 East Cabrillo Boulevard.

U.S. Census records for 1870, 1880, 1900, 1910, 1920, 1930, 1940.

U.S. Congress. *Report of the Committee on Privileges and Elections of the United States Senate Relative to the Right and Title of William A. Clark to a Seat as Senator from the State of Montana.* 56th Cong., 1st sess. 3 vols. Washington, DC, 1900.

U.S. Congress. "Resignation Remarks of Senator W. A. Clark." *Congressional Record.* 56th Cong., 1st sess. Vol. 33, May 15, 1899.

Woodlawn Cemetery, the Bronx, New York City, lot cards and records for the W. A. Clark mausoleum.

Manuscript Collections

Butte Silver Bow Arts Foundation, Butte, MT.

Butte–Silver Bow Public Archives, Butte, MT.

Clarkdale Heritage Museum, Clarkdale, AZ.

Connellsville Area Historical Society, Connellsville, PA.

Corcoran Gallery of Art, Washington, DC.

Dunbar Historical Society, Dunbar, PA.

Durand-Ruel & Co., Paris.

Girl Scout National Historic Preservation Center, New York.

Grand Lodge of Ancient Free and Accepted Masons of Montana, Helena.

Harry S. Truman Library and Museum, Independence, MO.

Jerome Historical Society, Jerome, AZ.

Library of Congress, Washington, DC.

Mark Twain Project, University of California, Berkeley.

Montana Historical Society Research Center, Helena.

Montecito Historical Archives, Montecito Association, CA.

Museum of New Zealand Te Papa Tongarewa, Wellington, NZ.

Museum of the City of New York, New York.

National Archives and Records Administration, Washington, DC.

New Canaan Historical Society, New Canaan, CT.

New-York Historical Society, New York.

Northern Arizona University, Flagstaff.

Paul Clark Home, Butte, MT.

Santa Barbara Historical Museum, Santa Barbara, CA.

Save Our Seminary, Silver Spring, MD.

Seeley G. Mudd Manuscript Library, Princeton University, Princeton, NJ.

University of Nevada, Las Vegas.

University of Virginia Law School Foundation, Charlottesville.

William Andrews Clark Memorial Library, University of California, Los Angeles (UCLA).

World Museum of Mining, Butte, MT.

Letters and Other Unpublished Writings

Abascal, Elizabeth Clark. Unpublished memoir by W. A. Clark's sister, provided by her daughters, Mary Abascal and Anita Mackenzie.

Anderson, J. H. Letter from Anderson to John A. Stewart, March 13, 1925. Anderson was W. A. Clark's personal secretary; Stewart worked at the Sulgrave Institution, which fostered friendship among English-speaking peoples. The letter contains a biographical sketch of Anderson's recently deceased employer and mentions that W.A. was a supporter of the institution's efforts.

Beth Israel Medical Center. Medical records of Huguette Clark, 1991–2011.

Clark, Huguette. Personal papers, including drafts of her correspondence, and letters and financial documents received. They include more than four thousand pages in French, translated for the authors by Guillaine Dale Farrell.

Clark, W. A. "Biographical Sketch of W. A. Clark of Butte City, Montana." General office of William A. Clark, Butte, 1893.

———. "Early Days in Montana: Being Some Reminiscences Dictated by Senator William A. Clark and Written Down by Frank Harmon Garver," typewritten pages in the collection of the Montana Historical Society Research Center.

———. Letters to artist Paul Wayland Bartlett concerning plans for the Clark mausoleum at Woodlawn Cemetery in the Bronx, NY. Library of Congress.

———. Letters to W. M. Bickford, Martin Maginnis, and John S. M. Neill, collection of the Montana Historical Society Research Center.

Clark, W. A., Jr. Letters to George John Palé.

Grandjany, Marcel. Compositions in the collection of Kathleen Bride, Eastman School of Music, University of Rochester, Rochester, NY.

McCord, Beverly Bonner. "The Senator's Kin." Unpublished article of Clark history.

Newell, Paul Clark, Sr. Draft passages for a biography of W. A. Clark.

Speeches

Baeyens, André. "From Copper to Corot: The Two Lives of William Andrews Clark, Senator of Montana." President's Lecture Series, University of Montana, Missoula, October 10, 2005. A video is available for viewing in the Maureen and Mike Mansfield Library there.

Clark, W. A. Address to the Semi-Centennial Celebration of the Grand Lodge of Montana, Virginia City, 1916.

———. Address to the Society of Montana Pioneers, Livingston, September 5–7, 1917.

———. Address to the Society of Montana Pioneers, Deer Lodge, 1923.

———. Addresses to the Society of Montana Pioneers, *The Butte Miner,* March 3, 1925.

Gower, William B. "Depletion of Mines in Relation to Invested Capital." Paper presented at Conference on Mine Taxation, Annual Convention of American Mining Congress, Denver, November 16, 1920.

Books

Allen, James B. *The Company Town in the American West.* Norman: University of Oklahoma Press, 1966.

Alpern, Andrew. *Apartments for the Affluent: A Historical Survey of Buildings in New York.* New York: McGraw-Hill, 1975.

———. *Luxury Apartment Houses of Manhattan: An Illustrated History.* New York: Dover, 1992.

———. *The New York Apartment Houses of Rosario Candela and James Carpenter.* New York: Acanthus Press, 2001.

American Psychiatric Association. *Diagnostic and Statistical Manual of Mental Disorders,* fourth edition, text revision. Washington, DC: American Psychiatric Association, 2000.

Astle, John. *Only in Butte: Stories of the Hill.* Butte, MT: Holt, 2004.

Baeyens, André. *Le Sénateur Qui Aimait La France: Une Histoire des Relations Franco-Américaines.* Paris: Scali, 2005.

Barsness, Larry. *Gold Camp: Alder Gulch and Virginia City, Montana*. New York: Hastings House, 1962.

Bettman, Otto. *The Good Old Days—They Were Terrible!* New York: Random House, 1974.

Birchard, Robert S. *Silent-Era Filmmaking in Santa Barbara*. Charleston, SC: Arcadia, 2007.

Birney, Hoffman. *Vigilantes*. New York: Grosset and Dunlap, 1929.

Bond, Marshall, Jr. *Adventures with Peons, Princes & Tycoons*. Oakland, CA: Star Rover House, 1983.

Brewer, James W. *Jerome, A Story of Mines and Men*. 15th ed. Tucson, AZ: Southwest Parks and Monuments Association, 1979.

Bryant, William Cullen. *Thanatopsis and a Forest Hymn*. Boston: Joseph Knight, 1893.

Buck, Pearl S. *The Hidden Flower*. New York: John Day, 1952.

Burlingame, Merrill G. *The Montana Frontier*. Helena, MT: State Publishing, 1942.

Byrkit, James W. *Forging the Copper Collar: Arizona's Labor-Management War, 1901–1921*. Tucson: University of Arizona Press, 1982.

Calkins, Ray, ed. *Looking Back from the Hill: Recollections of Butte People*. Butte, MT: Butte Historical Society, 1982.

Callaway, Lew L. *Early Montana Masons*. Billings, MT: Western Litho-Print Press, 1951.

———. *Montana's Righteous Hangmen: The Vigilantes in Action*. Norman: University of Oklahoma Press, 1982.

Chesarek, Frank, and Jim Brabeck, eds. *Montana: Two Lane Highway in a Four Lane World*. Missoula, MT: Mountain Press, 1978.

Connolly, C. P. *The Devil Learns to Vote*. New York: Covici, 1938.

Conway, William E., and Robert Stevenson. *William Andrews Clark, Jr.: His Cultural Legacy*. Los Angeles: William Andrews Clark Memorial Library, 1985.

Coyle, Laura, and Dare Myers Hartwell. *Antiquities to Impressionism: The William A. Clark Collection*. London: Corcoran Gallery of Art, 2001.

Craven, Wayne. *Gilded Mansions*. New York: W. W. Norton, 2009.

Davis, George Wesley. *Sketches of Butte, from Vigilante Days to Prohibition*. Boston: Cornill, 1921.

Dimsdale, Thomas J. *The Vigilantes of Montana, or Popular Justice in the Rocky Mountains*. Norman: University of Oklahoma Press, 1953.

Dunaway, Wayland F. *The Scotch-Irish of Colonial Pennsylvania*. Chapel Hill: University of North Carolina Press, 1944.

Edmondson, Mary Dillon. *Profiles in Leadership: A History of the Spence School, 1892–1992*. West Kennebunk, ME: Phoenix, 1991.

Egan, Timothy. *The Big Burn: Teddy Roosevelt and the Fire That Saved America*. Boston: Mariner Books, 2009.

Emmons, David M. *The Butte Irish: Class and Ethnicity in an American Mining Town, 1875–1925*. Urbana: University of Illinois Press, 1989.

Everett, George. *Champagne in a Tin Cup: Uptown Butte and the Stories Behind the Facades*. Butte, MT: Outback Ventures, 1995.

Finn, David. *Sculpture at the Corcoran: Photographs by David Finn*. With Susan Joy Slack. Washington, DC: Ruder Finn Press, 2002.

Freeman, Harry C. *A Brief History of Butte, Montana*. 1900. Reprint, Caldwell, ID: Caxton Printers, 1969.

Gibson, Richard I. *Lost Butte, Montana*. Charleston, SC: History Press, 2012.

———. *Map: Ethnic Butte*. Butte, MT: Gibson Consulting, 2008.

———. *Mining Matters: The Why, What, How, and Where of Mining*. Butte, MT, 2008.

———, ed. *Vernacular Architecture Forum, 2009: Butte and Southwest Montana*. Butte, MT: Vernacular Architecture Forum, 2009.

Glasscock, Carl Burgess. *The War of the Copper Kings: Builders of Butte and Wolves of Wall Street*. Indianapolis: Bobbs-Merrill, 1935.

Hamilton, James McClellan. *From Wilderness to Statehood: A History of Montana*. Portland, OR: Binfords and Mort, 1957.

Hedges, Cornelius. "Freemasonry in the State of Montana." In John Milton Hodson, William H. Upton, Jonas W. Brown, and Cornelius Hedges, *Masonic History of the Northwest*. History Publishing, 1902. Available online at http://www.freemason.com/library/norwst29.htm.

Hoffman, Hortense. *Long Beach from Sand to City*. Long Beach, CA: Royal Press, 1957.

Holbrook, Stewart H. *The Age of the Moguls: The Age of the Robber Barons and the Great Tycoons*. New York: Random House, 1985.

Howard, Joseph Kinsey. *Montana: High, Wide, and Handsome*. New Haven, CT: Yale University Press, 1959.

Hugo, Victor. *Les Misérables*. New York: Carleton, 1863.

Hutchens, John K. *One Man's Montana: An Informal Portrait of a State*. New York: J. B. Lippincott, 1964.

Hyslop, Donald, Alastair Forsyth, and Sheila Jemima. *Titanic Voices: Memories from the Fateful Voyage*. Phoenix Mill, UK: Sutton, 1997.

Important Dolls, Teddy Bears, Toys and Automata, London, Tuesday 18th May 1993. Auction catalog. London: Sotheby's, 1993.

James, Don. *Butte's Memory Book*. Caldwell, ID: Caxton Printers, 1975.

Jensen, Kristin H. *The Diary of a Dean: Excerpts from the Private Journal of William Minor Lile*. Charlottesville: University of Virginia Law Library, 2011.

Joralemon, Ira B. *Romantic Copper: Its Lure and Lore*. New York: D. Appleton-Century, 1934.

Josephson, Matthew. *The Robber Barons*. New York: Harcourt, Brace, 1934.

Kaplan, Fred. *The Singular Mark Twain*. New York: Doubleday, 1937.

Kaplan, Justin. *Mr. Clemens and Mark Twain: A Biography*. New York: Simon and Schuster, 2003.

Kathrens, Michael C. *Great Houses of New York, 1880–1930*. New York: Acanthus Press, 2005.

Kearney, Pat. *Butte's Pride: The Columbia Gardens*. Butte, MT: Skyhigh Communications, 1994.

———. *Butte Voices: Mining, Neighborhoods, People*. Butte, MT: Aircraft Printers, 1998.

King, Constance Eileen. *Jumeau: Prince of Dollmakers*. Cumberland, MD: Hobby House Press, 1983.

Klein, Maury. *The Life and Legend of E. H. Harriman*. Chapel Hill: University of North Carolina Press, 2000.

Klepper, Michael, and Robert Gunther. *The Wealthy 100: From Benjamin Franklin to Bill Gates—A Ranking of the Richest Americans, Past and Present*. Secaucus, NJ: Carol, 1996.

La Fontaine, Jean de. *Fables of La Fontaine*. Illustrated by Félix Lorioux. 1927. Reprint, New York: Dover, 2012.

Langford, Nathaniel P. *Vigilante Days and Ways: The Pioneers of the Rockies*. Helena, MT: American and World Geographic, 1996.

Lawson, Thomas W. *Frenzied Finance: The Crime of Amalgamated*. New York: Ridgway-Thayer, 1905.

Lebrun, Yves, and Claudine Lebrun. *Fables and Fantasies: The Art of Félix Lorioux*. Washington, DC: Trust for Museum Exhibitions, 1992.

Lewis, Sharon E. *Butte Under the Hill: A Brief Introduction to Mining and Geology*. Butte: Montana College of Mineral Science and Technology, 1989.

Limerick, Patricia Nelson. *The Legacy of Conquest: The Unbroken Past of the American West*. New York: W. W. Norton, 1987.

Lukas, J. Anthony. *Big Trouble: A Murder in a Small Western Town Sets Off a Struggle for the Soul of America*. New York: Simon and Schuster, 1997.

Magnificent Jewels. April 17, 2012, auction catalog. New York: Christie's, 2012.

Malone, Michael P. *The Battle for Butte: Mining and Politics on the Northern Frontier, 1864–1906*. Seattle: University of Washington Press, 1981.

Malone, Michael P., and Richard B. Roeder, eds. *The Montana Past: An Anthology*. Missoula: University of Montana Press, 1969.

Mangam, William D. *The Clarks of Montana*. Washington, DC: Service Printing, 1939.

———. *The Clarks: An American Phenomenon*. New York: Silver Bow Press, 1941.

Marcosson, Isaac. *Anaconda*. New York: Dodd, Mead, 1957.

Mather, R. E., and F. E. Boswell. *Hanging the Sheriff: A Biography of Henry Plummer*. Missoula: Historic Montana, 1998.

Maugham, W. Somerset. *Of Human Bondage*. New York: Grosset and Dunlap, 1915.

McCracken, Robert D. *Las Vegas: The Great American Playground*. Las Vegas: University of Nevada Press, 1996.

McCutcheon, Marc. *Everyday Life in the 1800s: A Guide for Writers, Students and Historians*. Cincinnati: Writers Digest Books, 1993.

McGrath, Jean, ed. *Butte's Heritage Cookbook*. Butte, MT: Butte–Silver Bow Bicentennial Commission, 1976.

McNelis, Sarah. *Copper King at War: The Biography of F. Augustus Heinze*. Missoula: University of Montana Press, 1968.

Metcalfe, June M. *Copper: The Red Metal*. New York: Viking Press, 1946.

Miller, Joaquin. *An Illustrated History of the State of Montana*. 2 vols. Chicago: Lewis, 1894.

Montana: Its Climate, Industries and Resources. Helena, MT: Geo. E. Boos, 1884.

Montana Writer's Project. *Copper Camp: The Lusty Story of Butte, Montana, the Richest Hill on Earth*. Helena, MT: Riverbend, 1943.

Murphy, Clyde Francis. *The Glittering Hill*. New York: Doubleday, 1944.

Murphy, Jere. *The Comical History of Montana*. San Diego: E. L. Scofield, 1912.

Murphy, Mary. *Mining Cultures: Men, Women, and Leisure in Butte, 1914–41*. Urbana: University of Illinois Press, 1997.

Myrick, David F. *Montecito and Santa Barbara*. Vol. 1, *From Farms to Estates*. Pasadena, CA: Pentrex Media Group, 1988.

———. *Montecito and Santa Barbara*. Vol. 2, *The Days of the Great Estates*. Glendale, CA: Trans-Angelo Books, 1991.

O'Farrell, P. A. *Butte: Its Copper Mines and Copper Kings*. New York: James A. Rogers, 1899.

O'Malley, Richard K. *Mile High Mile Deep*. Livingston, MT: Clark City Press, 2004.

Pace, Dick. *Golden Gulch: The Story of Montana's Fabulous Alder Gulch*. Self-published, 1962.

Paher, Stanley W. *Las Vegas: As It Began—As It Grew*. Las Vegas: Nevada Publications, 1971.

Paris, Leslie. *Children's Nature: The Rise of the American Summer Camp*. New York: NYU Press, 2008.

Pate, Alan Scott. *Ningyo: The Art of the Japanese Doll*. Boston: Tuttle, 2005.

Paul, Rodman Wilson. *Mining Frontiers of the Far West, 1848–1880*. Rev. ed. Albuquerque: University of New Mexico Press, 2001.

Peterson, Richard H. *The Bonanza Kings: The Social Origins and Business Behavior of Western Mining Entrepreneurs, 1870–1900*. Norman: University of Oklahoma Press, 1971.

———. *Bonanza Rich: Lifestyles of the Western Mining Entrepreneurs*. Moscow: University of Idaho Press, 1991.

Pfouts, Paris Swazy. *Four Firsts for a Modest Hero: The Autobiography of Paris Swazy Pfouts*. Helena: Grand Lodge of Ancient Free and Accepted Masons of Montana, 1968.

Place, Marian T. *The Copper Kings of Montana*. New York: Random House, 1961.

Powell, Ada. *The Dalys of the Bitter Root*. Self-published, 1989.

Progressive Men of the State of Montana. Chicago: A. W. Bowen, 1902.

Punke, Michael. *Fire and Brimstone: The North Butte Mining Disaster of 1917*. New York: Hyperion, 2006.

Purple, Edwin Ruthven. *Perilous Passage: A Narrative of the Montana Gold Rush, 1862–1863*. Helena: Montana Historical Society Press, 1995.

Quinn, Frank. *Memories of Columbia Gardens*. Self-published, 1975.

Raymer, Robert George. *A History of Copper Mining in Montana*. New York: Lewis, 1930.

Rodda, Jeanette, and Nancy R. Smith. *Experience Jerome: The Moguls, Miners and Mistresses of Cleopatra Hill*. Sedona, AZ: Thorne, 1990.

Rolle, Andrew, ed. *The Road to Virginia City: The Diary of James Knox Polk Miller*. Norman: University of Oklahoma Press, 1989.

Sale, Reno H. *Underground Warfare at Butte*. Caldwell, ID: Caxton Printers, 1964.

Sanders, Helen Fitzgerald. *A History of Montana*. Vol. 1. Chicago: Lewis, 1913.

———, ed. *X. Beidler: Vigilante*. Norman: University of Oklahoma Press, 1957.

Sanders, W. F., II, and Robert T. Taylor. *Biscuits and Badmen: The Sanders' Story in Their Own Words*. Butte, MT: Editorial Review Press, 1983.

Secrest, Meryle. *Duveen*. New York: Alfred A. Knopf, 2004.

Shoebotham, Hiram Minar. *Anaconda: The Life of Marcus Daly*. Harrisburg, PA: Stackpole, 1956.

Signor, John R. *The Los Angeles and Salt Lake Railroad: Union Pacific's Historic Salt Lake Route*. San Marino, CA: Golden West Books, 1988.

Sillig, Frédéric Edouard. *Douze Fables: Avec Traduction Littérale Allemande et Anglaise en Regard Suivies du Vocabulaire*. Vevey, Switzerland: F. Recordon, 1858.

Silver, Nathan. *Lost New York*. New York: Schocken Books, 1967.

Smith, David Lennox. *Murray M. Harris and Organ Building in Los Angeles, 1894–1913*. Richmond, VA: Organ Historical Society, 2005.

Spence, Clark C. *Territorial Politics and Government in Montana, 1864–89*. Chicago: University of Illinois Press, 1975.

Swibold, Dennis L. *Copper Chorus: Mining, Politics, and the Montana Press, 1889–1959*. Helena: Montana Historical Society Press, 2006.

Tarbell, Ida M. *All in the Day's Work*. New York: Macmillan, 1939.

Temianka, Henri. *Facing the Music: An Inside View of the Real Concert World*. Sherman Oaks, CA: Alfred, 1980.

Toole, John H. *The Baron, the Logger, the Miner, and Me*. Edited by William H. Forbis. Missoula, MT: Mountain Press, 1984.

Toole, Kenneth Ross. *Montana: An Uncommon Land*. Norman: University of Oklahoma Press, 1959.

Twain, Mark. *Autobiography of Mark Twain*. Edited by Harriet Elinor Smith et al. Vol. 1. Berkeley: University of California Press, 2010.

————. *Mark Twain in Eruption.* Edited by Bernard De Voto. New York: Harper and Brothers, 1940.

————. *Mark Twain's Correspondence with Henry Huttleston Rogers, 1893–1909.* Edited by Lewis Leary. Berkeley: University of California Press, 1969.

Tyer, Brad. *Opportunity, Montana: Big Copper, Bad Water, and the Burial of an American Landscape.* Boston: Beacon Press, 2013.

The United Verde Copper Company: A Series of Articles Describing the Organization, Operations, and Activities of This Company in the Jerome District of Arizona. Washington, DC: Mining Congress Journal, 1930.

Waldie, D. J. *Holy Land: A Suburban Memoir.* New York: St. Martin's Press, 1986.

Watson, Wendy M. *Italian Renaissance Maiolica from the William A. Clark Collection.* London: Scala Books, 1986.

Whiteside, Fred. *Three Hundred Grand: The Highlights of One Man's Life.* Bozeman, MT: Color World of Montana, 1980.

Wildman, Edwin. *Famous Leaders of Industry: The Life Stories of Boys Who Have Succeeded.* Boston: Page, 1920.

Willard, Daniel Everett. *Montana: The Geological Story.* Lancaster, PA: Science Press, 1935.

William Andrews Clark Memorial Library: Report of the First Decade, 1934–1944. Berkeley: University of California Press, 1946.

Wolle, Muriel Sibell. *Montana Pay Dirt: A Guide to the Mining Camps of the Treasure State.* Denver: Sage Books, 1963.

Wyman, Mark. *Hard Rock Epic: Western Miners and the Industrial Revolution, 1860–1910.* Berkeley: University of California Press, 1979.

Yellowstone Art Center. *The William A. Clark Collection: Treasures of a Copper King.* Billings, MT: Yellowstone Art Center, 1989.

Young, Herbert. *Ghosts of Cleopatra Hill: Men and Legends of Old Jerome.* Jerome, AZ: Jerome Historical Society, 1964.

————. *They Came to Jerome: The Billion Dollar Copper Camp.* Jerome, AZ: Jerome Historical Society, 1972.

Dissertations and Theses

Brogdon, J. Carl. "The History of Jerome, Arizona." Master's thesis, University of Arizona, 1952.

Farrell, Mary M. "William Andrews Clark." Master's thesis, University of Washington, 1933.

Foor, Forrest L. "The Senatorial Aspirations of William A. Clark, 1898–1901: A Study in Montana Politics." Ph.D. diss., University of California, 1941.

Peterson, Helen Palmer. "Landscapes of Capital: Culture in an Industrial Western

Company Town, Clarkdale, Arizona, 1914–1929." Ph.D. diss., Northern Arizona University, 2008.

Pitts, Stanley Thomas. "An Unjust Legacy: A Critical Study of the Political Campaigns of William Andrews Clark, 1888–1901." Master's thesis, University of North Texas, 2006.

Rodda, Jeanette. "William Andrews Clark: A Biography." Master's thesis, Northern Arizona University, 1990.

Articles and Essays

Bybee, Jay S. "Ulysses at the Mast: Democracy, Federalism, and the Sirens' Song of the Seventeenth Amendment." *Northwestern University Law Review* 91, no. 2 (Winter 1997). Available online at http://scholars.law.unlv.edu/facpub/350.

Clark, Helen. "Copper King in a Mining Camp." *Old West,* Spring 1973.

Connolly, C. P. "The Story of Montana." Pts. 1–5. *McClure's Magazine,* August 1906–July 1907.

Conviser, Josh. "The House on the Hill." *Santa Barbara Magazine,* September 2009.

Dean, Patty, ed. "Coming Home: A Special Issue Devoted to the Historic Built Environment and Landscapes of Butte and Anaconda, Montana." *Drumlummon Views* 3, no. 1 (Spring 2009).

Dedman, Bill. "The Clarks: An American Story of Wealth, Scandal, and Mystery." A series of articles and videos, msnbc.com, NBCNews.com, and the *Today* show, 2010–2013, http://nbcnews.com/clark/.

Doran, Barbara Hoelscher. "Behind the Gates of Bellosguardo." *Santa Barbara Magazine,* Winter 1996.

Gibson, Richard I. "The Nature-Built Landscape: Geological Underpinnings of Butte." Paper presented at Vernacular Architecture Forum Thirtieth Annual Meeting, Butte, MT, 2009. Available online at http://www.gravmag.com/gibson-geology.pdf.

High, James. "William Andrews Clark, Westerner: An Interpretive Vignette." *Arizona and the West* 2 (Autumn 1960).

"The House of Senator Clark." *Architectural Record,* January 1906.

Lynch, Don. "The Clark Family of Los Angeles." Pts. 1 and 2. *The Titanic Commutator,* 15 (Winter 1991) and 16 (May–July 1992).

Malone, Michael P. "Midas of the West: The Incredible Career of William Andrews Clark." *Montana: The Magazine of Western History,* Autumn 1983.

Montana Department of Environmental Quality, Mining District Historical Narratives. http://www.deq.mt.gov/abandonedmines/linkdocs/183tech.mcpx.

Rodda, Jeanette. "William Andrews Clark and Welfare Work in Arizona." *Montana: The Magazine of Western History,* Autumn 1992.

LIST OF ILLUSTRATIONS

In Text

ii–iii ANNA CLARK'S BEDROOM AT BELLOSGUARDO, C. 1940: Karl Obert.

6 W. A. CLARK HOME, NORTHEAST CORNER OF FIFTH AVENUE AND SEVENTY-SEVENTH STREET: Collection of the New-York Historical Society, George P. Hall & Son Photograph Collection, negative 58796.

10 SALON DORÉ, A ROOM FROM THE CLARK MANSION ON FIFTH AVENUE, AT THE CORCORAN GALLERY OF ART, WASHINGTON, D.C., 2013: © Patrice Gilbert.

11 MORNING ROOM IN THE W. A. CLARK MANSION ON FIFTH AVENUE, 1911–27: © Brown Brothers.

15 ANNA, ANDRÉE, AND W. A. CLARK IN THE EASTER PARADE ON FIFTH AVENUE, 1914: International News Service via *The New York Times*.

24 GOLD MINERS IN 1863 IN CENTRAL CITY, COLORADO: Collection of Newell family.

37 KATHERINE LOUISE "KATE" STAUFFER CLARK: Collection of Newell family.

53 W. A. CLARK, SIBLINGS, AND OTHER RELATIVES IN LOS ANGELES, 1908: Collection of Newell family.

56 W. A. CLARK GREETS CITIZENS IN LAS VEGAS FROM HIS PRIVATE RAILCAR, 1905: University of Nevada, Las Vegas, Libraries, Special Collections, image 0001, album 3, 12.2.

69 PIPE ORGAN IN ART GALLERY OF THE W. A. CLARK MANSION ON FIFTH AVENUE: Camera Craft. From the collection of Jim Lewis.

107 HUGUETTE CLARK WITH 1925 GRADUATING CLASS FROM MISS SPENCE'S BOARDING AND DAY SCHOOL FOR GIRLS: Collection of the New-York Historical Society.

109 HUGUETTE CLARK IN INDIAN COSTUME WITH HER FATHER, W. A. CLARK, C. 1912: The Estate of Huguette M. Clark.

118 SHOWGIRLS CLOWNING ON CONSOLE OF PIPE ORGAN, W. A. CLARK MANSION ON FIFTH AVENUE, BEFORE PUBLIC TOURS PRECEDING THE HOME'S DEMOLITION, 1927: © Bettmann/CORBIS, photo U374572INP.

119 BOTTOM OF MARBLE STAIRCASE ON GROUND FLOOR OF W. A. CLARK

MANSION, FIFTH AVENUE, C. 1905: Wurts Brothers, collections of the Museum of the City of New York, negative X2010.7.2.19249.

134 HUGUETTE CLARK POSING WITH CHAIR, C. 1925: The Estate of Huguette M. Clark.

135 WILLIAM M. L. (BILL) GOWER AT PRINCETON, C. 1925: Princeton University Library.

137 HUGUETTE CLARK IN HER WEDDING GOWN: *New York Evening Post*, August 28, 1928, p. 17.

140 NEWSPAPER FEATURE ON GOWER DIVORCE, 1930: International Feature Service, Hamilton Evening Journal.

149 EXTERIOR OF 907 FIFTH AVENUE, 2013: © John Makely. Collection of Bill Dedman.

156 PAUL CÉZANNE, *MADAME CÉZANNE IN A RED DRESS (MADAME CÉZANNE EN ROBE ROUGE)*, C. 1890: Museu de Arte de São Paulo.

163 ETIENNE ALLARD DE VILLERMONT IN 1936: *Stevens Point* (Wisconsin) *Daily Journal*, March 14, 1936.

166 LETTER FROM ETIENNE DE VILLERMONT TO HUGUETTE CLARK, MARCH 21, 1965: The Estate of Huguette M. Clark.

167 CABLE FROM HUGUETTE CLARK TO ETIENNE DE VILLERMONT, JULY 17, 1959: The Estate of Huguette M. Clark.

198 MUSIC ROOM OF BELLOSGUARDO, C. 1940: Karl Obert.

207 FURNITURE COVERED IN LIBRARY OF BELLOSGUARDO, 2011: The Estate of Huguette M. Clark.

209 1933 CADILLAC SEVEN-PASSENGER LIMOUSINE IN THE GARAGE AT BELLOSGUARDO, 2011: The Estate of Huguette M. Clark.

209 1949 LICENSE PLATE ON 1933 CADILLAC AT BELLOSGUARDO, 2011: The Estate of Huguette M. Clark.

214 FRONT OF LE BEAU CHÂTEAU IN NEW CANAAN, CONNECTICUT, 2012: © John Makely. Collection of Bill Dedman.

215 BEDROOM BUILT FOR HUGUETTE CLARK IN THE 1950S AT LE BEAU CHÂTEAU, 2012: © John Makely. Collection of Bill Dedman.

216 PAINTBRUSH MOTIF ON BALUSTER OF STAIRWELL LEADING FROM HUGUETTE CLARK'S BEDROOM TO THE ARTIST'S LOFT AT LE BEAU CHÂTEAU, 2012: © John Makely. Collection of Bill Dedman.

321 W. A. CLARK MAUSOLEUM AT WOODLAWN CEMETERY, THE BRONX, NEW YORK: © Paul Clark Newell, Jr.

344 LETTER FROM HUGUETTE CLARK TO SANTA BARBARA MAYOR SHEILA LODGE, JUNE 10, 1988: Collection of Sheila Lodge.

437 W. A. CLARK, SIBLINGS, AND OTHER RELATIVES IN LOS ANGELES, 1908, WITH IDENTIFICATION KEY: Collection of Newell family.

Insert One (between pages 196 and 197)

HUGUETTE CLARK, C. 1943: The Estate of Huguette M. Clark.

CLARK MANSION IN BUTTE, MONTANA, BUILT 1884–88, 2012: Nicholas K. Geranios © The Associated Press.

HUGUETTE CLARK WITH HER DOLLS ON THE PORCH OF THE CLARK MANSION IN BUTTE, C. 1910–11: Collection of Paul Clark Newell, Jr.

W. A., ANNA, ANDRÉE, AND HUGUETTE CLARK, C. 1912: Collection of Paul Clark Newell, Jr.

ANNA EUGENIA LACHAPELLE CLARK, C. 1912: The Estate of Huguette M. Clark.

SALON DORÉ, A ROOM FROM THE CLARK MANSION ON FIFTH AVENUE, AS INSTALLED AND RENOVATED AT THE CORCORAN GALLERY OF ART, WASHINGTON, D.C., 2001: © Cris Molina.

EDGAR DEGAS, *THE DANCE CLASS* (*ECOLE DE DANSE*), C. 1873: Corcoran Gallery of Art, William A. Clark Collection, 26.74.

W. A. CLARK WITH DAUGHTERS ANDRÉE, LEFT, AND HUGUETTE, AT COLUMBIA GARDENS IN BUTTE, MONTANA, C. 1917: Montana Historical Society Research Center Photograph Archives.

DEMOLITION OF THE W. A. CLARK MANSION AT FIFTH AVENUE AND SEVENTY-SEVENTH STREET, MAY 1927, VIEWED FROM CENTRAL PARK: Philip G. Bartlett, collections of the Museum of the City of New York, negative MNY219182.

Insert Two (between pages 228 and 229)

SELF-PORTRAIT BY HUGUETTE CLARK, UNSIGNED, C. 1928: The Estate of Huguette M. Clark.

PAINTING BY HUGUETTE CLARK OF VIEW DOWN FIFTH AVENUE IN SNOW WITH WINDOW AND JAPANESE LAMP, UNDATED: The Estate of Huguette M. Clark.

PAINTING BY TADÉ STYKA OF HUGUETTE CLARK PAINTING A NUDE MALE MODEL, C. 1925: The Estate of Huguette M. Clark.

PAINTING BY HUGUETTE CLARK OF BAREFOOT GEISHA, UNDATED: The Estate of Huguette M. Clark. Collection of Bill Dedman.

HUGUETTE CLARK, C. 1928: © The Associated Press. (Often cited as 1930 at the time of her divorce, but apparently from 1928 at the time of her honeymoon.)

AERIAL VIEW OF THE CLARK ESTATE, BELLOSGUARDO, IN SANTA BARBARA, CALIFORNIA, AUGUST 2011: © John L. Wiley, http://flickr.com/jw4pix/.

AERIAL VIEW OF SANTA BARBARA BEACHES, BELLOSGUARDO, AND THE ANDRÉE CLARK BIRD REFUGE: © Buddy Moffet.

LIBRARY AT BELLOSGUARDO, C. 1940: Karl Obert.

ANNA CLARK'S BEDROOM AT BELLOSGUARDO, C. 1940: Karl Obert.

ANDRÉE CLARK, C. 1917: Girl Scout National Historic Preservation Center.

ANDRÉE'S COTTAGE, BELLOSGUARDO, 2011: The Estate of Huguette M. Clark.

SIGN AT ANDRÉE'S COTTAGE, BELLOSGUARDO, 2011: The Estate of Huguette M. Clark.

AERIAL VIEW OF LE BEAU CHÂTEAU, HUGUETTE CLARK'S COUNTRY RETREAT IN NEW CANAAN, CONNECTICUT: © Stefenturner.com via Barbara Cleary's Realty Guild.

VINES GROWING THROUGH SHUTTERS OUTSIDE THE KITCHEN WINDOW OF LE BEAU CHÂTEAU, 2013: © John Makely. Collection of Bill Dedman.

Insert Three (between pages 260 and 261)

ETIENNE DE VILLERMONT WITH HIS DAUGHTER, MARIE-CHRISTINE, AND A TOY DONKEY, CADICHON, GIVEN TO HER BY HUGUETTE CLARK, C. 1967: The Estate of Huguette M. Clark.

ANTIQUE FRENCH DOLL BY JUMEAU PURCHASED BY HUGUETTE CLARK ON MAY 18, 1993: Sotheby's, London.

ANTIQUE FRENCH DOLL BY THUILLIER PURCHASED BY HUGUETTE CLARK ON MAY 18, 1993: Sotheby's, London.

MODEL OF AN AUTHENTIC JAPANESE BUILDING CONSTRUCTED FOR HUGUETTE CLARK TO HER DESIGN BY AN ARTIST IN JAPAN: The Estate of Huguette M. Clark.

JAPANESE HINA DOLL OWNED BY HUGUETTE CLARK: The Estate of Huguette M. Clark.

PHOTO OF HUGUETTE CLARK WITH EASTER FLOWERS, C. 1955: The Estate of Huguette M. Clark.

FURNITURE IN HUGUETTE CLARK'S BEDROOM, 907 FIFTH AVENUE, APARTMENT 8W, 2011: The Estate of Huguette M. Clark.

ONE OF THREE CHECKS FOR $5 MILLION WRITTEN TO HADASSAH PERI BY HUGUETTE CLARK: Surrogate's Court of New York County, case 1995-1375A.

HADASSAH PERI: Peri family.

EDGAR DEGAS, DANCER MAKING POINTS (DANSEUSE FAISANT DES POINTES), 1879–80: Nelson-Atkins Museum of Art, Kansas City, Missouri.

VIOLIN "LA PUCELLE" BY ANTONIO STRADIVARI, 1709: The Fulton Collection, © David Fulton.

ART DECO DIAMOND AND MULTI-GEM CHARM BRACELET, C. 1925, OWNED BY HUGUETTE CLARK: Christie's, New York. Other jewelry in her collection is pictured at http://nbcnews.com/clark/.

EMERALD, PEARL, AND DIAMOND EAR PENDANTS BY CARTIER, EARLY TWENTIETH CENTURY, OWNED BY HUGUETTE CLARK: Christie's, New York.

ART DECO DIAMOND BRACELET BY CARTIER, C. 1925, OWNED BY HUGUETTE CLARK: Christie's, New York.

ART DECO EMERALD AND DIAMOND BRACELET BY CARTIER, C. 1925, OWNED BY HUGUETTE CLARK: Christie's, New York.

VIEW FROM THE ROOF OF 907 FIFTH AVENUE, 2013 © John Makely. Collection of Bill Dedman.

VIEW FROM HUGUETTE CLARK'S LAST REGULAR ROOM AT BETH ISRAEL MEDICAL CENTER, ROOM 3K01, THIRD FLOOR, KARPAS PAVILION, 2012: © Bill Dedman.

W. A. Clark is pictured here in 1908 in Los Angeles with most of his siblings, as well as other relatives. The photo without the key appears on page 53.

1. *W. A. Clark.* **2.** *Mary Margaret Miller, W.A.'s sister, who with her husband, Ted, established department stores in Jerome and Clarkdale to serve W.A.'s Arizona mining towns.* **3.** *James Ross "J. Ross" Clark, W.A.'s brother and partner in banking and other businesses.* **4.** *Miriam Evans Clark, wife of J. Ross; Miriam's sister Margaret married Marcus Daly, W.A.'s adversary in Montana business and politics.* **5.** *Walter Clark, son of J. Ross and Miriam, who died four years later, at age twenty-seven, in the sinking of the Titanic.* **6.** *Virginia McDowell Clark, Walter's wife, who survived the Titanic disaster in a lifeboat with Madeleine Astor (Mrs. John Jacob Astor IV) and soon remarried, beginning a battle with her in-laws over custody of her son.* **7.** *Amanda "Elie" Clark, onetime belle of Butte and widow of W.A.'s brother Joseph Kithcart Clark.* **8.** *Anna Belle Clark, unmarried sister of W.A.* **9.** *Effie Ellen "Ella" Clark Newell, youngest sister of W.A. and grandmother of co-author Paul Clark Newell, Jr.* **10.** *The Reverend James Newell, husband of Ella and grandfather of co-author Newell.* **11.** *Elizabeth Clark Abascal, sister of W.A., who traveled to Paris with her two daughters as chaperone for Anna LaChapelle before Anna became W.A.'s second wife.*

12. *Anita Abascal, daughter of Elizabeth, niece of W.A.* **13.** *Mary Abascal, daughter of Elizabeth, niece of W.A.* **14.** *Alice McManus Clark, wife of W. A. Clark, Jr., and stepmother of W.A. III.* **15.** *Paul Clark Newell, nephew of W.A. and father of co-author.* **16.** *W. A. Clark III, grandson of W.A., known by the family as Tertius.* **17.** *Mrs. Groshan, not a relative. The only siblings of W.A. who lived to maturity but who are not pictured here died before 1908: Sarah Ann Clark Boner and Joseph K. Clark.*

APPENDIX: INFLATION ADJUSTMENT

What $1,000 Then Would Be Worth Now

A sum of $1,000 in 1840 had the same buying power as about $23,200 in 2013, according to the tables used by most economists.* To convert a dollar figure in 1840 to today's dollars in rough terms, multiply the older value by 23.2.

1840: $1,000 = $23,200 in 2013 (multiply by 23.2 for today's value)
1850: $1,000 = $27,800 in 2013 (multiply by 27.8)
1860: $1,000 = $25,700 in 2013 (multiply by 25.7)
1870: $1,000 = $18,300 in 2013 (multiply by 18.3)
1880: $1,000 = $23,900 in 2013 (multiply by 23.9)
1890: $1,000 = $25,700 in 2013 (multiply by 25.7)
1900: $1,000 = $27,800 in 2013 (multiply by 27.8)
1910: $1,000 = $24,800 in 2013 (multiply by 24.8)
1920: $1,000 = $11,700 in 2013 (multiply by 11.7)
1930: $1,000 = $14,000 in 2013 (multiply by 14.0)
1940: $1,000 = $16,700 in 2013 (multiply by 16.7)
1950: $1,000 = $9,700 in 2013 (multiply by 9.7)
1960: $1,000 = $7,900 in 2013 (multiply by 7.9)
1970: $1,000 = $6,000 in 2013 (multiply by 6.0)
1980: $1,000 = $2,800 in 2013 (multiply by 2.8)
1990: $1,000 = $1,800 in 2013 (multiply by 1.8)
2000: $1,000 = $1,400 in 2013 (multiply by 1.4)

* These conversions use the consumer price index from the U.S. Bureau of Labor Statistics for the years beginning 1913 and *Historical Statistics of the United States* (Washington, DC: Government Printing Office, 1975) for earlier years. Some researchers contend that these conversions greatly underweight the true change in the value of the dollar.

What $1,000 Now Was Worth Then

A sum of $1,000 in 2013 had the same buying power as about $43 in 1840. To convert between those years, divide the newer value by 23.2.

1840: $43	= $1,000 in 2013 (divide the newer value by 23.2)
1850: $36	= $1,000 in 2013 (divide by 27.8)
1860: $39	= $1,000 in 2013 (divide by 25.7)
1870: $55	= $1,000 in 2013 (divide by 18.3)
1880: $42	= $1,000 in 2013 (divide by 23.9)
1890: $39	= $1,000 in 2013 (divide by 25.7)
1900: $36	= $1,000 in 2013 (divide by 27.8)
1910: $40	= $1,000 in 2013 (divide by 24.8)
1920: $85	= $1,000 in 2013 (divide by 11.7)
1930: $71	= $1,000 in 2013 (divide by 14.0)
1940: $60	= $1,000 in 2013 (divide by 16.7)
1950: $103	= $1,000 in 2013 (divide by 9.7)
1960: $127	= $1,000 in 2013 (divide by 7.9)
1970: $167	= $1,000 in 2013 (divide by 6.0)
1980: $357	= $1,000 in 2013 (divide by 2.8)
1990: $556	= $1,000 in 2013 (divide by 1.8)
2000: $714	= $1,000 in 2013 (divide by 1.4)

INDEX

Page numbers in *italics* refer to illustrations.

Abascal, Anita, 48*n*, 381, *438*
Abascal, Elizabeth "Lib" Clark,
    19–21, 48*n*, 381, *438*
Abascal, Mary, 48*n*, 381, *438*
Adams, John, 19
Adriatic, RMS, 93
Agadir, 94
Agamemnon, HMS, 41
Albert, Agnes Clark, 105, 152, 153,
    154, 157, 158, 305
Albert, Clare, 331–32
Albert, Paul, 315, 325*n*, 400, 414
Alder Gulch, 25
Amalgamated Copper Company,
    85–86
Amati family, 155–56
Ambien, 312
American Friends of New Commu-
    nities in Israel, 272
American Girl (doll), 186
American Mining Congress, 136–37
Amsterdam Nursing Home, 246
Anaconda, Mont., 73, 145
Anaconda Copper Mining
    Company, 73, 85, 142, 145, 193,
    384
Anaconda Smoke Stack State Park,
    145
Anaconda Standard, 59, 76, 78
anarchists, 95
Anderson, Nora S., 349

Andrée Clark Bird Refuge, 199, 346,
    355, 400
annuities, 284
Antibes, 222
antitrust, 86
Antoinette, Marie, 9, 11, 244
Arbuckles', 164
Arc de Triomphe, 112
Architectural Record, 12
Arizona Territory, 50
Armstrong, Alma, xxvii, 208–9,
    261, 355
Armstrong, Walter, xxvii–xxviii,
    138, 194, 204
Arps, Edith von, 178
arsenic, 44
Associated Charities of Butte, 254
Associated Press, 131
Astor, Brooke, 316
Astor, Caroline, 65
Astor, Madeleine, 93, *437*
Astor, Vincent, 119
Astoria, N.Y., 246
Atlantic Richfield Company
    (ARCO), 145
Au Nain Bleu, 174, 179–80, 240,
    244, 355
automatons, mechanical, 244

Baeyens, André, xxi, 310, 325*n*, 327,
    346–47, 355
Baeyens, Jacques, 177
Baeyens-Clerté, Jacqueline, 153,
    325*n*, 414

Baeyens, Patrick, 325*n*, 414
Bannack, Mont., 25–28, 30, 377–78
Barbie dolls, 174, 243, 244
Barbizon school, 68
Barnum, P. T., 12
Bartholdi, Frédéric-Auguste, 42
Bartlett, Paul Wayland, 45
Baugh (miner), 25
Baxter, George White, 220
Beare, Charles, 274, 275
Beasley, W. W., 79
Beau Château, Le, xiii–xiv, xv
Bell, Alexander Graham, 41
Belle Epoque, 94
Bellevue Hospital, 246
Bellosguardo, xv–xvi, xx, xxii,
    xxvii–xxviii, 113–14, 136, 138,
    169, 193–209, *207*, 216, 235, 243,
    251, 294, 300, 332, 343, 349, 355
    cars at, xxviii, 204, *209*
    cost of, 194
    dining room of, 200
    forty-eight-hour rule at, 200, 205
    gardens of, 196, 201–2, 208
    memorials at, 197–99
    music room of, 196–97, *198*
    public fascination with, 193
    in World War II, 203–4
Bellosguardo Foundation, 296, 299,
    326, 338, 345–46, 355
Belmont mine, 97
Bergen, Edgar, 198
Berkeley Pit, 145
Berker, Gurbild, 151
Berle, Milton, 257
Bernhardt, Sarah, 43
Berry, Kip, 325*n*
Berry, William, 325*n*
Beth Israel Medical Center, 279–80,
    282–87, 297, 298, 300, 310, 311,
    325, 326, 343, 345, 346

    conflicts of interest in, 286
    financial difficulties of, 282–83
Beth Israel North, 279–89
Binet, Alfred, 128
Bitterroot Mountains, 31
Bloch, Henry, 291
Bluette (doll), 186
Bobtail Hill, 23
Bock, Wallace "Wally," 266, 267,
    268, 271–72, 273, 274–75, 281,
    286, 289, 292, 294, 305, 312–13,
    314, 316, 317–19, 320, 322, 326,
    331, 333–34, 335, 337, 345, 349
    and Huguette's wills, 294–300
    malpractice claim against, 342
Bonwit Teller, 251
Boutet de Monvel, Louis-Maurice, 7
Boy Scouts, 207, 345
Briarcliff Manor, N.Y., 103
British School of Heraldry, 19
Broadway Theatre (Butte), 43
Bryant, William Cullen, 102
Buck, Pearl S., 185
Buffett, Warren, 114
Bullock, Steve, 386
Burns, Robert, 22
Butte, Mont., 4, 39, 41, 43–44, 47,
    66, 75, 98, 144–46, 254, 380
    Broadway Theatre of, 43
    Columbia Gardens in, 97, 113, 145,
    235
    Copper King Mansion of, 43
    Grand Opera House of, 43–44
    Paul Clark home of, 113, 170,
    254–56
Butte Miner, 43, 75–76, 78

California, University of, Los Angeles,
    143
Calumet, Mich., 47

Camp Andrée Clark, 103–4, 170, 199

Canova, Antonio, 68, 116

Carlson, Hilda, 150

Carnegie, Andrew, 8, 113

Carnegie libraries, 113

Carrere & Hastings, 12

cartoons, 223, 235, 280, 281, 339, 356

Catholicism, 7

cedar, 182

Centennial Exhibition, 41–42

Central City, Colo., 23, *24*

Central Fund of Israel, 272

Cézanne, Paul, 155, 268

Chaplin, Charlie, 120, 133

charitable gift annuity, 284

Charles of London, 126

Chase, William Merritt, 306

Choice of a Model, The (Fortuny), 68

Christian Dior, 177, 180, 355

Chrysanthemums (Renoir), 128

Citibank, 290–91, 348

Citizen Kane, 399

Civil War, U.S., 21–22, 25, 96

Claris de Florian, Jean-Pierre, 11

Clark, Alice McManus, *438*

Clark, Alma, Effie, and Addie, 114–15

Clark, Amanda "Elie," *437*

Clark, Anna Belle, 20*n* , 382, *437*

Clark, Anna Eugenia LaChapelle,
    xvii, xx, xxiii, 3–4, 15, *15*,
    46–49, 59–62, 65, 70, 94, 100,
    111, 117, 235, 254

    Andrée's quarrel with, 98–99

    and Bellosguardo, 194–95, 196–
    97, 200–202, 203–4

    chamber music loved by, 154–58

    deafness of, 154

    death of, 170

    Fifth Avenue apartment of, 125–27,
    132, *149*, 150–51

    friendships of, 148

    goddaughters of, 147–50

    and Huguette's marriage, 135

    and Huguette's wedding, 138

    humor of, 48

    inheritance of, 113–14

    photos of, 4

    politics and, 149

    proof of marriage required from,
    62

    Rancho Alegre bought by, 204

    religion of, 7

    shyness of, 60, 65

    step children and, 152–54

    and Villermont family, 164

    and W.A.'s death, 112–13

Clark, Carr & Ellis, 147, 294

Clark, Charles Walker, 38, 39, 53,
    74, 80, 83, 105, 113, 114–15, 139,
    142, 152

Clark, Christopher, 325*n*

Clark, Francis Paul, 38, 254

Clark, George, 21*n*

Clark, Huguette Marcelle, xv–xvii,
    xxvii–xxviii, 47, 72, *107, 109,*
    137, 159–60, 353–57

    and Andrée's death, 103

    arrival in U.S. of, 3–4

    art collecting by, 128

    as artists' patron, 188–90

    auction days and, 244, 255

    Bellosguardo and, 200–202,
    205–9

    beneficiaries of, 296–300

    cancers of, xxv–xxvi, 227, 230, 232

    cartoons enjoyed by, 223, 235,
    280, 281, 339, 356

    challenges to will of, 325–29,
    337–40

    childhood home of, *see* Clark
    mansion

Clark, Huguette Marcelle (*cont'd*):
childhood summers in France of,
    95–96
Christmas gifts given by, 240
as Corcoran Gallery patron, xx
Corcoran show of, 131
daily hospital routine of, 233–37
death of, xxii, 320–22
as debutante, 134–35, *134*
desire for authenticity by, 182–83
as difficult patient, 229
divorce of, 140–41, 159
Doctors Hospital seclusion of,
    227–76
dolls and dollhouses of, xvi,
    152–53, 177–80, 182–85, 201,
    223, 227, 240, 242–45, 255–56,
    280, 356
dwindling staff of, 223–24
education of, 105–8
Efrat donation of, 271–72
extravagant spending by, 251–53
eyesight of, 235, 315
and father's death, 112–13
Fifth Avenue apartments of, xvi,
    xxv, 125–27, 132, *149*, 150–51,
    219, 223–24, 240–41, 329,
    348–49
French film library of, 223
friendships of, 148
as frightened of new people, 231,
    288
generosity of, 179, 180–81, 186,
    188, 201–2, 207, 249–50, 261
as germophobic, 173
gifts to Peri family by, 260–70
hallucinations of, 316, 342
Hawaiian vacation of, 110–11
hearing of, 235–36
and Hérouard, 188–89
income of, 252

inheritance of, xvii–xviii, 114–15
initial standard assessment of,
    229–30
Japanese dolls of, 183–85
Japanophilia of, 129–31
last known photo of, xix
last photograph of, 169
Le Beau Château and, 213–17
liquid diet of, 234
and Lorioux, 186–90
marriage of, 135–39
mental competence of, 338–42
missing jewelry of, 290–91
money stolen from, 291
monthly expenses of, 247, 251
mother's death and, 170–72
in move to Beth Israel, 288–89
at Mowitza Lodge, 96–97, 98–99
musical instruments collected by,
    218
and Ninta Sandré, 246–48
as outdoor girl, 5
painting by, 128–33, 201
paintings collected by, 218–19
painting stolen from, 291–93
parties thrown by, 106, 135
Paul Clark Home and, 254–56
personal assistant of, *see* Sattler,
    Chris
photography by, 169–70, 200–201
politics and, 149
post-marriage friendship with
    Gower of, 220–22
privacy and, 245, 281, 290
as reclusive, xviii, xx, xxi, 165,
    178, 228, 230, 245, 248, 305,
    315, 354
religion of, 7
remodeling of apartment of,
    238–39
royalty admired by, 244

sale of possessions of, xviii–xix
sales of collections and property
of, 274–76
self-portraits of, 129
settlement negotiations over estate
of, 342–47
shyness of, 109, 111, 155, 159, 224
solitaire played by, 234–35
stepsiblings and, 152–54
surgeries of, 230
taxes owed by, 252, 268, 297
taxes owed by estate of, 333–36
transatlantic trips of, 93–94
and Villermont, 163–75
Wanda Styka and, 257–59
wedding of, 137–38
wills of, xxii, 294–300
Clark, James Ross, 39, 52, 72, 93,
382, *437*
Clark, Jessie, 38
Clark, John, 18–19, 20
Clark, Joseph, 39, 53, 382, *437*
Clark, Katherine Louise, 38, 60, 66,
103, 117, 135–36, 144
Clark, Katherine Louise Stauffer,
37–38, *37*, 44, 61
death of, 45
Clark, Louise Amelia Andrée, xvii,
xxiii, 5, 7–12, *15*, 47, 59, 61,
197, 235
childhood summers in France of,
95–96
diary of, 102–3
Girl Scouts and, 100–101
illness and death of, 101–2
at Mowitza Lodge, 96–97
quarrel with Anna of, 98–99
transatlantic trips of, 93–94
Clark, Mary, 152
Clark, Mary Andrews, 19, 20, 52,
255, 382

Clark, Mary Joaquina, 38, 60, 117
Clark, Miriam Evans, 72, *437*
Clark, Patsey, 152, 330
Clark, Sarah Ann, 19, 382
Clark, Virginia McDowell, 93, *437*
Clark, Walter Miller, 93, 94, *437*
Clark, William, 18–19, 31*n*
Clark, William Anderson, 114–15
Clark, William Andrews, xvii–xviii,
xx, xxiii, 3–12, 15, *15*, *24*, *53*,
56, 93, 97, *109*, 135–36, 349,
437
ambition of, 21
ancestry of, 19
and Andrée's death, 102
art collection of, 44–45, 66–67,
68–69, 116–17
arts interest of, 33
attempted street robbery of, 59
as banker, 39, 40, 41
Bellosguardo bought by, 194
birth of, xviii
bribery by, 75–76, 79–80, 384–85
business holdings of, 52
as businessman, 16
Butte mansion of, 43–44
childhood of, 18–20
Civil War and, 21–22
collapse of empire of, 142–44
in Colorado, 23
copper mining by, 41, 50–51
death of, 112–13
decline of, 111–12
early naiveté of, 25–26
eccentricities of, 57
education of, 20, 21, 375–76
eggs sold by, 27
elected to Senate, 88
entrepreneurship of, 30–31, 38, 41,
50–51
estate of, xvii

Clark, William Andrews (*cont'd*):
Europe trips of, 44–45
family crest created by, 9
female protégées of, 46
gold mining by, 26
honesty of, 38, 86–87
journal of, 31–32
last will and testament of, 112–15, 116
Las Vegas started by, 55–56
legacy of, 144–46
Los Angeles businesses of, 53–54
mail delivery contract of, 30–33
marriage to Anna, 59–62
marriage to Kate, 37
as Mason, 28–29
military commission of, 39
mining claims bought by, 40
in move to Montana, 23–25
near drowning of, 32–33
nervous energy of, 23
and New York mansion, 4–12
Paris apartment of, 48, 93
paternity suit against, 48–49
personality of, 16–17
philanthropy of, 113
political career of, xvii, 16, 71–81
pottery collected by, 67
railroads acquired by, 54
religion and, 7
reputation of, 307
self-assessment of, 146
Senate appointment scheme of, 82–85
Senate election of 1898 and, 74–78
Senate testimony of, 80
social ambitions of, 65–67, 68, 71, 89
as teacher, 21
threats on life of, 44
Twain on, 71

union relations of, 97–98
United Verde and, 50–51
and Vigilantes, 28–29
wealth of, 39, 41, 114, 371–72
westward move of, 20–21
wholesale mercantile business of, 38
work ethic of, 16
World War I and, 95–96
Clark, William Andrews, Jr., 38, 53, 60, 61, 96, 112, 113, 142–44
Clark, William Andrews, III, 144, *438*
Clark County, Nev., 56
Clark Fork, 31, 145
Clark Holding Company, 252
Clark mansion, New York, 4–12, *6*, 65–66, 69, 89, 100, 112, 118–20, 126, 235, 303, 353
art galleries of, 66–67, 69–70, *69*
cost of, 7–8
critics of, 12
demolition of, 120
library of, 11–12
marble staircase of, *119*, 120
morning room of, 10, *11*
pipe organ in, 69–70, *69*, *118*, 120, 383
quarantine suite in, 9, 101
sale of, 118–20
Salon Doré in, 9, *10*, 117, 373–74
sculpture hall of, 67–68
tower of, 9, 12
Clark Road, *see* San Pedro Los Angeles & Salt Lake Railroad
Clarkdale, Ariz., 51, 113, 144
Clarks, The: An American Phenomenon (Mangam), 376
Clinton, Bill, 234
Clover Creek Canyon, 54
Coelho, Alice Gray, 325*n*

Coffey, Geraldine Lehane, 100, 233, 261, 265–66, 321, 402

Cognin, Monsieur, 173–74

Cold War, 213

Columbia College, 40

Columbia Gardens, 97, 113, 145, 235

Colusa mine, 40, 41

Connellsville, Penn., 18, 37

Connick, Harry, Jr., 214, 349

Continuum Health Partners, 282–83

Coolidge, Calvin, 112, 117

copper, 40–41, 43, 44, 50–51, 85–86, 97, 144, 380
  copper mining, xvii, 16, 72, 97

Copper King Mansion, 43–44, 379

Corcoran Gallery of Art, xx, 117, 131, 170, 293, 300, 303–6, 315, 325, 332, 343–46, 395
  Clark family reunion at, 306–7, 311, 411–12

Corliss, John, 386

Corot, Jean-Baptiste-Camille, 68

Corrupt Practices Act (1912), 386

Courbalk, Artine, 187

"Cricket, The" (Florian), 358–59

Cross Keys School, 20

Cruz, Kati Despretz, 234, 265

Cummings, Celia Gray, 325*n*

Curly (goose), 217

Curtis, Cyrus H. K., 114

Curved Dash Oldsmobile, 6

Dadakis, John D., 336

Daly, Marcus, 72, 73, 74, 76, 79, 87, 88, 142, 145, 151, 307, 384

Daly, Margaret Price, 151

Dancer Making Points (Degas), 128, 219, 291–93

Davis, Marvin, 206

Day, E. C., 80

"Dead Man's Statute," 345

Deer Lodge, Mont., 38

Degas, Edgar, 68, 128, 219, 291

Deglane, Henri, 5

De Lobel, Pauline, 150, 223

Democratic National Convention (1896), 48–49

Democratic National Convention (1904), 61

Democrats for Willkie, 149

Denver Post, 48

Devine, Ian Clark, 307, 310–13, 318–19, 325*n*

Devine, Rodney, 325*n*

Dior, Christian, 177, 355

Disney, Walt, 186

divorce, 140–41

Doctors Hospital, xxvi, 227, 229–30, 247, 260, 279, 282, 285, 287, 289
  see also Beth Israel North

Donald Duck, 186

Don Antonio (horse), 204

Donnell, Clark & Larabie, 38

Donnell & Clark, 38

Doran, Barbara Hoelscher, 197, 200, 201–2

Douglas, John C., III, xv, xx, 205, 209, 216, 299

Dreams (Kurosawa), 185

Dresden, 45

Dreyfus, Alfred, 82

Dublin Gulch, 75

Duffy, Margaret, 151

Dunbar Township, Penn., 18–20

Duncan, Isadora, 105–6

Durant, W. C., 126

Dutch John, 28

Duveen, Joseph, 69, 116

Earthenware Jug (Cézanne), 268
Edgerton, Keith, 146
Edison, Thomas, 41
Efrat, 271–72
Ehnes, James, 275
Elder Abuse Unit, 316
Elements of Geology (Hitchcock), 22, 40
Ellis, George, 147–50
Ellwood Oil Field, 203
El Palomar, 142
Empire State Building, 107, 126, 132, 288
Erickson, Anna, 151
erysipelas, 254
estate tax, 308–9
Evanston, Wyo., 330–31
Eve (Rodin), 67
Evry-sur-Seine, 95

Fabrizio, Ann, 224
Family Corner dolls, 244
FAO Schwarz, 223
Farlin, Bill, 41
FBI, 291
Federation of French War Veterans, 227
Fergus County Bank, 80
First Army, German, 96
First National Bank of Deer Lodge, 39, 41
First National City Bank, 290
FitzGerald, Edward, 159
Flatley, Anna, 151
Flintstones, The (cartoon), 223, 235, 281
Florian, Jean-Pierre Claris de, 358–59
Flynn, Errol, 163
Forbes 400, 114
Ford, Henry, 114

Fort Bridger, 23–24
Fortuny, Marià, 68
Fox Software, 275
Franciscan Friars of the Atonement, 170
French Revolution, 9, 176, 190
Friedman, Carla Hall, 304–5, 307, 310–13, 318–19, 325*n*, 411
full metal jacket bullet, 41
Fulton, David, 275, 407

gallows frames, 145
Gambetta mine, 40, 41
Garr, H. H., 79
Gates, Bill, 114
Gates of Hell, The (Rodin), 67
Gehry, Frank, 304
Geiger, John H., 79
General Motors, 126
George V, King of England, 93
George Washington, RMS, 94
Gettysburg, Battle of, 25
gift taxes, 252, 267, 297, 335, 336
Girl Fishing at San Vigilio (Sargent), 219
Girl Scouts, 100–101, 103–4, 170
Girls Playing Battledore and Shuttle-cock (Renoir), 219
Girl with Parasol (Renoir), 218–19
Glass House, 214
Glen, Kristin Booth, 415
Goewey, Mallory Devine, 325*n*
Golden, Shyra, 151
Goldman, Emma, 95
gold rush of 1849, 21
Gonzalez, Martin, 299
Gordon, Irving, 249
Gottlieb, Karen, 236
Gould, Jay, 136
Gower, Constance Toulmin, 220, 222

Gower, William Bleckly, 136–37

Gower, William MacDonald, 135–39, *135*, 141, 220–22, 355, 401–2

Gracie Mansion, 229

Graham, Geraldine, 197, 399

Graham, Lee Eleanor, 193–94, 197

Graham, William Miller, 193, 197

Grand Opera House (Butte), 43

Grandjany, Marcel, 149

Grasshopper Creek, 23

Gray, Christopher, 12

Gray, Jerry, 152, 325*n*, 338–39, 414

Gray, Ruth, 260

Gray, Timothy, 330–31

Great Depression, 128, 144

Greenhalgh, Paul, 306, 411

Greenwich, Conn., 109

Griffin, Ethel J., 415

G. T. Marsh and Company, 183

Gump's San Francisco, 263

Guy, Alma, 100–101

Hall, Jack, 325*n*

Hall, Katherine Morris, 137, 303

Hall, Lewis, 325*n*

H&R Block, 291

Harriman, E. H., 54–55

Harrower, Leontine Lyle, 147–50, 170, 197–99

Hauger, Paula, 151

Hawaii, 110–11, 138, 141, 393

Healey, Delia, 223–24

Hearst, William Randolph, 116

Hedges, Cornelius, 29

Helena, Mont., 37–38, 73

Helena Hotel, 77

Helena Independent, 84

Henry-Bonnard bronze foundry, 5

Hérouard, Chéri, 188–89, 355, 398

Herrmann, Emil, 157

Hidden Flower, The (Buck), 185

hina dolls, 183, 185

Hina-matsuri (Girl's Day), 183

Hirosaki Castle, 182

Hobson, S. S., 80

Hoelscher, Albert, 203, 205

Hoelscher, Barry, 203, 204

Hoelscher, Lorraine, 208–9

Hollywood Bowl, 143

Holter, Tom, 97

Home Pong, 223

Hope, Thomas, 68

Hope Venus (Canova), 67–68, 69, 116

Hopper, Edward, 131–32

Hughes, Howard, 142

Hugo, Victor, 3, 87

Hurley, James H., 273, 299

Hyman, Morton, 281, 283, 285, 286, 311

Idaho Territory, 23, 25, 31

Iessel, Manon, 179, 188, 355

Immigration Act of 1924, 214

Impressionism, 68, 130, 218

incentive spirometer, 233–34

Indian massacres, 31

industrial revolution, second, 18

Industrial Workers of the World, 97

inflation, 439–40

inherited wealth, 328–29

Institute for Crippled and Disabled Men, 89

In the Roses (Renoir), 218, 274, 304

Iowa, 22

Iowa Wesleyan University, 21, 375–76

IQ test, 128

Iseman, Frederick, 349

Islamic Revolution, 206
Israel, 271–72
Itō, Michio, 246
Ives, Helen, 150

Jackson, Michael, 229
Jaklitsch, Anna, 178, 181, 355
Jaklitsch, Rudolph, 178–79, 180–81,
    355
J. & W. Seligman, 136
Japan, 182, 183
Japanese Americans, internment of,
    203
Japonisme, 129
Jeff Davis Gulch, 25, 26
Jenkins, Gwendolyn, 249–50, 355
Jerome, Ariz., 50–51
Jetsons, The (cartoon), 235
Joan of Arc, 7, 67, 94, 177, 218, 275,
    306, 316
Johns, Jasper, 137
Johnson, Philip, 214
Johnson, Reginald, 194
Joint Commission, 282
Jones, Joseph, 151
Joseph, Chief, 39
JPMorgan Chase, 315
Judgment of Midas, 116
Juilliard School, 149, 170
Jumeau Company, 244
Jumeau triste pressed bisque doll, 255

Kabuki, 242
Kahanamoku, Duke, 111, 235, 353
Kamsler, Irving, 251–52, 260, 266,
    267, 268, 289, 296–300, 308–9,
    315, 317–19, 321, 326, 331, 335–36,
    337, 345, 349, 412, 413
  arrest of, 307–8

conviction of, 313–14
  false returns prepared by, 333–34
  malpractice claim against, 342–43
Kasakyan, Linda, 178–79
Katherine Stauffer Clark Kindergarten
    School, 113
Kawakami, Saburo, 182, 183, 355
Kelly, Grace, 244
keshi-bina, 185
Klebanoff, Louise, 341–42, 356
Knoedler & Co., 157, 219
Koch brothers, 114
Kurosawa, Akiro, 185

LaChapelle, Anna E., 261
LaChapelle, Philomene, 47, 48
LaChapelle, Pierre, 47–48
Ladies' Home Journal, The, 114
Lady (horse), 204
La Fontaine, Jean de, 11
Landscape (Pissarro), 128
La Pucelle (violin), 218, 274–76,
    317, 407
Larsen, Niels "Slim," 207
Larsen, Oda, 207
Las Vegas, Nev., xvii, 16, 55–56
Laube, Hattie Rose, 48, 59
Laurel Hill Academy, 20
Lawson, Thomas B., 86
Le Beau Château, 213–17, *214,* 296,
    310, 349, 401
  bedroom of, 215, *215*
  sale of, 274, 349
  stairway of, *216,* 217
Lee, Gypsy Rose, 128
Legion of Honor, 227
Levy, David C., 304, 305
Lewinsky, Monica, 234
Lewis, Lisa Berry, 325*n*
Lewis, Meriwether, 18–19

Lewis and Clark Expedition, 18–19, 31*n*

Lewiston, Idaho, 28

Liberty Enlightening the World (Bartholdi), 42

lightbulb, 41

Lindbergh, Charles, 144

Little, Frank, 97, 98

Lloyd's of London, 290

Lodge, Sheila, 194, 206, 299, *344*, 355

Loewenguth String Quartet, 155–56

Loewy, Elizabeth, 316–17, 356

Long Island Society for the Prevention of Cruelty to Children, 308

Look, 220

Lorioux, Félix, 186–90, 355

Lorioux, Lily, 188

Los Angeles, Calif., xvii, 52–54, 56–57

Los Angeles Philharmonic Orchestra, 143

Los Angeles Times, 55

Los Vegas Rancho, Nev., 55

Lotos Club, 65

Luce, Clare Boothe, 229

Lyle, William Gordon, 101, 112

Lynch, Jack, 144

Maas, Robert, 156–58

MacGuire, Edith, 325*n*

McCall, Karine, 105, 154, 155, 318–19, 325*n*, 327, 414

McCormick, Cyrus, 18

McCormick, Harold Fowler, 399

McKinley, William, 88

McLaughlin, H. W., 79

McNellis, Mary, 48–49, 59

Madame Cézanne in a Red Dress (Cézanne), 155, *156*, 157

Madame Cézanne with Unbound Hair (Cézanne), 155

Maison Jean Patou, 172

Malone, Michael, 85

mame-bina, 185

Manet, Edouard, 219, 283

Mangam, William D., 139, 143, 376

Man with a Sheet of Music (Rembrandt), 116

Mapplethorpe, Robert, 304

Marie, Adele "Missie," 147

Marne, First Battle of the, 96

Marsh, Caterina, 182–83, 185, 234, 243, 355

Mary Andrews Clark Memorial Home for Women, 56–57, 113, 255

Masons, 28–29, 113, 378

Maya the Bee (cartoon), 235

Mellick, Edward, 371

Mellon brothers, 114

Mercier, Jean, 188, 355

Metropolitan Museum of Art, 116, 219, 389

Metropolitan Opera, 139

Mickey Mouse, 186

Microsoft, 275

Miller, Mary Margaret, *437*

Miller, Ted, *437*

Millionaires' Row, 4, *15*, *121*

Missoula, Mont., 30

Missoula Gazette, 38

Miss Spence's Boarding and Day School for Girls, 105–8, 135, 152

Moana Hotel, 110, 111

Mohiuddin, Primrose, 234

Monet, Claude, 219, 240, 268, 300, 343

Monroe, Marilyn, 229

Montana, 23, 41, 71–73, 82

campaign fraud in, 73–75, 386

Clark's legacy in, 144–46

Montana (cont'd):
  as lawless, 28–29
  statehood for, 73
Montana Pioneers, 29
Montana Ranch, 53–54
Montecito, Calif., 195, 399
Moody's Investment Service, 282
Morales, Sylvia, 209
Morgan, J. P., 8, 65
Morken, John R., 326, 346
Mormons, 27, 55
Mormon Tabernacle Choir, 70
Morning Press, 138
Morris, Katherine, 93
Morse, Samuel, 18
Morton, Thomas, 200
Mountain Chief mine, 40
Mount Sinai Hospital, 287
Mowitza Lodge, 96–97, 143, 300
Murdoch, Rupert, 114
Music Academy of the West,
  206

National Arts Club, 65
National City Bank of New York, 86
NBC News, 316
NBC Nightly News, 214
Negri, Pola, 133, 163
Neill, John S. M., 84
Nelson-Atkins Museum of Art,
  292–93
Nevada, University of, 143
New Canaan, Conn., 213, 214
Newell, Effie Ellen "Ella" Clark,
  21*n*, 56, 57, 377, 381–82, *438*
Newell, James, *438*
Newell, Paul Clark, Jr., xix–xxii,
  21*n*, 305, 353, 355, 377, *438*
Newell, Paul Clark, Sr., xx, 57–58,
  438

Newman, Robert, 279, 280, 281–82,
  283–87, 297
New Orleans, La., 50
New York Association for the Blind,
  101
New York Herald, 83, 139
New York Times, xvii, 9–10, 112,
  233, 246, 371–72
New-York Tribune, 81
New York Yacht Club, 65
Nez Percé War of 1877, 39
Niagara, USS, 41
Nippon Music Foundation, 395

Obama, Barack, xviii
Odd Fellows Hall, 37
oil paints, 128–29
O'Keeffe, Georgia, 132
Olds, Ransom, 6
Old Sledge (card game), 28
Oloroso, Gicela Tejada, *see* Peri,
  Hadassah
O'Neill, Eugene, 229
Oratorio Society of New York, 154
Oregon Trail, 24
Original mine, 40, 97
osteopenia, 231
Outdoor School of Santa Barbara, 207
Overland Trail, 23

Paganini, Nicolò, 157
Paganini Quartet, 157–58, 195, 198,
  218
Pahlavi, Mohammad Reza, 206
Palé, George, 143–44
Panama Canal, 88, 136
panic of 1837, 18
panic room, 44
Panther (German gunboat), 94

Paris Match, 243

Parsons on Contracts, 22

Paul Clark Home, 113, 170, 254–56

Pearl Harbor, Japanese attack on, 203

Pend Oreille River, 145

penicillin, 102

Peonies (Manet), 219, 283

Perfect Moment, The (Mapplethorpe), 304

Peri, Abraham, 261, 263

Peri, Daniel, 232, 263, 267

Peri, David, 263, 269

Peri, Geula, 263

Peri, Hadassah, 139, 229, 231–33,
    235–37, 281, 285, 287, 288, 294,
    310, 311, 312, 322, 325, 333, 336,
    337, 342, 354
  Huguette's gifts to, 260–70
  and Huguette's will, 296–97, 298,
    299
  and settlement negotiations, 343,
    345

Pernault Workshops, 238

Perry, Janet, 220–21

Pershing, John J. "Black Jack," 196

Petit-Bourg, château de, 95–96,
    204, 213–14, 235

Phelps Dodge Corporation, 144

Philadelphia, Penn., 41–42

Phil Kearney, Fort, 31

Phillips Academy, 254

Picasso, Pablo, 187

Pierre, Jules, 227, 261, 267–68

Pierre, Suzanne, 227–28, 230, 234,
    240, 259, 261, 265, 267–68,
    288, 297, 310, 312, 327, 336, 354

Pierre's (restaurant), 135, 152

Pinchon, J. P., 188, 189, 355

Pissarro, Camille, 68, 128

placer mining, 26

Plummer, Henry, 28, 29

pneumonia, 234, 294, 296

Poems of Robert Burns (Burns), 22

Point de Vue, 243–44

pollution, 44, 145

Poplars on the Epte (Monet), 219

Pratt, Herbert Lee, 126

Presbyterian Church, 19

Princesse Merveilleuse, Une, 174–75

Princeton University, *135*, 136

private-duty nurses, 232

Pro Arte Quartet, 156

Prohibition, 107

Pure Food and Drug Act of 1906, 88

Rancho Alegre, 204, 205, 206–7,
    213, 345, 400

Rancho Los Alamitos, Calif., 53–54

Rangeley Lakes, 101

Raynolds, Ann Ellis, 147–50, 164,
    170, 197–99

RCA Victor, 157

Reagan, Ronald, 252

Red Cross, 170

Red Jacket, Mich., 47

Reed, David Aiken, 214

Reed, John S., 291

Rembrandt, 116

Reno, Nev., 140–41

Renoir, Pierre-Auguste, 128,
    218–19, 274, 304

Riverside Hotel, 141

Rockefeller, John D., 114, 126, 149,
    371, 384

Rockefeller, Nelson, 149

Rockefeller Center, 113

Rockefeller Foundation, 113

Rodda, Jeanette, 206

Rodin, Auguste, 67

Rogers, Henry Huttleston, 85–86

Ronald McDonald House, 255

Rooftops of Capri (Sargent), 219
Roosevelt, Franklin, 203
Roosevelt, Theodore, xviii, 65, 88, 117, 128
Royal Hawaiian Hotel, 110
Royal Leamington Spa, 96
Rubens, Peter Paul, 116
Rubin, Eduard, 41
Rudick, Jack, 230, 281, 298
Rudolph Wurlitzer Company, 218
Ruggiero, Tony, xiv, 216, 299

safety cages, 87
Saint Anthony's fire, 254
St. Thomas Church, 102, 112, 303
Salmon Lake, 96
Salt Lake City, Utah, 27, 28, 54
Salt Lake Temple, 27
Samuels, Robert, 224
Sandré, Madame, 94, 95, 138, 246
Sandré, Ninta, 246–48, 252, 261, 355
Sandy, Hurricane, 343
San Francisco, Calif., 52
San Pedro, Calif., 54
San Pedro Los Angeles & Salt Lake Railroad, 54–55, 57–58
Santa Barbara, Calif., xv, xx, 193, 199, 203, 299
    earthquake in, 136, 138, 194
    Japanese submarine off, 203
    water shortages in, 208
Santa Barbara Cemetery, 15, 195, 206
Santa Barbara Foundation, 294
Santa Barbara Museum of Art, 195, 206, 208
Santa Fe railroad, 50–51
Santa Ynez Valley, 204
Sargent, John Singer, 219
Sarrazine, La, 222

Sattler, Chris, 165, 213, 234, 240–45, 259, 269, 272, 273, 275, 283, 288, 289, 294, 299, 304, 310, 322, 325, 336, 345, 354
Saturday Evening Post, 114
Sautereau, Mr. and Mrs., 261
Scarsdale, N.Y., 103
schizoid personality disorder, 339, 416
Schneiderman, Eric, 343
School Art League, 89
School of Mines, 40
Schram, Peter S., 354, 415
Schwab, Charles M., 65
Selby, Lloyd, 28
Semaine de Suzette, La, 186, 187, 189
Semple, Amelia, 159, 170, 235
Semple, T. Darrington, 159
Semple, T. Darrington, Jr., 159–60
Senate, U.S., 16, 48, 79, 88, 349, 386
    Committee on Privileges and Elections, 79–81, 82
September 11, 2001, terrorist attacks of, 273, 326
Seventeenth Amendment, 85, 386
Shoshone Indians, 24
Silver Bow Creek, 145
Simon, Paul, 214
Singman, Henry, xxv–xxvi, 227, 230–31, 233, 234–36, 279, 281, 285, 287, 291, 292, 299, 312, 345, 354, 358
Sioux City, Iowa, 37
Skinner, Cy, 26
Sleeping Beauty, 154, 177, 179, 189
Sleepy Hollow Country Club, 65
Sloan, Judith, 317
Smith, Claire, 164
Smith, James, 151
Smith, Robert B., 82, 83, 84
Smithsonian Institution, 304
Smurfs, The (cartoon), 235, 280, 281, 339

Social 400, 65, 89
Sotheby's, 255, 268, 274, 283, 298
Southern Pacific Railroad, 52
speakeasies, 107
Spence, Clara, 105–6, 356
Spitzer, Eliot, 316
Spriggs, A. E., 82, 83
"Stack, the," 145
Standard Oil, 85, 126, 384
Statue of Liberty, 42
Stewart, Martha, xvi
Stewart Ranch, Nev., 55
stock swindles, 85–86
Storke, Thomas M., 400
Stradivari, Antonio, 152, 218, 269
Stradivarius violins, xviii, 152, 195,
    196–97, 218, 269, 274, 275,
    316, 317, 349
Strasheim, Lyn, 246, 248
Stuart, Gilbert, 6
Styka, Adam, 391
Styka, Doris, 257–58, 261
Styka, Jan, 391
Styka, Tadeusz, "Tadé," 128–33, 135,
    196, 197, 201, 203, 257, 391–92
Styka, Wanda Magdaleine, 257–59,
    261, 273, 296, 300, 325, 326,
    336, 338, 355
Summit Bank of New Jersey, 252–53
sumptuary laws, Japanese, 182
Sun Flower Troop, 100–101
Super Chief (train), 198
Superfund environmental disaster
    fund, 145
Supreme Court, U.S., 386
Tarbell, Ida, 85
Tax Reform Act of 1986, 252
telegraph, 18
    transatlantic, 41
telephone, 41
Temianka, Henri, 150

Texaco Star Theater, 257
"Thanatopsis" (Bryant), 102, 112,
    143, 322
Three Poplars in Gray Weather
    (Monet), 268
Thuillier pressed bisque doll, 255–56
Thurber, James, 229
Titanic, RMS, 93, 94
Today, xix
Tokyo String Quartet, 395
Tonopah Banking Corporation,
    252
tracer patients, 282
transfer tax, 333
Traveler (violin), 218, 275
Tremaine, Emily Hall, 137
Trinity School, 136
Trouville, 93–94, 163, 175, 235
Truman, Harry, 128
tubercular meningitis, 101–2
Twain, Mark, 43, 65, 71, 85–86, 87
typhoid fever, 45

undue influence, 336, 338
Union League Club, 85
Union Pacific Railroad, 41, 54
unions, 97–98
Unique Book and Handcraft Salon,
    89
United Hospital Fund of New York,
    170
United Verde mine, 50–51, 52, 136,
    142, 144
Utah & Northern Railway, 41
Utah Territory, 27

Valentino, Rudolph, 133
Valley Club, 195, 208
Van Buren, Martin, xviii

Vanderbilt, Cornelius, Jr., 141
Vanderbilt, Frederick W., 193
Vanderbilt, Gloria, 165
Vanderbilt, Mrs. Cornelius, 119
Venus (goddess), 68
Vermont Copper Company, 164
Vigilantes, 28–29, 98, 378
Villermont, Elizabeth de, 166,
    171–72, 176, 261, 355
Villermont, Etienne Allard de,
    163–68, *163*, 171–76, 294, 355,
    397
Villermont, Henri de, 173, 174
Villermont, Marie-Christine de, 167,
    171–72, 173, 175, 176, 261, 296,
    297–98, 355
Villermont family, 163, 174, 252
Virginia, University of, 143
Virginia City, Mont., 28, 29
voting rights, 72, 87, 148

W. A. Clark & Brother, Bankers,
    39, 80
Waikiki Beach, 110–11, 353
Walker, Jimmy, 107
Wallace, Donald, xx–xxi, 206, 217,
    247, 249, 251–52, 260, 266,
    272, 289, 291, 295–96, 317–18
Walla Walla, Wash., 30
Walska, Ganna, 399
Warhol, Andy, 137
Warner, D. G., 79
Warner, Ty, 206
Warren, Dorothy, 107–8
Washington, George, 6, 19, 126
Washington Post, 306
Washington Territory, 30
Water Lilies (Monet), 140, 219, 240,
    300, 332, 334, 343

Watt, Louise, 107
Weinstein, Boaz, 348
Wellcome, John B., 75
Welles, Orson, 399
Wexler, Marvin, 286
Whiteside, Fred, 75
Wild Bill (horse), 39
Wilde, Oscar, 143
Williams, Brian, 214
Williams, Kathryn, 46, 59
Willkie, Wendell, 149
Wilson, Marc, 292
Winchell, Walter, 164
Wobblies, *see* Industrial Workers of
    the World
Wolff, John, 230–31, 355–56
Woman in a Green Hat (Cézanne),
    155
women, voting rights for, 72, 87, 148
Woodlawn Cemetery, 45, 102, 113,
    170, 254, 320, *321*
Woolworth Building, 7–8
workday, 88
Worker's Marseillaise, The, 95
World's Columbian Exhibition, 45
World's Industrial and Cotton
    Centennial Exposition (1885), 50
World Trade Center, 273
World War I, 95–96, 112, 137
World War II, 189, 203–4
Wright, Myron, 227, 246, 248
Wynn, Steve, 274
Wyoming Territory, 23

Yellow Peril (car), 101
Young, Brigham, 27
Young Women's Christian Associa-
    tion (YWCA), 57, 255
Ysit, Christie, 311

ABOUT THE AUTHORS

======

BILL DEDMAN introduced the public to heiress Huguette Clark
and her empty mansions through his compelling series of
narratives for NBC, which became the most popular feature
in the history of its news website, topping 110 million page views.
He received the 1989 Pulitzer Prize in investigative reporting
while writing for *The Atlanta Journal-Constitution*
and has written for *The New York Times, The Washington Post,*
and *The Boston Globe.*

. . .

PAUL CLARK NEWELL, JR., a cousin of Huguette Clark, has
researched the Clark family history for twenty years, sharing
many conversations with Huguette about her life and family. He
received a rare private tour of Bellosguardo, the mysterious
oceanfront Clark estate in Santa Barbara.

. . .

emptymansionsbook.com

ABOUT THE TYPE

———

This book is set in Fournier, a typeface named for Pierre-Simon Fournier, the youngest son of a French printing family. Pierre-Simon first studied watercolor painting, but became involved in type design through work that he did for his eldest brother. Starting with engraving woodblocks and large capitals, he later moved on to fonts of type. In 1736 he began his own foundry, and published the first version of his point system the following year.